Elementary Classroom Management

SIXTH EDITION

C. M. Charles
Professor Emeritus, San Diego State University

Gail W. Senter
California State University San Marcos, Retired

PEARSON

Boston Columbus Indianapolis New York San Francisco Upper Saddle River
Amsterdam Cape Town Dubai London Madrid Milan Munich Paris Montreal Toronto Delhi
Mexico City Sao Paulo Sydney Hong Kong Seoul Singapore Taipei Tokyo

Vice President, Editor in Chief: Paul A. Smith
Managing Editor: Shannon Steed
Editorial Assistant: Matthew Bulchholz
Marketing Manager: Joanna Sabella
Production Editor: Paula Carroll
Editorial Production Service: Shylaja Gattupalli
Manufacturing Buyer: Megan Cochran
Electronic Composition: TexTech International
Photo Researcher: Annie Pickert
Cover Designer: Linda Knowles

Credits and acknowledgments borrowed from other sources and reproduced, with permission, in this textbook appear on appropriate page within text.

Library of Congress Cataloging-in-Publication Data

Charles, C. M.
    Elementary classroom management / C. M. Charles, Gail W. Senter.—6th ed.
        p. cm.
    ISBN-13: 978-0-13-705541-8
    ISBN-10: 0-13-705541-2
    1. Classroom management.   2. Education, Elementary.   I. Senter, Gail W.   II. Title.
    LB3013.C465 2012
    372.11'024—dc22

                                                                        2010050279

10 9 8 7 6 5 4 3 2 1 RRD-VA   14   13   12   11

www.pearsonhighered.com

ISBN-10: 0-13-705541-2
ISBN-13: 978-0-13-705541-8

Contents

Preface

It is noble to be good.
It is nobler to teach others to be good, and less trouble.

—Mark Twain

As with prior editions, this sixth edition of *Elementary Classroom Management* focuses on the improvement of instruction and learning through good classroom management. When it is done well, classroom management helps establish learning environments and instructional programs that are well organized and efficient, where communication is good, and where teachers, students, and others are considerate of each other and dedicated to learning. As teachers improve their skills in classroom management, they find that students also become more cooperative, make responsible choices, and happily engage in learning activities.

New to This Edition

Educators agree that effective classroom management is essential for successful teaching and learning. This book attempts to present management considerations in a logical order for readers to organize the elements for success. The following changes are new to this edition, and should be especially interesting and helpful:

- *MyEducationLab for Classroom Management,* a website with interactive simulations, assignments, activities, and classroom videos, is integrated throughout the new edition.

- Chapter 1 describes a new teacher through a modern parable: The Beginner, Next Generation. The story is that of Alexa Smart, a new teacher for a 4/5 multi-age class.

- Chapter 2 discusses curricular needs for today's students. It also includes templates for planning with design questions for backward design and for planning thematic units of instruction using an updated curriculum wheel and the multiple intelligences.

- Considerations related to technology are included throughout this book. In particular, Chapter 3 shows sample floor plans with classroom computers, and Chapter 4 includes mention of the work by Eileen VanWie regarding democratic learning communities in technology-rich environments.

- Discussions of bullying and cyberbullying are included in Chapters 4, 7, and 9.

- Revised summaries of student needs are presented in Chapter 5, along with five principles of brain-friendly teaching.

- Chapter 6 now includes the description and grade-appropriate ideas for Problem-Based Learning (PBL) as an instructional approach. Also, cooperative learning is expanded to support how it helps to minimize four interrelated crises in education.

- Chapter 8 is reorganized for better flow of the content and current data about various special groups. Children with exceptionalities and special needs are discussed in the first portion of the chapter. Children with other challenges—language, family, and economic situations—are discussed in the second section. A section on children who are homeschooled is included in this later section because these children may spend some of their time in elementary classrooms. Additionally, updated history and details regarding legislation about inclusion, the discrepancy or failure model, and the Response to Intervention (RTI) process now are found in Appendix A.

- Several new topics are explored in Chapter 9. In addition to bullying and cyberbullying, sections present special challenges related to economic realities and neurological-based behavior (NBB). The self-discipline pyramid of Villa, Thousand, and Nevin is revised, and the work of Harry and Rosemary Wong and updated views of Marvin Marshall, all contemporary authorities on discipline, are included.

- Chapter 10 includes clarified definitions of assessment terms: formative, summative, criterion-referenced, norm-referenced; alternative and authentic; performance- and problem-based assessment, peer assessment, and self-assessment. Mention is made of electronic record keeping, and examples are included for keeping written records.

- The 2001 revision of Bloom's taxonomy of the cognitive domain appears in Chapter 11.

- Chapter 12 provides some information regarding advocates for students with special needs.

- Further classifications of trauma, definitions and factors that contribute to teacher burnout and teacher rustout, and mention of professional learning communities appear in Chapter 13.

- The capstone activity that appears in Chapter 14 is written as a problem-based learning task for students to work in teams to develop a grade-level management plan.

- Real teachers' voices, presented as case studies and vignettes, are interspersed throughout the chapters.

- The extensive webliography and bibliography of resources at the end of each chapter and at the back of the book—have been carefully updated for maximum usefulness to readers.

Help for Readers

The text is written in an informal, inviting tone to make information accessible for readers. Each chapter begins with a *Preview–Review Guide*. By responding in the column labeled *Preview* before reading a chapter, readers are able to record what they know, don't know, think they know, or assume about the chapter topics. After reading the chapter, readers can reflect on their earlier responses by responding to the same statements in the *Review* column.

Many of the statements are intentionally worded to not be clearly true or false; consequently, reflective discussions can be organized for use in class based on these statements, and reader responses. Websites, along with case studies and vignettes, are infused in the chapters to provide additional resources and experiential perspectives and discussions. To help readers strengthen their learning and acquire a sense of progressive accomplishments, checklists, practice applications, and discussion questions are included at the end of chapters.

MyEducationLab

The Power of Classroom Practice In *Preparing Teachers for a Changing World,* Linda Darling-Hammond and her colleagues point out that grounding teacher education in real classrooms—among real teachers and students and among actual examples of students' and teachers' work—is an important, and perhaps even an essential, part of training teachers for the complexities of teaching in today's classrooms. MyEducationLab is an online learning solution that provides contextualized interactive exercises, simulations, and other resources designed to help develop the knowledge and skills teachers need. All of the activities and exercises in MyEducationLab are built around essential learning outcomes for teachers and are mapped to professional teaching standards. Utilizing classroom video, authentic student and teacher artifacts, case studies, and other resources and assessments, the scaffolded learning experiences in MyEducationLab offer preservice teachers and those who teach them a unique and valuable education tool.

For each topic covered in the course you will find the following features and resources:

Connection to National Standards Now it is easier than ever to see how coursework is connected to national standards. Each topic on MyEducationLab lists intended learning outcomes connected to the appropriate national standards, and all of the activities and exercises in MyEducationLab are mapped to the appropriate national standards and learning outcomes as well.

Building Teaching Skills and Dispositions These learning units help students practice and strengthen skills that are essential to quality teaching. After presenting the steps involved in a core teaching process, students are given an opportunity to practice applying this skill via videos, student and teacher artifacts, and/or case studies of authentic classrooms. Providing multiple opportunities to practice a single teaching concept, each activity encourages a deeper understanding and application of concepts, as well as the use of critical thinking skills.

Simulations in Classroom Management One of the most difficult challenges facing teachers today is how to balance classroom instruction with classroom management. These interactive cases focus on the classroom management issues teachers most frequently encounter on a daily basis. Each simulation presents a challenge scenario at the beginning and then offers a series of choices to solve each challenge. Along the way students receive mentor feedback on their choices and have the opportunity to make better choices if necessary. Upon exiting each simulation students will have a clear understanding of how to address these common classroom management issues and will be better equipped to handle them in the classroom.

Course Resources The Course Resources section on MyEducationLab is designed to help students put together an effective lesson plan, prepare for and begin their career, navigate their first year of teaching, and understand key educational standards, policies, and laws.

Certification and Licensure The Certification and Licensure section is designed to help students pass their licensure exam by giving them access to state test requirements, overviews of what tests cover, and sample test items.

Visit www.myeducationlab.com for a demonstration of this exciting new online teaching resource.

Help for Instructors

The following features are included in the *Instructor's Manual* that accompanies the text to help instructors manage the course or topic effectively and efficiently:

- Suggestions for introducing the textbook to students
- Course organization options, including both goals and calendar considerations for semester, quarter, and weekend courses, and topics that can be part of a broader course
- Additional activities
- Evaluation expectations and procedures

And as already mentioned, instructors can direct students to *MyEducationLab*, where they can apply the content of the textbook using a variety of media resources. The Instructor's Manual is available for download from the Instructor Resource Center at: www.pearsonhighered.com/irc.

Acknowledgments

The authors gratefully acknowledge the valuable contributions to this edition by the following teachers who generously shared their experiences. It is their stories that make this book real: Gloria Anderson, Kim Anderson, Eileen Andreoli, Jearine Bacon, Kay Ballantyne, Janet Beyea, Mary Brewer, Dyanna Burak, Bernardo Campos, Della Casteñeda, Ruth Charles, Tim Charles, Sherry Coburn, Debbie Comer, Marilyn Cox, Rebecca Cumming, Beth Davies, Chris De Cramer, Ginger DeNigro, Julie DePew, Linda Foote, Hollie Foster, Stacy Ganzer, Devora Garrison, Jennifer George, Betsy Goff, Jan Gretlein, Lynne Harvey, Deseré Hockman, Ellen Hodgers, Lisa Johnston, Rose Mary Johnston, Pam Klevesahl, James Kolp, Kathryn Krainock, Ginny Lorenz, Karen O'Connor, Patti Peterson, Charlotte Rodzach,

Ronda Royal, Jamie Ruben, Nancy Rutherford, Linda Tyler, Debbie Teudt, Ted Saulino, Stephen Ulmer, Shaylene Watkins, and Candace Young.

Professional Analysts

The quality of any textbook is heavily dependent on critical analyses and suggestions made by knowledgeable experts. The authors express their sincere gratitude to Dr. C. Bobbi Hansen, University of San Diego, and Dr. Kimberly Woo, California State University San Marcos, whose suggestions helped to improve this book.

The authors would like to thank the reviewers Lisa Hazlett, The University of South Dakota; Sharon L. Smith, Fairmont State University; and Steven W. Neil, Emporia State University of this edition for their valuable comments.

The authors also gratefully acknowledge the assistance provided by Shannon Steed, Editor at Pearson Allyn & Bacon, and Matthew Buchholz, Editorial Assistant at Pearson Allyn & Bacon.

> *On this journey*
> *You will encounter all different paths:*
> *paths of hardships,*
> *paths of beauty,*
> *paths of trial,*
> *and paths of error.*
> *You may get lost,*
> *but if you give up,*
> *you will not reach your destination.*
> *If you did not want to reach your destination,*
> *Why did you begin the journey?*
> *Be strong.*
> *Keep faith.*
> *The journey,*
> *you know in your heart,*
> *is worth it.*

Written by Dyanna Burak during teacher training.
Dyanna went on to teach second-grade.

Relating This Book to Standards for Teachers

In recent years, national standards for teacher preparation and performance have been identified by a number of agencies. Notable efforts include the Interstate New Teacher Assessment and Support Consortium (INTASC) standards, the Praxis™ Series of tests and the Framework of Domains and Components described by Charlotte Danielson, ISTE's National Educational Technology Standards (NETS) for Teachers Project, and the National Board for Professional Teacher Standards (NBPTS). In fact, INTASC, NBPTS, and the National Council for Accreditation of Teacher Education (NCATE) have worked together to create a compatible set of performance-based standards that span the teaching career. On the following pages, you will find brief descriptions of the standards, along with their connections to relevant chapters.

INTASC Principles

INTASC stands for Interstate New Teacher Assessment and Support Consortium (see http://www.ccsso.org/projects/Interstate_New_Teacher_Asesssment_and_Support_Consortium). This consortium, which consists of more than 30 states that have developed standard and assessment procedures for initial teacher certification, has issued licensing standards that should be met in order to teach in public schools. The INTASC core standards are based on 10 principles of effective teaching, which focus on the integration of content knowledge and pedagogical understanding.

INTASC Principles	Chapter Coverage
1. **Making content meaningful** The teacher understands the central concepts, tools of inquiry, and structure of the discipline(s) he or she teaches, and creates learning experiences that make these aspects of subject matter meaningful for students.	2, 6, 8
2. **Child development and learning theory** The teacher understands how children learn and develop, and can provide learning opportunities that support their intellectual, social, and personal development.	4, 5, 8, 9
3. **Learning styles/diversity** The teacher understands how students differ in their approaches to learning and creates instructional opportunities that are adapted to diverse learners.	3, 6, 8
4. **Instructional strategies/problem solving** The teacher understands and uses a variety of instructional strategies to encourage students' development of critical thinking, problem solving, and performance skills.	6, 8
5. **Motivation and behavior** The teacher uses an understanding of individual and group motivation and behavior to create a learning environment that encourages positive social interaction, active engagement in learning, and self-motivation.	5, 9
6. **Communication/knowledge** The teacher uses knowledge of effective verbal, nonverbal, and media communication techniques to foster active inquiry, collaboration, and supportive interaction in the classroom.	4, 11, 12, 13

7. **Planning for instruction**   2, 6, 7

   The teacher plans instruction based on knowledge of subject matter,
   students, the community, and curriculum goals.

8. **Assessment**   10

   The teacher understands and uses formal and informal
   assessment strategies to evaluate and ensure the continuous
   intellectual, social, and physical development of the learner.

9. **Professional growth/reflection**   1, 11, 12, 13, 14, Appendix A

   The teacher is a reflective practitioner who continually evaluates
   the effects of his or her choices and actions on others (students,
   parents, and other professionals in the learning community) and
   who actively seeks out opportunities to grow professionally.

10. **Interpersonal relationships**   11, 12, 14

    The teacher fosters relationships with school colleagues, parents, and agencies
    in the larger community to support students' learning and well-being.

Source: The Interstate New Teacher Assessment and Support Consortium (INTASC) standards were developed by
the Council of Chief State School Officers and member states. Copies may be downloaded from the Council's website at http://www.ccsso.org or at http://cte.jhu.edu/pds/Resources/INTASC_Principles.htm.

Council of Chief State School Officers. (1992). *Model standards for beginning teacher licensing, assessment, and development: A resource for state dialogue.* Washington, DC: Author. http://www.ccsso.org/content/pdf/corestrd.pdf.

Praxis™ Series and Danielson's Framework for Teaching

The Praxis Series™ is a series of assessments for beginning teachers. Developed and dissem-
inated by the Educational Testing Service (ETS), the Praxis Series™ assesses academic skills,
subject knowledge, and classroom performance during the early states of a beginning
teacher's career, from entry into teacher education to the first year of teaching. Praxis™
I measures basic skills in reading, writing, and mathematics and may be used as an admis-
sions tool for teacher education programs. Praxis™ II measures prospective teachers'
knowledge of the subjects they will teach, as well as pedagogical skills and knowledge. It
includes tests on principles of learning and teaching, specific subject assessments, and multiple subject assessments. Praxis™ III measures the classroom performance of beginning
teachers. It includes instructional planning and teaching, classroom management, and student assessment and may be used as a licensure tool.

Charlotte Danielson, one of the Praxis™ III test developers, was concerned that teachers have or make little opportunity to discuss teaching with others. Her framework of four
domains, shown here, aligns with the domains of Praxis™ III. Danielson's intent was to give
teachers a means of discussion to enrich their professional lives and teaching. Her revised
framework of domains, components, and elements appears in her book, *Enhancing Professional Practice: A Framework for Teaching* (2007). For more about Danielson's efforts and
books, consult http://www.ascd.org.

Based on Praxis™ III, Danielson's Domains and Components of the Framework for Teaching	Chapter Coverage
Domain 1: Planning and Preparation • Component 1a: Demonstrating Knowledge of Content and Pedagogy • Component 1b: Demonstrating Knowledge of Students • Component 1c: Setting Instructional Outcomes • Component 1d: Demonstrating Knowledge of Resources • Component 1e: Designing Coherent Instruction • Component 1f: Designing Student Assessments	2, 6, 7, 8, 9, 10
Domain 2: The Classroom Environment • Component 2a: Creating an Environment of Respect and Rapport • Component 2b: Establishing a Culture for Learning • Component 2c: Managing Classroom Procedures • Component 2d: Managing Student Behavior • Component 2e: Organizing Physical Space	3, 4, 6, 7, 8, 9, 13
Domain 3: Instruction • Component 3a: Communicating with Students • Component 3b: Using Questioning and Discussion Techniques • Component 3c: Engaging Students in Learning • Component 3d: Using Assessment in Instruction • Component 3e: Demonstrating Flexibility and Responsiveness	5, 6, 7, 8, 10, 11, 13
Domain 4: Professional Responsibilities • Component 4a: Reflecting on Teaching • Component 4b: Maintaining Accurate Records • Component 4c: Communicating with Families • Component 4d: Participating in a Professional Community • Component 4e: Growing and Developing Professionally • Component 4f: Showing Professionalism	10, 11, 12, 13, 14, **Appendix A**

Source: From *Enhancing Professional Practice: A Framework for Teachers*, 2nd ed. (Figure 1.1, p. 3) by Charlotte Danielson. Alexandria, VA: ASCD. © 2007 by ASCD. Adapted with permission. Learn more about the ASCD at http://www.ascd.org.

ISTE'S National Educational Technology Standards (NETS) for Teachers Project

Sponsored by the International Society for Technology in Education (ISTE), NETS "defines the fundamental concepts, knowledge, skills, and attitudes for applying technology in educational settings." The infusion of technology into teacher education programs is based on the NETS Project. The standards, first published in 2000, have expanded to include

ISTE's NETS	Chapter Coverage
1. **Facilitate and inspire student learning and creativity.** Teachers use their knowledge of subject matter, teaching, learning, and technology to facilitate experiences that advance student learning, creativity, and innovation in both face-to-face and virtual environments.	5, 6, 10
2. **Design and develop digital-age learning experiences and assessments.** Teachers design, develop, and evaluate authentic learning experiences and assessment incorporating contemporary tools and resources to maximize content learning in context and to develop the knowledge, skills, and attitudes identified in the NETS-S.	2, 5, 6, 8, 10
3. **Model digital-age work and learning.** Teachers exhibit knowledge, skills, and work processes representative of an innovative professional in a global and digital society.	6, 11, 12, 13
4. **Promote and model digital citizenship and responsibility.** Teachers understand local and global societal issues and responsibilities in an evolving digital culture and exhibit legal and ethical behavior in their professional practices.	11, 12, 13
5. **Engage in professional growth and leadership.** Teachers continuously improve their professional practices, model lifelong learning, and exhibit leadership in their school and professional community by promoting and demonstrating the effective use of digital tools and resources.	11, 12, 13, 14

Source: NETS for Teachers: National Educational Technology Standards for Teachers, 2nd ed. © 2008, ISTE (International Society for Technology in Education), http://www.iste.org/content/navigationmenu/nets/forteachers/2008standards. All rights reserved.

NETS-S, NETS-T, and NETS-A. Each project—student, teacher, and administrator—identifies specific characteristics and responsibilities for the technology literacy of the target group.

NBPTS Standards

The National Board of Professional Teaching Standards (NBPTS), created in 1987, is an organization that has established standards for highly accomplished teaching as seen in the National Board's central policy statement, *What Teachers Should Know and Be Able to Do.* NBPTS has developed five core propositions on which voluntary national teacher certification is based (NBPTS, 2003).

NBPTS awards professional certificates to master teachers—those with vast professional knowledge and highly developed teaching skills. Certification candidates submit a portfolio that includes video or digital tapes of classroom instructions, samples of student work, and the teacher's reflective comments. Trained NBPTS evaluators who teach in the same grade level or field as the candidate judge all elements of assessments. See http://www.nbpts.org/the_standards/the_five_core_propositions.

NBPTS Standards	Chapter Coverage
Proposition 1: Teachers are committed to students and their learning.	4, 8, 13
Proposition 2: Teachers know the subjects they teach and how to teach those subjects to students.	5, 6, 7
Proposition 3: Teachers are responsible for managing and monitoring student learning.	3, 6, 8, 9, 10
Proposition 4: Teachers think systematically about their practice and learn from experience.	2, 10
Proposition 5: Teachers are members of learning communities.	11, 12, 14

Source: http://www.nbpts.org/the_standards/the_five_core_propositions. Reprinted with permission from the National Board for Professional Teaching Standards. All rights reserved.

Classroom Management: Problems and Promises

CHAPTER 1

You make the path when you walk.

—Loosely translated from
Spanish poet Antonio Machado

Preview Review Guide

Before you read the chapter, and based on what you know, think you know, or assume, take a minute to put a check mark in the **Preview** column if you agree with the statement. When you finish the chapter, take time to reread the statements and respond in the **Review** column. Reflective discussions can develop because many of the statements are not clearly "yes" or "no."

Preview   **Review**

1. _____ A primary purpose of classroom management is efficiency and
effectiveness in teaching.   _____

2. _____ The *psychosocial environment* refers to class parties and other
social events that occur in the classroom.   _____

3. _____ *Feedback* is a term used to indicate student responses
to a teacher's questions.   _____

4. _____ When new teachers fail in their jobs, most often it is because their
management skills are fine but their content knowledge is weak.   _____

5. _____ The Cardinal Principles mainly have to do with how teachers
should organize and present lessons.   _____

6. _____ Three fundamental questions in education are: What should
students learn? How do they learn? and How should they be taught?   _____

7. _____ It is suggested that students begin each day with a quiet activity.   _____

8. _____ The term *monitor* is used to indicate a student who helps with chores
in the classroom.   _____

9. _____ Lesson management, like other management chores, requires
ongoing attention.   _____

10. _____ In addition to their classroom responsibilities, teachers are expected
to handle extracurricular duties.   _____

Chapter Objective

After reading Chapter 1, students will demonstrate understanding in broad terms of the realities and complexities of teaching through their active participation in discussions and the end-of-chapter activities for reflection.

This book is about managing the elementary classroom. A problem to solve or an essential or guiding question for this chapter might be: *How can I plan for and handle all the management skills I will encounter in such a way so as to make teaching and learning pleasant and successful experiences for everyone?* This chapter begins to answer this question by revealing a multitude of management skills that lead toward artistry in teaching and pleasure in learning. These skills, among the most important you will encounter in all of teaching, rarely occur naturally and cannot be taken for granted. They can, however, be taught and learned. Some skills can be acquired quickly; others are built up over time. Beginning teachers, in particular, often struggle because their management skills have not yet developed adequately. Such was the case for Alexa Smart, a promising new teacher who found that teaching involved considerably more than she anticipated.

A Modern Parable: The Beginner, Next Generation

Alexa Smart is a first-year elementary teacher, and is she having trouble! Teaching runs in her family. In fact, we described her aunt Mercedes Bright and her cousin Janna Smart in earlier editions. Just like them, Alexa did well in school and her teacher preparation program. Her professors saw her as a "natural," and her cooperating teachers and student teacher supervisors ranked her high. Growing up, Alexa had spent hours in her aunt and cousin's home, and on many occasions she had listened when they spoke with friends about school, their work, and the children they taught. Based on her years of observing and helping in classrooms Alexa thought she was well informed about the realities of elementary classrooms, and well prepared to teach.

At a time when districts everywhere were faced with cutbacks and budget challenges, Alexa spent the summer interviewing for jobs. Local districts began school right after Labor Day, but it wasn't until late September that she was offered a position to teach a multi-age class of fourth and fifth graders. Because neither grade had enough students to create a new single-grade class, the administration created the multi-age class. Class sizes had been raised from 25 to 30 students this year, and while Alexa would begin with only 26 students, hers was the class that would receive the first new enrollees. She accepted the position without hesitation.

Alexa knew she was qualified, and she felt very comfortable about teaching. Everything seemed to fall into place, and she felt ready to begin her year.

Alexa was hired on a Wednesday afternoon and would first meet her students the following Monday—she had four full days to prepare. That day she looked at the room that would be her classroom. It had been a room off the multipurpose room that now was converted to a classroom. She walked around the school with the principal and met two of her team members. She also received copies of the books her students would study this year. On Thursday Alexa reviewed the curriculum and standards for both the fourth and fifth grades.

"Okay, which one of you has the cell phone ringtone that sounds like a class bell?"

Bob Vojtko Cartoons on Facebook. Reprinted with permission.

Over the weekend some of her friends helped with her room while she planned activities that would help everyone get acquainted. Her friends made bulletin boards and an inviting art exhibit related to exploration, the first social studies unit the fifth graders would study. They placed some plants to cheer the room and arranged a reading center with a few large colorful pillows. They put several computers in different spots about the room. And they created a nature center with a terrarium for food, water dishes, and leafy plants, and Ziggy, Alexa's iguana and soon-to-be class pet.

Alexa was a little nervous when her students arrived on Monday morning, but she felt ready to begin the day. A few parents even stopped by the room on the way to their jobs. She greeted everyone warmly. The students were quite well behaved, although they were a little reserved from having had to change from their original classrooms. Alexa took time to tell a little about herself and played a memory game so she could begin to learn everyone's name. Soon after that she took time to tell the students her rules for the year. Because the students had come from other classrooms, Alexa was able to give her first math lesson to the fifth graders and begin a core chapter book with the fourth graders. At the end of the day, Alexa felt she had made a good beginning.

As her cousin before her, Alexa was confident that the second day would be even better, but to her shock, things did not go perfectly. Because these were fourth and fifth graders, Alexa assumed they would remember how to enter the room in a quiet and orderly manner. To her dismay, however, most did not. It took her much longer than expected to get them settled. As the day went on, those who had at first been cooperative became slow to follow directions. When Alexa tried to work with the fourth graders on their curriculum, the fifth graders fooled around and played with electronic devices from their backpacks. That made her uneasy, and it bothered her when some began showing disrespect.

By Wednesday afternoon, Alexa was struggling. She had several confrontations with students who talked, called out, wandered out of their seats, would not listen to directions or pay attention, sharpened pencils needlessly, and repeatedly asked to go to the restroom. When dismissed for lunch, three boys raced out of the room and down the corridor. As the day progressed, almost every child had tapped on the terrarium glass, and it seemed they simply could not leave Ziggy alone.

The fourth day moved toward chaos. Every boy seemed bent on making unpleasant sounds and every girl on looking at herself in a mirror. No one seemed at all willing to listen to Alexa or do as she requested. When Alexa worked with the fourth graders, the fifth graders wandered around the room or used their cell phones to text each other. When assigned seatwork had been completed (or not completed, or completed incorrectly, or messed up impossibly), students shouted, waved their arms, and annoyed the few who still were trying to work. Many seemed never to have heard of standards of human civility, much less of classroom behavior. Alexa's efforts to plan for two grades and the curricular needs for each child only added to her struggles.

By the fifth day, Alexa was in despair. Students now blatantly broke rules and seemed unaffected by her kindest, most sincere counseling. It was not so much that they were cruel or hostile toward her—they simply disregarded her and clowned, giggled, fussed, fought, and shouted. She was frustrated with the double curricula and the broad ranges of age and maturity within the two grades.

Other surprises caught Alexa off-guard as well. After school on Monday, Alexa told her administrator that she had only enough math books for her current fourth graders and was one short for her fifth graders. She was concerned about not having enough books for any new students who were sent to her class. He told her that it was not likely she would get more books because of budget cuts; she would have to make do with the books she had. On Tuesday, a student who was legally blind was transferred into her room, along with her service dog and a paraprofessional who was assigned to assist her as needed. On Wednesday, two mothers arrived to help in the room. Because Alexa didn't know what to have them do, they spent the day watching her sweat and struggle. Two new girls arrived on Thursday; one spoke little English and the other spoke none at all. On Friday, a child with learning disabilities was brought in to be included in her room. The student called out incessantly and made noises, which the other students found bizarre and delightedly mimicked. He also vomited during the math lesson, which made everyone laugh. Unable to get the class to refocus on the lesson, Alexa shouted at the students about being cruel and inconsiderate and made them put their heads down on their desks.

These events almost obscured the fact that on Tuesday two boys got into a fight and ruined a new pair of jeans. When Alexa was called to the phone after school, she was reprimanded by the parent on the other end about the cost of jeans and her lack of control. On Wednesday, another parent confronted her, swearing and complaining that her son was being bullied on the playground and demanding that Alexa put a stop to it. After school both the principal and vice principal called her into their offices to talk about the incidents. And by Friday, most of the scripts for the social studies readers' theatre were either unreadable from scribbles or simply missing, the computers were making distracting noises, the book and supply areas were jumbled, and no one seemed to know where Ziggy was. On Friday, Alexa also found two notes in her mailbox. One informed her that her support provider, an experienced teacher assigned by the district's Beginning Teacher Support Assistance program to work with Alexa during her first year, intended to visit her classroom the following week. The second was from the parent of her new student with learning disabilities, who wanted to schedule a meeting in the next week or two with her and the student advocate to discuss Alexa's plans for working with her child.

Spirits crushed and mind in turmoil, Alexa dragged herself home. She now doubted that she would ever get those nine-, ten-, and eleven-year-olds to behave like civilized boys and girls, much less learn. She cried for two hours and seriously contemplated moving to Australia, then called a friend. They met at a coffee shop, where Alexa talked and cried some more. That took her mind off escaping to Australia, however, and by the next morning her personal determination was beginning to return.

That night she faced the fact that most of the problems had to do with three things: her own instruction, her curriculum planning and organization, and her ability to manage the class.

Previously, she had been confident about her ability to instruct. Now she knew her lessons were not running smoothly. Some were too long, some too short, and most too easy or too difficult. Though interesting to Alexa, some were obviously boring the students, and she could see why they might lose interest and look for something more stimulating. In addition, the two grade levels of curricula and standards and the problem of not having enough textbooks for all her students only added to her challenge.

She realized, too, that she was having trouble monitoring seatwork while she worked with one grade or the other and with smaller groups. Students, often several at a time, were forever coming up to her with questions, usually about what she had carefully explained only minutes before. Also, she noticed that most anything took the students off-task, and she could hardly get them back.

While at her university, she remembered hearing about using technology in the classroom, about curriculum standards, and about teacher and student rights. She realized how little she knew about technology, let alone about the equipment that was being brought into her classroom or that was already at her desk. While she was aware of the standards in general, she was not overly familiar with the specific standards for fourth and fifth grades. She also realized that she knew little about the rights and responsibilities that applied to her situation and her students. She knew that students who were learning English and students with special needs had rights that would affect her decisions, her ability to include them in her class, and her ability to instruct them so they could be successful.

On Saturday morning, she made several phone calls—one to her cousin Janna, one to her Aunt Mercedes, and one to a teacher who had taught in the school for a few years. She also called her support provider. With all four she swallowed her pride and confessed her difficulties. She learned that Janna had had very similar experiences her first days and that these experiences were hardly unusual. She also listened to and accepted a number of suggestions for redoing the operations of her classroom. That afternoon she went to school and in calm solitude took her first steps in taking back control of her classroom. On Sunday afternoon, she met with the teacher from her school who went over the school rules (about electronic devices—cell phones and iPods, in particular), coached her in some of the basics for using the electronic equipment at her desk, and talked to her about what she might expect working with parents and student advocates.

When students returned on Monday, Alexa seated them farther apart and separated those who had been encouraging each other's disruptive behavior. She had moved all the computers to a separate area in the room, moved her desk to the side of the room where she could see her students while she operated her computer equipment, and repositioned the small-group area so she would be closer to the rest of the class. She found she was better able to quickly reach all her students with this new arrangement. She set up, taught, and practiced a signal system of kinesthetic signs that students could use to ask for help during the lesson and seatwork. This allowed her to better pace her lessons because she taught her students to signal when she was going too fast or the material was over their heads. The signals allowed her to go to students during independent work, not vice versa, and gave the students fewer opportunities to get into trouble. She also planned several classbuilding and teambuilding activities to bring everyone together, and was prepared with quick brain and movement energizers for when students showed signs of needing a break.

With determination, Alexa spent time reteaching and practicing the school and class rules. After her new student introduced her service dog, Alexa reaffirmed that the dog was a working dog and how they as a class would help with appropriate care and attention. She then had the students describe how responsible and irresponsible behavior looked, sounded, and felt, so each rule was more concrete and students had some solid options for appropriate actions to solve problems. She planned to repeat the practice often until the rules and responsible choices were second nature to her students.

With resolve she also began to use the basic instructional technology her colleague had taught her. Although these were fourth and fifth graders, Alexa spent time reviewing basic guidelines for using the computer. She also watched her students for potential technology leaders, peer mentors, and troubleshooters.

She installed a new system of distributing and collecting materials, with students assigned to help. In fact, she assigned special responsibilities to every student in the class. She added more structure to her lessons and organized them so students were quickly and actively involved. She printed simple directions on the board, using separate areas and different colors for each grade, and referred students to them. She firmly began to follow through on insisting that students complete their work and fulfill their obligations, and she set up record-keeping and parent communication systems to ensure that they did so. She also put into place a system of incentives and activities for students when they worked and behaved responsibly. Although she initially saw such systems as bribes, especially for older students—it seemed to her that older students should already know and follow the rules and act responsibly—she now saw their value. By using activities for learning and for incentive, she encouraged the students to save time by working hard and behaving well, and she allowed them to do fun activities that she wanted to include anyway, if time permitted.

Most of her changes worked, and by the end of the second week Alexa was almost back to where she had started, which she considered a grand achievement.

The Lesson: The Weight of Minor Details

Similar to what had happened during Janna's first days, Alexa's challenges point to one of the most significant realities in teaching, one that continues to be especially important to beginning teachers. Simply put, no matter how much you know of educational philosophy, child psychology, and the subject matters you teach, teaching will inevitably expose an enormity of minor details that require attention. If these details are not dealt with quickly, they can overwhelm everything else you are trying to do. In fact, many describe teaching as "a career in which the greatest challenges and most difficult responsibilities are faced by those with the least experience" (Glickman, Gordon, & Ross-Gordon, 2007, p. 24).

Fortunately, Alexa was determined to withstand defeat. She also was helped in her effort by a story that had inspired both her aunt and cousin and by some readings in her university courses. Her aunt often repeated a story to the girls that she had read in *Teacher and Child* (1972), a book by Haim Ginott. The story was about a river boatman who was ferrying a passenger across the river. The passenger, a scholar, asked the boatman, "Do you know philosophy?" "I can't say I do," answered the boatman. "Then you have lost a third of your life," declared the scholar. After a time the scholar asked, "Do you know literature?" "I can't say I do," answered the boatman. "Then you have lost another third of your life," said the scholar. After a while the boat was seized by the current, dashed against a boulder, split, and began to sink. The boatman asked the scholar, "Do you know how to swim?" "No," cried the scholar. "Then you have lost all your life," concluded the boatman. Alexa knew the theories and subject matter and was determined that she would learn how to swim.

When Alexa was younger and aspiring to become an elementary teacher just like her cousin and her aunt, she read two books Janna had found to be inspiring. Jesse Stuart told his story in *The Thread That Runs So True*, first published in 1949. The book detailed his twenty years of teaching in the mountain region of Kentucky, but seemed to be almost a mini-history of education in the United States. Just a few years older than some of his students, he had only a teaching certificate and three years in high school when he entered his first one-room school. These qualifications did little to prepare him for the ruffian group of older students—boys who delighted in the fact that they had "run off" their previous teachers. Though the boys set out to make the new teacher's life miserable, Stuart was determined to give them the best he had and to never be chased out of the school, no matter what they tried to do to him. Like Janna before her, Alexa decided that she, too, would not be chased away.

In *Marva Collins' Way* (1990), Collins told about how she had turned hopeless, hostile youngsters into eager and ambitious achievers. It was her attitude that made children learn, her constant "You can do it" that convinced students that there was nothing they could not achieve. Collins greeted her children daily with endless encouragement. "The first thing we are going to do here, children, is an awful lot of believing in ourselves." Inspired and determined, "I can do it" also became Alexa's mantra.

Alexa knew she could and would succeed, just as Mercedes and Janna had done. She was a quick learner who now knew that to succeed, she must prevent as many problems as possible and immediately handle those that did arise and threaten to drag her under. She knew (or thought she knew) how to create a class team and how to prepare and present good lessons for one grade level, but not for two grades at the same time. She also realized that she knew very little about the other things that required her attention during the day: taking attendance, collecting lunch money, integrating technology and equipment effectively in her lessons, keeping paper and other supplies available and in good order, distributing and collecting worksheets and other materials, moving students from one place to another, timing the day's activities, correcting student work in helpful ways, ensuring that students kept materials and displays in good order, and generally nipping disruptive behavior in the bud. She realized that somehow or another the plants in the room had to be watered, and Ziggy's habitat had to be cleaned, the computers and audiovisual equipment dealt with, the notices sent out, the duplicating done, classroom visitors dealt with in positive ways, and provisions made for students with special needs or with limited English proficiency and for new students who were transferred into her class now that the year was under way. The first week she found that she was spending enormous amounts of time repeating instructions, cajoling students, and then waiting exasperatedly for them to follow directions. She added insult to her own injuries by spending evenings, though exhausted, reading papers, preparing material for the next day, and contacting parents or guardians about countless matters. Her schooling had not prepared her for all of that. She discovered quickly how heavy the mass of minor details could be.

What Teachers Try to Accomplish and How

Certainly, lists of specific things teachers try to accomplish during a year would fill the remaining pages of this book. Instead of lists, what you will find here is highly summarized information and examples that are important to your understanding of the linkage between teacher intentions and the managerial tasks that make their accomplishment possible. We'll begin with some very general goals and move toward specific examples.

In broad terms, teachers want to help their students become productive citizens, able to live life fully and well. Teachers everywhere sincerely want their students to make responsible choices and to discriminate between right and wrong. They would like for their students to be healthy and to appreciate life's beauty and joy, but also to be able to deal with adversity. Teachers want all of this for the students they teach. (Of course, teachers also wouldn't mind a bit of appreciation, fond regard, and remembrance, though they don't expect too much of it.)

In more specific terms, teachers aim their efforts toward the goals that have guided modern education for decades. These goals were well articulated in the 1918 *Cardinal Principles of Secondary Education,* though they certainly were evident before that publication. In 1918 goals were (1) health, (2) command of the fundamental processes (communication and math), (3) worthy home membership, (4) vocation, (5) civil education (good citizenship), (6) worthy use of leisure, and (7) ethical character. These goals are not equally emphasized now, if indeed they ever were. While little attention presently is given to worthy home membership or worthy use of leisure, the remaining five goals still figure strongly in the curriculum.

The very specific outcomes of teaching—as well as the procedures designed to bring them about—are published in curriculum guides and state frameworks and nationwide standards that describe what is to be accomplished at each grade level and in every area of the curriculum. And now in response to various reform legislations and the interest in a nationwide curricula, many states (most notably California, Texas, and Florida) have statewide textbook adoptions that dictate the textbooks schools and districts can use. The states select the textbooks they deem correspond most closely with curriculum standards and frameworks. As a result, major publishing houses now tailor books and other materials accordingly.

The Instructional Package: Content, Instruction through Experience, and Management

Management is closely linked to teaching—in fact, classroom teaching hardly can occur in its absence. As will become evident in later chapters, the management component of teaching varies according to subject, grade level, and method of teaching. Kindergarten is run quite differently from a sixth-grade classroom; multi-age classes are run differently from single-grade rooms. Reading is taught differently from art, music differently from math, spelling differently from social studies. Record keeping, activities, groupings, materials, and even expectations and work products for students are likely to differ as well.

It is difficult, if not impossible, to describe in precise detail exactly what is included and what transpires in the totality of classroom teaching. Identifiable key elements of teaching can be thought of as decision points that call on teachers to decide how they should proceed in the classroom. Let us examine some of teaching's key considerations and decision points by analyzing the following statement:

> Education begins with three fundamental questions that, when considered in light of learner traits and conditions, link to elements of teaching, which have certain identifiable characteristics and typical focuses.

Think of it this way—education begins with three fundamental questions that are entwined with learner traits and conditions.

1. *What should learners know?* The answer to this question is determined by deciding what is best for individuals and society. What learners should know—the contents and curricula of education currently identified by the content standards—is a central question to philosophy. Chapter 2 presents some considerations and definitions of curriculum.

2. *How do learners learn?* The answer to this question is determined by investigating the process by which individuals acquire, remember, and put knowledge to use. It is a central question to educational psychology. For further enlightenment, this question of how students learn must be considered in light of certain learner traits and conditions known to affect learning. Several chapters consider these points, in particular, Chapters 5, 8, 9, and 13. Chief among these learner traits and conditions are the following:

   - Intelligence and aptitude, which include inborn abilities and proclivities that vary from student to student
   - Individual learning styles and rates
   - Motivation as indicated by students' willingness to work at the experiences and activities provided them
   - Group behavior, which differs significantly from individual behavior
   - Social and economic realities, which are known to affect individual ability and motivation to learn

3. *How should learners be taught?* The answer to this question is determined by which experiences, instructional strategies, activities, and materials best promote student learning. It is a central question in pedagogy, or methods of teaching, and the focus of Chapter 6.

Consideration of these questions links to structures called elements of teaching, which are the content to be taught (what learners should learn according to content standards) and the instruction through experiences and activities (how learners learn and how they should be taught). Underlying these elements is another element—management—the primary focus of this book. When everything is taken into account, it becomes clear that for a classroom to run smoothly, management techniques must fit the activities and expectations of specific subjects and students' ages, maturity, and ability levels. In other words, curriculum, instruction, and management must go hand in hand.

These three elements of teaching are judged against the following criteria:

- Content must be relevant to the learners, worth learning in itself, and further contribute to the overall goals of education.

- Instruction through experiences must be given clearly, must guide and assist learning, must be relevant to both subject matter and students' lives, and must be attractive and enjoyable.

- Management must help teaching run more smoothly and efficiently.

Further, these criteria must be linked as follows: Worthwhile *content or curricula* are delivered through instructional strategies, which include *experiences and activities* that are relevant and attractive, clear and helpful, with the entire process enhanced through *management* that promotes smoothness and efficiency.

Alexa Smart Revisited

Mindful of the difficulties Alexa Smart experienced, and with the introduction of classroom management now completed, let us see how Alexa might have minimized the troubles she encountered. We will give attention to what she could have done before the school year began, or in this case before she first met her students, during the first days and weeks, and as a continual process through the year. This presentation is general for now but will be elaborated in chapters to come.

"THE FIRST WEEK OF SCHOOL IS JUST REVIEW. YOU KNOW. SCENES FROM LAST YEAR'S EPISODE."

© Martha F. Campbell. Reprinted by permission.

Before the School Year Begins

Before students are scheduled to arrive, teachers need to take care of several matters, of which the following five are especially important. First, teachers should familiarize themselves with the school facilities and meet as many of the school personnel as possible—administrators, clerical and custodial staffs, and other teachers. Alexa Smart did this well: As the principal introduced her and showed her around the school on the afternoon she was hired, she quickly began to establish friendly relationships with him, the staff, and the teachers she met. She learned the locations of the library, playgrounds, restrooms, the cafeteria, the nurse's office, the custodians' station, and the teacher workroom and lounge. She introduced herself to people at school whenever possible.

Second, teachers should familiarize themselves with the curriculum and content standards for their particular grade level, and with textbooks and other materials provided them. Alexa did this fairly well. She reviewed curriculum guides and standards for both the fourth and fifth grades, studied the various textbooks, familiarized herself with material present or typically used in her room, and reviewed some of the available websites and media.

Third, teachers should lay out a tentative calendar for the year, with specific detailed plans for the first two or three weeks. Alexa, who prided herself on attention to detail, had the first month of topics and lessons broadly outlined before her first day with the students. She later found it necessary to modify her plans substantially, but most teachers frequently do.

Fourth, teachers should organize and set up the physical environment of the classroom to include flexible seating; convenient work areas adjacent to needed materials, any special areas in the room such as computer areas, science corners, or reading centers; and storage centers for materials and equipment. Alexa thought her well-meaning friends had done a good job of this, though she soon found they included things that were too distracting (the terrarium and iguana). She realized that she had put too much emphasis on classroom appearance and not enough on efficiency of procedures, activities, and student movement.

Fifth, teachers should give thought to the kind of psychosocial climate they hope to establish and maintain, together with the procedures designed for bringing it about. Here was where Alexa made a major mistake. She knew that students needed to feel a sense of belonging, especially because they were moved so abruptly to a new class with a new teacher after the school year had begun. She knew that they also needed to experience pleasure in their work. Alexa also thought that because they were older students, the fourth and fifth graders would know and follow school rules and class routines that were made to avoid chaos. Alexa believed students would behave responsibly and reciprocate with their own kindnesses. She thought she could simply remind the students of rules and routines and establish those feelings of belonging just by being nice to students and accepting what they did. When she found they didn't, she had no effective means for putting an immediate end to chaos, disrespect, poor manners, inconsiderate behavior, and irresponsible choices. She had to learn that rules, order, and consideration of others must be firmly established, practiced, and taught before a class can move ahead.

The First Days and the First Weeks

What teachers do in the beginning is crucial to setting tone, expectations, and the likelihood of compliance. Good managers make sure the first days of school are orderly, which calls for tight structure. They explain rules and procedures, introduce materials and various parts of the classroom, monitor students closely, and let them know when they are behaving responsibly and appropriately. They explain and practice routines, a first step in making them habitual. They use a few appropriate classbuilding activities to help create a caring community for the students. Teachers also talk with students about how they must accept responsibility for their own conduct. Alexa did not do this well. Of course, everything in the program can't be introduced on the first day of school, but by the end of the first week, several issues should be settled.

Attendance and Opening Procedures From the first day onward, students should begin the day in their seats with a quiet activity. During this time the teacher should take attendance while walking around and observing the students.

Older students should learn at once that they are to go to their assigned seats and begin work immediately. They can be given specific assignments such as five-a-day math problems, journal writing, or reading their library books. Younger students, not yet able to work on their own, are taught to go directly to the circle (kindergarten), to an assigned center, or to their seats. In the past, on the first morning students were told: "Now we are in school, and the first thing we do here is sit down, fold our hands, and close our lips. If we need to say anything, we must raise our hand." The teacher then went directly into calling the roll and other opening activities, such as flag salute, calendar, counting, song, or sharing. When students showed themselves capable of doing other activities with self-control, the teacher may have changed the opening. In any case, the beginning tone was businesslike and was quickly made routine. Considerable reminding and practice were necessary at first, but quiet self-control was—and still is—essential to everything in the program.

Jones (2007), Kagan and Kagan (2009), and others encourage teachers to greet students in a manner similar to this (and yes, it is all right to smile): "Welcome everyone. I'm very glad you are with me this year. I know we will have fun and learn a lot, and learning will be fun. There will be time for you to talk and move, and also time to sit. I will use a quiet signal like this when I want your attention on me." Every day teachers should give their students structured activities that allow them to move and talk—two basic human needs.

Seating Arrangements and Orientation to the Classroom Teachers should explain seating arrangements. Introductions to the uses of the various parts of the classroom, including interest centers and work areas, the materials they contain, and what is to be done there, can be accomplished with teacher demonstration or guided student exploration and discovery. Older students may enjoy a scavenger hunt of the classroom and its resources.

Class Rules and System of Discipline On the first day teachers should go over the expected rules of responsible student behavior in such a way that the expectations are concrete for the students. There should be no more than four rules for younger children and six for older children; greater numbers cannot be remembered. Have in mind what is acceptable to you, but encourage students to give input, ask questions, or discuss the various rules, incentives, and consequences. Make sure students understand the rules, the reasons behind them, and enforcement procedures you will use, and make sure they see the system as fair. If students are old enough, you may have them sign their names on a "class contract" of the rules to indicate they understand the rules, find them fair, and fully intend to abide by them.

Orientation to the School and School Rules Unless new to the school, older students already will be acquainted with the buildings and grounds. Still, it is advisable to spend time orienting students to restrooms, drinking fountains, playgrounds, the cafeteria, the library, the principal's office, the reception desk, and the nurse's station. Many teachers take their students on a walking tour of the places sometime during the first or second day of school.

Students are expected to follow certain rules that pertain to the school, as distinct from the rules of the classroom. These rules tell how to behave in common areas such as corridors, on the playground, in the library, in the cafeteria, at bus and parking areas, and at street crossings. They also state the policies and consequences regarding electronic devices such as cell phones, iPods, and other things students like to bring with them to school. It is the teacher's responsibility to thoroughly familiarize students (and aides and visiting caregivers as well) with these school regulations and procedures.

The Daily Schedule The daily schedule should be explained in a way that makes clear what activities are to occur during each part of the day and how students are to work and behave for each. The schedule should be posted where students easily can see it for reference. Along with a discussion of the schedule and activities, the teacher previews books and materials to be used on a regular basis—where they are located, how they are obtained, how they are cared for, and how they are returned after use. The teacher also reviews guidelines for computer use.

Monitors (Classroom Assistants) Many teachers use class members to help with the numerous classroom chores. Often called *monitors,* these helpers are selected during the first week of classes and changed several times during the year. Some teachers assign monitors to their duties, whereas others take applications, ask for volunteers, or make prized assignments (such as feeding a classroom animal) contingent on special accomplishment. A list of duties for which assistants can be particularly helpful may be found in Chapter 7. It is desirable to assign some special job to every student in the class, in order to increase interest and promote a sense of ownership and responsibility.

Miscellaneous Needs Students continually need help while working independently. They also need to sharpen pencils, get drinks, go to the restroom, and sometimes call their parents or guardians. Procedures and routines must be established and practiced for all such matters, so students understand how they are to proceed.

Traffic Patterns Students must be instructed and given the opportunity to practice how to enter the room, how to leave when dismissed, what to do during emergency drills, and how to move from one area to another. Congestion, prevalent around the teacher's desk and classroom animals, should be eliminated by instructing students on how they are to move about and how many may be out of their seats at a given time.

Managerial Matters That Require Ongoing Attention

To the extent possible, matters just described should be discussed with the class and put into place during the first week of school. In addition, several managerial matters require ongoing attention throughout the year. Having regained control of her classroom, Alexa placed herself in a position from which she could attend to these matters. Such ongoing matters are mentioned here briefly and are discussed more fully in later chapters.

Curriculum Management The curriculum is the program for learners, which is aligned to standards that are described by the state and the school. Its management entails the selection, organization, and presentation of subject matter, plus arrangements for student work and accountability. These matters fluctuate throughout the year and require continual adjustment.

Lesson Management Lesson management involves selecting and organizing learning activities, grouping students, giving explanations and directions, providing for student accountability, monitoring and giving feedback, assessing performance, and reteaching as necessary. In such management, teachers find that the pacing of lessons is very important. Pacing means that lessons cover what is intended, with immediate student participation, within the allotted time, with steady momentum but without rush or delay. Also important are the transitions between lessons, which should be made smoothly and quickly, allowing for no dead time.

Record Keeping, Assessment, and Reporting Records should be kept that tell the student, teacher, caregivers, or administrator, at a glance, a student's achievement levels, work in progress, strengths and challenges, and future needs. In the past, this requirement was most easily met by keeping records sheets for the entire class plus separate records files or folders for each individual student. The folders included individual progress charts together with samples (good or poor) of student work. As districts, schools, and caregivers move into technology, many teachers are asked to keep current records on the computer and be able to share those records upon request with caregivers and others who have interest in the student's performance and progress. As for reporting, each school district has its own system. Many still use report cards to show achievement made in different subjects and may also include effort expended by the student and general behavior or comportment, although some also use some form of electronic reporting.

Special Groups Teachers now instruct students with diverse abilities and in varied settings. All teachers are expected to welcome, value, and educate all students, including those with special needs. Teachers who instruct in inclusive or multi-age classrooms, or who instruct students with language and cultural diversities, have additional management challenges related to curriculum and lessons, record keeping, and paraprofessionals. Teachers, students, and caregivers all have rights and responsibilities that affect these matters.

Communication Teachers are constant communicators. They direct, instruct, and motivate students through lessons. They work with paraprofessionals, support providers, volunteers, and substitute teachers, all of whom have potential to enrich lessons. They communicate with caregivers in a variety of ways. They also interact with administrators and colleagues.

Extracurricular Activities Teachers' duties range far beyond those of simply organizing and presenting lessons. The following are a few of the important tasks they frequently perform that contribute to children's education but rarely are considered part of teaching.

Plays and Performances Teachers are called on to organize, coach, direct, and stage various types of performances, which usually involve organizing help from caregivers and volunteers.

Field Trips When the class is able to leave the school to visit places of special interest, the teacher must oversee transportation, permission slips from parents and guardians, volunteers to help supervise students, and advance preparation to make the trip smooth and beneficial.

Fairs and Carnivals Many schools put on fairs, carnivals, and other money-raising activities. Even when such events are under the direction of the parent–teacher organization, teachers are called on to help plan, prepare, and work at the events.

Back-to-School and Open House Almost all schools have one or more evenings during the year in which caregivers and the public are invited to visit the school and classrooms. At these events, teachers describe their programs, activities, and expectations for the year and display samples of student work.

Family Math Nights Some schools try to involve entire families in their children's learning by holding family math nights. Caregivers join their students to investigate a series of math activities set up and monitored by teachers.

Assemblies Teachers sometimes are put in charge of assemblies for their school, which requires much planning and organization. At other times they are responsible only for the movement of their class to and from the assembly, as well as the behavior of their students while there.

Clubs Teachers often assume leadership roles for special clubs or other activities such as student council, safety patrol, cheerleading, athletics, photography, scouts, science groups, after-school recreation, and so forth. Occasionally, these extra tasks bring a little extra pay, but typically, they are an expected part of the teacher's overall duties.

"DO YOU REALIZE THAT THEY PAY OUR TEACHER TO COME TO SCHOOL EVERY DAY AND WE DO IT FOR FREE?"

Managerial Matters That Relate to Professionalism and Professional Growth

Teachers also are likely to find themselves dealing with managerial matters related to professionalism and professional growth. On occasion they will need to manage the work of other adults in their classroom or meet with student advocates. Additionally, teachers may need to manage emotional trauma and even their own job-related stress.

Paraprofessionals, Volunteers, and Advocates Particularly in lower grades, many teachers have aides and volunteers working in their rooms, and perhaps even cross-grade partners and cross-age tutors. Some experienced teachers have student teachers assigned to them. The duties of each should be very clear, as should the extent to which they are to correct and discipline students. When assigned to do clerical work, adult helpers should be provided with a comfortable workstation and appropriate materials. Teachers also may need to meet and communicate with advocates of students with special needs. Read more about these matters in Chapter 12.

Preparing for Substitute Teachers From time to time, every teacher must rely on a substitute. The class should be able to continue with its normal routines under the direction of a substitute. To make this possible, the teacher must prepare the class to work with, not against, the new teacher. Discussions with the class can clarify students' responsibilities in helping the process. Whenever possible, complete lesson plans should be left for or e-mailed to the substitute, and one or two class monitors should be assigned to inform substitutes of routines, locations of materials, and normal work procedures.

Here we end our introductory chapter on classroom management, having laid the groundwork for what is to come. The next chapter will deal with how to manage the curriculum and the calendar. Before proceeding to that topic, take a moment to consider these parting thoughts, and review and reflect on what has been presented so far.

Parting Thoughts

What is important is not what happens to us, but how we respond to what happens to us.

J. Sartre

If you have built castles in the air, your work need not be lost; that is where they should be. Now put foundations under them.

Thoreau

Summary Self-Check

Check off the following as you either understand or become able to apply them:

- ☐ Three fundamental questions about education
  - What should students know?
  - How do learners learn?
  - How should learners be taught?
- ☐ Aspects of classroom management that require attention
  - Before the year begins: familiarity with personnel and facilities, curriculum and content standards, calendar; preparation of the classroom; planning for the emotional tone of the class
  - First days and weeks of school: attendance and opening procedures; seating arrangements and classroom organization; orientation to the school, classroom, and school rules; the daily schedule; guidelines for computer use; books and materials; selection of student helpers (monitors); miscellaneous routines; traffic patterns and regulations; use of volunteers and paraprofessionals; preparation for substitute teachers

☐ Continual attention throughout the year: curriculum selection and organization; lesson management; special groups; record keeping, assessment, and reporting; extracurricular activities

☐ Aspects of professionalism and professional growth
  • Working with others

Activities for Reflection and Discussion

1. Take a moment to review the statements in the Preview–Review Guide at the beginning of this chapter. Put a check mark in the *Review* column next to any statement with which you now agree. How have your thoughts changed since reading this chapter?

2. Interview at least two teachers about the problems they experienced their first year(s) of teaching. What is the best advice from the teachers you interviewed regarding the first days of school or first year of teaching?

3. From what you have seen or heard, how realistic is the Alexa Smart story?

4. What distinction, if any, can be made between instruction and management? Describe what you believe each entails. What overlap do you see?

5. Have you known teachers who failed, gave up early, or lived through immense frustration? If so, what seemed to be the major difficulties with which they had to contend?

6. The point was made that the instructional program cannot proceed until a semblance of good order is established, practiced, and maintained in the classroom. Why do you agree or disagree with that? What if it takes a week or two (or longer) to get the class under control?

7. This first chapter presents a fairly thorough overview of classroom management. Was it worth your time reading it, or did you feel that you more or less knew all these things before you decided to become a teacher?

References and Recommended Readings

Bureau of Education. (1918). *Cardinal principles of secondary education*. Bulletin #35. Washington, DC: Department of the Interior, Bureau of Education.

Evertson, C., & Emmer, E. (2009). *Classroom management for elementary teachers* (8th ed.). Upper Saddle River, NJ: Pearson.

Glickman, C., Gordon, S., & Ross-Gordon, J. (2007). *SuperVision and instructional leadership*. Boston: Pearson.

Ginott, H. (1972). *Teacher and child*. New York: Macmillan.

Jones, F. (2007). *Tools for teaching: Discipline Instruction Motivation* (2nd ed.). Santa Cruz, CA: Fredric H. Jones & Associates.

Kagan, S., & Kagan, M. (2009). *Cooperative learning*. San Clemente, CA: Kagan Publishing.

Kozol, J. Letters to a young teacher. *Phi Delta Kappan* 89(1), 8–20.

Wong, H., & Wong, R. (2009). *The first days of school* (4th ed.). Mountain View, CA: Harry K. Wong Publications, Inc.

Trade Books

Collins, M., & Tamarkin, C. (1990). *Marva Collins' way*. New York: G.P. Putman's Sons.

Sollman, C., Emmons, B., & Paolini, J. (1994). *Through the cracks.* Worcester, MA: Davis Publications.

Stuart, J. (1949). *The thread that runs so true.* New York: Simon & Schuster.

PEARSON
myeducationlab

Go to the Topic: **Establishing Classroom Norms and Expectations** in the MyEducationLab (www.myeducationlab.com) for your course, where you can:

- Find learning outcomes for **Establishing Classroom Norms and Expectations** along with the national standards that connect to these outcomes.
- Apply and practice your understanding of the core teaching skills identified in the chapter with the Building Teaching Skills and Dispositions learning units.
- Examine challenging situations and cases presented in the IRIS Center Resources.
- Use interactive Simulations in Classroom Management to practice decision making and to receive expert feedback on classroom management choices.

Laying Out the School Year

A good plan executed right now is far better than a perfect plan executed next week.

—George S. Patton

Preview–Review Guide

Before you read the chapter, and based on what you know, think you know, or assume, take a minute to put a check mark in the **Preview** column if you agree with the statement. When you finish the chapter, take time to reread the statements and respond in the **Review** column. Reflective discussions can develop because many of the statements are not clearly "yes" or "no."

Preview   **Review**

1. _____ Curriculum is defined as the contents of textbooks and other materials   _____
children use.

2. _____ Teachers are expected to redesign curriculum guides to meet their own   _____
specifications.

3. _____ Ideally, teachers should lay out the yearly calendar before they finalize   _____
units of instruction.

4. _____ Curriculum maps reveal repetitions and gaps in content and skills.   _____

5. _____ Backward design planning begins with target goals and assessment.   _____

6. _____ Essential or guiding questions are intended to check ongoing student   _____
understanding of the fine points of their study.

7. _____ Authorities recommend that, when planning units, teachers begin by   _____
listing the broad objectives they hope to have their students attain.

8. _____ Thematic plans integrate several subjects into each unit of instruction.   _____

9. _____ Awareness of what students already know or are able to do provides   _____
helpful information to teachers as they plan.

10. _____ How the curriculum is managed is much more important to education   _____
than is the subject matter contained in the curriculum.

Chapter Objectives

After reading Chapter 2, students will demonstrate understanding of

■ various views and definitions of "curriculum"

■ how to organize the instructional program for the school year, a unit of study, and single lessons

through their active participation in discussions and the end-of-chapter activities for reflection.

Teachers are faced with numerous management tasks, but one that should be completed at least tentatively before the school year begins is that of laying out the intended instructional program for the year. While national, state, and district standards direct what students are to study at each grade level, the reality of schooling is that the curriculum is more flexible than the calendar and time schedules. Because the curriculum must be adjusted to the dates and times available for instruction as published by the district and school, effective teachers plan ways to interweave curriculum with the calendar. As you read this chapter, consider this problem to solve or this essential or guiding question: *How can I plan or arrange my school year, my school day, and my lessons to increase my teaching effectiveness and maximize student learning?*

This task is more challenging for elementary teachers than for secondary teachers, because elementary classes deal with so many different subject areas on a daily basis—reading, math, social studies and current events, science, health, safety, physical education, music, art, penmanship, and now technology and character education. Elementary teachers are challenged to find ways to deal with, and do justice to, all these subjects for all the children they teach. They accomplish this task in two steps. First, they note what the year's calendar allows in terms of instructional days and time. Then they organize their instructional programs to fit within time constraints while providing proper emphasis, duration, and continuity over weeks, grading periods, and the entire year. These two steps fall into place naturally behind teachers' understandings of the goals of school curriculum, and their awareness of the knowledge and skills their students need to be successful in today's world.

The Goals of the School Curriculum

The school curriculum is intended to expose students to important subjects and topics, thereby causing them to acquire certain knowledge, skills, attitudes, and values. These goals were partially expressed in the Cardinal Principles mentioned in Chapter 1, especially command of the fundamental processes of communication and mathematics and, more recently, ethical character. In addition, the curriculum is intended to produce (1) attitudes of openness to ideas, willingness to try, and acceptance of others; (2) knowledge of facts and their application; and (3) growth in thinking skills such as analysis, synthesis, evaluation, and creation. As Eisner asserts, "Curriculum is and needs to be a course of action that advances understanding" (2002).

All of this is to be worked on in school although, in truth, much of it—especially concerning attitudes and values—occurs more potently in the home and community. Published character-building curricula such as *Character Counts* are available for adoption by districts, schools, or individual teachers. These programs offer guided activities so teachers and schools can focus on a character trait or quality each week. However, for teachers to best help students acquire attitudes of good character, they must infuse these qualities into the way they instruct. They also must provide students with constant opportunities to practice the attributes and attitudes of good character within the natural events of their class.

What Is the Elementary School Curriculum for Today's Students?

In past decades, elementary curriculum was simple: reading, 'riting, and 'rithmetic, three basic skills for getting along in the world. But the world has changed and is changing, and so is the curricula. Sharon Robinson (AACTE) had this to say: "We used to develop in students a passion to learn all the right answers. We want 21st century students to have a passion for asking new questions" (http://www.youtube.com, accessed 3/27/2010). Skills and knowledge for twenty-first-century survival are much more expansive. Sternberg (2008) suggests another Three R's as an alternative to the original three: reasoning, resilience ("persistence in achieving goals despite the obstacles life places in our way"), and responsibility (ethics and morals). Wagner's list (2008) is longer. He identifies seven skills for surviving in the new world of work: (1) critical thinking and problem solving, (2) collaboration and leadership, (3) agility (flexibility) and adaptability, (4) initiative and entrepreneurialism, (5) effective oral and written communication, (6) accessing and analyzing information, and (7) curiosity and imagination. Elementary school is the first step toward all of these goals.

Business and education leaders are talking about skills for the twenty-first century. The Partnership for 21st Century Skills, based in Tucson, Arizona, presents a framework of knowledge and skills, a "vision for student success in the new global economy." With similarities to Wagner's list, the *P21 Framework Definitions* (2009) embrace skills in four distinct but interconnected elements: (1) core subjects and twenty-first-century themes (global awareness; financial, economic, business, and entrepreneurial literacy; and civil, health, and environmental literacies); (2) learning and innovation skills (creativity and innovation; critical thinking and problem solving; and communication and collaboration); (3) information, media, and technology skills (information, media, and ICT [information, communications, and technology] literacies); and (4) life and career skills (flexibility and adaptability, initiative and self-direction, social and cross-cultural skills, productivity and accountability, and leadership and responsibility).

A Brief Word about Standards and Reforms

In the 1980s and 1990s, state and federal governments responded to *A Nation at Risk* by implementing a series of laws for standards-based reform. With the Improving America's Schools Act of 1994 (IASA) and Goals 2000: Educate America Act, the federal government moved standards-based reform to policy and encouraged states to adopt content standards in the core subject areas of mathematics, English language arts, reading, and science. The No Child Left Behind Act (NCLB) of 2001, originally known as the Elementary and Secondary Education Act, was made into law to improve education for all students in public schools. NCLB, now setting 2014 as the year for all students to meet state grade-level academic content and performance standards, has made standards-based reform a national education policy. In 2009 President Barack Obama took this goal further with Race to the

Top (RTTP), a competitive grant program. The program provides incentives to states that invest in education innovation and reform, improve student outcomes, and show significant gains in achievement, closures in achievement gaps, improved high school graduation rates, and stronger preparation for success in college and careers.

The current U.S. Department of Education supports the alignment of a national curriculum and standards with internationally "benchmarked" standards developed by UNESCO, the education arm of the United Nations (U.S. Department of Education, 2003). To this end, the administration's federal plan is that all schools in all 50 states will teach the same content.

In light of current reforms across the nation, standards have become a driving force for content and curriculum performance, opportunities to learn, and technology. This has been particularly true of literacy and math for some time, although now all individual subject areas have identified content standards as well. States and districts have created or revised learning goals and have identified benchmarks and competencies to define skills, knowledge, and content mastery for students of varying ages and grades.

Curriculum from the Management Perspective

Our concern here is with managing the curriculum, not with preparing and organizing it. A goal of curriculum management is to bring about purposeful interaction between students and the information and skills they are intended to learn. A concurrent goal is to accomplish this interaction as effectively and efficiently as possibly.

Teachers usually think of curriculum as the basic material they are expected to teach or the textbooks they use. In efforts to align curriculum across the country and to help state departments of education and teachers themselves identify and plan their curricula, national, state, and local organizations of content areas have published standards that describe the specific topics and content for each grade level. Just as you find specific standards connected to each chapter in this book, target standards now are laid out in the teacher editions of the textbooks designed for the students they are instructing. In preparing those textbooks, authors and publishers do their best to interpret and address the published standards, make the books both effective and easy to use, and provide appropriate ancillary materials. Older textbooks were supplemented with transparencies and black lines. Many newer textbooks now have accompanying websites and weblinks; CDs, DVDs, or videos; differentiated activities; and banks of test questions.

However, for the sake of accuracy, we must note that textbook contents and curriculum are not synonymous terms. For as long as schools have existed, there has been dispute about what the curriculum ought to be. Even today there is no real consensus as to what the term *curriculum* means. It has been defined as experiences under the auspices of the school (Rosales-Dordelly & Short, 1985); a series of planned events intended to have educational consequence (Eisner, 1985); and activities, processes, and structural arrangements intended for and used in the school and classroom as a means of accomplishing the educative function (Goodlad, 2004). Doll suggests that "curriculum is what happens when the door is closed," although he more formally describes curriculum as formal and informal content and process used to help learners in knowledge, understanding, skills, attitudes, appreciation, and values (1995). Ralph Tyler (1949), one of the twentieth century's most influential writers on curriculum, didn't really define it at all. Instead, he devoted his efforts to describing how curriculum is studied, developed, and evaluated.

Some authorities view curriculum as "explicit" or formal, "implicit" or hidden, and "extra." The *explicit* curriculum is what is published. This generally aligns with standards and grade-level expectations. The *implicit* curriculum includes socialization and learning environments, rules and guidelines, and behavior. The *extra* curriculum includes athletics, band, clubs, and other such activities.

Current educational policies and reforms further influence the definition of curriculum. Inspired by NCLB, a contemporary twist to the definition is the idea of "curriculum narrowing." Academic subjects of reading, math, and science are given time and resource priorities over other subjects (social studies, physical education, foreign languages, and the arts).

Although there is little agreement about the definitions of curriculum, there is perhaps even less agreement about curriculum content. Philosophers, educators, politicians, critics, individuals with axes to grind, and countless special-interest groups struggle to shape curriculum contents, as each believes proper. Hirsch and others have published volumes by grade level of what every child should know.

Laying Out the School Year

As you begin to consider the curriculum for your grade (or grades, if yours is a blended or multi-age class), you should carefully consider three things: what you are supposed to teach (content and standards), available materials, and your students. Once you do that, you will find yourself marking a calendar for the year. Templates or books for lesson planning can be found online, are furnished by schools, or are available for purchase. They usually provide a year's calendar formatted as blank boxes for each day of each month and contain spaces to enter your daily plans week by week. Choose the format you find easiest to use.

National holidays will be shown in your plan book, as well as some non-holidays, such as Halloween, Election Day, and Valentine's Day. As you prepare the overview of your instructional calendar, you can mark all the holidays, vacation times, teacher in-service or professional growth days, and days when students will not be present. Your school district calendar, separate from the plan book and available on the district's website, will indicate teaching days, professional growth days, parent–teacher conference days, and dates when report cards are due. Your school site calendar, available on your school's website, is likely to include back-to-school and open house nights, and perhaps dates for school assemblies, school carnival, family math nights, and other school or community events. While these events may seem to interfere with teaching continuity, they also can motivate and energize students and provide themes that you can use to good advantage.

Anticipating Upcoming Events

Considerations about the yearly calendar are annotated below to remind teachers of outside forces that can influence or distract from instruction, not to imply that the calendar is the driving force behind curriculum organization. Once you mark the yearly calendar in this way, you will have a more accurate view of the blocks of time available for teaching. Now you can make additional notations that offer an even more complete picture of what the months will bring. Depending on your actual school year, you will find it helpful to anticipate the following realities.

Summer Many districts schedule orientations and workshops in July or August, before the school year begins. New teachers who are hired before the school year begins are expected to attend these events.

Mid-July, Late August, Early September Schools that follow a trimester or year-round schedule may begin as early as July. In most areas of the country, school begins the week before or after Labor Day, although in some areas school begins even earlier in August. No matter when the school year begins, everyone is excited, and those first days tend to be a time of fairly good student behavior. Students are unsure of the new setting and usually hope they have a teacher who will treat them well. This is a good time for high-interest lessons that will help you get off to a good start with your students. Because you can expect that your students will test you very early in the year, as they did with Alexa Smart in Chapter 1, these first days are the time to establish—and practice—clear expectations and routines. This also is a good time for classbuilding activities that will help create a sense of community among the students and for teambuilding activities that will encourage cooperation. By closely observing your students these first weeks, you can develop an informal sense of their academic, social, and physical abilities before diagnostic and placement testing begins. For teachers and students alike, the first days of school usually are a time of watchfulness and promise.

Most of today's classrooms are likely to have at least a few students of varied cultural and ethnic backgrounds, and it important to remember and respect traditions of your community members. The Jewish New Year and High Holy Days, from Rosh Hashanah to Yom Kippur, occur in September and October. Ramadan, which may be observed by older Muslim students, can begin as early as August. Check with your building principal regarding the school's policy of drawing attention to religious holidays and discussing their history, meaning, and significance.

September and October Back-to-school nights usually are scheduled soon after the school year begins. You will be expected to describe your program to those who attend, answer questions, talk with caregivers, and show samples of each student's early work. Although your program should already have been communicated to caregivers through a class website or newsletter, this is a good time for reminders.

Parent–teacher conferences may be scheduled close to the back-to-school night, depending on when the school year began. In some areas, students are dismissed early or do not have school on those days; in other areas, conferences are scheduled at the end of the school day. These conferences call for considerable preparation on your part (as will be explained in Chapter 11). You will need to plan out what you would like to discuss with each student's caregivers. You also will need representative samples of each student's work, showing strengths and areas for growth.

Columbus Day is observed the second Monday of October, and for many districts this provides a three-day weekend. Teachers may give some attention to Columbus's explorations through stories and art activities. Halloween falls on the last day of the month. Although many schools downplay Halloween, students nevertheless will be excited and distracted by it. Many teachers use the event to combine reading, writing, art, and technology standards with the Halloween theme through stories, writing, research, and art activities. Again, check with your principal about district and school policy and practice.

November Early in November, most parts of the United States will "fall back" the clocks to standard time. This time change affects the energy levels of both teachers and students. Also, three events of particular interest occur this month. Election Day, the first Tuesday of the month, is not a school holiday, but usually is of interest to older students. Veterans Day, November 11, a school holiday, is accompanied by little fanfare in most places, and some school districts move the observance date in order to provide a three-day weekend. In contrast, Thanksgiving, the fourth Thursday of the month, generates much excitement. At least two days (in some districts, three days or even the entire week) are non-school days. Students will be interested in the origins of Thanksgiving, making this a good opportunity to blend writing, drama, research, and art activities with academic standards and technology.

December The first two-thirds of the month may be a time of excited anticipation over Hanukkah, Christmas, and Kwanzaa, and the last one-third will be given to vacation. Check school policy regarding mention of these events, but recognize that, regardless of policy, the children will be thinking about family celebrations and customs, travel, gifts, special foods and treats, and decorations, and will likely be more excitable and distracted than usual. These weeks are especially good times to connect academic standards and technology with activities in art, music, drama, and stories of the season.

January Teachers and students return from holiday excitements to the normal school routine with varying degrees of interest, but overall, this is a time for everyone to settle back into a productive routine. Observance of Martin Luther King Day, celebrating Dr. King's birthday on January 15, normally is scheduled to provide a long weekend in the middle of the month. That day, along with the entire month of February, Black History Month, provides opportunities to celebrate African American and Black heroes in history, music, art, and literature. Depending on the locale, winter weather also may be a topic of interest, or a challenge to planning because of unexpected snow days.

February This month marks the approximate midpoint of the school year. The month seems to pass especially quickly because it is short and contains events of interest to children. Many students will be interested in the professional football playoffs, with high interest in the Super Bowl early in the month. Winter Olympic Games, if they are held that year, offer interest and lesson opportunities. Children usually enjoy Groundhog Day (February 2) and Valentine's Day (February 14). Lincoln's birthday (February 13) and Washington's birthday (February 20) may also spark student interest and often are observed with one, or sometimes two, long weekends. Many elementary schools and teachers enjoy celebrating the one-hundredth day of school with a variety of math, literature, and art activities.

It is likely that teachers will have to prepare midyear report cards sometime in February or March. They also may be expected to hold midyear conferences with caregivers.

March After the fast pace of February, March may seem rather slow, and student enthusiasm may wane. However, with fewer outside distractions, teachers can focus on content standards, and children can concentrate better on schoolwork, making this a good time to complete longer units of study. Dr. Seuss's birthday is March 2, encouraging many teachers and librarians to plan celebration activities on that day. Also, Saint Patrick's Day may receive

"IT RAINED ALL WEEK AND THEY HAD TO STAY IN AND DRAW."

© Martha F. Campbell. Reprinted by permission.

some attention on March 17. Clocks that were changed in the fall will be moved ahead from standard time to Daylight Savings Time sometime during the month. Energy levels again are affected because of the time change.

April Most schools take a weeklong spring break in March or April. Students and families often travel or have visitors during this time. Also, April frequently brings commemorations of Passover and Easter. Check with your principal about school policies regarding these holidays.

May and June Sometime in May, schools typically extend another formal invitation for caregivers to visit the school. This is when teachers and students display some of their accomplishments of the year, and classrooms usually are decorated accordingly. Mother's Day occurs in May, and students often do art activities in which they make something to give the special women in their lives. Memorial Day falls on May 30 but usually is observed on the last Monday of the month to make a long weekend. Flag Day and Father's Day in June may attract some attention.

The end of the traditional school year comes in mid-May or June, depending on when the academic year began. Unexpected weather days during the year may extend the published end of school by a few days. Whenever school ends, the final weeks are a time of activity and distraction. Teachers are concerned about report cards. Students' minds are on summer, and a few are concerned about promotion or moving to another school.

Summer In districts with trimester or year-round school calendars, Independence Day, July 4, will affect planning for the first week of July. Some years, Summer Olympics Games and the national political primaries can provide interesting topics of study, particularly for older students.

Let us repeat: the yearly calendar is not the driving force behind curriculum organization. It is annotated here in this manner to remind teachers of outside forces that can influence or distract from instruction. Keep the notations at hand as you use your curriculum guide, grade-level standards, and textbooks to plot out the selected topics of instruction for your students. Use sticky notes or a pencil to block out your plans on a separate chart, blank calendar pages, or web template. You probably will make a number of changes before you finalize your plans. Two points to remember: First, to the extent possible, begin instructional units on Mondays (or the day following a long weekend) and have them end just before holidays, long weekends, or vacation times, because it is difficult to recapture student enthusiasm after such breaks. Second, while you may need to shorten or even bypass some of the units or lessons included in your grade and textbooks to fit everything into your schedule, always look for meaningful thematic approaches to content, and always try to integrate all relevant standards into your planning.

Laying Out the School Day

Once you have the year's calendar blocked out, but before you begin to plan specific lessons and units, it is a good idea to set up the day's schedule within the structure of the school's schedule, as you would like it to be. Although the school establishes times for recess, lunch, and dismissal, and your grade-level team may adjust schedules to create team teaching opportunities, you may have considerable discretion in deciding on the schedule of teaching you prefer. However, you should view the daily schedule as more than a matter of convenience. Certain subjects, such as math or language arts, are best studied when students are fresh, alert, and able to concentrate for a long while. Other subjects, such as physical education or singing, are best scheduled to relieve tension from long concentration. Still others that may involve cooperation and talking are good for later in the day when students are getting tired.

Daily Schedules

Stacy Ganzer teaches 30 half-day kindergarten students, many of whom are learning English. In addition to considering the short attention spans and the language diversity of her students, she must plan all her lessons and activities for a shorter time frame than teachers in other K–6 grades.

Hollie Foster and members of her grade-level team teach all-day kindergarten in a K–8 school. During their daily 35- to-40- minute prep, the teachers are able to meet and plan as a team. Their students attend school for the same length of time as the first through eighth graders. This year Hollie has 25 students. While she has no students who are learning English, she does have one with an IEP. Last year she had two students with behavior and academic IEPs. Hollie follows a schedule that takes into consideration many of the same issues that face Stacy.

Because Hollie's school is fairly new and has a high focus on technology and science, technology is integrated into all classrooms and all of the daily routines. All teachers in the school use the *Proxima,* an overhead projector, when they instruct. They also use a united streaming website and are able to show educational "movies."

Marilyn Cox and Bernardo Campos are partners in a fifth-grade team. In their district, fifth graders may participate in several special programs such as band and safety patrol that must be considered as the team plans the daily schedule.

Library is scheduled for one day a week. The school's computer lab is only available by sign-up and often is used for project-related work. Marilyn and Bernardo plan to use a portable computer lab, a cart with 30 laptop computers that can be moved from room to room, more often this year and will need to sign up for it accordingly. Many students serve on Student Council, which meets one day a week before school, or on Safety Patrol (in rotating groups of five each day). Because of their responsibilities, these students arrive shortly after the bell rings in the morning and leave the classroom five to ten minutes before general dismissal. This year's school budget still allows for band, and most of Marilyn and Bernardo's students participate in band as an elective. Band students are grouped according to the

Half-Day Kindergarten

Stacy's Schedule

7:45–7:50	Students place all their folders in the collection bin; attendance
7:50-8:00	Math problem solving of the day
8:00-8:20	Calendar activities/story
8:20-8:30	Shared writing
8:30-9:30	Reading/math groups (two groups of five children)
9:30-9:55	Snack/PE
9:55-10:10	Story/sharing
10:10-10:20	Daily phonemic awareness activities
10:20-10:50	Language and math centers/English language development groups
10:50–11:00	Free exploration (if time allows)
11:00-11:10	Clean-up
11:10-11:12	Line-up and dismissal

Reading and math groups alternate days except on Wednesdays when the groups are replaced with individual journal writing activities or whole-class science or social studies lessons.

Full-Day Kindergarten

Hollie's Schedule Tuesday through Friday

9:10–10:40	Reading
10:40-11:10	Writing
11:10-12:05	Lunch and recess
12:05-1:05	Science
1:05-1:45	Prep
1:45-2:00	Science
2:00-2:10	Snack break
2:10-3:25	Math
3:25-3:45	Social studies
3:45	Dismissal

Hollie's Monday Schedule

Monday is a short day for all the students in the school. While the kindergarten schedule is the same through lunch as the rest of the week, content segments for Monday afternoon are longer to better fit the earlier dismissal time:

12:05–12:28	Science
12:28-1:03	Prep
1:03-1:25	Science
1:25-1:35	Snack break
1:35-2:15	Math
2:15-2:45	Social studies
2:45	Dismissal

Marilyn and Bernardo's Schedule

8:55	Students gather on the playground with their classmates and enter their classrooms together to begin the day.
9:00–11:05	Reader's workshop and writing
11:05-11:20	Recess
11:20-12:45	Math (students are separated by ability groups, and the teaching team rotates to different groups when units change)
12:45-1:00	Homework assignments and explanations
1:00–1:40	Lunch
1:40-2:00	Reading aloud
2:00-2:20	Word study
2:20-3:00	Social studies/science
3:00-3:20	PE/art
3:20	Dismissal

instrument they play and meet with the band teacher one day a week. Also, in anticipation of a school Winter Olympics event, the fifth-grade team plans for eight rotations over a three-week period before winter break. Students participate in the school Olympics in February or March. The daily schedule is changed to allot 2:50 to 3:30 for these rotations.

Stacy, Hollie, Marilyn, and Bernardo teach in elementary schools where they are responsible for the entire curriculum. Some schools, particularly middle schools, also have specialist teachers for physical education, music, art, and occasionally other subjects, although budget cuts may already have eliminated these positions. These schools may schedule common preparation time for grades and subjects such as social studies and language arts to permit teachers to plan together and then team-teach. Other schools may have a regularly scheduled time for teachers to use for planning. In middle schools that include sixth grade, teams of teachers may share two or more groups of students every day. In teams of two, one teacher may teach students language arts and social studies while another teaches math and science. Where there are teams of four, teachers may each have separate subjects and simply rotate in order to teach the same content to all the students in the grade.

Sherry Coburn is the social studies teacher for a sixth-grade team at her middle school. Every day she teaches four groups of students for a 56-minute period. The other three teachers on her team teach language arts, math, and science. Sherry has a typical weekly plan for when her students study a chapter in their textbook. On Monday, Sherry assigns eight district geography questions. After some whole-class review, students use their textbooks and other resources to search for the answers. At the start of the year, students need a great deal of help with this activity, but they become more proficient as time goes by. On Tuesday and Wednesday, students complete activities using vocabulary from the chapter in the textbook. This work is turned in as homework on Thursday. To help students with their reading, Sherry creates study guides that include questions and missing words. Students use class time on Thursday to search the chapter and complete the study guides. On Friday, after a quiz from their reading, students play review games such as vocabulary concentration and Jeopardy.

Mapping the Big Picture

"To make sense of our students' experience over time, we need two lenses: a zoom lens into this year's curriculum for a particular grade and a wide-angle lens to see the K–12 perspective" (Jacobs, 1997, p. 3). Heidi Jacobs describes a procedure she calls curriculum mapping, which involves individual, team, and whole-school input and promotes alignment within and across grade levels by revealing gaps and redundancies in content and skills. A website that can lead you to more about curriculum mapping is http://www.curriculum21.com. In addition to initial and follow-up training sessions, the process of curriculum mapping has multiple steps:

■ After initial training in the process, teachers independently identify the major elements that make up the curriculum—the emphasized standards, benchmarks, content, skills, assessment, technology, and essential questions.

■ In a first read-through, each teacher scans the maps for the entire building (or team), to gather information and identify areas for future examination. Each teacher notes repetitions (of standards, content, and skills), gaps (between standards and goals and what actually is taught), meaningful assessments, matches with content standards and objectives, potential areas of integration, and timeliness (availability of current materials and resources and knowledge of current best practices).

■ If the curriculum-mapping project is large enough (for a school or the district), teachers who do not teach together then meet in teams of six or eight. They share their individual findings and create a composite list of their observations for review by the larger group.

■ In an all-faculty (or all-team) review, observation findings from the smaller sessions are charted, and the focus still is on the nonjudgmental review of what was observed. When teachers begin to edit, revise, and develop, they remain together as one large group or move into smaller instructional units.

■ Faculty members begin to sift through the data from the observation findings and determine areas that can be revised immediately and easily by faculty members, teams, and administrators.

■ Faculty members also determine areas that require more long-range research and development. These areas may require structural decisions, more in-depth investigation, or more consideration of the potential long-range consequences before changes can be made.

■ The steps in the whole curriculum mapping process then are repeated, because curriculum review is active and ongoing. Periodic reviews ensure that (1) essential questions focus instruction, (2) content is appropriate, (3) skills are aligned with content, and (4) assessments are appropriate and aligned with skills (Jacobs, 2004, p. 21).

Backward Design Planning

In an effort to help teachers better plan curriculum and assessments that will result in student *understanding* (as opposed to simple student *knowing*), McTighe and Wiggins (2004) offer another approach to planning. What they call backward design is an alternative to coverage and activity-oriented plans. Teachers plan through three stages. Here's an intentionally simplified explanation. Teachers who use backward design planning first identify the desired results. Then they determine acceptable evidence, the products students will provide to demonstrate their understanding. Finally, teachers plan and sequence the instruction and learning experiences. McTighe and Wiggins developed two templates to help teachers with their backward design planning. Figure 2.1 guides teachers to focus on important content. Figure 2.2 gives teachers a set of planning questions to consider as they plan a unit of study.

According to Wiggins and McTighe, teachers must reflect on several things as they consider the desired results of the teaching and learning. Teachers must identify the understandings students will gain. They must form essential or guiding questions—broad questions that will guide and focus the teaching and learning. They must identify key knowledge and skills students will acquire as a result of the study. Teachers also must consider the possibilities of evidence, such as performance, quizzes, tests, work samples, and student self-assessment, and determine what evidence they will expect and use for students to demonstrate their understanding.

Task analyses of performance tasks and assessment greatly help teachers determine acceptable evidence, the second step of backward design. It makes sense in this step to articulate content standards and the desired understandings to be assessed through tasks. It also makes sense to clarify the purpose of the assessment tasks—whether they are diagnostic, formative, or

Figure 2.1

Planning Template

Stage 1—Desired Results	
Established Goal(s): ⓖ	
Understanding(s): ⓤ *Students will understand that . . .*	**Essential Question(s):** ⓠ
Students will know . . . ⓚ	*Students will be able to . . .* ⓢ

Stage 2—Assessment Evidence	
Performance Task(s): ⓣ	**Other Evidence:** ⓞⓔ

Stage 3—Learning Plan
Learning Activities: ⓛ

Source: From *Understanding by Design Professional Development Workbook* (pp. 30–31) by Jay McTighe & Grant Wiggins, Alexandria, VA: ASCD. © 2004 by ASCD. Reprinted with permission. Learn more about the ASCD at http://www.ascd.org.

summative. GRASPS is a simple acronym that can help with this: Goals, Role, Audience, Situation, Product or Performance, and Standards (Wiggins & McTighe, 2005). Identifying the criteria as well as the scoring tool for evaluating student products and performances (rubric, checklist, or other) is as important to this step as identifying the assessment tool itself.

Only after teachers identify what they want students to understand and be able to do and consider the evidence they will expect and accept from the students to determine those

Figure 2.2

Planning Template with Design Questions

Stage 1—Desired Results

Established Goal(s):
- What relevant goals (e.g., content standards, course or program objectives, learning outcomes) will this design address?

Understanding(s): **Ⓤ**	**Essential Question(s):** **Ⓠ**
Students will understand that . . .	• What provocative questions will foster inquiry, understanding, and transfer of learning?
• What are the big ideas?	
• What specific understandings about them are desired?	
• What misunderstandings are predictable?	

Students will know . . .   **Ⓚ**   *Students will be able to . . .*   **Ⓢ**
- What key knowledge and skills will students acquire as a result of this unit?
- What should they eventually be able to do as a result of such knowledge and skill?

Stage 2—Assessment Evidence

Performance Task(s): **Ⓣ**	**Other Evidence:** **OE**
• Through what authentic performance task(s) will students demonstrate the desired understandings?	• Through what other evidence (e.g., quizzes, tests, academic prompts, observations, homework, journals) will students demonstrate achievement of the desired results?
• By what criteria will "performances of understanding" be judged?	• How will students reflect upon and self-assess their learning?

Stage 3—Learning Plan

Learning Activities: **Ⓛ**
- What learning experiences and instruction will enable students to achieve the desired results? How will the design

W = Help the students know Where the unit is going and What is expected? Help the teacher know Where the students are coming from (prior knowledge, interests)?

H = Hook all students and Hold their interest?

E = Equip students, help them Experience the key ideas, and Explore the issues?

R = Provide opportunities to Rethink and Revise their understandings and work?

E = Allow students to Evaluate their work and its implications?

T = Be Tailored (personalized) to the different needs, interests, and abilities of learners?

O = Be Organized to maximize initial and sustained engagement as well as effective learning?

Source: From *Understanding by Design Professional Development Workbook* (pp. 30–31), by Jay McTighe, & Grant Wiggins, Alexandria, VA: ASCD. © 2004 by ASCD. Reprinted with permission. Learn more about the ASCD at http://www.ascd.org.

understandings are they in a position to plan the learning experiences and instruction. Hence, the process name of *backward design planning*.

It is important to note here that the backward design process can be applied to multiple levels of planning. Teachers can use the process to organize the overview of the entire year, as well as to develop unit plans. It even can be used to plan single lessons. The process is the same: First, identify the desired results of the study. Then determine acceptable evidence to demonstrate student understanding. Finally, plan and organize the instruction and learning.

Implementing the Curriculum

Activities in teachers' daily schedules are delivered through individual lessons that, in most cases, are episodes within larger units of instruction rather than isolated events. Units consist of closely related lessons that build toward larger understandings, and most are designed to be completed in one to four weeks.

Frequently preorganized units are found in teacher editions of student textbooks, but almost all teachers plan or adapt a number of units of their own to better match their students' needs. Unit topics are numerous, and they spread across the spectrum of the curriculum—dinosaurs, weather, the family, pets, poetry, fractions, graphing, physical endurance, landscape drawing, immigration, media, and so on. These diverse units are built mostly around concrete concepts. Generally, students do not do well in units on intangibles such as prejudice, self-esteem, or feelings until they are able to think abstractly. Some attention is given in elementary classes to patriotism, freedom, quality, and breaking barriers, though mostly in terms of the beliefs and deeds of heroes and heroines such as George Washington, Abraham Lincoln, Martin Luther King, Jr., Harriet Tubman, Clara Barton, Rosa Parks, and Taylor Gun-Jin Wang.

Something to Think About

It has long been said that when humans learn, they remember approximately:

- 10 percent of what they read
- 20 percent of what they hear
- 30 percent of what they see
- 70 percent of what they say
- 90 percent of what they do

And yet in many classrooms, education still most strongly emphasizes reading and hearing.

Organizing Units of Study

Units can be planned in a variety of ways. A current trend is called problem-based learning (PBL, described in greater detail in Chapter 6), where student learning comes about as they confront and solve relevant real-world problems. Authorities in curriculum and instruction believe that once the topic is selected, units should be planned as follows:

1. Review the local, state, and national standards to determine which may be addressed in the unit of study.

2. Formulate an overall problem that you want your students to solve, a goal that you want them to achieve, or an essential or guiding question for them to answer. Several considerations are fundamental to forming essential questions or problem-based learning statements. They are open-ended, allow for divergent solutions, and have multiple correct answers. They also encourage students to interact with the broad community outside school as they examine, solve, and present their findings and solutions to their real-world problems.

    For example, an appropriate problem for students to solve as they study a unit entitled "Community" might be: "In emergency situations, how can services work together to provide the greatest help to community members?" A goal for a unit on community might be: "Students will be able to construct a model of a community that includes physical structures as well as evidence of meaningful services." An appropriate essential or guiding question might be: "How does my community affect my life?" For a unit entitled "Maps as Tools," a problem for students to solve might be: "How can we find our way out of the jungle in South America when we do not have a guidebook or map?" An overall goal might be: "Students will be able to construct a series of maps offering information about a country or region from which some of their ancestors came." An essential or guiding question might be: "In what ways have maps been useful tools for humans?"

3. Formulate several interim subordinate objectives, whose attainment moves learners progressively toward the overall goal. Interim objectives for the unit on community might ask students to be able to list community members and their services, or compare their neighborhood community to one from another time and place in history (such as ancient Greece or Rome, the mid-1800s, the early 1900s). The unit on maps might call on students to locate points using latitude and longitude, interpret and use maps in reference books, and make population and climatic maps for a selected country such as Peru.

4. Organize instructional lessons and activities that lead to the attainment of each of the interim objectives. Consequently, the unit on community could include a number of individual lessons on the nature and meaning of community and neighborhood and on local jobs. The unit on community could be integrated with the map unit, with lessons on map reading; interpreting map legends; pinpointing specific buildings, businesses, and services; creating a map of the area where one lives; and learning how different types of maps convey specific information. Materials will be needed for the lessons, as well as appropriate space and arrangements for engaging in the activities. All of this will have to be planned and managed carefully if you are to keep students productively on-task.

5. Provide assessment activities that will give the students opportunities to demonstrate what they now understand, what solution they have to solve the problem, or how they reached the objective or were able to answer the essential or guiding question.

Note that while this approach does not follow the three stages of backward design unit planning, it does emphasize the curriculum standards, real-world problems or essential or guiding questions, or the objectives—what you hope students will know or be able to do as a result of their working through the unit—and assessment opportunities.

Case Study 2.1   How Two Teachers Plan and Manage Curriculum for Multi-Age Classes

FOCUS QUESTIONS

Two teachers consider parents' understandings, their students, and the curricula for their multi-age 4/5 classes. Shaylene Watkins's challenge was to educate parents about a new multi-age program. Lisa Johnston, who teaches in an established program, groups her students. What concerns/resistance might caregivers have about multi-age classes? How would you respond? How do Mrs. Watkins's blended team approach and Ms. Johnston's student groups help them to manage and successfully deliver the curriculum to their students? What are your thoughts about teaching teams distributing content instruction? What are your thoughts about heterogeneous rather than homogeneous grouping within the class for planning and delivering the curricula? What are the challenges of both? The advantages of both? What changes might Ms. Johnston make to manage curriculum for students in a single grade? for first graders? sixth graders?

Shaylene Watkins teaches a 4/5 multi-class that was newly formed this school year:

Last spring, to plan for the class, my school hosted a parent information night. The goal of the evening was to use open communication from the beginning to dispel misconceptions parents had about fourth graders "being promoted" or fifth graders "being held back." We had a very successful night as a result of the informative PowerPoint and question/answer format. We were able to build a list of parents who were interested in a blended multi-age classroom, and we used teacher input to carefully screen students who would benefit from the class.

Once the class was built, the upper grade team worked together to come up with a supportive curriculum model. The biggest curriculum challenge for my multi-age program revolves around the grade-specific social studies and science standards. Our team decided to have me, the multi-age teacher, teach science to my fifth graders every afternoon. Our upper grade special education resource teacher teaches fourth-grade social studies at that time to her small group of students and my fourth-grade cluster. The beauty of this blended approach is twofold: the mainstreaming benefits for the students who are in special education and the fact that we teachers can teach one content area.

Lisa Johnston teaches a 4/5 multi-age class in an established program:

It is important to me that all my students receive adequate instruction in the appropriate grade-level content areas. At the beginning of the year, I decide on the themes that will organize my teaching and provide structure for my students to make meaningful connections throughout the year. I plan my curriculum after I review the state and local standards for the two grade levels. In order to engage and help everyone be successful, I then carefully consider my students. I mentally divide them into three categories based on their readiness, interest, and learning profile for the topic or concept: advanced, average, and struggling learners. Then I plan different ways to approach the topic for each of the three groups. For example, I provide different reading materials to differentiate the content. I vary the process by which students make sense out of their study. I also suggest different ways for students to demonstrate their understanding and extend their learning.

The Way Many Teachers Organize Units

Curriculum standards and objectives are key considerations for planning. However, many teachers do not begin to organize units from the basis of objectives, authentic problems, or essential questions. Rather, they plan with thoughts of desirable experiences. In planning, those teachers follow a process of self-questioning somewhat like the following:

1. What topics or problems do the standards, textbook, curriculum guide, achievement tests, and my personal beliefs and experiences suggest that I ought to cover this year?

2. What beneficial experiences or activities can I provide for my students within each of these topics? What will students find enjoyable and worthwhile? What websites, books, pictures, media, and other materials and objects (or maybe even guests) can I use?

3. Which district, state, and federal standards will be addressed through these activities?

4. How can I organize these activities to fit into the time allotments I have available?

5. How will I evaluate my students' work, and how can I let them show their caregivers and others how much they have learned?

You can see that after identifying standards, this procedure for organizing instructional units evolves from a list of experiences or activities that teachers believe good for their students, not from a list of objectives. The teachers still have objectives or outcomes in mind, but they think first about quality experiences.

Organizing Thematic Units of Instruction

Thematic units of instruction that weave together several appropriate content and performance standards and integrate teaching from several different subject areas are strongly popular and can be highly efficient. To show how thematic units are planned, let's consider a unit entitled "Breaking Barriers." For this unit we want to integrate content and appropriate grade-level standards that will contribute to a greater understanding of the broad scope of barriers (including physical, emotional, social, and artistic), and the circumstances of individuals who fought to remove or at least minimize barriers for themselves and others.

So we begin by identifying the broad central theme. That theme and unit can be visualized as the hub of a wheel, whose spokes are composed of the various subjects to be integrated—social studies, language arts, science, math, the arts, PE and movement, technology, and character education and community. Figure 2.3 is an example of such a curriculum wheel for this thematic unit on Breaking Barriers.

Figure 2.3

Interdisciplinary Curriculum Wheel: Concept Model: Breaking Barriers

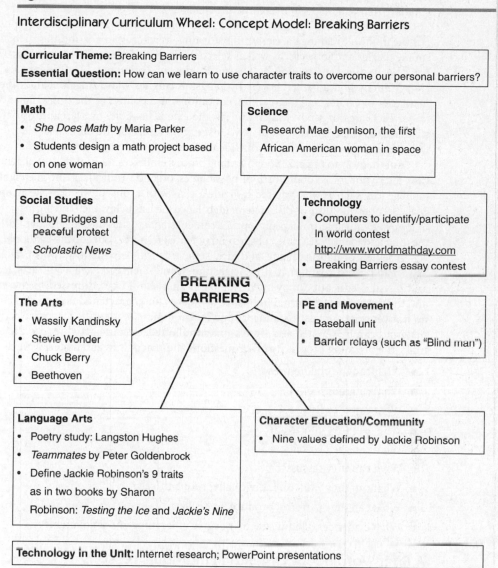

Curricular Theme: Breaking Barriers

Essential Question: How can we learn to use character traits to overcome our personal barriers?

Math
- *She Does Math* by Maria Parker
- Students design a math project based on one woman

Science
- Research Mae Jennison, the first African American woman in space

Social Studies
- Ruby Bridges and peaceful protest
- *Scholastic News*

Technology
- Computers to identify/participate In world contest http://www.worldmathday.com
- Breaking Barriers essay contest

BREAKING BARRIERS

The Arts
- Wassily Kandinsky
- Stevie Wonder
- Chuck Berry
- Beethoven

PE and Movement
- Baseball unit
- Barrier relays (such as "Blind man")

Language Arts
- Poetry study: Langston Hughes
- *Teammates* by Peter Goldenbrock
- Define Jackie Robinson's 9 traits as in two books by Sharon Robinson: *Testing the Ice* and *Jackie's Nine*

Character Education/Community
- Nine values defined by Jackie Robinson

Technology in the Unit: Internet research; PowerPoint presentations

Source: Gail Senter and Shaylene Watkins, Poway Unified School District (CA) Teacher of the Year, 2010. This is an adaptation of the work first produced by Heidi Hayes Jacobs. Reprinted with permission.

To better focus your planning, identify the unit goal, or write an appropriate essential question or PBL statement. Better awareness and understandings of personal challenges one must face in order to break personal barriers might be a goal for a unit on breaking barriers. An essential question might be: How do character traits help individuals break barriers? A problem might be: Select a personal barrier and describe what character traits you have that will help you overcome the challenge.

Next, brainstorm relevant standards and content, materials, and activity possibilities. For the unit on Breaking Barriers, brainstorming may result in possibilities such as primary source diaries and journals, as well as selected fiction and picture books such as *The Year of the Boar and Jackie Robinson* by Sharon Robinson, *Teammates* by Goldenbrock, and *She Does Math* by Marla Parker; poetry by Langston Hughes, Maya Angelou, and others; documentaries of events; and the realities, conditions, and politics of the times. Balance the lists under each area of study. Match and, to the extent possible, overlap appropriate content standards as you begin to formulate your specific lessons for the unit. Also, identify relevant websites and potential resources outside the textbook.

Another way to organize your planning process embraces the multiple intelligences. In this case, after your initial brainstorm of possibilities, organize your ideas into the eight multiple intelligences, such as what you see in Figure 2.4. As with a concept wheel, write an appropriate goal, essential question, or PBL statement; balance the lists below each intelligence; match and, to the extent possible, overlap appropriate content standards as you begin to identify lessons for the unit; and identify relevant websites and potential resources outside the textbook.

A review of national, state, and local standards will help identify appropriate language arts (reading and writing), math, social studies, and science, as well as the arts, technology, and physical education/movement standards that should be addressed in the grade level and the unit of study. Formal published standards for character education and community do not yet exist. Once the standards and lesson topics are identified, specific activities and materials can be selected and time segments allotted. Because activities are the crux of all units, the planning process involves questions about activities and materials such as:

- What can the children read?
- What can they look at?
- What can they listen to?
- What can they construct?
- What can they write?
- What can they discuss?
- What can they work on individually? cooperatively?
- What can they perform, produce, or display?
- What evidence will indicate their degree of learning and enjoyment?

A Brief Word about Organizing Individual Lessons

Units of instruction are accomplished through the individual lessons that comprise each unit. Just as you do when you plan units of study, individual lessons should be planned carefully so that activities, materials, work, space, procedures, homework, and means of assessment all can be communicated clearly to students.

A Brief Word about Writing Unit or Lesson Objectives

Teachers are asked to teach to the standards and to objectives. However, the language of the objectives falls under debate. Simply, objectives are what students *should know or be able to*

Figure 2.4

Multiple Intelligences Curriculum Wheel: Breaking Barriers

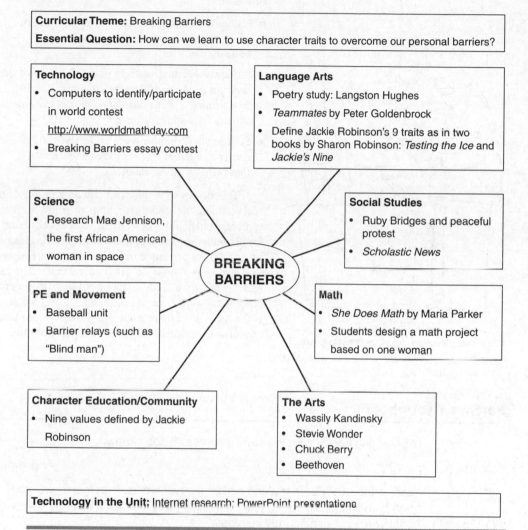

Curricular Theme: Breaking Barriers

Essential Question: How can we learn to use character traits to overcome our personal barriers?

Technology
- Computers to identify/participate in world contest http://www.worldmathday.com
- Breaking Barriers essay contest

Language Arts
- Poetry study: Langston Hughes
- *Teammates* by Peter Goldenbrock
- Define Jackie Robinson's 9 traits as in two books by Sharon Robinson: *Testing the Ice* and *Jackie's Nine*

Science
- Research Mae Jennison, the first African American woman in space

Social Studies
- Ruby Bridges and peaceful protest
- *Scholastic News*

BREAKING BARRIERS

PE and Movement
- Baseball unit
- Barrier relays (such as "Blind man")

Math
- *She Does Math* by Maria Parker
- Students design a math project based on one woman

Character Education/Community
- Nine values defined by Jackie Robinson

The Arts
- Wassily Kandinsky
- Stevie Wonder
- Chuck Berry
- Beethoven

Technology in the Unit: Internet research; PowerPoint presentations

Source: Gail Senter and Shaylene Watkins, Poway Unified School District (CA) Teacher of the Year, 2010. This is an adaptation of the work first produced by Heidi Hayes Jacobs. Reprinted with permission.

do because they participated in a lesson, watched a webclip, read the text, participated in a WebQuest, interviewed someone, went on a field trip, and so on. Objectives are clear statements of what teachers expect students to learn, and they help define the direction for the lesson. They are *not* the activity. Objectives also state the learning outcome that will be observed or measured. Normally, the language is better kept relatively short, as shown

"I've been reviewing your lesson plans."

Bob Vojtko Cartoons on Facebook. Reprinted with permission.

in these examples, rather than detailed and lengthy. Objectives, if written using the following template, clearly identify the broad content *and* the performance outcome:

■ Students will demonstrate understanding of (*concept or content*) by (*performance activity/ outcome*).

■ Students will demonstrate understanding of *the basic concepts of planning a grade-level curriculum* by *outlining a year's units of meaningful study for a grade level of their choice.*

■ Students will demonstrate understanding of *the basic concepts of lesson design* by *creating a lesson that includes all the elements.*

This brings to a close our discussions for organizing and planning the school year, units of study, individual lessons, and curriculum objectives. More specific suggestions for planning, sequencing, and communicating lessons to all concerned are presented in Chapter 6. Next, however, serious attention should be given to several other management concerns, including the physical environment of the classroom—how it should be organized and managed. This is the topic of Chapter 3. Before proceeding to Chapter 3, take time to explore these end-of-chapter activities.

Parting Thoughts

All learning begins with the simple phrase, "I don't know."

Anonymous

Here is the truth about making a plan: It never works. (Not in the way you plan it, that is.) If, however, you do make a plan, the chances of getting what you want significantly increase.

John-Roger and Peter McWilliams

Summary Self-Check

Check off the following as you either understand or become able to apply them:

☐ Before planning a year's program for students, mark published and important dates on a calendar (vacations, celebrations, special events, school assemblies, conferences, and report card dates), note grade-level themes and content and performance standards, and highlight available blocks of time.

☐ In curriculum management we hope to bring about a purposeful and efficient interaction between students and what they are supposed to learn in school.

☐ *Curriculum maps* help identify redundancies and gaps in standards, content, and skills.

☐ In the *backward design* process of planning, teachers identify desired results and determine acceptable evidence for determining understandings before they plan the learning experience and instruction.

☐ Federal, state, and local *standards* identify knowledge and expected content mastery, along with performance skills for students.

☐ A large portion of elementary teaching is done through *instructional units,* which are related lessons that work together to build larger learnings.

☐ Before planning specific units of instruction, decide on the daily and weekly schedules, and then overlay the desired instructional units for the year.

☐ Appropriate national, state, and district standards must be considered when planning instructional units.

☐ Often preorganized units are found in teacher editions of student textbooks, but most teachers plan or adapt many units on their own.

☐ Objectives are clear, specific statements of what students should know or be able to do *because* of their study.

☐ Problem-based learning (PBL) encourages students to investigate and solve real-world problems.

☐ Essential or guiding questions are broad questions—rather than fact-based questions—related to the topic of study that guide and focus the instruction and learning.

☐ Thematic units that integrate several standards and subject areas are popular and efficient.

☐ Backward design planning can be used for planning the year's curriculum, as well as for unit planning and daily lessons.

☐ Activities are of prime importance for all units, and teachers should think continually in terms of questions such as: What can children read? look at? listen to? construct? write? discuss? work on individually or cooperatively? perform, produce, or display? What evidence will indicate their degree of learning and enjoyment?

Activities for Reflection and Discussion

1. Take a moment to review the statements in the Preview–Review Guide at the beginning of this chapter. Put a check mark in the *Review* column next to any statement with which you now agree. How have your thoughts changed since reading this chapter?

2. Interview at least two teachers about their planning. What do they consider for their personal situations regarding the organization of their days? What advice do these teachers offer regarding how best to plan the school year? units? daily lessons? How does their planning align with what authorities recommend?

3. In Chapter 1, Alexa Smart had to learn the standards and curricula and plan for a multi-age class. Check the fourth- and fifth-grade standards and curricula for your state. What suggestions can you make to her regarding this challenge?

4. Suppose that January 3 falls on Monday. Lay out the January calendar to determine teaching days and any celebration days that might influence your curriculum and decisions.

5. How do lessons, instructional units, and thematic units differ? How are they similar? Why is so much of the elementary curriculum organized into units? Illustrate your conclusions by summarizing what might be done in a short primary-grade unit on dinosaurs, first as a traditional unit and then as a thematic unit.

6. Suppose you want to plan a very short unit (perhaps consisting of only a lesson or two) on the life cycle of the trumpeter swan. After identifying your grade level and standards, work in teams to plan in three ways:

   a. First, make a plan beginning with two or three specific objectives, written in terms of what you later can actually see or hear students do as a result of what they learn (e.g., "Students will demonstrate understanding of the trumpeter swan's habitat by describing the unique environment in which it lives and indicating its nesting area on a map of North America"). Your lesson activities should be aimed directly at helping students reach your stated objectives.

   b. Second, make a plan beginning with two or three experiences you'd like your students to have concerning the trumpeter swans. Your lesson activities and materials should be expressions of the experiences you named.

   c. Third, use the idea of problem-based learning to make a plan. Your lesson activities should allow students to demonstrate their ability to solve the problem you propose.

   What do you see as the comparative advantages and disadvantages of these three planning approaches?

7. For a grade level of your choosing, work in teams to outline the major elements of the language arts/literacy curriculum found in a local district or school. This is step one of curriculum mapping. List the standards, processes, skills, essential content and topics, and the products and performances that are expected to demonstrate student learning.

Webliography

Character Counts: http://charactercounts.org
Curriculum Designers: www.curriculum21.com
Partnership for 21st Century Skills: http://www.21stcenturyskills.org
Partnership for 21st Century Skills: Teaching 21st Century Learners: http://www. youtube.com/watch?v=el_IjOKTawg

U.S. Department of Education. (2003). U.S. Re-enters UN's education arm—UNESCO. Speech of U.S. Secretary of Education to UNESCO General Conference: http://www.edwatch.org/updates06/022006-unesco.htm

References and Recommended Readings

Doll, R. (1995). *Curriculum improvement: Decision making and process* (9th ed.). Boston: Allyn & Bacon.

Eisner, E. (1985). *The educational imagination: On the design and evaluation of school programs* (2nd ed.). New York: Macmillan.

Evertson, C., & Emmer, E. (2009). *Classroom management for elementary teachers* (8th ed.). Upper Saddle River, NJ: Pearson.

Fisher, D., & Frey, N. (2007). *Checking for understanding: Formative assessment techniques for your classroom.* Alexandria, VA: ASCD.

Goodlad, J. (2004, 1984). *A place called school: Prospectives for the future.* New York: McGraw-Hill.

Jacobs, H. (1989). *Interdisciplinary curriculum: Design and implementation.* Alexandria, VA: ASCD.

Jacobs, H. (1997). *Mapping the big picture: Integrating curriculum and assessment K–12.* Alexandria, VA: ASCD.

Jacobs, H., ed. (2004). *Getting results with curriculum mapping.* Alexandria, VA: ASCD.

McTighe, J., & Wiggins, G. (2004). *Understanding by design: Professional development workbook.* Alexandria, VA: ASCD.

Partnership for 21st Century Skills. (2009). *P21 Framework Definitions.* Tucson, AZ: Author. http://www.21stcenturyskills.org.

Rosales-Dordelly, C., & Short, E. (1985). *Curriculum professors' specialized knowledge.* Lanham, MD: University Press of America.

Sternberg, R. (October, 2008). Excellence for all. *EL Educational Leadership* 66(2), 14–19.

Tomlinson, C., & McTighe, J. (2006). *Integrating differentiated instruction and understanding by design: Connecting content and kids.* Alexandria, VA: ASCD.

Tyler, R. (1949). *Basic principles of curriculum and instruction.* Chicago: University of Chicago Press.

Wagner, T. (October, 2008). Rigor redefined. *EL Educational Leadership,* 66(2), 20–24.

Wiggins, G., & McTighe, J. (2005). *Understanding by design* (expanded 2nd ed.). Alexandria, VA: ASCD.

PEARSON
myeducationlab

Go to the Topic: **Establishing Classroom Norms and Expectations** in the MyEducationLab (www.myeducationlab.com) for your course, where you can:

- Find learning outcomes for **Establishing Classroom Norms and Expectations** along with the national standards that connect to these outcomes.
- Apply and practice your understanding of the core teaching skills identified in the chapter with the Building Teaching Skills and Dispositions learning units.
- Examine challenging situations and cases presented in the IRIS Center Resources.
- Use interactive Simulations in Classroom Management to practice decision making and to receive expert feedback on classroom management choices.

Managing the Physical Environment of the Classroom

A bare room is like a boring teacher. Both lack the pizzazz which is the soul of teaching.

—Kathy Paterson

Preview–Review Guide

Before you read the chapter, and based on what you know, think you know, or assume, take a minute to put a check mark in the **Preview** column if you agree with the statement. When you finish the chapter, take time to reread the statements and respond in the **Review** column. Reflective discussions can develop because many of the statements are not clearly "yes" or "no."

Preview		Review
1. _____	The main purpose of bulletin boards should be to beautify the room.	_____
2. _____	Experience has taught that the most efficient elementary classroom environment still emphasizes the chalk- or whiteboards and rows of student seats.	_____
3. _____	Ceiling space is an important but often forgotten facet of the physical environment.	_____
4. _____	Modular clusters seem to provide the greatest seating advantages, including benefits for students with special needs.	_____
5. _____	A main disadvantage of modular clusters is that they encourage students to talk and interact with others, even when talking is not appropriate.	_____
6. _____	Computers should be placed randomly around the room to create a technology-rich classroom environment.	_____
7. _____	Any music can be used effectively in the classroom, as long as the children like it.	_____
8. _____	The main principle underlying management of physical space is that the physical classroom should enhance the activities included in the curriculum.	_____
9. _____	An important guideline for managing the physical environment is to keep it clean and in good order.	_____
10. _____	All students should have responsibilities for helping to maintain the physical environment.	_____

Chapter Objectives

After reading Chapter 3, students will demonstrate understanding of

■ the importance of attending to the physical classroom environment

■ six facets that make up the physical environment

through their active participation in discussions and the end-of-chapter activities for reflection.

As we stated earlier, attention to several managerial matters can and should occur before the school year begins, or before the teacher first meets his or her students. In the last chapter, we talked about ways the calendar and curriculum can be interwoven and tentatively set. In conjunction with these decisions, however, is another consideration. Attention must be given to organizing the interior of the classroom so it not only reflects but also substantially contributes to the learning and behavior goals. This can be done in elementary school classrooms better than anywhere else (with the possible exception of secondary school science labs and athletic facilities). Some elementary classrooms are works of art. They are richly equipped and beautifully laid out, and you would consider children fortunate to spend their days there. Other rooms are austere, dull, and uninspiring; you would pity students who are trapped in them.

Yes, classrooms often reflect the personality of the teacher. However, beautiful classrooms can be run by teachers who are punitive, harsh, and cold, and uninspired classrooms can be the domains of warm and nurturing teachers. This fact reminds us that quality of teaching cannot be judged solely on the basis of room appearance. That, however, does not detract from this basic point:

> The physical environment can and should be organized so as to further the program of instruction and activity.

This bears repeating and should be understood before you read on. What you put into your classroom should have instructional purpose. There is little point in loading it with decorations that have no instructional value and do not contribute to the program, except perhaps to charm caregivers and administrators. The classroom just as easily can be made attractive—and more usefully so—by setting it up with interesting activities and stimulating materials. Teachers have a free hand in setting up their workplaces—almost anything is permitted, within reason of course, and it begins with their own mental image of the classroom.

Take a minute to reread the description in Chapter 1 of Alexa's room arrangement and keep this in mind as you continue reading the chapter.

Upon Reflection

To prepare for meeting her students, Alexa reviewed curriculum and planned for her first days while her well-intentioned friends set up her room. Although the room looked interesting and attractive, what were some of the inherent problems in the room arrangement?

The Pictures We Hold in Our Heads

All of us hold some mental picture of what elementary school classrooms should look like. For some, the images still may be "old school," with straight rows of desks, chalkboard and teacher in front, one or two doors on the side wall, perhaps a coatroom or coat hooks in the back, and windows with shelves of dusty reference books. For others the images are clusters of tables filling the middle of the room, and chalk- or whiteboards, book shelves, small cubbyholes, and coat hooks lining the surrounding walls. In current times, class sizes again are increasing, and teachers are faced with challenges to design the physical arrangement of their classroom in a way that accommodates more students and still supports their program for instructing them. While those older classrooms in particular have been used to advantage by thousands of teachers over the decades to teach millions of students, there are better ways of setting up the classroom—ways that affect attitudes, efficiency, and overall learning. Suppose for example, you plan to have your students do the following:

- Make stick puppets to use in retelling a story
- Write and publish original poetry and stories
- Create a *Who's Who* book or CD of class members and school personnel
- Write letters to a class in a foreign country
- Build a model of a community
- Make graphs of daily weather phenomena
- Monitor and record the growth cycles of plants from seeds
- Compare the latitudes of foreign capital cities
- Research careers and plan and practice mock interviews in preparation for a Careers Day event with community guests

- Use computer software to create materials to supplement presentations about ancient Greece and Rome
- Learn a folk dance from another country
- Make a CD or video of life in the school or classroom

As you plan your curriculum and consider supporting activities, you begin finding hints for organizing the room. The problem to solve or the essential or guiding question might be: *How can my room best help me do justice to what I want my students to experience and learn?*

As the question suggests, the classroom should be made to accommodate and to further a variety of educational activities. Math and language arts, for example, may require students to work quietly at their seats with furnished materials. Social studies may call for active collaborative work in construction, drawing, or discussion. Science and art often require special workspaces and materials. Dance, music, and drama require open space for movement. Technology requires computer and printer access. Each type of activity calls for its own space, seating, movement, materials, and interactions.

Just how classrooms can be made both rich and flexible will be explained presently, but first let us take a moment to remind ourselves of a seldom remembered but fundamentally important fact: The room should be set up for the teacher's pleasure, too. Some teachers are more comfortable—and possibly more effective—when working in highly structured programs that hold students under tight supervision and that direct them through assignments. Other teachers are more comfortable—and possibly more effective—when giving students leeway in selecting activities, obtaining and using appropriate materials, and working collaboratively with fellow students. We go too far when we expect all teachers to teach in a single, specified way, especially when that certain way changes from year to year, as is often the case. Teachers are different and have different styles, and most of them would benefit from being allowed to use their talents to their fullest.

Remember, too, that just as teachers show different styles of teaching, so will they set up their classrooms differently. Some prefer their rooms to be richly furnished with materials, charts, pictures, animals, decorations, and slogans, believing that this keeps the classroom fully stimulating. Others prefer their rooms to be clean and efficient, with materials at hand only when relevant to what is being studied at a particular time. These teachers find heavily decorated classrooms distracting and believe students also find them distracting. Effective teaching—and learning—can occur in both these physical settings, which again suggests the desirability of allowing serious-minded teachers to rely on their own best judgments. Regardless of their differing styles, teachers should consider all areas of the classroom when they organize the physical environment.

Six Facets of the Physical Environment

This analysis breaks the physical classroom into six components: (1) floor space, (2) wall space, (3) countertop space, (4) shelf space, (5) cupboard and closet space, and (6) ambience. Many teachers use a seventh facet as well—the ceiling. While the ceiling does offer many possibilities, it is not considered here because attaching materials to it may increase fire hazard and often is a violation of local fire codes. Let's explore some of the possibilities offered by the other six facets.

Floor Space

One of the first things a teacher has to decide is how to position students for the various activities that involve individual work and group interactions. This not only affects seating arrangements but also traffic patterns and work/activity areas (including computer stations, interest centers, and the teacher's station). Because today's classrooms are inclusive and teachers can expect physical and language diversity among their students, it also is important to consider floor space as it relates to any special needs for students, including proximate space for associated service providers.

Seating   In the not-so-distant past, student desks were anchored to wooden or metal runners, where they remained unmoved until rusted out or ripped up. You won't see that now except in museums. Seating in today's schools is intended to be flexible so various groupings can be made and space opened for multiple purposes, according to the needs of the subjects taught. Teachers arrange seating at their discretion, keeping in mind two cautions. First, students shouldn't be placed so they face windows and have to look directly into strong outdoor light—the resulting strain causes tension and makes concentration difficult. Investigators, including Hathaway et al. (1992), Chan and Petrie (1998), Freiberg (1999), and Berry (2002), have documented the possible health effects of lighting. Second, when students are asked to rearrange their desks and tables, they show a penchant for shoving, bumping, making noise, and pestering each other. Accept this as a fact of teaching and be proactive to avoid the potential misbehaviors. Take time to teach and have students practice responsible behavior for times such as this. Then when you ask students to rearrange their seating areas, remind them in a positive tone to do so in accordance with class rules and procedures they have practiced.

When students are taught as a total group, they should be seated as near to the teacher as feasible, facing a chalkboard or dry erase board where the teacher writes or projects instructional information. Primary students may come together on a small carpet area for whole-group instruction. The teacher may sit with them on the carpet or in a chair, often near a small board or an easel. Well-behaved students can be placed close together, but some students may have to be separated a bit. Designating marks or colored carpet squares on the room carpet are common methods of separation and arrangement. During

Contestants, note: Ben, Tommy, and Sarah cannot sit near each other. Fanchon is to be kept away from the other girls, and most of the boys should be kept away from the window. You may create your seating chart... NOW!!

Alejandro Yegros. http://alejandroyegros.com. Reprinted with permission.

guided study, students sometimes will be asked to work alone and sometimes in cooperative groups. Normally, the teacher will circulate among students to monitor and help. For ease of movement, aisles and gaps in seating should be maintained, but the distance between the teacher and the farthest student should be as minimal as possible.

When students are taught in small groups, they may go to a special area or to centers where extra chairs are kept, or to which they bring their own chairs. With a well thought out floor plan, teachers working with small groups will have full view and be in fairly close proximity to students working at their desks. Teachers must be able to oversee everyone in the class, and this watchfulness should be evident to the students.

Popular seating arrangements include rows, circles, semicircles, and long tables. Jones (2007) advocates creating an interior loop or walkway, with the least distance and fewest barriers between the teacher and every student in the classroom, so the teacher can easily and efficiently "work the crowd" (see Figure 3.1). Others find that modular clusters seem to best meet the demands of modern classrooms, where large- and small-group instruction, cooperative group and teamwork, and individual seatwork routinely are interchanged. Kagan and Kagan (2009) recommend group arrangements that enable students to engage in classbuilding and teambuilding activities for successful cooperative learning. For example, four students sitting in pairs on opposite sides of a table (or with their desks touching and placed so students face each other) can work as shoulder partners, as face partners, or as teams of four. Kagan further suggests that placing students with comparable language and achievement abilities on the same side of the table so they can work as shoulder partners ensures the best mix for partnering and processing information and tasks (see Figure 3.2).

Modular clusters of five or six students afford fairly good eye contact among students and between the teacher and individual students, enable easy transition into cooperative work, allow good traffic flow, and provide the flexibility for obtaining extra floor space when needed. Such small-group clusters also are more effective in facilitating the inclusion of students with special needs. Figure 3.3 shows an example of modular seating for 36 students.

Vignette 3.1   Modular Cluster Seating

Beth Davies prefers modular cluster seating in her fifth-grade classroom:

Initially I choose the places where the children sit. Once they become acquainted I let them contract to sit by a person of their choice, but still within their original cluster. By this time they understand my right to teach and their right to learn without disruption. My students know that I will immediately move any person who abuses the contract. In each cluster of desks, I try to balance the lower-achieving students with the higher-achieving, in order to mix minds and provide help during group work.

UPON REFLECTION

Based on your personal experience and your observations, what are your thoughts about cluster seating versus rows or other configurations? How do you feel about students choosing their own seats?

Figure 3.1

Jones's Interior Loop
Walkways that allow teachers to "work the crowd" with the fewest steps are created by bringing students forward and packing them sideways.

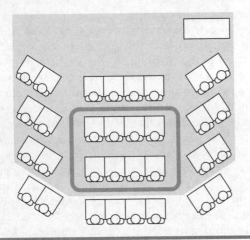

Source: Fred Jones, *Tools for Teaching,* 2007, http://www.fredjones.com. Reprinted by permission.

Figure 3.2

Kagan encourages group arrangements so students can interact with shoulder partners, face partners, and teams of four.

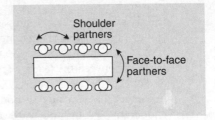

Figure 3.3

Modular Cluster Seating

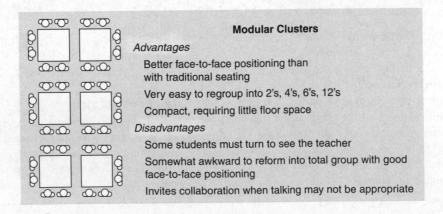

Modular Clusters

Advantages

Better face-to-face positioning than with traditional seating

Very easy to regroup into 2's, 4's, 6's, 12's

Compact, requiring little floor space

Disadvantages

Some students must turn to see the teacher

Somewhat awkward to reform into total group with good face-to-face positioning

Invites collaboration when talking may not be appropriate

Work, Activity, and Special Areas Work and activity areas are affected by the room's seating arrangement. Compact seating makes space available to begin with, and rearranging the seats provides still more space. Of course, you don't need extra space for all activities. Frequently, reading, math, spelling, handwriting, and guided seatwork are conducted with students in their assigned seats. Activities in social studies, science, art, music, drama, and dance often involve movement and require extra space. Some activities may involve technology. Computers are most beneficial when they are located in designated areas of the classroom.

Space is needed for other purposes as well. Most teachers like to include one or more special centers, corners, or interest areas. An art center with easels may be present. Free-standing learning centers may be on the floor, though they are placed more commonly on tables or countertops. Frequently, special centers for quiet reading, science projects, map and globe study, or individual investigations are seen in the room.

Some teachers also like to set aside a special space in the classroom as a reward for responsible student behavior or good work. Here teachers may put cushions, a thick rug, a computer, interesting books and magazines, individual slide viewers, and headsets for listening to music or stories.

Computer Stations Technology is steadily finding its way into elementary classrooms. In fact, now most classrooms have at least one, often several, computers for students to use in writing, math, research, and other areas. Eileen VanWie, a professor at New Mexico State University, is a strong proponent of democratic learning communities (DLC) in technology-rich environments (TRE). In Chapter 4 we will discuss how she believes these elements support the psychosocial tone in classrooms. However, computers require additional considerations because of their operating noise, lighting needs, and potential distractibility. Teacher Jearine Bacon, who makes extensive use of computers in her primary classroom, describes some of the cautions to keep in mind concerning classroom computers:

> Classroom computers are extremely motivating and useful in the classroom, but care should be taken in their use. Computers should be away from liquids, dust, and extreme heat, and some distance from the chalkboard. They also should be placed so they face away from students so images on the screens are not distracting to others. Additionally, students should be reminded frequently of the rules for use and care of the computers. Computers are expensive to repair and frustrating to use when not working properly.

Figure 3.4 shows a hypothetical floor space arrangement for elementary classrooms with three to four student computers. In contrast, Figure 3.5 shows a classroom arrangement where every student, probably in an upper grade, has direct access to a personal computer.

Teacher's Station Today's teachers are up and moving among students throughout the entire day. In newer schools' designs, teachers may share a small office area adjacent to their classrooms, but most still have a desk somewhere in the classroom. Their station in their classroom—normally a desk—should be placed in a position that oversees the entire class, ideally to the side or back of the room. It is a good idea to make the teacher's station attractive and special, as it enhances one's position as authority and can help students feel honored when called there. It should begin with a clean desk (a good example for students), an

Figure 3.4

Floor Space Arrangement with a Few Computers for Younger Grades

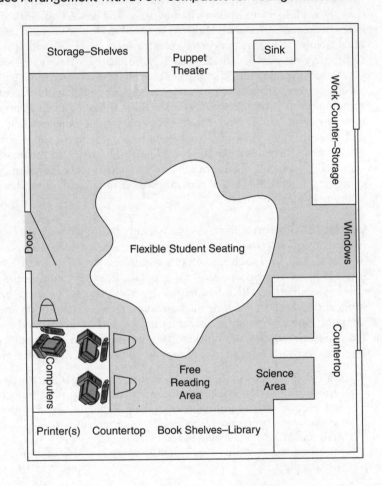

attractive file cabinet, and shelves for a small collection of personal books. Photographs of family, friends, former students, or pets add touches that students like. Artifacts, weavings, and art prints contribute tastefully. One or two articles of high prestige for students can be kept there, such as a puppet, a sports team pennant, or a large toy animal. A special chair for students can provide a pleasant place for individual conferencing.

Location and organization of the teacher's desk are especially important in schools where technology is in place as a frequently used teaching tool. Teachers may use a document camera projection system (such as *Proxima*) and interactive whiteboards (such as *Promethean Activboards*) as they present or review information to the whole class. From their desk or work table, teachers can display the architecture of an ancient Greek temple,

Figure 3.5

Technology-Rich Classroom for Upper Grades
Every student has a laptop, smart board, and student response system. The teacher uses a document camera to project or record from his/her desk.

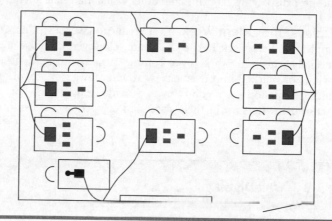

Source: Adapted from Deseré Hockman. Reprinted with permission.

model the steps in solving math problems, review spelling rules, show the various layers of the earth, demonstrate how to draw in perspective, and so on.

Traffic Patterns Student movement around the room must be given careful attention, because congestion, waiting, and unnecessary contact usually lead to disruptive behavior. For students with disabilities, traffic patterns must be free from barriers and allow easy access to materials. Students routinely enter and exit the room, obtain and return materials, sharpen or exchange dull pencils, get drinks, go to learning centers, feed the fish or class pet, approach the teacher, and so on. Traffic routes for such movements must be kept open, a concern not to be taken lightly when deciding on the layout of the room.

Wall Space

Classroom walls are rarely used to full advantage, but they offer excellent instructional possibilities. Chalkboards and whiteboards remain among the most valuable of all teaching tools. They are used routinely to post daily information, assignments, math problems, and vocabulary words. Most teachers use them for explanations and demonstrations. Often overlooked, however, is the delight many students experience in going to the board to work.

Bulletin Boards Bulletin boards, though present in practically every classroom, tend to be used mostly for decoration and rarely for instruction. Decorations can make a room pleasant to look at, but with a bit of thought they also can serve the important purpose of instruction. More valuable than mere decoration are displays such as puzzles that draw students' attention and make them think, clippings from newspapers and magazines that serve as focal points for class discussion, and interactive and creative ideas and problem situations that stimulate writing and debate. Perhaps best of all, bulletin boards are excellent places for displaying art prints and other visual materials, including student work.

Displays of Student Work It's advisable to give all students the opportunity to display samples of their work in the classroom. However, not just any work should be shown, especially when the work is not commensurate with student ability. When excellence is obvious or marked improvement is evident, putting that work on display—with the student's permission—is a good way to provide recognition. This recognition gives students a sense of ownership in their classroom, as well as a sense of accomplishment and the

---

Vignette 3.2 Wall Displays

Adelheida Montante Castañeda, a sixth-grade teacher, has a large bulletin board across the room from the entry door, visible to anyone who comes into her room. There she displays four of her favorite posters, which she has treasured over the years because they emphasize positive learning, good citizenship, challenge, and determination.

1. My greatest challenge in life is doing what others think I cannot do.

2. Tell me, I forget.
   Show me, I remember.
   Involve me, I understand.

3. How to Get Better Grades
   a. Be on time and ready to work.
   b. Follow directions.
   c. Work neatly and accurately.
   d. Ask for help when you need it.
   e. Check your work.
   f. Find a time and place to study.
   g. Take responsibility for yourself.

4. My Classroom Rights
   a. I have the right to be happy and to be treated with compassion in this room.
   This means that no one will laugh at me or hurt my feelings.
   b. I have a right to be safe in this room. This means that no one will kick me, punch me, push me, or hurt me.
   c. I have a right to hear and be heard in this room. This means that no one will yell, scream, shout, or make noises.
   d. I have a right to learn more about myself in this room. This means that I will be free to express my feelings and my opinions without being interrupted or punished, as long as the rights of others are not infringed.

UPON REFLECTION

Take time to visit some elementary classrooms in the area. What visual displays do you see on the walls? What purpose do they have in the classroom?

Idea: Take pictures of what you see with a camera phone, or digital or disposable camera, and create a personal file for future reference.

understanding that others care about their performance. It also builds self-esteem and is highly motivating.

Art Prints and Other Visual Materials Art prints that relate to the curriculum tend to be overlooked by students unless attention is drawn to them in art lessons. The same can be said for most maps, globes, and charts, though students often enjoy simply exploring maps once they learn how to use them.

Wall space should be used for posting graphic models, visual instructional plans, and reminders. Such materials are chronically underutilized given the help they provide to students and teachers. Thoughtful visual instructional plans become helping tools for students to become more autonomous as they do their independent work. These visual materials illustrate and help explain products or procedures such as parts of a business letter, elements of sentences and paragraphs, steps in long division, proper use of the computer, proper editing annotations and publishing procedures, and any number of explanations and reminders that teachers must otherwise repeat, sometimes to the point of exasperation.

Read more about the use of effective visual materials in Chapter 6.

Countertop Space

A good deal of useful space is available in classrooms with windows and countertops beneath the windows. In these rooms, because they are near natural light, such countertops are well suited to many kinds of science activities, especially those involving living plants. They also are good places for aquariums and terrariums if the outside light is not too strong or hot. Other kinds of science projects find useful placement here as well—experiments; projects in progress; and models of human torsos, sense organs, skeletons, dinosaurs, atoms, molecules, and the like. Kits of various kinds that are in most classrooms, often on countertops, typically contain science projects or materials to supplement instruction in reading, spelling, social studies, and mathematics. Globes fit nicely on countertops and can be wonderful instructional devices since they show not only the shape of the earth but also the relative locations and distances between landmasses, oceans, countries, and cities. They are important to the study of history, geography, astronomy, and current events.

Shelf Space

Shelves, if not built into classrooms, can be inexpensive additions to rooms. Inexpensive shelves or easy-to-assemble kits are available for purchase, or shelves can be made by stacking pine boards on concrete blocks. Typically, textbooks, reference books, class libraries, and other special materials are stored or displayed on shelves.

Textbooks usually accompany the core curricular areas: reading, language arts, mathematics, social studies, and science. Many teachers keep the textbooks on shelves and distribute them to students when needed.

Internet searches on class computers are steadily gaining as a preferred reference resource, especially for studies above primary grades. However, reference books still have value and a place in classrooms. Normally, they are kept on shelves and typically include dictionaries, encyclopedias, almanacs, atlases, thesauruses, and special reference books such as the *Guinness World Records* and *The Farmer's Almanac*.

If not kept on a book carousel, a small class library often is found on classroom shelves. A class library usually consists of easy-to-read books of high interest to students, plus age-appropriate magazines such as *National Geographic Kids* and *Ranger Rick*. Teachers look into many sources to find such materials at low prices, and students' caregivers may donate to class libraries. The library also may include student-written and illustrated materials that have been laminated or bound into small books.

Special materials to motivate and extend students' experiences are kept on shelves in most classrooms. Examples include video and audio DVDs, CDs, and tapes; games and puzzles; puppets and other toys; photo collections; collections of shells and fossils; and the like. Some teachers create a lending library that includes videotapes or CDs of the children as they work on projects and activities during the year. Of course, before children are taped, caregivers must grant permission, and when taping, equal time must be given to every child. The tapes are kept on a library shelf and checked out to be viewed at home by parents, grandparents, and others who are not able to be in the classroom during the day. You will read more about this in Chapter 11.

Cupboard and Closet Space

Classroom cupboards and closets are useful places for keeping student supplies, worksheets, computer and printer supplies, audiovisual equipment, physical education or subject-specific materials, and cleaning supplies. They also are good places to store materials used for special occasions such as sports days and certain times of the year such as the winter holidays.

Student supplies include such things as writing paper, construction paper, pencils, scissors, glue, paint, crayons, rulers, and pens. When district budgets are able to provide teachers with basic supplies, smaller quantities are kept in classroom cupboards, while larger quantities are stored in a central teachers' supply workroom.

Vignette 3.3 Student Publishing

Rebecca Cummins has taught third grade for many years. She has her students publish and share their stories:

My third graders write, illustrate, and bind their own stories into books. They read the books aloud to the class and then take them home to read to their parents. When the books are returned, they are placed on a special shelf in the classroom. When children finish their work, they may select a classmate's book to read. These books are treated like genuine treasures. At the end of the year, the children take their books home, though I always beg to keep a few to show next year's class.

UPON REFLECTION

What standards and goals—academic and social—can be met when students write, publish, and share their stories?

Manipulatives for math are kept in appropriately sized storage containers. Plastic boxes that are the same size, stackable, and clear for easy viewing of the contents work well for this purpose and can be purchased on sale and over time at many stores.

Worksheets still are used—overused, many believe—in great quantities in many classrooms. Usually, the teacher, aide, or volunteer duplicates them. Worksheets are useful for drilling skills and preparing students for timed tests, but they are of little value when used only to keep children busy.

In older schools, audiovisual equipment usually is kept in a central area of the school and checked out when needed. If not provided by the school, many teachers bring their own iPod, MP3 player, CD player, or boom box to their classroom. Many classrooms now have their own television and VCR, either mounted on a wall or on a movable cart. Classrooms also may have overhead projectors, tape recorders, headphones, smaller three-dimensional models, and sometimes slide viewers. Some of these are kept on tables and others in cabinets, to be brought out when needed. More expensive items, such as micro-projectors, larger models (such as human torsos), large art collections, motion picture projectors (although these mostly have been replaced by VCRs), and so forth, are checked out from a central repository for short-term use. In many places around the country, designs for new schools and improvements to older schools are embracing technology. As new schools are built and older schools are renovated, the buildings are given school-wide Internet connections and other electronic equipment as standard features in the classrooms.

Equipment used for specific content areas is kept in containers and stored in closets. Physical education equipment, often consisting of little besides balls and jump ropes, and perhaps a parachute, with the room number clearly written on each, is kept in closets, frequently in large plastic garbage bins.

Each room's personal set of cleaning materials also is found in the classroom closet and usually includes a broom, dust cloths, cleanser, paper towels, and rags. A small vacuum or sweeper broom is very useful but probably will not be provided by the school. These materials permit students and teachers to take care of routine spills, dusting, and other necessary cleaning that is beyond what the custodians are available to do. Student monitors can be helpful in this regard.

Finally, collections of special materials for Presidents' Day, Valentine's Day, Saint Patrick's Day, Thanksgiving, winter

"I DON'T GET TOO FAR AT HOME COMPLAINING ABOUT MY CUBICLE. MY WIFE'S CUBICLE HAS THIRTY-FOUR CHILDREN IN IT."

and spring holidays, and other themes are usually kept in large, clearly labeled plastic or cardboard file boxes and stored in or on top of closets.

Ambience

Ambience refers to the totality of intangible impressions that pervade the physical classroom—an atmosphere that at its best conveys excitement, aesthetics, comfort, security, and pleasure. It is created in large part by the contents of the room, which many teachers further enhance with art and music. Most schools or district media centers make available prints, carvings, weavings, and photographs, which provide focal points for learning about artists and media. CDs and cassette tapes can provide music that is excellent for relaxation and mood setting, not to mention the opportunity they provide for learning about composers and performers.

Music Researchers continue to investigate the effectiveness and use of music in the classroom. Because of studies, including the "Mozart Effect" study (Rauscher et al. [1993]; see also Campbell (2000, 2002)), we now know that music effects changes in the mind and body. With this knowledge, teachers can play the right type of music for the desired objective: thinking, relaxing, learning, destressing, concentration, inspiration, and productivity.

Appropriate music can help reduce stress and heighten alertness, excitement, relaxation, and emotional well-being, as well as creativity. Sometimes we want students to reflect and relax. Music with 50 to 60 beats per minute, as well as environmental sounds of birds, waterfalls, and the like, work best for this. Sometimes we want students to work independently or quietly, for example, during journal writing, creative writing, or problem solving. For these times we should use music that has 60 to 70 beats per minute. Best for this is baroque-style music and some of the "gentle modern classics" of the nineteenth and twentieth centuries by Beethoven, Chopin, Debussy, and others. Sometimes we want to energize students. Upbeat music with 120 beats per minute, such as many of the songs of the 1960s and 1970s, works well for energizing students and managing transitions.

We know that music contributes to the classroom ambience. As an aside, it is important to be knowledgeable about the ethics and legalities of using music. As general rules of thumb, if you use music only with your students and in your classroom, you do not need a license. If, however, you use music in other venues (workshops or other presentations), a license may be required.

2008 Alejandro Yegros

"Field trip"? Actually, due to budget cuts, this is now our classroom.

Alejandro Yegros. http://alejandroyegros.com. Reprinted with permission.

When in doubt, you should contact the performing rights organization. You can e-mail questions to Broadcast Music, Inc. (BMI) at genlic@bmi.com or call them directly at 877-264-2137. Their website is http:// www.bmi.com.

Special Themes Many teachers enhance ambience through special themes built around children's literature, professional athletes, popular music, cartoon characters, favorite motion pictures—whatever seems to attract students' interest. Both the room and lessons can reflect elements of the selected theme—characters, emblems, photographs, drawings, colors, sayings, music, and so forth. Students respond well to such themes and often like to help in their selection and organization.

Other Special Touches Finally, a number of special touches and events add to the room ambience—videos, popcorn parties, classroom pets, a stuffed animal mascot, favorite plants, class murals or quilts, and time lines that depict the history of the year's dates, events, and accomplishments. Ambience deserves this attention because it helps teachers provide students comfort, enjoyment, stimulation, and satisfaction.

Confusing or Engaging?

Attention to physical environment should not result in a confused mess, and it is the teacher's responsibility to ensure that it does not. Each of the six facets that comprise the classroom's physical environment should be considered carefully and used to best advantage. As mentioned, the best advantage for some teachers means keeping the environment relatively lean, efficient, and nondistracting, whereas others may see it differently. It depends on the teacher and students. In any case, the physical environment should always be kept clean and in good order.

Toward that end and to the extent their maturity allows, students should be given major responsibility in taking care of the classroom and the materials it contains. As they keep things orderly and clean, students have the opportunity to build sound values of aesthetics, ecology, and responsibility.

This brings us to the end of our brief exploration of purposes, arrangements, and contents of the physical environment of the classroom. It also concludes our attention to considerations teachers should tend to *before* the school year begins or before they first meet their students. Now we are ready to shift attention to what teachers attend to once the school year begins and they first meet their students. Before proceeding to Chapter 4, which deals with the psychosocial environment of the classroom, take time to explore these end-of-chapter activities.

Parting Thought

Vision is the ability to make a dream a reality.

Summary Self-Check

Check off the following as you either understand or become able to apply them:

☐ The physical environment of the classroom should be arranged and managed so as to enhance the activities called for in the curriculum. Keeping in mind preferences of teachers and students, give attention to six facets of the physical environment:

- Floor space: seating, work, activity, and computer areas; teacher's station; special centers; traffic patterns; students with disabilities and special needs
- Wall space: chalk- and whiteboards; bulletin boards and display areas; student work, prints, maps, and charts
- Countertop space: science projects, kits, models, and globes
- Shelf space: textbooks, reference books, popular library books, special materials
- Cupboard and closet space: student supplies, worksheets, computer and printer supplies, audiovisual equipment, physical education or subject-specific materials, and cleaning supplies, special decorations or collections
- Ambiance: art objects, background music, themes, other special touches

Activities for Reflection and Discussion

1. Take a moment to review the statements in the Preview–Review Guide at the beginning of this chapter. Put a check mark in the *Review* column next to any statement with which you now agree. How have your thoughts changed since reading this chapter?

2. Interview at least two teachers about their room arrangements, or visit and photograph several elementary classrooms. How do the teachers design the physical organization of their classroom to support their program? How do the arrangements differ to best meet primary and upper elementary needs?

3. Again review the description in Chapter 1 of Alexa Smart's room as her friends had set it up for her the weekend before she met her students. Also reread the section that describes the changes she made after her first week with her students. How will these changes better serve the needs of Alexa and her students? How do they align with the suggestions that are described in this chapter?

4. Discuss your feelings concerning the degree to which you would like your classroom to include various items (materials, photos, models, collections, and the like.). Comment on (1) your personal preferences concerning the richness/leanness of classrooms you have attended; (2) student interest, involvement, and motivation; and (3) how you would manage the types of items you would use.

5. For which aspects of physical classroom management would you assign student responsibilities, not only to help but also to increase the sense of student ownership of the classroom? Consider how the responsibilities need to vary depending on the grade level, age, and maturity of your students.

6. The statement was made in the text that "the room should be set up for the teacher's pleasure, too." To what specifically do you think that statement refers? Why do or don't you consider it a valid point?

7. Suppose you teach a third-grade class. In the afternoon you like to rearrange the seating to provide additional floor space for movement activities. Describe specifically how you would train your students to move furniture so that everything is done quickly, correctly, and with no horseplay.

8. Schools provide custodians whose duties include cleaning the classrooms. To what extent, if any, would you want your class (and yourself) to be responsible for cleaning and tidying the room? Justify your opinion in terms of its value to students and their program.

Webliography

Broadcast Music, Inc (BMI): http://www.bmi.com

References and Recommended Readings

Berry, M., principal investigator. (2002). Healthy school environment and enhanced educational performance, prepared for Carpet and Rug Institute. Report is available at www.jjcommercial.com/pdf/10-CharlesYoungElementary.pdf.

Campbell, D. G. (2000). *The Mozart Effect for children: Awakening your child's mind, health, and creativity with music.* New York: HarperCollins.

Campbell, D. G. (2002). *The Mozart Effect: Tapping the power of music to heal the body, strengthen the mind, and unlock the creative spirit.* New York: HarperCollins.

Chan, T., & Petrie, G. (1998). The brain learns better in well-designed school environments. www.nea.org/teacherexperience/braik030312.html.

Evertson, C., & Emmer, E. (2009). *Classroom management for elementary teachers* (8th ed.). Upper Saddle River, NJ: Pearson.

Freiberg, J. H. (Ed.). (1999). *School climate: Measuring, improving and sustaining healthy learning environments.* New York: RoutledgeFalmer.

Hathaway, W., Hargreaves, J., Thompson, G., & Novitsky, D. (1992). *A study into the effects of light on children of elementary school age—A case of light robbery.* Unpublished manuscript, Planning and Information Services, Alberta Department of Education, Edmonton, Alberta, Canada.

Jones, F. (2007). *Tools for teaching. Discipline Instruction Motivation* (2nd ed.). Santa Cruz, CA: Fredric H. Jones & Associates.

Kagan, L. (2007). *The successful dynamic trainer: Engaging all learners course workbook.* San Clemente, CA: Kagan Publishing.

Kagan, S., & Kagan, M. (2009). *Kagan cooperative learning.* San Clemente, CA: Kagan Publishing.

Rauscher, F., Shaw, G., Levine, L., Ky, K., & Wright, E. (1993). Music and spatial task performance. *Nature, 365,* 611.

PEARSON
myeducationlab

Go to the Topic: **Organizing Your Classroom and Supplies** in the MyEducationLab (www.myeducationlab.com) for your course, where you can:

- Find learning outcomes for **Organizing Your Classroom and Supplies** along with the national standards that connect to these outcomes.
- Examine challenging situations and cases presented in the IRIS Center Resources.

Managing the Psychosocial Environment of the Classroom

Don't be out in front of them to rescue or over them to punish, but as they are falling down, stand beside them and guide them. One of the ways we guide them is with the six critical life messages: I believe in you . . . I trust you . . . I know you can handle this . . . you are listened to . . . you are cared for . . . and you are very important to me.

—Barbara Coloroso

Preview–Review Guide

Before you read the chapter, and based on what you know, think you know, or assume, take a minute to put a check mark in the **Preview** column if you agree with the statement. When you finish the chapter, take time to reread the statements and respond in the **Review** column. Reflective discussions can develop because many of the statements are not clearly "yes" or "no."

Preview

Review

1. _____ The qualities of good character should be embedded into the way we teach rather than taught as separate lessons. _____

2. _____ Cyberbullying appears to be replacing other forms of bullying, but it is not a concern for educators. _____

3. _____ Looping is a modern concept in which teachers and students stay together for two or more years. _____

4. _____ Students cannot learn in an environment that is harsh, cold, punitive, and rejecting. _____

5. _____ In addition to words, teachers communicate with tone of voice and body language. _____

6. _____ Giving regular personal attention to students is best done by speaking with them individually every day about their work in school and their academic progress. _____

7. _____ Verbal reinforcement should be directed at students' character traits rather than at their efforts. _____

8. _____ Teachers should help students acknowledge that learning is their main responsibility in school. _____

9. _____ Modeling refers to teaching through example so students can learn through imitation. _____

10. _____ It is the students' responsibility (with teacher guidance) to maintain a warm, pleasant, and supportive environment. _____

Chapter Objectives

After reading Chapter 4, students will demonstrate understanding of

- positive and negative aspects of the psychosocial environment

- factors that contribute to the psychosocial environment

through their active participation in discussions and the end-of-chapter activities for reflection.

Psychosocial environment encompasses the overall emotional climate or "feeling tone" that exists in every classroom, a mixture of pleasure, distress, intrigue, boredom, happiness, sadness, excitement, love, fear—all human emotions seem to be included. This environment is intangible, yet all teachers and students are aware of it. Its effects on learning, productivity, and self-concept are even more powerful than those exerted by the classroom's physical environment.

Think about this as it applies to you. Like most other people asked to recall their educational experiences, don't you find yourself remembering your most intense interactions with teachers or groups of students—those who enlivened, invigorated, and supported your efforts, or those who embarrassed or threatened you? As you read on, the problem to solve or the essential or guiding question might be: *What decisions and actions can I make to best create a positive psychosocial environment for my students?*

On the Positive Side of the Psychosocial Environment

During our own years as students, most of us experienced or witnessed the extremes—both positive and negative classroom environments. The positive side of the psychosocial environment is the warmth, caring, and support that make the classroom a friendly, pleasant, encouraging place. Most students flourish best in such an environment. But the psychosocial environment can have a negative tone as well—cold, uncaring, harsh, punitive, aloof, and sarcastic—further burdening children whose psychological well-being already is threatened by social ills outside the school, and even fear from bullies in school.

When the climate feels threatening because of the actions or attitudes of other children or the teacher, students fear making errors, hope they will not fail or be embarrassed, and pray that if they make mistakes, the teacher will not take reprisals against them. Few students do well in such environments, though there are exceptions. For most, achievement in such climates is suppressed and pleasure is nonexistent.

Perhaps you recall from experience that learning can occur rapidly within a climate of fear, provided the fear is not paralyzing. Fear has long been used to motivate learners, but it is doubtful that fear of physical or psychological hurt should ever be used in today's class-rooms. At best it has a short-term effect, and it is known to produce detrimental side effects of stress, anger, and resentment, all of which are counterproductive to what we hope to accomplish with young learners. Teachers who succeed in making their classrooms enjoyable, engaging places in which to work and learn leave positive impressions on their students.

On the Negative Side of the Psychosocial Environment: Bullying

Today bullying is a regular occurrence, both in and out of school. When asked to define bullying, most agree that three elements are present: (1) willful harm-doing, (2) recurrence over time, and (3) a target who is someone with less power than the bully (Nansel et al., 2001). Individuals who intentionally instill fear in others are bullies; they intend to hurt, and they enjoy it. Both boys and girls bully. Boys tend to be more direct in their bullying, while girls are more indirect. Elementary-aged bullies frequently use verbal or physical bullying, often while bystanders do nothing to stop them. However, not all bullying takes place through obvious verbal or physical actions. Relational bullying, which is more difficult to recognize, undermines the bullied child's sense of self by shunning, isolating, excluding, or ignoring. Hate motivates

Case Study 4.1   Memories

FOCUS QUESTIONS

Take time to recall a teacher who had an effect on you. What do you remember about the teacher and the class? Based on your memories of how the teacher looked, sounded, and acted, how are your memories positive or negative?

Carlos Bachicha doesn't remember much about his fourth-grade teacher or school, except that he rode the bus with his brother and carved a soap elephant that looked more like a pig. His sixth-grade year is even more blank. But his fifth—that's a different story. His teacher was Miss Osborne, and she had red hair and freckles and was forever having her students do something interesting in class. They performed plays while wearing paper costumes they cut and stapled together—and the students thought they looked real enough. For Johnny Appleseed's birthday, they ate foods made with red and green and yellow apples. In October they had a pumpkin day and tasted pumpkin seeds, breads, pies, cookies, and even pumpkin ice cream. That month they also parched corn and smashed it into cornmeal, and a mom baked cornbread and they ate it with butter. In November Miss Osborne roasted an enormous turkey, and parents brought in all kinds of other food for everyone to share in a Thanksgiving meal. One day Miss Osborne set up her real spinning wheel in class and let the students take turns running it. She even started a lunchtime chess club and taught interested students how to play the game. That was a long time ago, but Carlos remembers her and that year like they were yesterday.

"You think maybe I lost my marbles, based on the psychosocial environment of my classroom?"

http://www.DansCartoons.com

bullying that focuses on culture, race, religion, or sexual orientation. And now with the growing prevalence of technology and the Internet in classrooms and homes, teachers and students must contend with another yet type of bullying—online or cyberbullying. Cyber bullies use electronic media to inflict willful and repeated harm on others (McGrath, 2007, and Shariff, 2008, cited in Larrivee, 2009, p. 94).

All too frequently nowadays, we hear in the news stories of victims who reach ultimate despair. Some are triggered to go on a killing spree. Shootings at Columbine and schools in Southern California were the results of bullying. Other victims are so despondent they take their own lives, for to them suicide is the only escape.

Bystanders and peers of victims also suffer from bullying. For several reasons, bystanders may appear to support—even encourage—bullies, or they may do nothing to stop the action: Bystanders may feel guilty, helpless, or unsafe because they don't act or stand up to the bully. They may avoid associating with the victim because they are afraid of payback from the bully. Because of their fear of being seen as an "informer" or "snitch," they may not report incidents of bullying. And thus the cycle of bullying continues.

Read more about bullying in Chapter 7.

Toward an Optimal Psychosocial Environment

Fraser and O'Brien (1985) found that psychosocial classroom environments tend to focus on five factors: satisfaction, friction, competitiveness, difficulty, and cohesiveness. While it is the teacher's responsibility to establish and maintain a positive psychosocial environment, students can and should help in this effort. Teachers may proceed safely on the premise that classrooms function best when they provide a positive and structured climate, one that reflects warmth, support, and pleasant circumstances with very low levels of fear. Fear should be limited to anxiety of not living up to one's own potential, of letting other people down, or of not acting in one's best interest. It should never be a fear of personal danger.

However, before you conclude that such climates are devoid of structure, expectations, or enforcement, be assured that this is not the case. In fact, it is doubtful that a positive climate can be maintained in the absence of well-enforced regulations governing interpersonal conduct.

Because establishing a positive climate is the teacher's responsibility and because such a climate usually is best for enhancing learning and building good self-concept, this chapter explores what you can do to ensure that your classroom environment provides the warmth and support prized by students and teachers alike.

Some teachers set the tone at the beginning of each year when they describe their students as their school family. They tell their students that everyone is special and important. They also explain that while they might not always agree on everything, just as in any family, everyone is expected to be respectful and well behaved in the classroom and on the school grounds. Some teachers teach and emphasize the Golden Rule: *Do unto others.* For example, if you don't want to be called names, then don't call other people names. If you want people to listen to you, then be sure to listen to others. And most important, if you want to have friends, then be a friend.

Gloria Anderson has taught every elementary grade. However, when she teaches fifth or sixth grade, she explores the psychosocial environment in an unusual way:

> I begin the year with an unusual writing prompt. I show students a *No Hunting* sign, the kind you can buy in a sporting goods store. The students are to write about what they think about the sign and why I have it in the classroom. The next day, after I have read all the quick writes, the students and I discuss what the sign means in our room. This discussion leads to their development of class rules and expectations.

A Quick Look at Looping

Looping, a concept that dates back to the one-room schoolhouse, is practiced in some parts of Europe and is reappearing in some areas of this country. Decisions to loop teachers and classes may result from school budgets, student enrollment numbers, or a belief in a best practice, but whatever the reason, a teacher keeps the same group of students for two or more consecutive years. The first year of looping is very typical—teacher and students get to know one another. The second year, however, has some unique benefits, several of which are related to the psychosocial environment: familiarity, stability, continuity, and strong communication. During the second year they are together, teachers know the strengths, contributions, and abilities of their students, and students know the teacher's expectations and routines. Looping provides stability, particularly for children who might be experiencing difficulties outside the school. Teachers, students, and caregivers have more opportunity and a longer time to bond and work together as a team for the children's success.

Case Study 4.2   Benefits of Looping

FOCUS QUESTION

When Marilyn Cox and neighborhood students moved into a new school, she was able to loop with her fourth graders from the year before. She found the experience to be rewarding for everyone. Here she describes several advantages when she looped with her students; list them. What other advantages can you think of? What challenges or disadvantages?

"What a wonderful experience this year has been. I've taught for thirty years, but this is my first fifth-grade class. Being new to fifth grade has been infinitely easier because I brought my students along with me. (Last year I taught them in fourth grade in another nearby school.) As the year started I didn't lose the usual chunk of time from my schedule needed to build the classroom environment. It was established last year. We just caught up on each other's summer experience and moved right into fifth grade.

"This is my first experience with looping. Having the privilege of starting a brand new grade level at a brand new school gave me the opportunity to take a risk on an entirely new concept to me! It has been wonderful to see how great the students have responded to this new environment. Our relationship, established last year, gave us a history to build on. We didn't have to start from dirt and build up from there. Our structure was already in place.

"Not only did I know the students and their strengths and weaknesses, I also knew their parents, and I wasn't the least bit hesitant about contacting them. Back-to-School Night was well attended. In the past it has been the rule that parent participation goes down drastically by the time students get to fifth grade. That hasn't been true with this class. At parent conference time all meetings went smoothly, due in no small part of their having done this with me last year. Parent helpers are coming out in droves to help in the classroom. Forms are returned faster. It seems incredible that we continue to work as such a tight team. Having the same parent group for two years has afforded me a tight relationship with the families. And having the same students again definitely has kept unacceptable behavior in the classroom down to a minimum."

Democratic Learning Communities in Technology-Rich Environments (DLC in TRE)

In recent years, Professor Eileen VanWie at New Mexico State University has researched aspects of Democratic Learning Communities in Technology-Rich Environments. She believes strongly in the goal of DLC in TRE—to bring together diverse learners so they can collaborate, use digital technology to engage in real-world studies and experiences, and learn from that process.

VanWie says *Democratic Learning Communities (DLC)* have several layers, with special benefits to students. First, these communities go beyond just the students. They are groups of people—students, teachers, families, and the public who work together to promote meaningful learning. Students are able to participate in interesting activities and projects. They have an opportunity to practice life and social skills because they choose, share responsibility, problem solve, and self-govern. They also have opportunities to communicate, interact, and share leadership.

VanWie defines *Technology-Rich Environments (TRE)* as physical and virtual spaces that use technology and electronic tools to engage students in critical and creative thinking, communication, and networking. In TRE classrooms, technology is used extensively to help students learn content knowledge, processes, and social and emotional skills.

Successful technology-rich environments are more likely when teachers feel comfortable with the technology, or at the least are willing to commit to possibilities and take reasonable risks. Teachers do not have to be expert in technical knowledge and skills, but they do need to have available student or adult support teams of "technicians" who can help them and less knowledgeable students as they acquire skills. Teachers may need help with designing curricula and lessons that use technology effectively. Finally, they also may need help with "educating" others—students, caregivers, other educators, and the public. If technology-rich environments exist schoolwide, school technology assistance teams can be organized to manage these tasks.

As budgets and the physical space allow, teachers should create flexible room arrangements, with attention to color and lighting, wireless and wired connections, and their plans for teaching, learning, and student interactions with materials and equipment. (Refer back to Chapter 3 for floor plan examples of technology-rich classrooms.) The contributions such technology-rich classrooms make toward a positive psychosocial environment are great.

Other Factors That Contribute to the Psychosocial Environment

Many other factors contribute to and significantly influence the psychosocial environment of the classroom. Factors under control of the teacher can be grouped into three categories: human relations skills, teacher and student responsibilities in human relations, and maintenance of the psychosocial environment.

Human Relations Skills

Good human relations enable people to interact pleasantly and productively, both of which are essential to a participative environment that promotes learning. Four aspects of human relations skills merit attention here: (1) general human relations skills, (2) human relations skills with students, (3) human relations skills with colleagues, and (4) human relations skills with parents and guardians.

General Human Relations Skills
Certain skills in human relations are pertinent to all people in almost all situations. Those skills involve maintaining a positive attitude, being friendly, demonstrating the ability to listen, and offering genuine compliments.

Maintaining a positive attitude is a skill that should be kept foremost in mind. Generally, we show it by looking on the bright side of things and avoiding complaining, backbiting, fault-finding, or hurtful gossiping—behaviors known to undermine positive climates. We maintain a positive attitude by remembering that although all of us have difficulties in our lives, we also have some measure of control over how those difficulties affect us. People with positive attitudes believe that no problem exists that cannot be solved, and they focus on dealing with problems rather than complaining or making excuses for them.

Friendliness is a trait that is admired everywhere, yet many of us have difficulty being friendly toward others, especially when we find ourselves in threatening situations or with people we dislike. We can, however, learn to be friendly even toward people who do not please us, by smiling, speaking in a considerate way, using their names, asking how they are, and inquiring about family and work. When we do these simple things, we find that others tend to respond to us in the same manner.

Ability to listen is a skill we appreciate in others but often have trouble practicing. Most of us would rather talk than listen, but demonstrating the ability to listen is very helpful in promoting good relationships. It shows genuine interest in the other person, indicates that the other's experiences and observations are valued, and enhances the quality of communication by bringing about a genuine exchange of ideas.

Ability to compliment genuinely is not often discussed but is a skill of considerable power. Both the giving and receiving of compliments make most of us uncomfortable for a time, partly because people sometimes use compliments to manipulate others. Too often, compliments are worded to sound like criticisms rather than acknowledgments or appreciations for what someone does. But it is evident that most people like to receive compliments, even when they are unable to accept them gracefully, and that they react positively toward individuals who compliment them.

Effective compliments are both genuine and explicit. For example, when complimenting someone on a presentation, we might say, "I found your talk entertaining and helpful, especially your suggestions on conducting evaluation conferences between principals and teachers." Ask yourself how you react to people who give you genuine compliments. In all likelihood, you feel good, and you also feel interested in working with and associating with those persons.

Human Relations Skills with Students   General human relations skills can be applied in all situations, but when dealing with students, there are additional skills that serve teachers well. Before all else, teachers should (1) infuse qualities of good character into the way they teach. They also should (2) model courtesy and good manners, (3) give regular attention, (4) display genuine caring, (5) show continual willingness to help, and (6) use verbal and behavioral reinforcers.

When teachers *infuse qualities of good character* into the way they teach, they go beyond lessons that teach about specific ideals. Lessons are single events. Teachers too often miss opportunities for students to acquire and practice qualities of good character when they simply teach about ideals. For example, when they teach about honesty, they merely provide students with a definition that may or may not be learned. On the other hand, when teachers uphold honesty as an ideal of good character and provide opportunities for students to practice being honest, honesty is more likely to become a characteristic of each student. In other words, teachers should continually be aware and "walk the talk" of good character.

Modeling courtesy and good manners closely complements this way of teaching and is extremely important in establishing a positive classroom climate. Teachers should hold high standards of decency and courtesy, and should model these qualities when dealing with students. They should never act cruelly, speak sarcastically, or show favoritism. Nor should they allow students to bully, be cruel, or speak sarcastically. Laughing and joking are not forbidden; they are prized, but never used hurtfully. Courtesy and other qualities of good character, when held as ideals, are embedded into the way we teach and practiced at all times.

Giving regular attention is best done by speaking personally with each student every day, on matters not necessarily related to schoolwork or behavior. In most classrooms, the majority of the teacher's attention goes to two small groups of students—those who do exceptionally well academically and those who chronically misbehave. Now that classrooms are inclusive, a third group also requires extra attention—students with disabilities or special needs. This leaves a large group of students who receive relatively little attention. Because this group causes teachers neither special joy nor special annoyance or challenge, it is natural that they tend to be overlooked. If these students are to do their best, however, they too need attention from the teacher.

Some teachers make a point of speaking to students as they first enter the room each day. Others speak with students while taking attendance. Still others speak with them individually during small-group instruction. To help them distribute personal attention equitably, some teachers keep class rosters at hand and put tally marks beside names as attention is given.

Displaying genuine caring should be both verbal and visual. All of us want to believe that we are cared for and that others value what we say and do. Because we want to feel that we belong and are able to contribute to the group, we look and listen for signs from others that this is so. Perhaps surprisingly, a fairly small percentage of what a teacher communicates to students is done with actual word choices. A much larger percentage is communicated through the sounds of words and through facial expressions and body language. Teachers need to make sure that what they say and what their body says really are the same. Teachers should be able to say to students, "I care for you and I want to support you in all that you do here," and then be able to show it.

Continual willingness to help is another trait that is universally admired but seldom seen. We almost confer sainthood on people such as Albert Schweitzer, Mother Teresa, Nelson Mandela, and others who devote their lives to helping others, including the abject poor. You should not expect your students to look upon you as saintly (though some will) when you show that you will do whatever you can to help them learn. Let it be enough that your students gravitate to you, admire you, and remember you positively in later years. How often we adults are heard to say of our teachers, "That Mr. Heck was strict, but he always went out of his way to help us."

Verbal and behavioral reinforcers are the teacher's words and actions that show support, encouragement, and approval. Reinforcers increase student attention and work output. Some teachers use tangible reinforcers such as stars, tokens, and even food and candy. However, in most classes gestures and verbal reinforcers are sufficient—a wink, nod, smile, thumbs up, "Nice going," "I can see how much work you have put into this," "You must have thought about this a great deal," and "You are improving every day."

Again, reinforcement should be given to all students, not only for achievement but also for effort and improvement. Notice the fine distinction between reinforcing a student's *efforts* and reinforcing *character traits*. Be careful of saying things like "You are very intelligent" or "You are a good boy" when commenting on work. Praise of this type often brings undesirable side effects of uneasiness, inhibited communication, and an increased need for personal validation. It is preferable to say, "I see you worked hard. Thank you."

Human Relations Skills with Colleagues Every teacher spends a good deal of time working or dealing with colleagues—fellow teachers, administrators, support staff for students with special needs, beginning teacher support providers, student teachers, secretaries, librarians, custodians, nurses, and others. It is very important to be able to interact well with colleagues. In addition to the general skills of polite attitude,

---

Vignette 4.1   Communicating with Students

Mary Brewer, an itinerant resource specialist, offers several suggestions for communicating with each individual student. "My students use a daily journal entry where they can express their feelings in a nonthreatening place via personal written conversations. I also schedule regular 'office hours' throughout the week. Students who want to discuss something with me sign up for the time(s) that are best for them.

"Students who otherwise are reluctant to express themselves often are eager to draw pictures that illustrate their feelings. If it's appropriate to do so, I use the services of bilingual personnel to draw out hidden concerns. Students new to the school are reticent about expressing themselves, often because they feel themselves to be 'outsiders,' unwelcomed in the 'in' group. I pair them with students who are more at ease. Cooperative learning provides many opportunities for this type of pairing."

UPON REFLECTION

Effective teachers make a point of talking to or interacting with every student every day. Mary Brewer suggests several ways to communicate with individual students; list them. What other ways can you think of?

---

friendliness, listening, and complimenting, four other considerations should be kept in mind: (1) supporting others, (2) sharing the load, (3) compromising, and (4) leading or following as appropriate.

Supporting others means standing behind them and what they are trying to accomplish, unless you absolutely cannot do so. Professional Learning Communities (PLC) offer one way to accomplish this. Members are able to give active support, as when actual assistance is given to colleagues, or passive support, as when acceptance and encouragement are shown.

Sadly, this attitude of support is not found in overabundance, and it seems that the larger the school, the shorter the supply. Unfortunately, all too often school district personnel denigrate the work of colleagues, make snide remarks, and belittle efforts and accomplishments—behind the colleague's back, of course. It has been documented that in faculty lounges, about 90 percent of teachers' comments are negative in nature. Negativism such as this is very detrimental to good working environments.

The paucity of support that teachers show for each other probably is due in part to teacher isolation, frustration, and the absence of tangible success. When we don't feel the world is treating us fairly, we tend to lash out at others who have little if anything to do with the real problem.

Another unattractive trait of human nature is that we all want to look good, in our own eyes as well as in the eyes of others, and we seem to believe that we can build ourselves up by tearing others down. As they look worse, we think that we look better in comparison. The result, of course, is never what we had hoped. For example, those who gossip and malign in an attempt to show their superiority hardly ever lack an attentive audience. But does that audience hold the complainer in high regard? Rarely. Complainers and backbiters seldom earn the sincere trust of others. As they tear others down, they taint their own reputations.

If you want to build yourself up, the way to do so is by building others up. If you learn only one thing from this chapter, let it be what you have just read.

Sharing the load is one thing you must do if you hope to earn the respect of your colleagues. In any school there are many tasks to complete: committee work that no one likes very much; team, student concern, and Individual Education Plan (IEP) meetings; open houses and parent–teacher meetings; family math nights; school musicals and carnivals; student council and safety patrols; curriculum groups; materials evaluations; and professional growth and in-service education sessions. Typically, a few people carry most of the load, while the rest do far less than their share. If we are to get along well with colleagues, and it is essential to our professional lives that we do so, we must undertake our part even when it is unpleasant. Sharing the load builds trust; shirking produces resentment.

Compromising is a way of life for those who get along well with others. Compromise doesn't mean giving in to others any more than it means demanding to have your own way all of the time. It is a matter of give and take, with resolution coming after everyone has had a say. In any professional group there will be strong differences of opinion regarding purpose, procedure, and workload. You will want to express and stick by what you believe, but also try to understand others' feelings and points of view. If a faculty's work is to go forward in a positive way, an acceptable middle ground must be found.

Both *leading and following* are important in any endeavor, especially when undertaken democratically. We should assume leadership roles in which we can effectively plan courses of action, obtain resources, guide decisions, and rally support. When others lead, we should do our best to help make decisions that share the load. This does not mean following the leader's dictates uncritically, but it does imply that criticisms and countersuggestions should be expressed in open forums, and support should be given once a group decision has been made.

Teachers who work together as partners have an even greater responsibility to practice these skills. *Teaching teams* may be an entire grade-level team of teachers, teaching partners who share one or two classes of students every day, or two teachers who share a contract for one class of students. Ideally, teaching teams are the result of mutual agreements that accentuate the strengths of the partners. Teaming allows teachers to arrange students and instruction in a variety of ways to best support both teaching and learning. In addition to giving teachers more time for students, team teaching encourages reflection and evaluation of what the partners themselves are doing. In teams, partners have someone who

" I REALIZE YOU'RE OVERWORKED, AND THAT'S WHY YOU'RE SO VALUABLE. "

Permission by Dave Carpenter.

can provide feedback on their ideas, someone whose strengths they can build on, and someone who will support their successes and challenges.

To be most effective and efficient, successful team teaching and planning require all the qualities we just discussed, and a few more: excellent communication, cooperation, mutual respect and trust, and careful planning. For team teaching to work, partners must share a mutual philosophy, respect, trust, and compatibility. Successful teaching teams require a lot of give and take, and the shared mindset that this is our classroom, and teaching partners must work together for the success of their program and students.

Beginning Teacher Support Programs In many school districts, beginning teachers now find themselves communicating directly with district support persons. Attention and efforts of the support personnel are intended to help beginning teachers grow in their professional skills. It's critical that novice teachers are comfortable and able to communicate classroom realities and concerns so support providers can mentor and assist efficiently.

Additional Cautions about the Teachers' Lounge Throughout the teaching day, teachers are likely to find themselves in close working relationships with other adults. Additionally, on most school campuses the teachers' lounge can be an excellent place to be with colleagues during prep time or lunch. Teachers are out of their classrooms, away from their students for a short while, and in a place where they can meet, plan, or socialize with other adults. However, a word of caution is important. Teachers' lounges also can be a hotbed where some teachers come to vent or complain. Again, remember that backbiters and complainers seldom earn respect or trust. Their negativity often adds to stress that weighs on teachers. In Chapter 12, we talk more about potential concerns and negativity that might be found in teachers' lounges as they relate to professionalism. To this end, it is wise for teachers to take the time to discuss with paraprofessionals and volunteers the dangers of gossip, backbiting, and complaining. In other words, take responsibility and do what you can to maintain a positive environment and healthy relations with colleagues.

Human Relations Skills with Caregivers

Teachers have the responsibility to communicate and work with the parents or guardians of the students they teach. Some teachers avoid this contact as much as possible, though such avoidance, under most circumstances, is counterproductive. Fortunately, many teachers accept the responsibility willingly and capitalize on it. Why? Alliances with caregivers—teachers working with parents or guardians in a collaborative effort—further the goal of supporting the student. Teachers who communicate well with caregivers often find that they enjoy increased home support in matters of discipline and curriculum. As an extra bonus, parents and guardians tend to give higher ratings to teachers who take the trouble to communicate about what caregivers consider the most important element of schooling—their child.

How teachers reach out to caregivers makes a difference in the response they get from them. When communicating with parents or guardians (more details will be presented in Chapter 11), keep in mind these four traits: positive attitude, friendliness, listening, and genuine compliments. Also make sure to (1) communicate regularly and clearly, (2) describe your program and expectations, (3) emphasize the child's progress while downplaying his or her shortcomings, (4) mention future plans for the child's instruction, and (5) arrange for productive parent conferences.

Vignette 4.2   Team Teaching

First-grade teachers Jamie Rubin and Patti Petersen have more than 30 years of combined teaching experience and have shared a teaching contract for many years.

The past years have been the most rewarding and the best, and we would not teach any other way. Being friends for six years prior to team teaching helped in making the situation a strong one. Once, when a child was asked the name of the teacher for whom he was running an errand, he replied without pause, "Mrs. Rubinsen."

Jamie: Our teaching styles are very similar and compatible. We both exhibit organization, fairness, structure, and a sense of fun in a fairly strict classroom. We each have our own strengths. One of us has a master's degree in reading and is very strong in language arts. The other loves science and music. When parents ask how their child will be able to balance two teachers in a first-grade classroom, our response is, "If the child is lucky enough to have a two-parent family, then so it is in this classroom."

Patti: What makes our partnership work and thrive? First, our friendship. We respect, trust, and love each other. We often try to outdo each other in the kindnesses we perform so that the next day's workload for our partner is lessened. Second is our communication. We e-mail each other daily with information about the day. Rarely is there a time when either of us is left in the dark concerning anything, be it related to parent, student, or peer.

UPON REFLECTION

What are the advantages of team teaching for the teachers and students? What are the disadvantages? What makes a successful teaching team work?

Communicating regularly and clearly establishes a basis of mutual interest and concern about the child. As a general rule, some kind of communication should go to caregivers every week—a note, instructions for homework, a written commentary about a piece of student work, a class newsletter, or a phone call. Most teachers now have a computer and Internet access for e-mail. They also have access to computer programs for creating and maintaining classroom websites. However, teachers never should assume that parents or guardians have a computer or Internet access at home or work that they can use for communication with the teacher.

Caregivers of a student with a disability or other special need should be involved actively in their child's educational program. In fact, parental knowledge and involvement are a significant part of the legislation for inclusion, the Individuals with Disabilities Education Act (IDEA), and the Response to Intervention (RTI) process. Also, when language diversity is a consideration, arrangements should be made to translate communications into the primary language of the caregivers. The importance of frequent regular communications cannot be overemphasized; a system should be implemented at the beginning of the year and followed thereafter.

Sometimes class rosters are available a few days before the first day of school. Third-grade teacher Pam Klevesahl often found notes regarding behavior and/or academic concerns by the names of some of her students. In order to develop a strong working relationship with caregivers and these students from the beginning, she would call and make the effort to meet with students and families in their homes for about 20 minutes:

> After I introduced myself I would ask the child if he or she was looking forward to the start of school. I would describe a little about the year and the plans I had for our studies, and then ask if he or she had any questions about our year together. Next I asked the parents if they had any questions or concerns that I could answer. Frequently, parents told me that their child has difficulty paying attention, working quietly, or the like. When I heard this, I would turn directly to the child and say, "Oh, my gosh! I sure hope that doesn't happen this year." I then explained that the students in my class are growing up and will be expected to work independently, and that if they do not, they will have to complete their work during recess. In this way I let both the child and the parents know my expectations and consequences. I then would explain my behavior plan to the parents while the child, of course, was listening.

Selective home visits worked well for Ms. Klevesahl. She found this to be an efficient and effective way to meet caregivers and clarify expectations for a few students and their families before the school year even began. However, not every district or school encourages home visits. Fourth-grade teacher Karen O'Connor explains why she routinely calls the parents and guardians of her students:

> I still remember a reaction the first year I taught from the mother of a student who was chronically disruptive in class. The mother said resignedly, "Oh, hello, Mrs. O'Connor. What has Bobby done wrong today?" When I reassured her that I was calling to tell her what an interesting oral report Bobby had given in front of the class that day, I heard her relief, even disbelief, as she listened to the details.
>
> I think we need to break the "no news is good news" mindset by taking time to make positive phone calls about our students. That one phone call to Bobby's mother turned a potentially adversarial relationship into a partnership that helped both of us support Bobby's efforts.

Regular communication must be done very clearly, with no possibility of parental misunderstanding. Education is filled with jargon and acronyms, such as grade-level benchmarks, curriculum standards, inclusion, IEP, RTI, GATE, SAT, multi-age classrooms, cooperative learning, authentic assessment, portfolios, rubrics, PBLs and problem-based learning—you probably can add several others. Don't take it for granted that caregivers understand any of these terms. Avoid such terms if you can, but if you must communicate about them, explain what they mean.

Describe your program and expectations early in your communication, and repeat them occasionally. Some caregivers will forget, but many may prove to be so interested in what you have to say that they will actively help their child achieve your stated goals. Inform them of the daily schedule. Tell them something about the activities you will use to reach your goals. Let them know about homework, the grading system, and anything else central to your program. They will appreciate it and will become more predisposed to cooperate.

Emphasize progress when communicating about the child. Also identify the child's difficulties, indicate your plan for remedying these shortcomings, and ask for parental help. Caregivers' thoughts about their child are fragile. They see their child as an extension of themselves, the child's difficulties as their own, and criticisms of the child as leveled at them. Dwelling on a child's shortcomings probes at the most sensitive feelings of the caregivers.

When discussing a student, consider this sequence: (1) mention something positive about the child personally, (2) show the progress the child has made and is making, (3) describe plans for producing still greater achievement in the child, and finally, (4) mention difficulties that are interfering with the child's progress. Assure caregivers that you are working to overcome these difficulties, that you have a plan for doing so, that you need their support in your efforts, and that you will appreciate any insights or suggestions they might offer. Most caregivers respond well when treated in this manner. They want their child to learn and behave in school, and when the teacher shows interest, they usually provide support and help.

Future plans for individuals and for the entire class should be communicated. If a student has unusual difficulty in math, formulate a definite plan you can share with the student and caregivers. If a child excels in science, plan how that child might stretch that talent or move into other topics. If the class shows unusual ability in music or art, plan to further those abilities, perhaps through a special performance or exhibit for caregivers.

Conferencing productively with caregivers, although closely related to the points already made, refers specifically to the parent–teacher conferences scheduled early in the school year at most schools. Some schools and districts schedule conferences at each grading period. Have at hand the individual student's folder, which shows progress, strengths, weaknesses, and work samples. Greet the parents or guardians and have them sit beside you at a table, not across from you. Engage them in a few words of small talk and make them feel at ease. Review the child's good qualities, strengths, progress, and difficulties, and your plans for increasing strengths and countering the difficulties. Request their help in supporting the child and, if necessary, in working with the child at home. In fact, if possible, help the caregivers create a home action plan that parallels and supports your plan. Assure the caregivers that you will do your best for the child and request their cooperation toward that end. Again, if English is not a strong language for the caregivers, invite a translator to join you for the conference. Further details of what should be included and said in parent–teacher conferences are presented in Chapter 11.

Responsibilities in the Psychosocial Environment

The psychosocial environment of the classroom rests on warmth, stimulation, and helpfulness. These qualities are unlikely to develop unless they are planned for, and an important part of that planning lies in recognizing who is responsible for what.

Teacher Responsibilities   The teacher is responsible for communicating and modeling the sort of psychosocial environment desired, initiating the conditions that lead to it, and maintaining a good environment once it is achieved.

The *desired environment,* as described previously, is one in which students work hard, help each other, and enjoy success, all in a pleasant setting of encouragement and absence of threat. You will want to talk with your students frequently about these desired conditions, in terms suited to their level of understanding and maturity. They will want the same conditions you do, and if allowed, they will make suggestions for achieving them. They will understand and support your reasoning. However, they will not always abide by what is necessary to keep the environment healthy.

Conditions that indicate and sustain the environment must be set forth by the teacher, through explanations, modeling, practice, classbuilding, and teambuilding. Students closely watch and often imitate the teacher's attitude and behavior. Teachers must set the tone by using appropriate classbuilding and teambuilding activities throughout the year. During classbuilding activities, students have the opportunity to meet and interact with all members of the class. Teambuilding activities give students opportunities to interact and support their teammates in positive ways. Kagan and colleagues (1995, 1997, 2009) offer numerous classbuilding and teambuilding structures (step-by-step sequences of action) that support a positive and safe class environment. For more information about classbuilding and teambuilding activity ideas, visit Kagan's website, http://www.kaganonline.com.

In addition to their own attitudes and behavior, as well as their classbuilding and teambuilding efforts, teachers must demonstrate the following as they establish and maintain a sound emotional environment in their class:

Enthusiasm Enthusiasm is a key element to which students react positively. They find it motivating, energizing, and contagious. Students like seeing teachers who enjoy what they do. Teacher enthusiasm should be shown for the curriculum as well as for working with children, in a stable, ongoing manner throughout the day.

Importance of the Individual The importance of every individual in the classroom should be established quickly. Teachers should communicate continually that students are worthy and have a place in school and society, that they have contributions to make, and that the class would be diminished without them. The feeling of importance will grow as students assume responsibilities in the classroom, experience success, and receive deserved acknowledgment from others.

Belonging Belonging is a primary goal in life—all of us want to know we are important to family, friends, class, and school. When that goal is not reached, students tend either to withdraw or misbehave, neither of which is good for the teacher, student, or class. Therefore, it behooves the teacher to foster a sense of belonging in every member of the class by stating, and repeating, that every student is important, will be valued, and will be treated fairly. It also helps to follow through with acknowledgment, friendliness, help, support, and assigned responsibility for some aspect of the room or program. Again, classbuilding and teambuilding efforts help affirm belonging and the sense of community.

Important underlying psychosocial values for inclusive classrooms are the ABC's (acceptance, belonging, and community) and the three R's (reading, writing, and relationships). Inclusive classrooms also focus on how to support the special gifts of every child in the school community and how to meet students' needs to feel welcomed and secure and to become successful (Pearpoint & Forest, 1992).

Fairness Fairness is required if the psychosocial environment is to remain positive. Students don't like the teacher to play favorites or enforce rules unevenly. They expect standards but don't want them to be impossibly high. They expect rules and enforcement but don't want them to be harsh. In other words, students will comply with standards and rules if they consider them to be reasonable and fair. In classrooms that are perceived to be fair, students will trust that irresponsible choices and poor behavior will not be tolerated, and behavior expectations will be maintained and enforced in an evenhanded way. Students are not hurtfully punished. Rather, logical consequences should give students second chances and the opportunity to right their wrongs or make up for them.

Responsibility Responsibility goes hand in hand with belonging. It is important that all students accept their responsibility in furthering their own learning, as well as other classroom roles. Classroom monitors can be assigned responsibilities for many of the ongoing requirements of the class. (You will find additional discussion and suggestions for class monitors in Chapter 7.) Mirroring a popular business practice of today, some teachers use students as "one-minute managers" to help run the class. Group discussions should emphasize that every student has a stake in making things good for all students collectively, and for the teacher as well, and that this responsibility should carry over to friends and family. Such responsibilities do not weigh students down but instead give them a sense of purpose, with attendant motivation for supporting group endeavors.

Consistency Students want to know what to expect day to day from their teachers. They like surprises, but only pleasant ones. When their teacher vacillates between warm and cold or tolerant and harsh, students become uneasy and their own behavior becomes unpredictable.

Friendliness Friendliness projects the warmth and consideration that contribute to productive work. This is not "best-pal" friendliness, but that which is shown through having a pleasant demeanor, acknowledging individual students, speaking with them regularly and personally, and remembering something about family members or pets and even their birthdays. This friendliness dispels any sense of threat and helps reduce fearfulness while increasing the willingness to attempt difficult tasks.

Success Success should be established and maintained from the beginning. Success is highly rewarding, motivating, and effective in building a positive self-concept, although students should not believe that they always will succeed in what they do or that success always comes easily. Students should understand that mistakes are part of learning. In fact, mistakes are opportunities for teachers to instruct and for students to learn. Mistakes give students the opportunity to accept and act to correct a challenge or consequence, rather than make up excuses. It is important, however, that every student experience success, especially from diligent effort and improvement.

Understanding When students are struggling with personal difficulties, they want to be understood. Understanding includes recognition of illness, discomfort, personal problems, or traumatic occurrences, so that a greater than normal degree of tolerance justifiably can be shown. This is not to be confused, however, with unquestioning acceptance of whatever a student might say or do. We can be understanding of difficulties, excitements, and problems without approving or ignoring a student's disruptive or inappropriate behavior in the classroom.

Humor • Finally, humor should be a mainstay of the psychosocial environment. Humor is the trait most often identified by older students when asked what they most like in teachers. (Younger children most often identify niceness.) Students like to laugh, share jokes, and find the humor in situations, and they appreciate teachers who make humor a part of the environment. Unfortunately, students also like to laugh hurtfully at each other, and that is a problem. You never should allow your students to laugh at the expense of others. If everyone is enjoying a laugh, fine. But when it is done in demeaning or cruel ways, it is not to be tolerated. Simply point out that students will have a good time in their work and there will be plenty of humor and laughter, but there will be no horseplay, no abject silliness, and no laughing at another's expense.

Organizing the Conditions That Build a Good Environment   Conditions that include and sustain a positive psychosocial environment must be brought into play in an organized manner. You must be sure to show every student that he or she is cared for and wanted, will be treated fairly, will be encouraged, and will enjoy learning in a nonthreatening environment. Every student should have important responsibilities in the class. You should not leave such matters to chance or assume they will occur because of your good intentions. (Again, think of the description of Alexa Smart's first days with her students.) Even the smartest teacher cannot keep in mind all the conditions and responsibilities of a classroom. A simple checklist, kept in a record book or taped to the wall or board by the teacher's desk, serves as a useful reminder of the attitudes and conditions just discussed and ensures that they will be given attention thoroughly and consistently.

Student Responsibilities   Students have responsibilities to the psychosocial environment just as teachers do, and the act of discharging these responsibilities is very powerful in building the classroom environment. Responsibilities should be clarified in class discussions and reemphasized regularly. Students' main responsibilities include the following.

Learning   Learning is the main reason students are in school. They are there to acquire the skills, attitudes, values, knowledge, and understandings that will permit them to function to the fullest while contributing to the societal good. This also includes learning to make responsible choices for themselves. They should be helped to recognize that fact and comply with it as their fundamental responsibility in the classroom.

Contribution   Contribution to the class is a second major responsibility students have in helping maintain a good psychosocial environment. They are to participate in discussions, help with class duties, assist other students and the teacher, and conduct themselves in accord with class expectations and regulations. Students become more productive and secure, and gain more from educational experiences when they participate than when they merely act as passive or reluctant space-fillers.

Making Responsible Choices   Making responsible choices related to their learning situations as well as their behavior is an important skill for all students. Students benefit from watching and listening to teachers as they model how they make choices to solve situations and problems. Moreover, we all have the potential to learn from our mistakes. Students grow from the results of their decisions when they first are guided through the process, given opportunities to practice, and then trusted to make choices and decisions.

Being Dependable Dependability on the part of all students does wonders for the class environment. Students help create a climate of enjoyment and productivity when they do what they are supposed to do, well and on time. Students can help themselves fulfill this responsibility by using self-reminders concerning tasks and deadlines. Older students can employ checklists of duties; younger students can rely on verbal reminders. All students can be asked periodically to evaluate themselves in terms of dependability.

Being Considerate Consideration for others should be shown at all times. Everyone— fellow students, teachers, the principal, custodians, and staff—have difficulties, egos, and sensitive feelings. Students profit from practical discussions, and even role-plays, of the Golden Rule that help them decide how they can show friendliness, helpfulness, and consideration toward others throughout the day.

Supporting Others Support for others' efforts, shown through acceptance and encouragement, is another important student responsibility. Students must learn quickly that they are not to be passive captives in the classroom but active community members who help each other succeed. They should be helped to understand that the best way to be liked and helped is to like and help others.

Relating Positively Finally, relating positively means showing good manners, being polite and courteous, and avoiding words and actions that hurt others. Teachers can help students see that everyone profits when they get along with each other and that they should work to maintain that attitude.

Maintaining the Psychosocial Environment

The preceding discussion emphasized the many responsibilities of teachers and students in fostering a positive psychosocial environment—a place where students can learn in an atmosphere of helpfulness, encouragement, and the absence of threat. Responsibilities that fall mainly to the teacher, especially regarding what can be done to sustain a positive psychosocial environment once it is begun, include modeling, verbal reinforcement, help, class meetings, classbuilding and teambuilding activities, and private discussions.

Modeling Modeling refers to teaching through example to help students learn through imitation. In reality, the majority of our life learnings occur through this process. We see how others act, dress, and talk, and we imitate them. Modeling is especially powerful in social learning and making responsible choices, which are central to the psychosocial environment. Teachers should consistently model what they hope to see in their students and provide students with opportunities to practice and model for fellow students as well.

Verbal Reinforcement and Appreciations Verbal reinforcement was described earlier as a process in which verbal rewards and appreciations are given when you see behavior you approve in others. With words such as "Thanks," "Good work," "You tried hard on this," "This work shows a lot of thought," "I appreciate how helpful you've been," and "You showed that you cared about John's feelings," teachers encourage, guide, and support behavior that contributes to the good of the total class. Verbal reinforcers and appreciations should be short and describe the behavior being approved. Teachers also should teach their students how to give verbal reinforcement and express appreciation to others so behavior is encouraged when classmates behave in pleasing ways.

Help   Help should always be available to students, though it should generally be given after they make a serious effort on their own. Knowing that help is available provides a sense of security and support and engenders positive attitudes. However, there can be a downside to providing help. A "helplessness syndrome" occurs when students will not make or sustain effort without constantly seeking attention from the teacher. Often this occurs simply because students like the teacher's attention, and showing helplessness is a way of getting that attention. In this case, teachers should give the student attention when help is *not* needed, for example, when the student makes a good effort.

Class Meetings   Class meetings are a technique for dealing with class problems devised by William Glasser (1969). They call for the identification of concerns, followed by the search for solutions. Teachers and/or students can raise concerns in the meeting, no fault-finding or blaming is allowed, and the entire focus is on finding positive solutions. Students sit in a tight circle for these discussions so they can see each other face to face. Meeting topics should be appropriate for the grade level, age, and maturity of the students. Meetings can deal with social problems in the classroom or school (e.g., noise of playground fighting), academic problems (e.g., lack of class interest, effort, or progress), or problems outside of school (e.g., conditions that interfere with home study). Class meetings also provide an additional setting for discussions and practice of effective ways to deal with conflicts. Regular class meetings help students carry out their responsibilities in perpetuating a healthy classroom environment. Nelsen, Lott, and Glenn (2000) clarify the process further by detailing eight discrete building-block skill areas to ensure successful and effective class meetings. For additional information about class meetings and the building blocks for success, look at the following website: http://www.positivediscipline.com.

Classbuilding and Teambuilding   Classbuilding and teambuilding, according to Kagan, are essential for creating caring, cooperative classrooms and communities. Classbuilding activities, during which everyone stands up, moves around, and interacts with someone new, should be done at least once a week, beginning the first day of school. Random groups can be effective and efficient during the first three weeks as teacher and students get to know one another. Then teambuilding, with fun and easy activities in which everyone can participate, should occur at least twice weekly. Teambuilding activities are nonacademic and can be very quick. Their purpose is to strengthen team functioning.

Private Discussions   Private discussions should be held with individual students when necessary to solve problems that are not appropriate for group discussions, such as refusal to work, defiance, theft, vandalism, or personal home or health problems. Individual conferences can focus on conflict resolution or on problem solving when appropriate. Kagan, Kyle, and Scott (2004, 2007) share numerous step-by-step suggestions, including *Same-Side Chat,* to use with individuals at the moment of disruption, for follow-up, and for long-term solutions. Consider looking at their suggestions, found at Kagan's website, http://www.kaganonline.com.

This concludes our review of purposes and responsibilities in managing a quality psychosocial environment in the classroom. Chapter 5 focuses on encouraging students toward greater effort and productivity in the classroom. Before proceeding to the next chapter, take time to explore these end-of-chapter activities.

Parting Thought

Teachers have the right to teach.

Students have the right to learn.

And no one has the right to interfere with either of these events.

Author unknown

Summary Self-Check

Check off the following as you either understand or become able to apply them:

- ☐ Teachers strive for an emotional tone in their classrooms that is warm, supportive, and pleasant, as opposed to cold, rejecting, and unpleasant.
- ☐ Bullying occurs in many forms: verbal, physical, rational, and now cyberbullying.
- ☐ Because looping keeps teachers and students together for at least two consecutive years, the climate for the second year actually is created during the first.
- ☐ Achieving the desired emotional tone calls attention to:
  - General human relations skills: maintaining a positive outlook, being friendly, demonstrating the ability to listen, offering genuine compliments
  - Relations with students: infusing character into the way we teach, modeling a good manners, giving regular attention, displaying genuine caring, showing helpfulness, providing reinforcement
  - Relations with colleagues: being supportive, sharing the load, compromising, leading or following as appropriate, teaching teams, support programs for beginning teachers
  - Relations with caregivers: communicating regularly, describing program and expectations, emphasizing the child's progress, giving future plans for the child's instruction, conducting productive parent–teacher conferences

- Teacher responsibilities in the psychosocial environment: communicating the desired environment, setting conditions that initiate and sustain the environment, classbuilding and teambuilding, showing enthusiasm, stressing responsibility, showing consistency, exhibiting friendliness, ensuring success for all, showing understanding, being helpful, showing a sense of humor, doing all in an organized way
- Student responsibilities in the psychosocial environment: learning, contributing, making responsible choices, being dependable, showing consideration, being supportive, being positive with others
- Maintaining a good psychosocial environment: modeling desired behavior, providing verbal reinforcement and appreciations, providing opportunities to practice, holding class meetings, using classbuilding and teambuilding activities to build community, holding private discussions as needed

Activities for Reflection and Discussion

1. Take a moment to review the statements in the Preview–Review Guide at the beginning of this chapter. Put a check mark in the *Review* column next to any statement with which you now agree. How have your thoughts changed since reading this chapter?

2. Interview at least two teachers about how they establish the feeling tone in their classrooms. How do they look, sound, and act when the school year begins? How do they sustain the tone through the year?

3. Review the description in Chapter 1 of Alexa Smart's efforts regarding the psychosocial environment—the feeling tone—of her classroom. What added challenges might she have been facing because the school year began before she first met her students? How do the changes she made her second week with students and her classroom align with the suggestions that are described in this chapter?

4. Suppose that you are meeting your class (select a grade level) for the first time and you want students to understand (a) the psychosocial environment you want for the class and why it is important, (b) the responsibilities you will assume in establishing and maintaining that environment, and (c) the responsibilities that students will need to assume in furthering that environment. What will you say to convey your ideas? To what extent will you expect or hope for student response and input? Also reflect on how your approach might be different if your class is older or younger.

5. Describe how you would begin the school year with a class that had looped with you from the previous year.

6. What will classbuilding and teambuilding look, sound, and feel like in your class? Describe some activities that you might use for each.

7. Class meetings and private discussions were suggested for maintaining a good psychosocial environment. For both a primary and an upper elementary class, list five topics you consider appropriate for each. How do you differentiate between topics to be discussed privately and those to be discussed in a group? What topics, if any, do you consider inappropriate for either class meetings or private discussions?

Webliography

Inclusion Press. Workshops, books, media, resources, newsletter: http://www.inclusion.com

Kagan Publishing & Professional Development. Online magazine, discussion board, Kagan Club, free articles and catalog, workshops, What's Hot: http://www.kaganonline.com

Positive Discipline. Parents, Teachers, workshops, products, news and events: http://www.positivediscipline.com

References and Recommended Readings

Building classroom relationships [Special Issue].(2003, September). *Educational Leadership 61*(1).

Charles, C. (2000). *The synergetic classroom: Joyful teaching and gentle discipline*. New York: Addison Wesley Longman.

Coloroso, B. (2002). *The bully, the bullied, and the bystander*. Toronto, Ontario, Canada: HarperCollins.

Fraser, B., & O'Brien, P. (1985). Student and teacher perception of the environment of elementary school classrooms. *Elementary School Journal 85*(5), 567–560.

Glasser, W. (1998). *The quality school: Managing students without coercion*. New York: Perennial Press.

Kagan, L., Kagan, M., & Kagan, S. (1997). *Cooperative learning structures for teambuilding*. San Clemente, CA: Kagan Cooperative Learning.

Kagan, M., Robertson, L., & Kagan, S. (1995). *Cooperative learning structures for classbuilding*. San Clemente, CA: Kagan Cooperative Learning.

Kagan, S., & Kagan, M. (2009). *Kagan cooperative learning*. San Clemente, CA: Kagan Publishing.

Kagan, S., Kyle, P., & Scott, S. (2004). *Win-win discipline*. San Clemente, CA: Kagan Publishing.

Larrivee, B. (2009). *Authentic classroom management: Creating a learning community and building reflective practice* (3rd ed.). Upper Saddle River, NJ: Pearson Merrill.

McGrath, M. J. (2007). *School bullying: Tools for avoiding harm and liability*. Thousand Oaks, CA: Corwin Press.

Mustacchi, J. (2009, March). R U safe? *Educational Leadership 66*(6), 78–82.

Nansel, T. R., Overpeck, M., Ramani, S. P., Ruan, W. J., Simons-Morton, B., & Scheidt, P. (2001). Bully behaviors among US youth: Prevalence and association with psychosocial adjustment. *Journal of the American Medical Association 285*(16), 2094–2100.

Nelsen, J., Lott, L., & Glenn, H. (2000). *Positive discipline in the classroom*. Rocklin, CA: Prima Publishing.

Pearpoint, J., & Forest, M. (1992). Foreword. In S. Stainback & W. Stainback (Eds.), *Curriculum considerations in inclusive classrooms: Facilitating learning for all students* (pp. xv–xviii). Baltimore: Paul H. Brookes.

The positive classroom [Special Issue]. (2008, September). *Educational Leadership 66*(1).

Siris, K., & Osterman, K. (2004, December). Interrupting the cycle of bullying and victimization in the elementary classroom. *Phi Delta Kappan 86*(4), 288–291.

Sapon-Shevin, M. (2008, September) Learning in an inclusive community. *Educational Leadership* 66(1), 49–53.

Shariff, S. (2008). *Cyber-bullying: Issues and solutions for the school, the classroom and the home.* London: Routledge.

Trade Book

Sollman, C., Emmons, B., & Paolini, J. (1994). *Through the cracks.* Worcester, MA: Davis Publications.

PEARSON
myeducationlab

Go to the Topic: **Understanding Students' Psychological Needs** in the MyEducationLab (www.myeducationlab.com) for your course, where you can:

- Find learning outcomes for **Understanding Students' Psychological Needs** along with the national standards that connect to these outcomes.
- Apply and practice your understanding of the core teaching skills identified in the chapter with the Building Teaching Skills and Dispositions learning units.

Managing Student Motivation to Learn

CHAPTER 5

Imagination is the true magic carpet.
—Norman Vincent Peale

Mistakes are simply invitations to try again.
—Dian Ritter

Preview–Review Guide

Before you read the chapter, and based on what you know, think you know, or assume, take a minute to put a check mark in the **Preview** column if you agree with the statement. When you finish the chapter, take time to reread the statements and respond in the **Review** column. Reflective discussions can develop because many of the statements are not clearly "yes" or "no."

Preview   **Review**

1. _____ Traditional teaching diminishes children's inborn interest in learning.   _____

2. _____ Students don't try very hard in school because lessons usually are not very interesting to them.   _____

3. _____ Unmotivated students rarely misbehave; they just sit and do nothing.   _____

4. _____ When teachers speak of *motivation* as part of their lessons, they refer to students' innate desire to learn.   _____

5. _____ Glasser claims that motivation and discipline cease to be problems when schooling is organized to meet students' needs.   _____

6. _____ Kagan would have teachers motivate students by using cooperative learning activities built around multiple intelligences and classbuilding and teambuilding experiences.   _____

7. _____ Students are better able to engage in instruction and demonstrate their learnings when teaching is enriched with multiple intelligences strategies.   _____

8. _____ Incentives should be given early in the day or week to ensure that students will continue to work hard the rest of the time.   _____

9. _____ With Preferred Activity Time (PAT), students are allowed to do anything they want as an incentive for work and good behavior.   _____

10. _____ True cooperative learning is more complicated than students working together in groups.   _____

Chapter Objectives

After reading Chapter 5, students will demonstrate understanding of

- internal and external motivation

- why individuals do or don't do what we want them to

- contributions relating to motivation by several authorities

- traits of good motivators to help increase student motivation to learn

through their active participation in discussions and the end-of-chapter activities for reflection.

Ask any group of elementary teachers what brings them the greatest professional pleasure and they almost certainly will mention working with students who have good intentions and who try hard to work. Conversely, if you ask those teachers what troubles them most about teaching, they will likely mention disruptive student behavior and an inability to get some of their students interested in learning. To that end, a problem to solve or an essential or guiding question for this chapter might be: *What motivates my students, and what can I do to increase their motivation?*

By learning, teachers of course mean school learning, for all students are interested in learning certain things and make intensive efforts to do so. The problem simply is that students' interests in learning often do not correspond with what teachers are required to instruct. Most students enter kindergarten eager and open to the entire curriculum, but within a year or two they have clearly distinguished between school activities that intrigue them and those that do not. From that point on, teachers continually search for ways to attract student attention and engage students in learning activities. In other words, they forever look for ways to motivate their students.

What Is Meant by Motivation?

The word *motive* comes from a Latin root meaning "to move" and is defined as an emotion, desire, or psychological need that incites a person to do something. Motive is the *why* of behavior. The associated term *motivation* has two meanings that are used rather differently. One of those meanings refers to a condition within individuals that disposes them toward an activity or goal, such as motivation to learn, motivation to succeed, or motivation to gain acceptance. For example, Mr. Garcia's sixth graders routinely forgot most of what they read about the Greeks and the Romans until he arranged a contest on ancient civilization facts against Ms. Woo's class. His students suddenly began to remember the material much better. Their internal motivation to learn and to succeed was increased.

Teachers frequently use a second, and different, meaning for the term *motivation*. This meaning refers to a process by which motives are instilled into students—that is, what one (such as a teacher) does to get students interested in lessons and to facilitate willingness to work at them. When teachers speak of motivation as a component of a lesson, they refer to what *they do* to attract students' interest and engage them more or less willingly in the work provided. Thinking in a short-term sense, they might ask themselves, "What can I do for motivation in this lesson?"

Why People Don't Do What We Want Them to Do

When we ask people to do something, sometimes they will do it, but sometimes they won't. Understanding the reasons why people will or will not do what we ask is a valuable insight for teachers as they think about how best to motivate students. Among reasons why people don't do what we want them to do are the following:

1. They don't know *what* to do. Students without requisite knowledge or who don't understand the expectations are not likely to do what teachers ask.

2. They don't know *how* to do it. The same is true regarding students' abilities and skills.

3. They don't know *why* they should do it. Students want to know the reason for and the importance of their work.

4. They *aren't suited or matched* to the task. For example, a student who is especially energetic will have a difficult time sitting still for a 40-minute presentation.

5. They don't *want* to do it. Sometimes it's simply a lack of will.

6. They *cannot reliably control* what they say or do because their cerebral processes do not occur in a "normal" manner. Behaviors that result from this condition are known as neurological-based behavior (NBB). (Read more about NBB in Chapter 9.)

Motivation and Lessons

Motivation that resides over time within individuals is *internal* or *self-motivation,* while motivation that is supplied from outside the individual is *external* motivation. Teachers would love to work with students who always are internally motivated to learn, but they know that most of the time they will have to supply at least some of the motivation for their students.

Teachers know that learning is both exciting and fun when it matches the interests and abilities of their students. They also know that most students enjoy hands-on activities. And they know that when they instruct the right way, motivation happens by itself.

Sometimes something as simple as a coupon booklet works. Students begin the year or the semester with coupons from the teacher (see Figure 5.1). For example, coupon booklets may include forgiveness coupons for single specific assignments, an assignment the student chooses (with teacher approval). Clever clip art designs and colored paper make these fun gifts. Students are allowed to redeem their coupons according to simple directions. Thus, an assignment forgiveness coupon might read, "This coupon is good for one assignment from any subject. Check with your teacher to see if the assignment is a coupon event. Coupons may be used only once."

Teachers also rely heavily on student wants. *Want* is an imprecise, nonscientific term that simply means something students desire, something they wish to have or do. Some

Figure 5.1

Sample Pages of a Coupon Booklet

READING LOG COUPON

THIS COUPON IS GOOD FOR
ONE NIGHT'S SIGNATURE
ON YOUR READING LOG.
IT MAY BE USED ONLY ONCE.

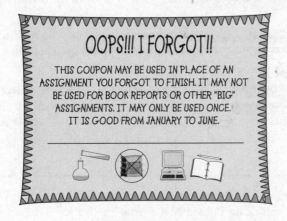

OOPS!!! I FORGOT!!

THIS COUPON MAY BE USED IN PLACE OF AN
ASSIGNMENT YOU FORGOT TO FINISH. IT MAY NOT
BE USED FOR BOOK REPORTS OR OTHER "BIG"
ASSIGNMENTS. IT MAY ONLY BE USED ONCE.
IT IS GOOD FROM JANUARY TO JUNE.

ASSIGNMENT COUPON

THIS COUPON IS GOOD FOR AN ASSIGNMENT
FROM ANY SUBJECT. CHECK WITH YOUR TEACHER
TO SEE IF THE ASSIGNMENT IS A COUPON EVENT.
IT MAY ONLY BE USED ONCE.

STUDENT SIGNATURE

Source: Virginia Lorenz. Reprinted by permission.

wants stem from *needs,* a scientific term referring to what students require in order to live enjoyably in reasonably good health. As Maslow pointed out (1943), everyone needs food, water, and air, and most of us need acceptance, love, and association with others. To say we need these things is to say that we feel best when we have them—healthy, content, fulfilled.

Most student wants have little to do with psychosocial needs. For example, students may strongly want to eat ice cream, watch a video or DVD, get a new comic book or video game, or play with a particular person—none of which, if denied, interferes with personal well-being. Nevertheless, such wants play important roles in students' lives, and they provide practical insights into how teachers can motivate students.

The major interests and wants of elementary students of different age levels have been documented and, in general, have remained fairly constant over time. Table 5.1 shows examples of wants and interests that predominate in elementary students.

Table 5.1   Age, Wants, and Interests

Age	Wants (things students seek and/or respond well to)	Interests (specific activities)
5 to 8 years	Assurance, physical activity, direct sensory experience, encouragement, praise, warmth, patience, concrete learning tasks	Relating experiences, stories, dramatic play, pictures, songs, poems, rhythms, and animals to organized games, models, dolls, jokes, gangs and clubs, collecting, comics, adventure books, animals, and foreign lands and people
9 to 10 years	Praise, physical activity, group membership, being admired	Riddles, jokes, puzzles, sharing, competitive games, trips, reading, maps, letters, animals, arts and crafts
Preadolescent	Affection, warmth, greater independence, peer group acceptance and belonging	Riddles, jokes, puzzles, gangs and clubs, sports, competitive and outdoor games, hobbies, construction, pets, movies, TV, comics, reading, drama
Adolescent	Acceptance by and conformation to peer group; kind, unobtrusive guidance by adults; security with independence	Music, dancing, cars, opposite sex, sports, trips, TV, movies, magazines, gossip, intrigue, adult roles

What Does Motivate Students to Learn?

The following is a review of information available to teachers about motivation, accumulated from experience and scholarly research. Also included is a review of contributions by William Glasser, Howard Gardner, Fred Jones, and Spencer Kagan.

Motivation for Elementary Classrooms

Brophy (2004) offers a helpful synthesis of research on classroom motivation. He presents a number of suggestions for teachers, of which the following are most pertinent to elementary grade teachers:

- Guide students toward achieving success rather than avoiding failure.
- Teach things that are worth learning in ways that help students appreciate their value.
- Emphasize reasons for the lessons—the value of the lesson and the outcomes.
- Create learning communities where students feel comfortable, cared about, empowered, safe, and secure.
- Give informative feedback. Mention both strengths and weaknesses.
- Make yourself and your classroom attractive to students.
- Include novelty and variety; include fantasy and simulations; provide for an active, hands-on response.
- Project your own enthusiasm.

Tomlinson (2002) describes what she calls *invitational learning* that embraces five student needs: affirmation (acceptance and significance), contribution, purpose, power, and challenge. Children want affirmation to feel they are significant in the classroom. They want to contribute and make a difference in the community. Students look for purpose when they come to school. They want to know that what they learn is useful and that their choices contribute to their success. Finally, students want to feel challenged and/or stretched. They want to feel that their work contributes to their success and the growth of others. Learning communities contribute to meeting these five needs.

Larrivee (2009) lists nine basic student needs for safe and successful learning communities, and categorizes them into three broad areas: belonging, importance, and power. Learning communities need a sense of *belonging* that is obtained through status among peers, safety, and affection. Learning communities need a sense of *importance*. Positive identity, recognition, and attention affect this need. Finally, learning communities need a sense of *power* that is achieved through competence, control, and freedom. Larrivee's organization of motivating elements aligns with research from other pioneering authorities on motivation, including Maslow, Erikson, Dreikurs, and Glasser. Students need a sense of belonging. To this end, they want to experience status among peers, emotional and physical safety, and affection. Students want to feel a sense of importance that comes with positive identity, recognition, and attention. Students also want a sense of power. Here, power does not mean brute force. Rather, power equates with personal competency, control, and freedom.

Consolidating the ideas of Brophy, Tomlinson, Larrivee, and others, the following generalizations are warranted and offer concrete, practical advice concerning student motivation:

- Students like to work with others at ideas, activities, and objects that they find novel, intriguing, relevant, and related to their perceived life concerns.

- Students seek out people and conditions that help meet needs important to their lives.

- Students try their best to avoid associating with people and conditions they find unpleasant.

- Students engage in tasks that are unpleasant to them in order to please people they see as important, including the teacher.

- Finally, remember, students detest looking bad in front of their peers; they don't want to appear stupid or to have their failures displayed.

As a teacher, therefore, you are well advised to capitalize on students' needs, interests, abilities, and curiosity. Use these to full advantage. Students will appreciate the effort you make, and because of their excitement, so will you. Also, you should encourage your students to help them feel secure. As you show your helpfulness and support, students will try to please you with effort, good behavior, responsible choices, and quality work.

These points generally hold true, and teachers who capitalize on them often accomplish much with their students. Nonetheless, experienced teachers find that these suggestions do not solve all problems of motivation. Consequently, some teachers set up systems of reinforcement for good student work, effort, and behavior. Many, however, are uncomfortable with such systems, feeling that they might be paying students for doing what they are supposed to do anyway. They wonder if children will learn to depend on others for approval and recognition and ask questions such as the following: What's in it for me? What's the payoff? Do you like it? Did you see me do it? Did I do it right? (Coloroso, 1994). But it is evident that elementary students become excited about receiving smiley faces, stickers, popcorn parties, extra time at recess or the computer, the honor of helping the teacher, the privilege of feeding the class pet, and many other similar rewards for their good effort. In fact, many students will study their spelling and arithmetic in order to get these rewards.

Teachers also have learned, many of them through distressing experiences when they themselves were students, that children can be frightened into working. Many students would rather do their homework than be yelled at, study for their tests than get failing grades, or feign paying attention than receive reprimands. But these days not all students will comply out of fear. Regardless of the work or behavior it induces, motivation through fear is an area for teachers to avoid. If you genuinely want your students to make an effort to learn and have a reasonably enjoyable time doing so, don't try to motivate through fear or intimidation. Ultimately, the results are not worth the costs. Students won't like you, you won't like them, and worse, you won't feel very good about yourself either.

It is much better to motivate students through what they enjoy and respond to positively and through things you feel comfortable with as well. Your program doesn't have to be insipidly easy; it can be rigorous and still be enjoyable.

William Glasser's Contributions

William Glasser is a psychiatrist-psychologist who writes and consults on behalf of school students. His landmark books on education are *Schools Without Failure* (1969), *Control Theory in the Classroom* (1998b), *The Quality School* (1998c), *The Quality School Teacher* (1998d), and *Every Student Can Succeed* (2000). For Glasser, motivation is virtually synonymous with needs

---

Case Study 5.1 Token Economy and Motivation

FOCUS QUESTIONS

Julie DePew describes a token economy that she uses (and now others at her school use similar systems in their classrooms). What potential positive and negative consequences do you see for using a token economy system? What might such a system look like in your classroom? What adjustments would you feel necessary for primary, middle, or upper elementary students?

Julie DePew, who now teaches third grade in a low-income school, uses *DePew Dollars* to run her class. "The two questions I am asked repeatedly about my classroom are: 'How do you keep the children so quiet and on task?' and 'Why don't you have problems with children not doing their homework?' The answers are much easier than one would think. My classroom runs on the *Gold Standard*! Yes, hard, cold, cash. Well, gold coins actually, which I can purchase at any party store. I use coins because they are indestructible. These coins are referred to as 'DePew Dollars,' and they are coveted by all.

"Gold coins have purchasing power at the weekly classroom store which I keep stocked with *quality* items that range from movie tickets, books, craft items, crayons, markers, and Beanie Babies, to the latest 'cool' stuff. I stock the store from discount shops, after-holiday sales, and parent donations, and each item has a price tag. Only students who have their weekly homework log signed by a parent can shop. I shuffle the logs and then call names for shopping privileges.

"So, how do students earn money? Easy! Everything I have my students do has a value. For example, to keep children fit and start our day on a positive note, our class runs laps around the track, and every lap earns a gold coin. Everything earns money: collected homework (one coin per assignment), finished class work, getting 'caught being good,' library behavior, returning library books on time earns money, and so on. There is no limit to what can be assigned value.

"On the flip side, I also fine students for poor behavior on the playground, incomplete or missing assignments, late library books and, yes, even extra bathroom trips. I was amazed how charging one coin per bathroom trip completely stopped the excess trips in just one day!

"This is truly the easiest system to put in place, and I can stress its importance by varying the value amounts. For fund raisers, I might award ten coins for returning a parent slip; a needed office form might earn five coins. Money truly gets the attention of my students. They understand it, and definitely want to have the option to shop and purchase. I have found children even save money to purchase a special item. I sell myself as a lunch buddy, and the shocking news is just how much they think I am worth!

"Another plus with this system is the mental math component that the children participate in without even realizing they are learning. My Gold Standard system works, and it is a lot of fun for everyone!"

---

satisfaction, specifically the needs he emphasizes in his writings. He maintains that when teaching and learning produce needs satisfaction, the motivation to work and to behave properly follows naturally.

Glasser (1998a) explains that "all of our behavior, everything we do, can be considered our best attempt to control ourselves so as to satisfy our needs" (p. 17). What are these needs we so desperately try to satisfy? According to Glasser, they are (1) to survive and reproduce, (2) to belong, (3) to acquire power, (4) to be free, and (5) to have fun. Glasser contends that these needs are in every one of us, from the toddler to the elderly, and he says that we can no more deny the urge to fulfill them than we can deny the color of our eyes. He also contends that schools, as traditionally designed, fall quite short of satisfying these needs.

Glasser goes on to say that education— schools, the classroom, and the teaching-learning process—should be reorganized and conducted so that students, while working at lessons, can satisfy their needs. Then students will behave well, take an interest in education, and learn. To this end, Glasser would have students work together in small learning teams and have teachers function as "lead managers" instead of bosses, emphasize quality in all student work, and transform the classroom environment into what he calls a "friendly workplace."

Glasser distinguishes between "boss style" and the "lead manager" in the preface to *The Quality School* (1998c):

A boss drives. A leader leads.

A boss relies on authority. A leader relies on cooperation.

A boss says "I." A leader says "We."

A boss knows how. A leader shows how.

A boss creates resentment. A leader breeds enthusiasm.

A boss fixes blame. A leader fixes mistakes.

A boss makes work drudgery. A leader makes work interesting.

Glasser feels that teams are inherently motivating and give students a sense of belonging. Stronger students find it need-fulfilling to help weaker students, and weaker students find it need-fulfilling to contribute to a team that is getting somewhere. Students with disabilities find themselves able to contribute and participate along with other team members. Teams provide freedom and fun as they function with less dependence on the teacher and are allowed to assume more authority and responsibility for their learning. In other words, many students working in teams find a good deal of belonging, power, freedom, and fun—the very things Glasser says we all seek in life.

Glasser has continually refined his thinking and did so again in *Choice Theory in the Classroom* (1998a) and *Every Student Can Succeed* (2000). Kathy Curtiss, senior faculty of the William Glasser Institute, helps educators and schools

LITERATURE

BOOK

DAVE CARPENTER..

"JUST THINK OF IT AS IF YOU'RE READING A LONG TEXT MESSAGE."

Permission by Dave Carpenter.

create their own unique learning environments that align with Glasser's ideas: classroom meetings, portfolios, assessment rubrics based on standards, character development as part of the curriculum, and student self-assessment and reflection. Choice theory advocates partnerships between teachers and students, and the use of instructional strategies that support student ownership and responsibility for learning. Curtiss also teaches the certification process to others. Visit these websites for additional details of their work and Glasser's choice theory: http://www. choicetheory.com/links.htm and http://www.kathycurtissco.com.

Howard Gardner's Contributions

Howard Gardner is a professor of education at Harvard and the author of several books, including *The Unschooled Mind: How Children Think and How Schools Should Teach* (1991), *Frames of Mind* (1993a), and *Multiple Intelligences: The Theory in Practice* (1993b). In 1983 Gardner first proposed his theory that human beings possess more than a single, fixed intelligence and learn in a variety of ways. Since then Gardner has identified eight intelligences and asserts that we all possess all eight, although each in varying degrees of strength. He also observes that schools tend to develop only two or three intelligences to any useful extent—verbal/linguistic and logical/mathematical. Overly simplified, the eight intelligences embrace the following understandings:

- Verbal/linguistic—capacity to use words and oral and written language effectively
- Logical/mathematical—capacity to use numbers effectively and to think in logical patterns and relationships
- Visual/spatial—ability to perceive the visual-spatial world accurately, with an awareness of color, line, shape, form, space, and the relationships among these elements
- Bodily/kinesthetic—expertise in using one's whole body to express ideas and feelings, with specific physical skills of coordination, balance, dexterity, strength, flexibility, and speed
- Musical—ability to perceive, discriminate between, transform, and express musical forms
- Interpersonal—ability to perceive and make distinctions in the moods, intentions, motivations, and the feelings of other people
- Intrapersonal—self-knowledge and the ability to act adaptively on the basis of that knowledge
- Naturalistic—ability to perceive and function in nature, with sensitivity to the interdependence of the plant and animal ecologies and to environmental issues

Gardner says teachers should not ask "How smart are my students?" but rather, "In what ways are my students smart?" Many now believe that understanding Gardner's ideas is essential to effective teacher thinking and planning—and key to student motivation.

For several years, Gardner, Spencer Kagan, and Robert Sylwester explored and exchanged ideas about multiple intelligences. If you are interested in reading more, you can find their triologue posted to Kagan's online magazine at http://www.kaganonline.com.

In the early 1990s, Gardner proposed a radical school restructuring: Students would spend most of their time engaged in project-based learning, both in and out of classroom settings. He believes that life is a series of projects and that school matters, "but only insofar as it yields something that can be used once students leave school" (Gardner, television interview, n.d.). By applying Gardner's ideas of multiple intelligences and project-based learning to motivation, students are transformed into active participants engaged in meaningful experiences that have real-world applications for them. They are motivated.

Fred Jones's Contributions

Fred Jones is a clinical psychologist and consultant who has made extensive field observations of effective teachers, particularly those he describes as "naturals." His observations are translated into ways to improve teacher effectiveness and motivate students.

Jones (2007) believes that students become actively involved in lessons to the extent they expect success, value successful completion of the tasks, and find the climate of interpersonal

---

Vignette 5.1   Using Multiple Intelligences to Deepen Student Understandings

Shaylene Watkins delivers content to her 4/5 multi-age class in ways that use multiple intelligences.

"In the first weeks of school, I use an online survey in the computer lab with my students to help build awareness of the multiple ways we learn. Throughout the year I present activities through the different modalities, and students often can select from a menu of learning activities to meet their needs.

"I know students are primarily kinesthetic, so I get them up and moving. Chanting math formulas and making up raps and movements help students store ideas. I have students use basic sign language to get them interacting and responding to lesson questions. They use body language to act out vocabulary. In science, for example, when students read about the new definition for atmosphere being a blanket around Earth, they make a fist and use their other hand to blanket their 'Earth' as they chant the defini-

tion. Visual students demonstrate their learnings through editorial cartoons, murals, and other creative opportunities.

"I use technology—interactive whiteboards with presentations, 'power points,' streaming videos—to reach my learners. Games make standards come alive for students. For example, I use a game show format to review language conventions and skills."

UPON REFLECTION

Based on her early informal inventory/assessment, Shaylene is able to design her class to *match* the dominant "intelligence" of her students, and *stretch* and *celebrate* the other intelligences (see the section on Kagan in this chapter to understand these three terms as they relate to multiple intelligences). Describe specific ways she can overlay multiple intelligences with her specific content areas: language arts, math, science, and social studies.

relationships acceptable. For elementary students, Jones believes academic needs include the following:

- Students must be quickly and actively involved in lessons.
- They experience success.
- They see learning modeled by adults as exciting and rewarding.
- They can relate the learning to their own lives.
- They have positive contact with peers.

Jones believes that effective teachers attend to these needs and are more successful in motivating their students.

Jones also gives a prominent place in his program to genuine incentives when he talks about motivating, managing, and instructing students. He found that most effective teachers use incentives systematically. Specifically relating to motivation (and behavior management) is his work that focuses on responsibility training though incentive systems.

Jones and others say that incentives are something outside of individuals that prompt them to act. Effective incentives are promised as the consequences for desired work or behavior, but they are delayed or provided later. One way teachers can use incentives as motivators is to apply Grandma's Rule to the classroom—students first do what they are supposed to do, and then, for a while, they can do something they want to do. A bonus of the incentive encourages students to save time they normally would waste in order to get it back in the form of preferred activities. It gives students a shared interest in cooperating to save time rather than wasting it in small bits throughout the day.

Jones has found that incentives work best when they are integrated within the context of the instructional program and the classroom structure. He describes this Preferred Activity Time, or PAT, as time allotted for activities such as learning games and enrichment activities. PAT activities are those that students enjoy, such as reading a class book for pleasure, using vocabulary words to play hangman, working on an art project, or working with manipulatives. When selecting activities for PAT, teachers must consider three things. First, the activity should be attractive to the students. Second, students should earn time toward PAT through their work effort and responsible behavior. And third, teachers should choose activities that are acceptable to them.

PAT can be earned in several ways. Mr. Kolp gives his fourth graders three minutes to put away their math work and prepare for language arts. Any unused time from the three minutes is added to their PAT. Mr. Bjorka gives the class two extra PAT minutes if everyone is seated and ready when the bell rings. However, the class loses the amount of wasted time if a few students continue to be noisy. PAT can be used the day it is earned, or it may be saved for the end of the week or for a future activity such as a field trip.

PAT has several important qualities that distinguish it from other motivation or reward incentive systems:

- PAT is genuine. In other words, Preferred Activity Time is desired and available to all students, in exchange for making the extra effort to obtain it.
- PAT has educational value because it is found in enrichment activities and team learning games. It's slightly misleading to say that students get to do anything they want. PAT activities that students do really are linked to a full program of academic work.

- PAT motivates all students by encouraging group concern for everyone to complete assigned work and behave well. Only then can students earn PAT for the entire class.

- PAT can be earned as an individual bonus. Teachers can work individually with the few students who would lose PAT for the class because of their irresponsible choices. With a contract, the teacher can give consequences to the individual student, but also can reward the whole class when behavior improves or the student makes responsible choices.

- PAT is easy for the teacher to implement and manage.

- PAT is as creative as teacher and student imaginations. Visit Jones's website, http://www.fredjones.com, where teachers continually share their PAT ideas.

Spencer Kagan's Contributions

Spencer Kagan is another clinical psychologist and consultant who specializes in teacher effectiveness in classrooms. He, too, has spent hours observing and researching effective teachers and their methods. Kagan sees close connections among curriculum, instruction, and management, with motivation affecting the success of all three. Kagan's work in classroom management gives considerable attention to using cooperative learning, classbuilding, and teambuilding, and the multiple intelligences as ways to motivate students. Based on his own research and the work of others, Kagan also applies current thinking about how the brain affects learning to his ideas of classroom management.

So how is cooperative learning a motivator? We realize that most of life and work involves interactions with others. Success, however, comes in learning how to work cooperatively. According to Kagan, the basic principles of cooperative learning rest on several critical questions, which he presents in a simple acronym he refers to as PIES:

- Positive Interdependence: Is a gain for one a gain for another? Is help necessary?

- Individual Accountability: Is individual public performance required?

- Equal Participation: How equal is the participation?

- Simultaneous Interaction: What percent are overtly active at once?

Cooperative learning groups (just like Glasser's learning teams) give students the opportunity to learn and apply these skills. Students collaborate with others on a project or task, with a degree of group autonomy to make decisions about the task, and have fun while they work.

And how are classbuilding and teambuilding motivators? Kagan (Kagan, Robertson, & Kagan, 1995) defined *classbuilding* as "the process by which a room full of individuals with different backgrounds and experiences become a caring community of active learners" (p. vi). Kagan's use of classbuilding as a verb reinforces that it is a process—classbuilding doesn't happen; it is done. Classbuilding activities have students, at least once a week, stand up, move around, and interact on non-content topics with students with whom they normally don't work. For example, they may share what they did over the weekend, talk about a favorite book or movie, or describe a favorite celebration or tradition.

According to Kagan, *teambuilding* sets a climate for learning. Teambuilding has five aims: (1) getting acquainted, (2) team identity, (3) mutual support, (4) valuing differences, and (5) developing synergy. Teambuilding activities are essential when students first form teams, but they also can be used effectively when energy lulls. Quick teambuilding takes only a minute or two away from instructional time, but reenergizes the learning potential. Occurring at least twice a week, teambuilding activities are fun, nonacademic, and well within the ability of all children. For example, students may come up with a team name and a team cheer, or try to find commonalities with their team members, such as favorite foods or places to visit.

How are the multiple intelligences motivators? Students are smart in different ways—remember Gardner's eight kinds of smart. Kagan has observed that classrooms seem to come alive when teachers (and students) use multiple intelligences strategies to instruct and show their learnings. In *Multiple Intelligences: The Complete MI Book* (Kagan & Kagan, 1998), Kagan describes enriched classrooms that have three MI visions: matching, stretching, and celebrating. The goal of *matching* is to maximize academic success by instructing to the intelligences of the students. The goal of *stretching* is to maximize the development of all intelligences by making every student more intelligent in more ways. The goal of *celebrating* is to applaud the uniqueness of every student and thereby sharpen students' abilities to understand and work with diversity.

And finally, how is current brain research connected to motivation? Kagan offers five principles of brain-friendly teaching:

1. *The brain seeks and processes information.* In order to process information, the brain looks for meaning, novelty, predictability, feedback. Students like to work on ideas, activities, and objects that they find novel, intriguing, relevant, and related to their perceived life concerns.

2. *The brain is social.* Position Emission Typography (PET) scans show that brains are dramatically more active when learning through interaction with others than when trying to learn alone, reading, or listening to a lecture. (See several brain imaging scans in Rita Carter's 1998 book, *Mapping the Mind.*) Working with others is a strong motivator for many students.

3. *The brain needs nourishment* (oxygen and glucose). Energy levels are more likely to dip when students sit quietly for prolonged periods of time. Movement, energizers, and brain breaks help send more oxygen to the brain. In fact, Kagan suggests that movement and interaction should occur on average about every 10 to 15 minutes.

4. *The brain needs psychological safety.* Anything that creates anxiety or threat decreases the probability of learning. We talked about the psychosocial environment in the last chapter, and you will find a very simplified discussion of the triune brain in Chapter 13.

5. *The brain is emotional.* Emotional experiences can affect interest, engagement, and retention. Student motivation can be whetted or derailed by content that is emotionally rich.

Kagan's work ties to student motivation. To motivate students to make responsible choices regarding their work and behavior, Kagan has written literally hundreds of step-by-step structures for teachers to use. Because the structures are content- and activity-free, they can be used in an infinite range of content areas. Visit http://www.kaganonline.com for ideas.

Personality Traits of Good Motivators

Teachers who are especially effective in classroom motivation are likely to possess several personality traits. As you reflect on these traits, remember that although nobody shows all of them all of the time, everybody shows some of them some of the time. Students greatly appreciate these traits, and you probably can increase them in your behavior.

Charisma

Charisma is hard to define and harder to acquire, but we all have seen it—that ephemeral quality of personality that attracts and inspires. It is very difficult to say what makes one person more charismatic than another. Reasonably attractive appearance makes one appealing, at first. So does a sparkling personality, though some of the most appreciated teachers could never have been the life of any party. Ability to envision potential helps, as does steadfastness of purpose and faith in students' capabilities. Add to that some wisdom, enlightenment, experience, normal human frailties, a measure of vulnerability, and determination to persist, and you are getting somewhere in the neighborhood of charisma. If you happen to be an individual fortunate enough to possess it, motivation won't be much of a problem for you.

Caring

Practically all teachers would prefer that their students learn and lead happy and productive lives. But caring in teaching implies considerably more than simple concern. It refers to teacher willingness to work on behalf of students, to keep trying when little progress is evident, and to persist even when students show no appreciation for efforts expended on them, as often will be the case. It means showing friendship—not to be confused with being a buddy—to every student, no matter how undeserving the student might seem. Depending on circumstances, it means encouraging, cajoling, supporting, or demanding. It may call for a warm heart or fire in the eye, but it always communicates that you are not willing to let any student drop by the wayside, to let students be less than they should be, or to say, "Oh well, what difference does it make anyway?"

Caring is a matter of effort and persistence and is within everyone's grasp. It brings occasional reward and frequent disappointment. How well you care depends on your personality, your level of conviction, and your ability to roll with the punches.

Enthusiasm

Up to a point, teacher enthusiasm motivates students. Enthusiasm is contagious, as is lack of it. But enthusiasm must be genuine. Students quickly spot a fraud. If you truly believe in the value of what you teach, and in the virtue of those with whom you work, your students will respond to your efforts, though perhaps not always exactly as you would like. But remember, it is difficult to achieve significant results overnight.

Trust

Trust has two sides. Students must trust that their teacher will support and guide them and be someone they can count on. Students also must think that their teacher believes in them and will let them make choices, decisions, and mistakes, and learn and grow from the results, without embarrassment, loss of dignity, harm, or reprisal.

Respect

Respect relates closely to trust. In fact, respect often comes from trust. Furthermore, respect should be mutual. Students must respect their teacher as a knowledge facilitator and as an adult who models good character qualities and the Golden Rule. Teachers must respect their students' right to learn, sometimes by making mistakes, and share responsibility for that learning.

Vignette 5.2   Focusing Attention

Kim Anderson learned several classroom management techniques during her student teaching experience.

"When I taught a multi-age first- and second-grade class, my cooperating teacher taught me a simple technique for managing expectations during instruction. She first would ask her students what she needed from them before she could begin the lesson. Eager to demonstrate their knowledge, students raised their hands and would list the five needs. My cooperating teacher would draw a simple descriptive icon on the board as students described each need.

"First, she needed students in *listening positions*, and she drew a chair to show that they needed to be sitting up straight. Second, she needed students to *raise their hands* if they wanted to speak, and she drew a hand below the chair. Third, she needed *mouths closed*, and she drew a set of lips below the hand. Next, she needed *eyes on her*, and she drew an eye. Finally, she needed

students to *listen to* the teacher and to each other. Her last icon was an ear. The icons stayed on the board through the entire lesson as easy reminders.

"I saw that this technique helped focus student attention on the lesson and simplified her management actions. If students needed to work on one skill, she simply pointed to the individual icon.

"My second student teaching placement was with a fifth-grade class, and I soon discovered that the technique worked for this level, too. After I taught them the five needs, all I had to say was 'listening position,' and the students immediately straightened up. They knew exactly what I expected of them."

UPON REFLECTION

Kim found that this technique for managing expectations during lessons worked in both the primary and upper grade classes she taught. Why do you think this is so? How would you teach this to both grade levels for success?

Good Motivators—What Do They Do?

Here, we move away from the nebulous area of personality traits to the more definitive realm of teaching skills, acknowledging the considerable overlap between the two. When personality traits are set aside, it is obvious that teachers good at motivation also perform certain skills particularly well. These skills can be learned, practiced, and perhaps even perfected. Teachers good at motivation frequently do such things as the following:

1. *Use novelty, mystery, puzzlement, and excitement* to energize their lessons. Mr. Samuel tells his students as they begin their reading lesson, "There may or may not be a double entendre somewhere on this page. If you think you find one and can explain its meaning, raise your thumb so I can see it."

2. *Use color, sound, movement, and student activity* to attract and hold attention. Mrs. Gomez uses songs, rhymes, and skits to help her students practice Spanish vocabulary, punctuation, and conversation.

3. *Assign individual and group projects* to encourage students toward responsibility and self-control, and as a means of adding a sense of purpose to what is being learned. Ms. Eggleston's students select and keep separate writing and art portfolios of some of their work to show their caregivers.

4. *State clear, reasonable expectations and requirements* to avoid confusion and enlist student cooperation. Mr. Timken uses visual instructional plans (VIPs), posts assignment details in consistent locations, explains to students, checks understanding by having students describe the assignments back to him, and leaves the VIP or chart on display while students complete their work.

5. *Provide continual support, help, feedback, and encouragement* to assist students through rough spots and keep them on track. As often as she can, Ms. Moore teaches her lessons in a cycle. She explains one step at a time, models the step, and then promptly engages her students by having them do the step in the process. When students cumulatively "teach" the step to a partner, they return to the beginning and work through the process to include the newest step. As the students work, she circulates quietly among them, making helpful suggestions and encouraging comments. Jones (2007) calls this Say, See, Do teaching.

6. *Listen to student concerns and remain flexible enough to change* when change is warranted. Mr. DeCramer holds brief class discussions at the end of each day. He asks students to comment on the lessons they liked best, those they liked least, and those they found most difficult. He listens to student suggestions and discusses his own ideas for improvement. In addition to asking students to share one idea they learned today, Mrs. Scott asks: "What can you do so you will learn more tomorrow?" and "What can I do to help you?"

7. *Provide numerous opportunities* for students to display their accomplishments to both the class and to larger audiences. Mrs. Cooper regularly displays student science and social studies projects, and toward the end of the year invites caregivers to view the displays.

8. *Emphasize student accountability* concerning behavior, work habits, and production of quality work. Mr. Adams requires his students to keep records of their work and effort and to periodically reflect on their personal improvement. Similarly, Mr. Wong has students keep private, ongoing charts and rate themselves each day on their behavior and work. He also schedules brief individual conferences with students to discuss the self-ratings. Mrs. Wilder's students are able to describe their own progress and achievement when they participate in student-led parent conferences.

9. *Use student-centered classroom assessment.* Mrs. Jacobs involves her students in student-centered assessment to better prepare them for writing term papers. By analyzing sample term papers, both outstanding and very poor, students are able to discern the qualities of the outstanding papers and apply their observations and understanding to their own work.

10. *Give students responsibility.* Students are allowed to make decisions about their learning and behavior that may be different from others around them. They know why they make their decisions and are comfortable with them. They are encouraged to be all they can be and are shown that they have options in what they do. And if they make mistakes—and sometimes they will—they experience the consequences the first time and then are given a second opportunity to try again.

11. *Differentiate instruction.* Mrs. Hodges thinks of alternative ways to provide content instruction, vary the process by which students can make sense of the content, or demonstrate the understanding and learning they take away from the content.

12. *Work to build espnit de corps* that, when successfully accomplished, mobilizes the class for better behavior and achievement. Ms. Iwai uses many classbuilding and team-building activities. She challenges her students to surpass expectations, to be their best, and to strive to make their lives works of art. She also shares and discusses their efforts as well as her own.

These are some of the things good classroom motivators frequently do. In fact, many of these suggestions bring the students into the process and make them feel as though they have some control. There are, as well, many things that good motivators diligently try *not* to do.

What Good Classroom Motivators Do Not Do

Most teachers are not born with the ability to be good classroom motivators. In fact, probably observation and experience have taught them to not do a number of things. Consider these six things teachers who are good motivators do not do:

1. *They don't bore students to death.* They plan against boredom, and at its onset they change the topic or activity, give a short brain break, insert a timely energizer, or simply say, "I know this is not very interesting, but it is important, and I need you to hang in with me for about five more minutes. Can you do that for me?"

2. *They don't confuse their students.* At least they try not to, though they recognize that all learners become confused at times. They make their directions short and explicit,

they give clear explanations, they show examples if they are able to do so, and, when possible, they use visual instructional plans to show and remind students of the steps. They check understanding: "Liam, please help us remember the three things we are supposed to do. Tell us what they are."

3. *They don't vacillate.* Hour after hour, day after day, they hold to their expectations and to the way they interact with students. They aren't hot one day, cold the next, a pal now, an enemy later. They work to get procedures correct and hold them steady. This is not to say they shouldn't be flexible enough to change when change is needed or that even the best teachers don't have good and bad days. Illness and personal problems affect all of us, and in turn affect our work and interactions. But there must be a steadying force in the classroom: the teacher.

4. *They don't frustrate their students.* Frustrated students sooner or later rebel. Frustration can come from two sources—unreasonable demands or work that is boringly difficult. Mr. Thaddeus is unreasonable when he says, "If the entire class doesn't make 100 on this test, nobody goes to recess for the rest of the day." He is unreasonable when he says, "You are to have all this [exorbitant amount of] homework finished by tomorrow or you get on F in the grade book."

5. *They do not intimidate their students* Most teachers tend to be intimidating at first, and others remain so despite efforts to the contrary. But they do not use a stance of autocratic superiority to make students work and behave, nor do they use sour personality, fierce physical stature, hostility, or thinly veiled threats. Rather, good teachers try to downplay intimidation, knowing that for whatever achievement it might inspire, intimidation certainly will produce a counterdesire to resist, vanish, or become transported elsewhere.

6. *They don't punish their students* for failure or other shortcomings. That is, they don't punish in the sense of inflicting pain, acute embarrassment, or loss of dignity. They do, of course, follow the provisions of the discipline system used in the class, which often invokes unpleasant consequences for irresponsible choices, disruptive behavior, or wanton failure to complete assignments. But that unpleasantness seldom entails more than missing recess or staying after school and, when possible, correcting whatever was done incorrectly. For students the impact comes from the certainty of receiving a consequence, not the fact that the consequence is a reward or a discipline. Good motivators rarely punish students for doing poor-quality work. They know they can achieve more through helpful correction than by hurting students' feelings or making them resentfully angry or withdrawn.

What Are Some Cautions in Motivation?

Although most teachers lament the lack of learner motivation, students can, at times, become overmotivated or overstimulated to such a degree that work and behavior suffer. If you bring a pet into the classroom during a lesson on animals, especially one as unusual as a skunk or raccoon, your lesson probably will be lost in the chaos that ensues. If you overemphasize the dire importance of an upcoming test, students may try so hard that they can't relax and think, and they will consequently do worse than if you hadn't mentioned it at all.

Aside from the harmful effects of overmotivation, what teachers do to instill motivation often raises unanswered ethical questions. For example, if novelty, puzzles, intrigue, and excitement are overlaid onto all lessons, do students come to believe that learning is only good when a wizard performs magic or a toy bounces and sings? If incentives and rewards are used to spur student work, do you perpetuate the belief that work is done only for a tangible reward and not for the personal satisfaction of learning or the sense of responsibility to oneself? Most teachers find such questions troublesome, but would rather see students working, even if the reasons do not seem praiseworthy, than find them not working at all. Taking to heart some of the ideas of Glasser, Gardner, Jones, and Kagan can ease some of the concerns considerably.

Their suggestions are important to keep in mind as we prepare to move into Chapter 6, the topic of which is managing instruction. Before proceeding to the next chapter, take time to explore these end-of-chapter activities.

Parting Thought

Learning is not attained by chance; it must be sought for with ardor and attended to with diligence.

Abigail Adams

Summary Self-Check

Check off the following as you either understand or become able to apply them:

☐ Teachers are more concerned about student motivation than about anything else in teaching, with the possible exception of discipline.

☐ To most teachers, the word *motivation* refers to what teachers do to get students interested in lessons.

☐ People do not do what we want them to do for several reasons: They don't know what to do, don't know how to do it, don't know why they should do it, aren't well suited or matched to the task, don't want to, or behave as they do because of the way their brain works.

☐ To motivate students, experienced teachers capitalize on students' known interests by including those interest topics or themes in their lessons. They also try to encourage students, help them feel secure and supported, and use systems of reinforcement for good work and responsible behavior.

☐ Some teachers still motivate through fear and intimidation, but the overall results rarely are satisfying.

☐ William Glasser has made some important contributions to education, including the following assertions concerning motivation:

- All behavior is people's best attempts to control themselves so as to satisfy their needs.
- Of the five predominant human needs, four relate closely to classroom motivation: to belong, to gain power, to be free, to have fun.
- Education should be organized so learning activities enable students to meet the four needs and feel they belong.
- This is accomplished when students work in small learning teams, and teachers function as "lead managers," stress quality in all student work, and transform the classroom into what students perceive as a "friendly workplace."

☐ Howard Gardner's theory of multiple intelligences identifies eight areas of intelligence: verbal/linguistic, logical/mathematical, visual/spatial, bodily/kinesthetic, musical, naturalistic, interpersonal, and intrapersonal.
- Teachers should ask, "In what ways are my students smart?"

☐ Fred Jones believes incentives work best when they are mixed with the content of the instructional program and the classroom structure.
- Preferred Activity Time (PAT) is the opportunity for learning and enrichment activities the teacher would have students do anyway, if time allowed.
- PAT is genuine, has educational value, encourages group concern, can work for individuals, and is easy to implement and manage.
- Visual instructional plans (VIPs) use a series of picture prompts to clearly show and guide students through the process or thinking.

☐ Spencer Kagan links motivation to cooperative learning, classbuilding, teambuilding, and multiple intelligences. He also considers how the brain affects learning.
- Three visions of multiple intelligences (MI): matching, stretching, celebrating.
- For brain-friendly teaching: brains seek and process information, are social, need nourishment, need safety, and are emotional.

☐ Traits of teachers good at motivation include charisma, caring, enthusiasm, trust, and respect.
- Teachers good at motivation use many skills as they plan and instruct.
- Teachers good at motivation try *not* to bore, confuse, frustrate, intimidate, or punish students for failure or shortcomings.
- Dangers of motivation include overstimulation of students and questions about the ethics of using rewards as incentives and payoffs.

Activities for Reflection and Discussion

1. Take a moment to review the statements in the Preview–Review Guide at the beginning of this chapter. Put a check mark in the **Review** column next to any statement with which you now agree. How have your thoughts changed since reading this chapter?

2. Interview at least two teachers about how they motivate their students, or describe one of your teachers from the past who seemed especially able to motivate you to work and learn. Which techniques seem better suited for primary grades (K–2), and which seem better suited for intermediate or upper grades (3–6)? What qualities and skills can you identify in that teacher that seem to contribute to student motivation?

3. The contention was made that good motivators do not intimidate their students. Yet successful high school and college football coaches everywhere yell, scream, swear, berate, and sometimes even strike their player-students, despite which the players usually try very hard and show great respect for their coaches. How do you account for this? The law aside, why or why not would such an approach be effective in the elementary grades?

4. Glasser contends that students will work at any subject if the process of doing so enables them to meet some of their needs. How would you organize the following social studies lessons to help students meet their needs: (a) a first-grade study of family, (b) a fourth-grade study of state geography, and (c) a fifth-grade study of U.S. history?

5. Gardner said, "School matters, but only insofar as it yields something that can be used once students leave school." To what extent do you agree or disagree with this statement? Give examples to demonstrate your viewpoint.

6. Reread Shaylene Watkins's description of her experience with an informal multiple intelligences assessment for her class (Vignette 5.1). How might her class look and function if students were dominant in one of the other intelligences?

7. Describe how you will use classbuilding, teambuilding, and multiple intelligences strategies in a grade of your choice to motivate your students.

Webliography

Fred Jones: http://www.fredjones.com
Howard Gardner: http://www.pz.harvard.edu/index.htm
Spencer Kagan: http://www.kaganonline.com
William Glasser: http://www.choicetheory.com/links.htm and http://www.kathycurtissco.com

References and Recommended Readings

Brophy, J. (2004). *Motivating students to learn.* Mahwah, NJ: Lawrence Erlbaum.

Carter, R. (1998). *Mapping the world.* Los Angeles: University of California Press.

Coloroso, B. (1994). *Kids are worth it! Giving your child the gift of inner discipline.* New York: Avon Books.

Gardner, H. (1991). *The unschooled mind: How children think and how schools should teach.* New York: Basic Books.

Gardner, H. (1993a). *Frames of mind* (10th ed.). New York: Basic Books.

Gardner, H. (1993b). *Multiple intelligences: The theory in practice.* New York: Basic Books.

Glasser, W. (1998a). *Choice theory in the classroom.* New York: HarperCollins.

Glasser, W. (1998b). *Control theory in the classroom* (rev. ed.). New York: Harper & Row.

Glasser, W. (1998c). *The quality school* (rev. ed.). New York: HarperCollins.

Glasser, W. (1998d). *The quality school teacher* (rev. ed.). New York: HarperCollins.

Glasser, W. (2000). *Every student can succeed.* Chatsworth, CA: Author.

Jones, F. (2007). *Tools for teaching: Discipline Instruction Motivation* (2nd ed.). Santa Cruz, CA: Fredric H. Jones & Associates.

Kagan, L., Kagan, M., & Kagan, S. (1997). *Cooperative learning structures for teambuilding.* San Clemente, CA: Kagan Cooperative Learning.

Kagan, S., & Kagan, M. (1998). *Multiple intelligences: The complete MI book.* San Clemente, CA: Kagan Cooperative Learning.

Kagan, S., & Kagan, M. (2009). *Kagan cooperative learning.* San Clemente, CA: Kagan Publishing.

Kagan, M., Robertson, L., & Kagan, S. (1995). *Cooperative learning structures for classbuilding.* San Clemente, CA: Kagan Cooperative Learning.

Larrivee, B. (2009). *Authentic classroom management: Creating a learning community and building reflective practice* (3rd ed.). Upper Saddle River, NJ: Pearson Merrill.

Maslow, A. (1943). A theory of human motivation. *Psychological Review* 50, 370–396.

Tomlinson, C. (2002, September). Invitation to learn. *Educational Leadership* 60(1), 6–10.

PEARSON
myeducationlab)

Go to the Topic: **Enhancing Student Motivation** in the MyEducationLab (www.myeducationlab.com) for your course, where you can:

- Find learning outcomes for **Enhancing Student Motivation** along with the national standards that connect to these outcomes.
- Apply and practice your understanding of the core teaching skills identified in the chapter with the Building Teaching Skills and Dispositions learning units.
- Use interactive Simulations in Classroom Management to practice decision making and to receive expert feedback on classroom management choices.

Managing Instruction

A teacher must be a prophet who can look into the future, see the world of tomorrow into which the children of today must fit, and then teach and test the necessary skills.

—Anonymous

Preview–Review Guide

Before you read the chapter, and based on what you know, think you know, or assume, take a minute to put a check mark in the **Preview** column if you agree with the statement. When you finish the chapter, take time to reread the statements and respond in the *Review* column. Reflective discussions can develop because many of the statements are not clearly "yes" or "no."

Preview   **Review**

1. _____ In essence, teachers and students share responsibility for the curriculum   _____
   in *direct teaching,* while *facilitative teaching* puts teachers in charge.

2. _____ *Direct teaching* typically has students use lower levels of thought.   _____

3. _____ Teachers who use *Say, See, Do teaching* explain, model, and give   _____
   students frequent structured practice.

4. _____ *Concept attainment* works better for older students than for younger   _____
   students and students learning English.

5. _____ Many teachers seem to prefer using cooperative learning over other   _____
   strategies of instruction.

6. _____ Productive and successful cooperative learning supports positive   _____
   interdependence, individual accountability, equal participation, and
   simultaneous interaction.

7. _____ Problem-based learning, project-based learning, and inquiry are   _____
   multiple names for one information processing strategy.

8. _____ *Problem-based learning* is best suited to older students who have   _____
   access to the Internet.

9. _____ Teachers who *differentiate instruction* make modifications to content,   _____
   process, and/or product.

10. _____ *Technology-assisted teaching* has everything to do with lesson design   _____
    and little to do with actual instruction and management.

Chapter Objectives

After reading Chapter 6, students will demonstrate understanding of

■ how to plan and manage instruction efficiently and effectively

■ several contemporary instructional approaches

■ considerations for planning lessons

through their active participation in discussions and the end-of-chapter activities for reflection.

The histories of curriculum and instruction are as old as time. Respected authorities have debated and identified areas of study, and teachers have devised and used a plethora of instructional methods believed to be best practice at the time. Some of the methods have endured, while others have faded with the changing realities of society and the world. Ask teachers about best practice and their responses probably reflect what they experienced in their own schooling and what they learned in their teacher preparation program. A problem to solve or an essential or guiding question for this chapter might be: *How can I match instructional approaches/strategies with curriculum content and design to increase student learnings?*

Curriculum and Instruction—A Short History Lesson

Fostering basic competencies in reading, writing, and arithmetic was established as law by the Massachusetts Bay Colony's Old Deluder Act of 1647 and has been a major ongoing purpose of elementary education in the United States. The law pointed out that Satan intended to lead people away from the paths of righteousness, so it was incumbent upon all citizens to learn to read the Scriptures as a means of thwarting Satan's unholy intentions. Thus, the primary schools became an instrument of God in His work against the devil.

For nearly 300 years thereafter, the content of the elementary curriculum remained much the same, and to a degree still does, although in the 1930s elementary education slowly began to change. Led by Francis Parker and John Dewey, educators radically suggested that schools be made consistent with young students' lives and attuned to their daily needs, aptitudes, and interests. Furthermore, schools should help prepare the young for constructive participation in a democratic society that requires cooperation, compromise, group decision making, and personal responsibility. The suggestion that schools should take the lead in preparing such citizens was revolutionary.

This progressive view gained popularity up through the 1950s. However, in 1957 when the Soviet Union launched *Sputnik,* the first orbital satellite, criticisms were aimed at schools in the United States—it was claimed that schools had gone soft, that they were asking students to do nothing but play, and that they had quit training young minds.

Over the years education has endured fierce criticism; certainly, this is true today. And over the years educators have tried to make things right. What teachers have known all along—to strive for balance between teaching students facts and teaching them to think for themselves—has not changed. Teachers still strive to help children acquire knowledge, skills, and concepts on the one hand, and develop cooperation, creativity, and good attitudes on the other, while emphasizing all learnings and slighting none.

Can such a balance be accomplished? And if so, how? The answer is deceptively simple. When students are asked to apply what they've learned to real-life situations, they become better at application. When students are asked to analyze problems and come up with solutions, they learn to problem solve. If students are given activities that require cooperation, they become better at cooperating. When students are asked to use technology for research and presentations, they learn technology as well as research skills. If students are given opportunities to demonstrate good moral behavior, they are likely to internalize the characteristics. In other words, students usually learn to do what we give them practice in doing. To this end, the intended outcomes indicate the instructional approach that teachers should use. Remember backward design planning (Chapter 2)? The logic of balance supports the steps of backward design: identify the desired results, determine acceptable evidence, and then plan learning experiences and instruction.

Three Instructional Approaches

The term *instructional approach* is used to mean a broad orientation to instruction, a general way of teaching that can lead to a variety of outcomes. Within each instructional approach fall a number of *instructional strategies*—specific ways to bring about the desired outcomes as teacher and students engage in the curriculum. Three broad instructional approaches—direct teaching, facilitative teaching, and differentiated instruction—are widely used in education today. Numerous instructional strategies, including many of the popular ones that are categorized and described by Joyce and Weil (2008), are used within these broad approaches. Cruickshank, Jenkins, and Metcalf (2006) describe 31 instructional alternatives that they define as "any teaching maneuver used to facilitate student learning and satisfaction" (p. 492). Let's briefly review the major instructional approaches and some of the strategies used in each.

Instructional Approach: Direct Teaching

Historically, direct teaching has been at the forefront of teaching practice and still enjoys great popularity. In the late 1970s and early 1980s, several studies focused on the basic academic areas of reading, mathematics, and English and found that students instructed with a structured curriculum and direct teacher involvement learned more than students taught with more individualized or discovery methods. Direct teaching continues to be used to advantage when goals are stated very precisely, content coverage is extensive, student performance is monitored closely, and feedback can be given immediately. Generally, it's agreed that direct teaching is excellent for skills development and for delivering large amounts of factual and conceptual information, but is not good for attitude development or for teaching creativity or problem solving.

Direct teaching gives teachers control of all aspects of instruction at all times. Teachers align the curriculum to the standards, set the objectives, plan the program, organize activities, arrange groups, give explanations, direct and correct student work, keep records, and evaluate results. While teachers may discuss all these matters with students, they primarily do so to help students understand what they are being asked to do. Teachers normally do not ask for student suggestions.

Instructional Strategy: Direct Instruction Direct instruction is referred to by some as the Hunter model or the five-step (six-, seven-, or nine-step) lesson plan. Direct instruction is a highly structured strategy that is intended to maximize student learning. The five-step lesson plan normally follows this sequence (Hunter, 1982):

1. An anticipatory set is used at the beginning of the lesson to orient, focus, or intrigue students as a means of motivating and guiding their work. As its name suggests, this first step helps student anticipate what is to come. Usually, the anticipatory set involves a verbal prompt or clue such as:

    "Friends, today there is a great surprise in store for us."

    "Class, have you ever wondered what it would be like if you could have your own pet dinosaur?"

    "Boys, and girls, today we are going to learn how to write haiku poetry."

Teachers may state objectives or explain the purpose of the lesson here or in step 2.

2. Teacher input of new information or skills follows the anticipatory set. Input possibilities vary. For example, the teacher can present it directly, or it can be contained in written material or visual media the teacher assigns or shows:

    "Boys and girls, watch carefully how I string these beads so you'll know how to string yours." (Teacher explains while demonstrating.)

    "Group Six, you are to use the computers to find out why dinosaurs are believed to have become extinct."

    "Class, watch the steps I follow when I do long division." (Teacher explains the steps of long division while referring to a chart or a visual instructional plan [VIP] with clearly numbered steps, then tells students that the chart or VIP will remain on display as a reminder.) Figure 6.1 shows an example VIP for long division.

3. Guided student practice follows teacher input. Students practice related work at their desks, individually, or in groups. The teacher circulates and provides guidance and immediate feedback, stopping class work if necessary to reexplain what the students seem not to understand.

4. Closure, following guided practice, further checks student understanding. In their own words, students explain concepts, list procedures, suggest how a new skill can be applied, or reflect on the value or purpose of the learning.

5. Independent practice occurs during homework and subsequent lessons where students review learnings and apply them in a variety of ways.

Teacher and Student Roles in Direct Teaching The teacher controls and directs instruction by presenting information in sequential steps and providing prompt feedback about students' efforts. Students do as directed and are not expected to give input about content or procedure.

Strengths of Direct Teaching This strategy is very effective for teaching information and basic skills to whole classes. It is highly structured and sequential, keeps students closely on-task, and gives them immediate feedback. Also, it enables teachers to cover a quantity of information in a relatively short period of time.

Limitations of Direct Teaching This strategy tends to emphasize lower levels of thought. Students are not called on to show much initiative, imagination, creativity, abstract thinking, or problem solving. The strategy's predictability can become boring for teacher and student alike.

Usability of Direct Teaching Direct teaching can be used at all grade levels to teach students of all levels of ability. Students learning English and others will appreciate the presentation pattern: smaller information segments followed immediately with practice and feedback. Its appropriateness for a given lesson depends on the curriculum standards, the lesson objectives, to some extent student ability, and the time available for teaching.

Instructional Strategy: Concept Attainment A concept is a general rule or notion we have about a certain thing—for example, about an object, idea, or procedures. We form the general idea by mentally combining that thing's perceived characteristics. Concepts are the essential elements of thought. To say that we think is to say that we review concepts and combine and manipulate them. This instructional strategy causes students to use analytical thinking and inductive reasoning. In other words, concept attainment—that is, the process by which we acquire and refine concepts—is an essential life skill and, consequently, of prime importance in education.

Concepts begin to develop as we encounter elements of life, whether these elements are tangible or intellectual, and whether we encounter them directly or vicariously. For example, our clear and accurate concept of a dog is the result of numerous experiences with dogs and what they do. Our concept of a tapir may be less clear and accurate because most of us have not had many experiences with that animal. And even less clear and accurate may be our concept of energy release that occurs in nuclear fusion, though most adults do have some idea about it.

We refine our concepts as we compare and contrast examples. For instance, a child refines the concept of an apple by experiencing apples (seeing, tasting, smelling, and touching them), and then contrasting apples' characteristics with those of oranges and bananas.

To help students attain concepts in school, we ask them to categorize objects and ideas on the basis of critical attributes. Apples, based on their attributes, go in one fruit box, and oranges, based on their attributes, go in another. Similarly, nouns go in one category of words, and verbs go in another. To help students further refine their concepts, we give them examples, called *exemplars,* that contain essential traits. In map study, for example, we teach students that representations of the earth's surface are called *maps.* We may show them, as one exemplar, a Mercator projection in which the earth's longitude and latitude are represented as straight horizontal and vertical lines. We may show them, as another exemplar, a polar projection in which the pole is in the center and lines of longitude and latitude look something like a circular spider web. From these exemplars and others, students acquire a concept of map that includes both Mercator and polar projections, but their concept of each differs from the other.

In using concept attainment, teachers first give exemplars and then ask students to develop and test hypotheses about them. Teacher and students then analyze the thinking process they used.

Teacher and Student Roles in Concept Attainment   The teacher selects, defines, and analyzes the concept to be developed, creates the lists of exemplars, and directs the activities. In concept attainment, the teacher controls the lesson but encourages student interaction and discussion.

Strengths of Concept Attainment   The strategy is valuable when teachers want to introduce or refine a concept or check student understanding of ideas and processes. Concept attainment causes students to use analytical thinking and inductive reasoning. Further, students enjoy lessons in concept attainment because the lessons seem like games to them. Some concepts can be exhibited as realia and artifacts. For example, items representing work and leisure can be displayed for students to organize by their essential traits. Rocks can be set out for students to arrange as sedimentary, metamorphic, and igneous, according to their composition traits. The strategy holds student attention and keeps them involved.

Limitations of Concept Attainment   The strategy is time-consuming, and teacher preparation is crucial for success. The teacher must prepare well to avoid the danger of students developing incorrect concepts.

Usability of Concept Attainment   With grade-appropriate concepts, the strategy can be used for all grade levels and most subjects. It can be used to introduce, identify, or refine and strengthen concepts, and to review and check student understanding. Concept attainment will not work well with students who are learning English or who do not have the vocabulary or basic knowledge to understand and then translate the concept exemplars and definition.

Instructional Strategy: Say, See, Do Teaching   Say, See, Do Teaching is an interactive technique developed by Fred Jones (2007). For successful teaching and learning, Jones says you have to consider three things—the way we remember, how much we remember, and how long we can remember it. Say, See, Do Teaching does this. Simply put, the Say, See, Do cycle has three steps: explanation (say), modeling (see), and structured practice (do), with frequent repetition of steps 2 and 3. For example, Mr. Wallace prepares to teach the steps for long division to his fourth graders. To ensure that they understand it, he uses Jones's Say, See, Do Teaching model, along with a visual instructional plan (VIP). The lesson consists of review, partner teaching, and frequent repetitions of the cumulative steps. As he and the class work through the steps of example problems, Mr. Wallace continually has the students repeat the entire process through the newest step and then again repeat the entire process as they teach their partner.

A visual instructional plan is a series of picture prompts that represents the process or thinking and clearly guides students through the process of the task and performance. As Mr. Wallace prepared his VIP, giving careful consideration of the complete task of long division, he followed three simple guidelines: one step at a time, a picture for every step, and minimal reliance on words. His VIP for long division looked like Figure 6.1.

Figure 6.1

A Visual Instruction Plan (VIP) shows every step of the lesson

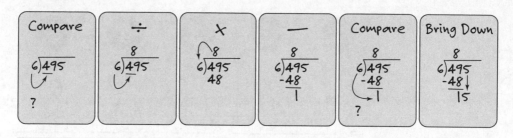

We can contrast VIPs with summary graphics and simple visual aids. Summary graphics do not include the individual steps of the lesson. For the lesson in long division, a summary graphic probably would look like Figure 6.2.

Simple visual aids are memory aids. Although they can be useful for test review, they omit information and details needed for students to acquire the skill or knowledge. Thus, a visual aid for the same long division lesson would look like Figure 6.3.

VIPs must answer in a concrete and visual manner the question students most ask when they need help: "What do I do next?" Performance illustrations, one type of VIP, are particularly useful for nonreaders because they show the performance steps. The performance illustration in Figure 6.4 shows younger students the classroom procedure for properly carrying a chair.

Mind maps are another type of VIP. Mind maps are any graphic that shows someone how to organize information or an idea, solve a problem, or perform a series of operations. Thus, mind maps may assume varied forms, such as those shown in Figure 6.5.

Figure 6.2

A summary graphic hides the individual steps of a lesson

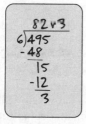

Figure 6.3

A memory aid is useful for test review, but it omits the information needed for acquisition

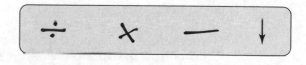

Figure 6.4

For students who cannot read, omit words

Source: Fred Jones, *Tools for Teaching*, 2007, http://www.fredjones.com. Reprinted by permission.

Jones found that visual instructional plans accelerate learning and support independent learning for three reasons. First, VIPs reduce the time needed for teacher prompting because students can be directed quickly to the next step—the explanation is "prepackaged." In other words, teachers can give efficient help in only a few seconds, by simply saying something like "Look at step 5 on the board. That's what you do next." Second, VIPs minimize the need for students to remember everything that is said because they can see and refer back to them. And third, because VIPs provide the steps for the entire lesson, students can help themselves rather than ask for help from the teacher.

Teacher and Student Roles in Say, See, Do Teaching The teacher uses the three-step cycle to reinforce the teaching and learning, frequently repeating steps 2 and 3. As students practice and solve the problems, they review each step completely by teaching it to a partner (partner teaching). All students are engaged actively in the learning process.

Strengths of Say, See, Do Teaching Say, See, Do Teaching reinforces the students' abilities to remember by reducing the amount of new information presented at one time and by quickly involving them in the lesson content. The very nature of the practice allows the teacher to observe students and give prompt feedback as it is needed. This is reinforced further when the teacher has students partner-teach the material as they review.

Limitations of Say, See, Do Teaching The teacher must plan instruction in discrete steps. Also, receiving limited pieces of information at a time can be distracting and disruptive for students who need to see the whole picture in order to master smaller steps.

Usability of Say, See, Do Teaching The strategy can be used at all grade levels and in most subjects. Because of its presentation pattern of explanation, modeling, and structured practice, Say, See, Do Teaching can be used to teach new content and skills, as well as to review prior learning. Students learning English will appreciate its inherent repetition and structured practice.

Figure 6.5

A mind map shows someone how to organize an idea, solve a problem, or perform a series of operations. In mind mapping, necessity is the mother of invention.

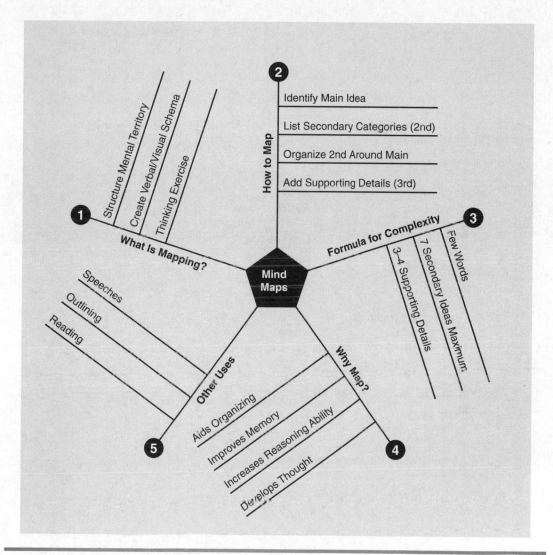

Source: Fred Jones, *Tools for Teaching*, 2007, http://www.fredjones.com. Reprinted by permission.

(*Continued*)

Figure 6.5

Continued

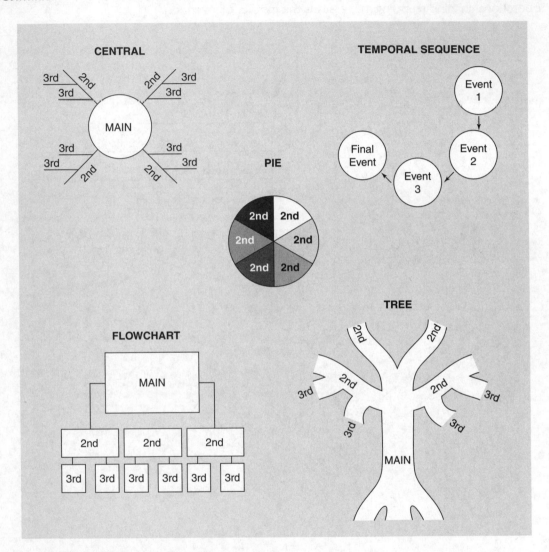

Instructional Approach: Facilitative Teaching

In direct teaching, the teacher rather tightly controls instruction. The teacher aligns the curriculum standards, sets objectives, plans and directs the lessons, and evaluates learning. The teacher can ask a guiding or essential question or even present an authentic problem to be solved. In facilitative teaching, first popularized by Carl Rogers (1969), students have a much more active role in giving input, delving into learning, reflecting on the meaning of what they are learning, and assessing the quality of their efforts. As the label implies, the primary role of the teacher is to facilitate or guide students' efforts and progress. Notice how these two approaches differ in the following lesson on capitalization:

1. *Direct Teaching* (*Direct Instruction Strategy*). The teacher introduces the lesson by stating rules concerning capitalization of first words in sentences, people's names, and cities and states and has examples of each rule on a chart to which students can refer. As a class, students do two practice sentences together with teacher direction, and then complete worksheets independently while the teacher observes and provides corrective feedback.

2. *Facilitative Teaching* (*Cooperative Learning Strategy—see below*). The teacher presents a written paragraph containing a number of capitalized words and informs the students that all capitalization is correct. Students, working with a partner or in teams, read the paragraph, circle the capitalized words, and then attempt to formulate, with consensus, rules that apply to the use of capital letters.

Note that in facilitative teaching the teacher remains in control of the class but does less lecturing and directing, and refrains from leading students to conclusions. Instead, students are encouraged to explore problems, come up with their own solutions, and examine the meaning of what they have learned.

Instructional Strategy: Cooperative Learning

Instructional Strategy: Cooperative Learning Cooperative learning involves two or more students working together to complete specific tasks. This strategy is used in facilitative teaching because it encourages good cooperation, requires positive give and take, shows the value of collective wisdom, and highlights the contributions that every student can make.

Cooperative learning is a valuable strategy for multiple reasons. When it's managed correctly, cooperative learning helps teachers counter four interrelated crises in education:

1. The achievement crises—"Academic performance in the United States is failing compared to other leading nations."

2. The achievement gap crisis—"Academic outcomes are inequitable for different races and socioeconomic classes."

3. The race relations crisis—"Racial tensions and discrimination create roadblocks to social harmony and justice."

4. The social skills crisis—"Students increasingly lack essential character virtues and social skills." (Kagan & Kagan, 2009, p. 2.1)

In other words, cooperative learning helps teachers more effectively address the needs of different learners and difficult students and thus begin to close the academic gap and lessen the crises they face with today's students.

Additionally, students with physical challenges are better able to participate in the learning community because the physical layout of the classroom is planned to best accommodate teams or cooperative learning groups. Also, students who are learning English are better able and more likely to communicate with their peers in the small groupings. As students participate in cooperative activities, they gain confidence in their language skills as well as insights into other cultures.

Spencer Kagan (1994; Kagan & Kagan, 2009) asserts that teachers' abilities to implement cooperative learning successfully relate to their skills in six key areas:

- *Teams.* Long-term, teacher-formed, and small enough for active participation by all members, teams can be heterogeneous (mixed gender, ethnicity, and ability), homogeneous, or random. Four- or six-member teams easily can be split for partner work.

- *Will.* Students must have the desire, the will to cooperate. Teambuilding and classbuilding activities strengthen that will.

- *Management.* Signals, clear responsibility and role expectations, and other management tools help ensure smooth and true cooperative learning experiences.

- *Skills.* Social skills help students work together effectively, and teachers can teach these skills in a variety of ways, including gambits (specific words to say), role-plays, modeling and practice, reflection, and planning.

- *Basic principles.* Four basic principles support cooperative learning, and all must be present for true cooperative learning to exist. PIES is an easy mnemonic for remembering the four principles: positive interdependence, individual accountability, equal participation, and simultaneous interaction. (Review PIES in Chapter 5.)

- *Cooperative strategies and structures.* An abundance of cooperative learning instructional strategies and structures exist, each designed to achieve different objectives and interactions for the instructional content. Kagan and Kagan (2009) define structures as content-free steps, the *how* of teaching, and apply them to cooperative learning in two simple formulas: structure + content = activity and activity + activity + activity = a lesson (p. 14.8). They offer hundreds of structures through Spencer Kagan's materials, workshops, and website, http://www.kaganonline.com.

Example of a Cooperative Learning Activity   Mr. Winston's sixth graders are studying whales. The class is organized into six heterogeneous cooperative learning teams, each of which has five members. From the beginning of the year the students have participated in classbuilding and teambuilding activities. Also, students have learned and practiced a variety of management tools and social skills for successful cooperative learning.

Mr. Winston begins by having students meet as "expert" teams to learn as much as they can about one specific large whale—gray whale, beluga whale, killer whale, pilot whale, right whale, or humpback whale. Students use reference materials in the room and from the library, as well as computers and the Internet to research their assigned whale. Although Mr. Winston provides the addresses for some websites, students are encouraged to find and share other helpful (and appropriate) sites. When the research is completed, students regroup into five "home" teams with six members each. Each team now contains one expert on each of the six types of whales. Using careful time management, each expert teaches the other five students in the home team about his or her whale: its appearance, where it lives, what it eats, and whether it is endangered. This process continues until all students have served as teacher for the home team. To ensure individual accountability, the other students are asked to listen and take notes on specific information. For their final products, every member of the class prepares a paper or web booklet of drawings and facts about each whale.

Teacher and Student Roles in Cooperative Learning Students principally work in small learning teams on activities that require them to assume various roles in the group. Example student roles include leader, encourager, questioner, researcher, reporter, artist, typist, summarizer, materials collector, or time manager. The teacher sets up activities, monitors the process, keeps order, and helps—but only when necessary.

Strengths of Cooperative Learning Students usually like cooperative activities and engage in them eagerly when they know how to participate effectively in cooperative learning teams. In well-planned cooperative activities, all students are able to participate and contribute to their maximum extent. Teams are relatively autonomous, with team members depending on each other. Students learn to think for themselves and show resourcefulness and creativity.

Limitations of Cooperative Learning For it to really work, cooperative learning must be taught, and the students must understand and practice the principles—this takes time before students can participate successfully in cooperative learning groups. Because students interact in groups, activities can become noisy. Some students move off-task easily, and some rely on others to do the work, which causes irritation. Also, the teacher may have difficulty assessing the quality of an individual student's work.

Usability of Cooperative Learning Cooperative learning is appropriate for all age levels and most subjects. However, for successful cooperative learning to occur, teachers must take into account the six key areas and the basic principles of PIES. Moreover, cooperative learning is more likely to be successful when activities and projects are designed so every student in the team has a specific role or task to perform. Students must possess adequate skills and self-control for appropriate behavior. With some guidance, students learning English can be successful contributors to group activities.

PRINCIPAL

"THEY TELL YOU TO BE A TEAM PLAYER, BUT TRY WORKING WITH YOUR NEIGHBOR ON A TEST."

Variations of Cooperative Learning Countless books have been written with cooperative learning structures. Among some of the more popular variations are jigsaw, student teams achievement divisions (STAD), teams-games-tournaments (TGT), think-pair-share, and numbered heads together. Additionally, numerous websites have been dedicated to cooperative learning. Articles and recommended reading-related links can be found at http://www.teach-nology.com.

Instructional Strategy: Problem-Based Learning (PBL) Three strategies closely
relate to information processing and fit well with technology-rich learning environments: project-based learning, inquiry-based learning, and problem-based learning. *Project based learning* focuses on developing a product of some kind. Students help to identify the problem in *inquiry-based learning,* an active approach that focuses the student on questioning, critical thinking, and problem solving. *Problem-based learning* (PBL) focuses on the process of solving an authentic problem and acquiring knowledge. Problem-based learning encourages students, individually or in teams, to investigate and solve challenging problems that have real-world applications. The curriculum-based real-world problems often are interdisciplinary. Well-designed activities embrace different styles of learning and demonstration of understandings, and the projects themselves become the assessments.

Generally, PBL activities involve four key elements: "(1) extended time frame; (2) collaboration; (3) inquiry, investigation, and research; and (4) the construction of an artifact or performance of a consequential task" (Sun Associates, 2003). Additionally, a series of steps guide the PBL:

1. Explore the issues to an authentic problem, list "What do we know?", and develop and write out a problem statement (which may be revised as new information is found).

2. Brainstorm solutions and list them from strongest to weakest.

3. List actions (what must we know and do to solve the problem?) and include a time line.

4. Write and submit a solution with supporting documentation to defend conclusions; present the project.

5. Review individual and group performance and celebrate the work.

Several steps may be repeated as new information becomes available and the problem is redefined: identifying what is known, the actual statement of the problem, possible solutions, actions, and time line.

Because the Internet frequently is a resource for problem-based learning, teachers should take time to teach students how to evaluate Internet resource sources. Harris uses the simple acronym CARS to help students remember a checklist for research source evaluation:

- *Credibility.* Is the source trustworthy? What are the author's credentials? What evidence is there of quality control? Students are looking for authoritative sources with some evidence that they can be trusted.

- *Accuracy.* Is the information current, factual, complete, and accurate? Students are looking for sources that are "correct today (not yesterday)," and that reveal the whole truth.

- *Reasonableness.* Is the source unbiased, objective, fair, and balanced? Students are looking for sources that convey content that is concerned with the truth, thoughtful, and reasonable.

■ *Support.* Are sources and contact information available? Are corroborations and supporting documentation available? Students are looking for sources that provide convincing evidence and support for their content claims, and that can be corroborated by at least two other sources (Badke, 2009, p. 56).

Teacher and Student Roles in Problem-Based Learning Students work individually or in small learning teams to investigate and solve challenging problems that have real-world applications. They also present their research and solutions, if possible, to an authentic audience. The teacher poses the original question or problem, monitors process, keeps order, and helps—but only when necessary. Teacher and students together may design the assessment rubric.

Strengths of Problem-Based Learning Students usually like PBL activities and engage in them eagerly. In well-planned team-designed PBL activities, teams can be fairly autonomous, and all students are able to participate and contribute to their maximum extent. As with cooperative learning, students learn to think for themselves and show resourcefulness and creativity.

Limitations of Problem-Based Learning When the activity involves team rather than individual work, students must be taught the principles of cooperative learning before they can participate successfully in PBL teams—this takes time. Time also should be given to teaching students how to find and evaluate Internet resource sources. As with cooperative learning, team activities can be noisy, some students move off task easily, and some rely on others to do the work. Also, the teacher may have difficulty assessing the quality of an individual student's work.

Usability of Problem-Based Learning PBL is appropriate for all age levels and most subjects. However, for activities to be successful and learning to occur, teachers must take into account the elements of cooperative learning. With some guidance, students who are learning English can be successful participants.

Examples of Topics for Problem-Based Learning *Note:* Thank you to Deseré Hockman (see Case Study 6.1). To access technology mentioned below and more, go to http://www.the21stcenturylearner.webnode.com.

Kindergarten–Second Grade: *Lemonade Stand. Essential question: "How can you make money?"* After focus discussions, student teams identify something they want for the classroom (new game, pencils). Based on the prices of the items, teams set up small businesses to raise the money and decide how they will start and launch their business within the allotted time frame. Successful businesses purchase the classroom item; if they earn more than the item costs, the class decides how to spend the overage. Rubrics guide the project.

Second Grade–Fourth Grade: *Natural Disaster Plan. Essential question: "How would you stay safe in a natural disaster?"* To focus, students discuss natural dangers that exist in the part of the country where they live. Students then are assigned to interest teams to examine one natural disaster and create public service announcements (PSAs) on the dangers, safety procedures to follow, and evacuation strategies. The project ends with teams presenting their safety plans and PSAs to the entire grade level. Rubrics guide the project.

Fifth Grade–Sixth Grade: *Archeological Dig.* Focus class discussions consider why this area of science is important and what archeologists have uncovered in the last century. Students are told that a first grader found an unknown item while digging in the dirt. The teacher reported the find to the archeological society. However, the society is short-funded and teachers are to lead students in an archeological dig and report all findings to the society for review. Teachers must demonstrate how to maintain control on a dig.

Multiple Grades and Schoolwide: *Outdoor Classroom.* In this school community builder, multiple grade levels plan and participate in the creation of an outdoor Exploratorium. Each grade is responsible for a specific section of the outdoor classroom. Examples of Exploratorium exhibits: local plant life, a pond, a butterfly sanctuary, an archeological dig site, a mural on the walls, an outside reading nook.

Multiple Grades and Schoolwide: *Eco-Friendly School.* Essential question: *"How can we make our school more ecologically friendly?"* Becoming ecologically friendly leads to a savings in spending, a challenge that is good for all and that every business and school now faces. Each grade level develops a part of the solution for the school, and then helps to enforce the policy they put into place. Student-created PSAs can be included in the daily announcements. Rubrics guide the project.

Worldwide PBL: *Local Community—For Upper Grades.* Students explore what job opportunities are available to them. Option 1: Students interview invited guests who talk about what it takes to get those jobs (in person during a career day, or via video conferencing). Option 2: At a career fair, students interview for jobs with professionals in fields of interest.

Worldwide PBL: *Around the World.* With CAPSpace, teachers can find other classrooms around the world with which to collaborate. *Focus question for the annual Iditarod: "Which*

Case Study 6.1   Planning for Problem-Based Learning

FOCUS QUESTION

Deseré Hockman now teaches grade 8 science, but has taught math and science to students in fifth through eighth grade. With the members of her eighth-grade team, she has created an entire year of problem-based learning units. How does Deseré's planning align with what you see in your elementary school observations and what you read in Chapter 2?

"One thing that I've learned over my career in education is how to integrate technology and authentic learning in the classroom. From experience I have learned that creating a good problem-based learning unit takes a lot of preplanning. It is important to practice backwards planning. The first thing I look at is the question I want students to solve. It is crucial I make this question a problem, not a project. The problem should be interesting and should meet the educational needs of my students. I need to understand my students and their needs given their grade level and developmental maturity, so I observe and do a task analysis. I also need to understand exactly what I want the final product to entail. I identify all the standards the unit will cover. I also consider choices to make differentiation possible. Finally, I arrange for an authentic audience—if possible, community leaders, experts in the field, publishing companies, and the like—to whom students can present their final products."

sled team do you think will win this year?" Students study the climate and weather, and map the area and the race route. As they follow the race, students continue to update charts, maps, and predictions. They also give live daily broadcasts on a *vlog* every day about the progress of their competitors.

Teacher and Student Roles in Problem-Based Learning Students assume a large responsibility for their learning as they work individually or in groups. Teachers may suggest or present the problem focus for the learning, but students decide how they will gather, verify, and interpret information. Students also decide how they will demonstrate and explain their conclusions, although to demonstrate knowledge and outcomes of problem-based learning, teacher and students together should create the evaluation rubric. The teacher may assist in any part of the process.

Strengths of Problem-Based Learning This approach more than the others teaches students valuable life skills of responsible research and problem solving. Students are motivated and able to learn on their own without the direct control of the teacher. Through problem-based learning, students often gain deeper understandings of the subject problem. The PBL process teaches them to confront a problem, gather information, and compose and support conclusions. The strategy encourages critical thinking and open-mindedness because students frequently encounter conflicting information and opinions.

Limitations of Problem-Based Learning The PBL process takes time and requires access to materials and resources, including books and even knowledgeable individuals to interview. Internet research requires access and technical knowledge and skill. Many teachers would rather devote time to other matters. Students may get stuck or waste time on inconsequential issues.

Usability of Problem-Based Learning With some modification, problem-based learning can be used at all grade levels in all subjects, especially social studies and science. To be successful in problem-based learning, primary children and students learning English require tangible problems and much more teacher guidance than do older students.

Instructional Approach: Differentiated Instruction

Students in today's classrooms bring with them varying languages, cultures, physical considerations, talents, and experiences. In many elementary schools, students work and study in classrooms with other students who are fairly close in age. In other schools, students work and study in multi-age classes where they interact with others of broader age ranges and very mixed levels of ability. Whether the class is traditional or multi-age, it is the teacher's responsibility to determine, plan, and begin instruction from where the students are, not from the first page of the curriculum guide or textbook. These adaptations are called, collectively, differentiated instruction. For Tomlinson (2000), differentiated instruction is a philosophy—one facet of expert teaching—that rests on a set of beliefs and principles:

■ Students who are the same age differ in many ways: their learning styles, academic and reading levels, interests, experiences, and life circumstances.

- These differences have a major impact on what students need to learn, including the support they need and the pace at which they need to work.

- Assessment is ongoing, responsive to students' needs and inseparable from instruction. Assessment and instruction are multimethod and multisource, with student performance determined by individual growth from a starting point.

- The teacher is clear about what is important in subject matter, and the tasks are meaningful. The teacher adjusts content, instruction, and products based on student readiness, interest, and learning styles. Activities and tasks encourage students to use more than one intelligence and encourage teachers to use varied instructional approaches, strategies, resources, materials, and assessment tools.

- All students participate in respectful work and help other students as appropriate. Multiple perspectives are sought and valued.

- The teacher and students collaborate to set both whole-class and individual learning goals, and the teacher equalizes group and individual expectations and standards.

- The teacher and students work together toward flexibility. Time and assessment are flexible and often are linked to students' needs. The teacher guides students toward self-reliance.

Teachers can differentiate instruction in a variety of ways. In primary grades, for example, flexible grouping and learning centers and stations allow teachers to set up varied materials and activities and thus differentiate instruction. Learning contracts differentiate instruction and assessment for older students. So do tiered activities, in which the teacher keeps the same focus for everyone, but provides opportunities of varying degrees of difficulty.

Technology-Assisted Teaching and Learning

While not generally perceived to be an instructional approach, technology-assisted teaching has been found helpful for teachers to better meet the needs of some students. The availability and affordability of classroom computers, broadband access and high-speed Internet service, and educational software in today's classrooms and homes have produced an upsurge in computerized instruction and distance learning (telecommunications) opportunities. System, program, and equipment costs have dropped, and the variety and sophistication of educational software have increased.

But, "Imagine a school with children who can read and write, but with teachers who cannot, and you have a metaphor of the Information Age in which we live" (Cochrane, n.d.).

"HOW DO YOU EXPLAIN LOSING SOMEONE, MISS MARSH? IT WAS A **VIRTUAL** FIELD TRIP."
Reprinted by permission.

For varied reasons, some teachers still avoid technology. They may not understand the advantages technology has to offer. They may be inexperienced in using the equipment or the programs or unskilled in *how* to effectively insert technology into their instruction. A 2004 survey by the National Center for Educational Statistics found that "public school teachers feel there is too little time to learn about, plan, and implement instructional technology in their everyday instructions" (Roblyer & Doering, 2010, p. 337). Or they simply may be uncomfortable with change. "Technology alters the limits of what can be done, but it does not ensure progress" (Armstrong, Henson, & Savage, 2009, pp. 287–288). Technology offers teachers new opportunities for instruction and management, but in the end it is their choice to use it or not. For those who use it, technology capabilities provide new potential for improving schooling and teaching.

Today, technology is moving beyond one or two classroom computers, TV monitors, and DVD and CD players. It is finding its way into classrooms and schools as budgets allow, new schools are built, and older schools are remodeled and updated. On average, federal funds account for about 25 percent of monies spent on educational technology, and discounts that are now available because of the Telecommunications Act of 1996 have helped many districts to increase their numbers of Internet-connected computers. A national survey completed in 2000 from the National Center for Education Statistics found that today "99% of schools have computers; 84% of teachers had at least one computer in their classroom; 38% had two to five computers, and 10% of teachers had five or more" (Armstrong, Henson, & Savage, 2009, p. 298). But again, remember that the presence of computers does not mean newer equipment, equal access, or even use.

Around the country, models of successful teaching with technology involve student participation in decision making and implementation. Students can serve as committee members to discuss and implement schoolwide policies of acceptable use. Students can function as mentors, technical support agents, and leaders who train and support peers, and who act as troubleshooters when necessary. Students can function as resource developers and communicators who "create curriculum resources, user manuals, documents, presentations, videos, and websites for class, school, or community use" (Martinez & Harper, 2008, p. 68).

"NO HOMEWORK FOR THE FIRST ONE WHO CAN SHOW ME HOW TO USE MY NEW PHONE."

MIKE SHAPIRO

Usability for Teachers Now, in many classrooms around the country, teachers are able to use computers and equipment such as document camera projection systems (e.g., Proxima) as tools to enhance their effectiveness—not replace it. They project information and images onto whiteboards or

TV monitors. Students then can participate in the lessons with personal interactive whiteboards (such as Promethean ActivBoards.)

Usability for Students Simkins et al. (2002) describe multimedia projects as "project-based multimedia learning . . . in which students acquire new knowledge and skills in the course of designing, planning, and producing a multimedia product" (p. 3). In other words, students demonstrate their understandings with technology-based presentations such as computerized slide shows, websites, or video.

Planning Approaches and Strategies

Bear in mind that all approaches and strategies require planning by the teacher. You can't rely on any approach to evolve naturally, but must envision your expectations and foresee what students are likely to do. Successful instruction evolves from this prior attention.

Long-range plans for the year and for longer units of instruction, discussed in Chapter 2, provide teachers with a map of the year's events, content, and activities. The steps in the backward design process—identify desired results, determine acceptable evidence, and plan learning experiences and instruction—help teachers organize their thinking and plan for the year and longer units.

Good daily lesson plans are needed for day-to-day work and, again, backward design can help. First identify the desired results. Then determine how students will demonstrate these results. As you plan the learning experiences and instruction, consider skills and knowledge the students need to have prior to the lesson. Then think about the beginning (how you will introduce the lesson), the middle (what you and the students will do), and the end (how you will end the lesson, what students will produce, and how you will evaluate and follow up). Here is an outline of considerations for teachers as they make their plans.

Considerations Before Instruction
- *Facts about the learners.* Who are they? How do they learn? Do they have the knowledge and skills to be successful?

- *Content and context.* Why should my students study this lesson or unit? What is the purpose of this learning? What are the grade level and content area? What content areas can be integrated? Where does the lesson fit into the unit? What are the national, state, and district curriculum standards? What are the learning goals, objectives, and/or essential or guiding questions or problems? How will prior knowledge and skills be assessed before the lesson? What do students need to review?

- *Product and assessments.* How will I be able to tell if students have learned well and enjoyed the work? In what varied and authentic ways will students demonstrate accomplishment of the objectives? What criteria will be used to judge students' success?

- *Management and discipline.* What materials and resources are needed? How will technology be used? How will the room be arranged? How much preparation time is needed? How much class time is available? How will students be grouped? How will transitions be managed? How will misbehavior be managed?

Considerations in Opening the Lesson

- How will students be motivated and focused?
- What will make students want to learn this material?

Considerations in Proceeding through the Lesson

- *Teacher input.* How much preparation time is available? How will I describe and model skills? What examples and nonexamples will I provide? How will I teach to the standards and objectives? How will I involve all students actively? What must I modify to make sure all students learn? What teaching skills and strategies will best help my students accomplish the learning? How will I best use technology in my instruction? What materials and resources will I need?

- *Guided practice/monitoring progress.* How will students practice alone, with a partner, or in cooperative groups? If students work in cooperative groups, how are the four principles of PIES satisfied? How will I check students' understanding?

- *Independent practice/summative assessment.* How will this occur? What will students do to demonstrate their understanding?

- *Closure.* How will I have students summarize and make meaning of their learning?

Considerations in Following Through after the Lesson

- *Transfer.* What opportunities will students have to continue practice and transfer learning? What follow-up activities and homework are appropriate and needed?

- *Reflection.* What went well with the lesson or unit? Was it relevant and worthwhile for the students? What evidence demonstrated this? What teaching skills and strategies worked most effectively? What changes can be made to enhance learning? What changes can be made to the use of technology to enhance the experience and learning? How will student learning and teacher effectiveness benefit from these changes?

Formalizing the Lesson Plan

Many experienced teachers plan lessons in their heads and write only fragmented notes in their plan book. Most new teachers need to be more deliberate and are wise to write out detailed plans to ensure coverage and not get lost in the lesson. Such plans can be written in a variety of ways. In fact, some teachers create a master template on paper or in their computer files so they easily can organize and record their planning ideas. Although you will need to find a format that works well for you, you probably will want to include the following considerations:

- Date
- Standard(s), objective(s), essential or guiding question(s) or problem, or intended outcomes
- Teacher input and student output

- List of activities or learning experiences and the time allotted for each
- Modifications for English learners and students with other special needs
- Technology and materials needed for each activity
- Closure
- Follow-up activities
- Evaluation procedures, scoring guides and answer keys, and criteria
- Management considerations for room set-up; material preparation; student groupings; content delivery, procedures, and transitions; and student behavior

Remember that objectives are clear, specific statements of what students will know or be able to do because of their participation in the study event. If you need to, return to the end of Chapter 2 and review the template for writing objectives.

This concludes our discussions of approaches and strategies you might use to present content to your students, and how you can match and organize your choices with curriculum content and design to increase student learnings. Chapter 7 looks at how you can manage your students at work.

Parting Thought

I talk and talk and talk, and I haven't taught people in fifty years what my father taught by example in one week.

Mario Cuomo

Summary Self-Check

Check off the following as you either understand or become able to apply them:
- ☐ Three broad instruction approaches are widely used today in teaching—direct teaching, facilitative teaching, and differentiated instruction.
- ☐ In direct teaching, the teacher plans, directs, monitors, and evaluates all aspects of instruction.
- ☐ In facilitative teaching, the teacher is in charge but allows much more student input, self-guidance, and responsibility.
- ☐ In differentiated instruction, the teacher modifies content, instruction and process, and product to best meet the needs and abilities of all students.
- ☐ Several specific instructional strategies bring about what is intended in learning:
  - Among strategies used in direct teaching: direct instruction, concept attainment, and Say, See, Do Teaching
  - Among strategies used in facilitative teaching: cooperative learning and problem-based learning

☐ In technology-assisted teaching, teacher and student assess instruction and resources via computers and the Internet, television, and cable.
- Technology-assisted teaching includes tutorials, distance learning, cyberspace connection.

☐ Teaching approaches and instructional strategies become translated into daily lesson plans. Experienced teachers often plan lessons in their head or with a computer template, giving attention to several important considerations before, during, and after the lesson.

☐ Objectives are clear statements of what students should know or be able to do *because* they participated in the lesson and can be written with this template: Students will demonstrate understanding of (*concept or content*) by (*performance activity/outcome*).

Activities for Reflection and Discussion

1. Take a moment to review the statements in the Preview–Review Guide at the beginning of this chapter. Put a check mark in the **Review** column next to any statement with which you now agree. How have your thoughts changed since reading this chapter?

2. Interview at least two teachers about how they plan and manage their instruction to satisfy the curriculum standards and the content itself and meet the needs of all their students.

3. If you were forced to teach mathematics in either a direct or facilitative approach, which approach would you choose? Explain your reasons, keeping in mind the accuracy, quantity, retention, usefulness, and enjoyment of learning for you and your students. Which approach would you choose for language arts? for social studies? for science?

4. You have just learned that a new species of animal named *zugu* has been discovered in the jungle rivers of Zaire. Devise a lesson plan to teach others verbally (no pictures exist yet) an accurate concept of zugu. Teach your plan to fellow students and check their understanding (and your teaching) by having them draw pictures of zugu.

5. Suppose you decided to teach a haiku lesson by using Say, See, Do Teaching. (A haiku is a poem that is concerned with nature and has three lines of five, seven, and five syllables. The first line often depicts a scene, the second an action within the scene, and the third the aftermath.) Describe how you would break the topic into small sequential steps and monitor each student's progress.

6. In what subjects typically taught in the elementary curriculum do you think you could best use problem-based learning? Bearing in mind that PBLs often are time-consuming, how much emphasis would you give to PBLs during the school year?

7. Describe how you would use problem-based learning and technology in your third-grade science or social studies program.

Webliography

Problem-Based Learning Clearinghouse: http://www.udel.edu/pblc

Cooperative Learning

Spencer Kagan: http://www.kaganonline.com

Teachnology, Inc. Teacher resources: lesson plans, free printable worksheets, rubrics, teaching tips, worksheet makers, web quests, math worksheets: http://www.teachnology.com

Problem-Based Learning: Activities

A 3-D floor planner: http://www.racedeck.com/floordesigner

ClassBrain.com: http://www.classbrain.com/cb_games/cb_gms_bag/lemonade.html

Johnson, L. & Lamb, A. (site managers), 2007. Project, problem, and Inquiry-based learning: http://eduscapes.com/tap/topic43.html

Legal Zoom.com. *Lemonade Stand:* http://www.legalzoom.com/legal-articles/Top-Ten-Small-Business-Owners.html

National Park Service and U.S. Department of the Interior. *Archeological Dig:* http://www.nps.gov/history/archeology/PUBLIC/kids/index.htm

Sun Associates, 2003. A project-based learning activity about problem-based learning: http://www.sun-associates.com/lynn/pbl/pbl.html

The 21st Century Learner. Problem-based learning activities: http://www.the21stcenturylearner.webnode.com

Problem-Based Learning: What is it?

USC California Science Project. Problem-Based Learning (PBL): http://www.usc.edu/hsc/dental/ccmb/usc-csp/Quikfacts.htm

WestEd Regional Technology Education Consortium. Exemplary Projects: Other Great Projects: http://www.wested.org/pblnet/other_gp.html

What is Project-Based Learning (PBL)? Attributes, issues, project examples, and teacher and student resources: http://imet.csus.edu/imet2/stanfillj/workshops/pbl/description.htm

Study Guides

Site is "researched, authored, maintained and supported by Joe Landsberger as an international, learner-centric, educational public service." Study guides and strategies: http://www.studygs.net/pbl.htm

Visual Instructional Plans

Fred Jones: http://www.fredjones.com

Other

The Cochrane Collaboration. [Cochrane's] Work/samples, talks and abstracts, including "IT Literate or Retired" (n.d.): http://cochrane.org

References and Recommended Readings

Armstrong, D. G., Henson, K. T., and Savage, T. V. (2009). *Teaching today: An introduction to education* (8th ed.). Upper Saddle River, NJ: Merrill.

Badke, W. (2009). Stepping beyond Wikipedia. *Educational Leadership 66*(6), 54–58.

Bernstein, D. (1992). *Better than a lemonade stand: Small business ideas for kids.* Hillsboro, OR: Beyond Words Publishing, Inc.

Cruickshank, D., Jenkins, D., & Metcalf, K. (2006). *The act of teaching* (4th ed.). Boston: McGraw-Hill.

Dlott, A. (2007, April). A (Pod)cast of thousands. *Educational Leadership 64*(7), 80–82.

Gee, J., & Levine, M. (2009, March) Welcome to our virtual worlds. *Educational Leadership 66*(6), 48–52.

Hunter, M. (1982). *Mastery learning.* El Segundo, CA: TIP Publications.

Jones, F. (2007). *The video toolbox.* Santa Cruz, CA: Fredric H. Jones & Associates.

Jones, F. (2007). *Tools for teaching: Discipline Instruction Motivation.* Santa Cruz, CA: Fredric H. Jones & Associates.

Joyce, B., & Weil, M. (with Calhoun, E.). (2008). *Models of teaching* (8th ed.). Boston: Allyn & Bacon.

Kagan, S. (1994). *Cooperative learning.* San Clemente, CA: Kagan Cooperative Learning.

Kagan, S., & Kagan, M. (2009). *Kagan cooperative learning.* San Clemente, CA: Kagan Publishing.

Lever-Duffy, J., & McDonald, J. B. (2008). *Teaching and learning with technology* (3rd ed.). Boston: Allyn & Bacon.

Martinez, D., & Harper, D. (2008). Working with tech-savvy kids. *Educational Leadership 66*(3), 64–69.

Roblyer, M. D., & Doering, A. H. (2010). *Integrating educational technology into teaching* (5th ed.). Boston: Allyn & Bacon.

Rogers, C. (1969). *Freedom to learn.* Columbus, OH: Merrill.

Simkins, M., Cole, K., Tavalin, F., & Means, B. (2002). *Increasing student learning through multimedia projects.* Alexandria, VA: ASCD.

Tomlinson, C. (2000, September). Reconcilable differences: Standards-based teaching and differentiation. *Education Leadership, 58*(1), 6–11.

Tomlinson, C., & McTighe, J. (2006). *Integrating differentiated instruction and understanding by design.* Alexandria, VA: ASCD.

Tomilson, C. A. (2008, November). The goals of differentiation. *Educational Leadership 66*(3), 26–30.

PEARSON
myeducationlab

Go to the Topic: **Planning, Conducting, and Managing Instruction** in the MyEducationLab (www.myeducationlab.com) for your course, where you can:

- Find learning outcomes for **Planning, Conducting, and Managing Instruction** along with the national standards that connect to these outcomes.
- Apply and practice your understanding of the core teaching skills identified in the chapter with the Building Teaching Skills and Dispositions learning units.
- Examine challenging situations and cases presented in the IRIS Center Resources.
- Use interactive Simulations in Classroom Management to practice decision making and to receive expert feedback on classroom management choices.

CHAPTER 7

Managing Students at Work

A school should not be preparation for life. A school should be life!

—Elbert Hubbard

Preview–Review Guide

Before you read the chapter, and based on what you know, think you know, or assume, take a minute to put a check mark in the **Preview** column if you agree with the statement. When you finish the chapter, take time to reread the statements and respond in the **Review** column. Reflective discussions can develop because many of the statements are not clearly "yes" or "no."

Preview　　　　　　　　　　　　　　　　　　　　　　　　　　　**Review**

1. _____ The problem with routines is that they inhibit individual thinking.　_____

2. _____ In the long run, the best way to begin the day is to allow students to relax and settle in before undertaking the day's arduous work.　_____

3. _____ Authorities agree that if classroom work is worth doing, it is worth being checked carefully by the teacher.　_____

4. _____ The use of classroom monitors is valuable in giving everyone some responsibility for what goes on in the classroom.　_____

5. _____ During independent work, it is possible to give students who are stuck all the help they need to resume work in just a few seconds.　_____

6. _____ Signaling devices are preferable to raising hands as a way for students to request the teacher's help.　_____

7. _____ Visual Instructional Plans give students written or picture steps so they can pace themselves with their work.　_____

8. _____ Modular cluster seating works well for teachers who wish to use cooperative learning.　_____

9. _____ Tattling is a normal part of childhood and therefore should not be a matter of concern for the teacher.　_____

10. _____ Student responsibility is shown adequately when students fulfill duties and obligations promptly, with concern for others.　_____

Chapter Objectives

After reading Chapter 7, students will demonstrate understanding of

- routines, signals, and assistance that help teachers manage students as they work

- incidentals and annoyances that can interfere with teachers' ability to manage students at work

through their active participation in discussions and the end-of-chapter activities for reflection.

It might seem that once a teacher has established the physical and psychosocial environments and has taken steps to increase students' desire to learn, students would work diligently with little supervision. Teachers who make that assumption are likely to find that the classroom quickly resembles Mr. Davis's room described below.

Such classes are familiar to every teacher, and they occur despite a good classroom environment and eager students. Missing in Mr. Davis's room are management procedures that bring students into the room and get them promptly focused and engaged in the work for the day. Essential or guiding questions or a problem to solve for this chapter might be: *What elements of classroom management affect students at work, and how can these elements be managed to support students as they work?* This chapter addresses these questions, giving attention to the following:

1. *Work routines* that involve opening activities, signals for attention, instruction, movement in the room, materials, completed work, student accountability and criterion of mastery, homework, and closing activities

---

Case Study 7.1   The Importance of Routine

FOCUS QUESTION

Mr. Davis does not have a place in his morning routine that sets the tone for a successful day. What management procedures could Mr. Davis install to reduce confusion and the amount of wasted time?

Mr. Davis is a beginning teacher. It is 7:55 in the morning and he is reading the revised agenda for the school day that he just received. There will be a fire drill at 10:15, an assembly for only the best citizens at 10:45, and the nurse will be on campus to check for lice sometime during the day. As Mr. Davis looks for his lesson plans, which he had placed somewhere in the middle of his desk amid numerous papers, utensils, and miniature toys, he sees an overdue slip for last week's video. Somewhere a bell sounds and suddenly 31 bright and shiny third graders, complete with loud voices, barge through the door.

"Good morning, teacher!" they cry. "Can I open the windows?" "Guy," one moans, "you always get to do that!" "Teacher! Here's my permission slip for our field trip!"

Mr. Davis stands there in a daze as 31 pairs of hands try to bless him with book reports and late homework assignments, and permission slips. His students are well intentioned; Mr. Davis simply hasn't taught them a better way to begin the day.

2. *Providing assistance* through the use of student assistants, giving efficient directions and feedback, and directing students in their requests for help

3. *Incidentals* such as seating, entering and exiting the room, sharpening pencils, using passes outside the room, controlling noise, and dealing with numerous other concerns, including procrastination, tattling, and bullying

All of these matters can be handled with routines and procedures that students learn as habits and comply with more or less automatically. Jones (2007), Wong and Wong (2009), and others agree that students' use of time is a major issue. Routine procedures, far from being restrictive, are very helpful in letting students know what to do, as well as how, when, and where to do it, thus reducing confusion and wasted time.

Work Routines

Opening Activities

How the teacher and students begin the day sets the tone and often sets the behavior. Teachers who are organized and friendly welcome students and get them started on something immediately. Teachers who are preoccupied and unorganized set up themselves and students for a day that is likely to be only minimally productive.

Teachers of younger children often greet their students on the playground and walk them as a group to the classroom. Either on the playground or at the door, teachers are able to greet each student individually, tell everyone a little about the day's activities, and remind them as a group of expected behavior.

Teachers of older students often have the children come into the room, stop talking, and get to work immediately on a silent activity, such as reading library books; writing in journals; seeing how many math problems they can do correctly in a given period of time; how many foods in each food group they can list; or some other content-specific challenge given to them by the teacher. While students work, the teacher quietly checks attendance, often using a seating chart. Some teachers have group monitors or table captains report who is absent from their group. Some post a daily opinion poll or survey and have students move their individual photos to indicate how they vote in response to the question for the day. Unmoved photos belong to absent students. Others use a clothespin system in which arriving students clip clothespins with their names to a group chart. Still others use a system in which students take sharpened pencils from loops attached beneath their photos or shadow profiles. The teacher checks attendance by noting which pencils remain.

Choosing, an opening routine that once was widely popular, still is favored by some primary and intermediate teachers. Choosing allows students to move to areas that contain attractive materials and activities when they enter the room. Some students might choose the art center to work with clay, paint, or weaving; others might choose the reading center to read books, magazines, or newspapers; still others might choose the computer center to engage in math or language activities. Once students have chosen their activities, they must be responsible for their conduct, keeping noise down, and taking care of the materials with which they are working. This procedure embraces the idea of multiple intelligences (Gardner, 1993; Kagan & Kagan, 1998) by helping provide a closer match between student interests, learning styles, and the classroom activities, and thereby improve learning and behavior.

Other opening activities popular with teachers are those that go by names similar to *five-a-days,* such as five math problems on the board to try to solve; five vocabulary words to define, learn to spell, and use; or five cities to locate on a map. These are only a few examples of opening activities that students enjoy and that involve them at once. Teachers can use the five-a-days as teasers for content that will be studied that day.

Some teachers open the day with a quick review of the previous day's work and activities. They use the overhead or a projector such as a Proxima or other document camera to show key transparencies or images from the earlier lessons. Others may review the prior day with a short podcast or mind map of events on transparencies or chart paper. They may preview the new day in a similar way. From time to time, opening activities should be changed to avoid a sense of staleness.

Signals for Attention

You never should try to instruct the class without everyone's attention. Normally, you just need to say something like "No talking; everyone's eyes on me" or "Listen carefully." But when students are busy working, especially in teams or groups with talking allowed, you can wear yourself out trying to talk over them. Instead, select and practice a signal that tells all students they are to stop immediately what they are doing and give you their attention. Primary teachers often use auditory signals, such as a clapping rhythm, sounding chords on the piano, ringing a wind chime or a bell, or turning a rain stick. Some just say, "Freeze!" Other teachers prefer a visual signal and simply flick the lights. Whatever signal you select, discuss it with your students and practice, practice, practice its use.

Instructions

For assigned work it is very important to inform students precisely what they are to do, and when and how they are to do it. Every teacher complains about students saying, "I don't know what to do" within seconds after receiving directions. Either students don't listen or there's too much to remember, but both problems can be avoided by stating what is to be done while jotting reminder notes on the board. For example,

> Boys and girls, all eyes on me. Everyone. Thank you. Listen very carefully. At your desks I want you to do problems 2, 4, 6, 8, and 10 on page 32 of your workbooks. [Jot "p. 32" and the problem numbers in the corner of the board.] You may work quietly with your partner. [Jot "quiet" and "partner" on the board.] You have 20 minutes to complete your work. [Jot "20 min." on the board.] When you finish, put your papers in the in-basket. [Jot "in-basket."] Then take out your library books and read until time is up. [Jot "library books." Draw a square around what you have listed on the board and repeat as you point to the notes:] Page 32, problems 2, 4, 6, 8, and 10. Work quietly with partner. Put finished work in the in-basket, and then read your library book until I call time. I'll circulate to help you if you need me. All right, let's get to work.

This procedure can apply to most assignments: Get all students' attention, tell them exactly what they are to do, and post abbreviated but clear reminders on the board or a

" MS. HOLT TAUGHT US TO WORK WELL WITHOUT SUPERVISION TODAY. THEN SHE LEFT."

© Martha F. Campbell. Reprinted by permission.

chart. To further support the instruction, Jones (2007) advocates the use of VIPs—visual instructional plans (see Chapter 6). You may wish to prepare reminder VIPs and charts beforehand and display them where everyone can see. This may seem unnecessary, but on many occasions it will save you having to repeat yourself several times. Moreover, VIPs eventually will help students learn to be self-directing and take responsibility for their own learning.

Movement in the Room

Movement is necessary before, during, and after many learning activities. Students must move from group to group, use the computers, obtain and replace materials, turn in completed work, get drinks or go to the restroom, use the wastebasket, come to your desk, perform their monitor duties, and so forth. Older students may be able to sit still for a while, but young students have to move; their natural behavior does not allow them to sit still and quietly for more than 10 or 15 minutes at a time. Teachers should alternate quiet, still activities with those that allow talk and movement, albeit restrained.

Movement management requires close attention because, although movement is necessary, it has high potential for creating or adding to discipline problems. Even when no trouble occurs, movement can cause congestion, wasted time, and annoyance. Therefore, you must discuss—and practice—movement with your students and establish appropriate guidelines. A basic rule should be that students are to remain seated and working unless otherwise directed. Some teachers like to use a code system that they post in front of the room to remind students of movement expectations for different activities. For example, a red sign tells students they should sit in their seats and talk only when called on. A yellow sign tells students they should remain in their seats, but they may whisper with their neighbors. This is allowed when partners, teams, or small groups collaborate and cooperate on activities. A green sign means that students may do group or individual project work, with quiet talking and movement allowed as necessary for obtaining materials and references.

Computers and Materials

Poor management can wreck efficiency, especially when it comes to classroom computers and other materials—textbooks, worksheets, paper, pencils, crayons, scissors, glue, paints, and brushes—that are used daily. Your room layout and the logistics of your management must allow for computers and materials to be stored out of the way yet remain easily obtained, distributed, and replaced.

Classroom Computers We have discussed that technology is finding its way into the elementary classroom. If you need to, take a few minutes to review some of the logistical concerns regarding classroom computers in Chapters 2 and 3.

Other Storage and Distribution Students with individual desks can keep many of the small materials there, especially textbooks, workbooks, pencils, crayons, rulers, and paper. Teachers use various techniques to encourage students to keep their desks orderly, ranging from simple inspections to procedures intended to be interesting and motivating. For example, some teachers have a box lid or shallow tub for each student that easily slides in and out of the desk space. These have several advantages: They confine the materials that are in the desk, they allow for easy retrieval, and they discourage students from playing with the desk contents when they should be working or listening. The class may earn time toward a preferred activity when they are able to quickly retrieve their supplies for the next lesson or activity because their desks are tidy and organized. Or, a "desk elf," an imaginary creature, might check all desks at the end of the day. When the elf finds desks that are especially neat, it leaves a small surprise, such as a sticker or a pencil.

When students sit at tables instead of desks, as is typically the case in primary grades, or when space limitations make it difficult for students to keep materials in their desks, other arrangements must be made for the storage of small materials. Some teachers provide each student with a container such as a small basket, dishpan, or tub marked with the student's name and kept on a shelf or in their cubbies. At appropriate times students or table captains go to their baskets for supplies to use at their table.

In rooms where student desks or tables are arranged in clusters, some teachers prefer to place a larger tub or basket in the center of each cluster. The tub contains materials that are arranged in the order they will be used for the day.

Often materials are distributed by the following procedures: (1) Teacher or aide distributes before school, during recess, or at lunchtime, so materials are available for students when they arrive. (2) Student assistants are trained to distribute materials as needed at recess, lunch, or during class activities. (3) Students get the materials as instructed.

Use and Care Use and care of materials present opportunities for students to practice conservation. Students should be instructed that they are to make good use of paper, crayons, and pencils, and are not to waste any materials. Likewise, books, workbooks, charts, and other materials that can be reused should be kept clean, undamaged, and orderly. The inherent value in taking proper care of materials is important in itself, especially in times of fiscal difficulties. When supply budgets dwindle, it becomes a matter of necessity for teachers and students alike to make better use of materials.

Vignette 7.1   Managing Materials and Supplies

Ted Saulino describes how he manages materials in his kindergarten class:

"I place a small, inexpensive yet durable plastic basket in the middle of each cluster of tables, full of the supplies that students will need on a given day: pencils, scissors, glue, markers, colored pencils, red correction pens, and rulers. The basket sits on top of a folder of good ruled paper and scratch paper.

"To avoid arguments and to distribute power to each station, I name rotating team captains. A wall chart, divided into sections representing the work stations, lists the students' names. The name at the top of the list is the first team captain. Next to the captain's name I clip a small star, which I move down to the next name when the week is over. The child whose name is below the captain's acts as the substitute if the captain is absent.

"Captains distribute the supplies and distribute and collect all handouts. If someone is absent at a station, captains start an absent folder for the child's return. At the end of each day, captains assess the team's supplies and replenish paper, sharpen pencils, and make sure the team has a clean station."

UPON REFLECTION
Mr. Saulino describes his management for kindergarten. What changes would make his management procedures work better for intermediate or upper grades, or for classrooms with individual desks rather than clusters of tables?

Replacement In addition to efficient distribution and care of materials, good management calls for attention to how materials are to be replaced after use. Typically, smaller materials and student work are handled in one of four ways: (1) students themselves quietly return the materials; (2) monitors collect and replace the materials; (3) students place materials in folders or containers that are collected later and reviewed by the teacher; or (4) the teacher or aide collects, organizes, and replaces the materials.

Large Materials Although newer schools are providing equipment alternatives that replace many of the larger materials found in this section, the fact remains that some of these materials are likely still to exist to some degree in most elementary classrooms. Larger materials that play keys roles in instruction also must be managed and used efficiently. These materials include maps and screens; reference books such as dictionaries and encyclopedias; globes, smaller maps, models, and art supplies; other items such as materials for aquariums and terrariums; physical education equipment; and audiovisual equipment. Although a few student assistants can handle most management duties associated with large materials, many teachers prefer to involve all students in procedures and responsibilities.

In many classrooms, larger maps and projection screens still are mounted on the wall or above the board so they can be pulled down and used as needed. Maps and screens on rollers can be used to cover materials, such as test items, visual instructional plans, and directions that have been written on the board, or to hide larger instructional props or resources until needed.

Newer or updated classrooms now are wired and equipped with computers; in these rooms classroom reference books may be minimal. However, when reference books are in the room, they should be kept on shelves at the side of the main seating area and easily accessible to students. Globes and models should be placed where students can easily see and approach them—on countertops or a special table. Art supplies are best kept near the classroom sink in cupboards with closable doors, and easels should be folded and stacked nearby. Materials for aquariums and terrariums, such as sand, plants, animal food, rocks, and cleaning equipment, should be kept in cupboards and used only by the teacher and designated monitors.

Physical education materials are best kept in plastic crates, large trash containers, or a small movable cart near or just outside the door until after school; then they are placed in the corner or a closet in the room.

Much of the media equipment now available for teachers' use to supplement instruction has been converted to video, DVD, or CD, and is projected through a television monitor or by document camera projection equipment (such as Proxima). Additionally, students may use interactive whiteboards (such as Promethean ActivBoards). A wheeled cart makes moving materials easy in classrooms where other audiovisual equipment is present. The top shelf can hold an overhead projector or a television (if one is not mounted on the classroom wall). Equipment such as CDs, DVDs, video and audiotapes, and tape or video recorders can be kept on the bottom shelf. In some schools, special projectors may be stored in a central equipment storeroom and available as needed for teacher checkout.

Completed Work

One of teachers' most time-consuming tasks is dealing with completed work. Teachers commonly take home stacks of daily papers to be checked, graded, recorded, and returned. The following suggestions are intended to help teachers manage this complex and burdensome task.

Should Teachers Check Everything? It is not necessary that all student work be checked in detail. Much independent work is for practice only, and necessary feedback should be given immediately as the teacher circulates and monitors student efforts.

Teachers should carefully check work that requires judgment or very accurate correction. However, there is nothing wrong with allowing students to exchange papers or check their own routine work. In fact, as much work as possible should be corrected by students in class, to relieve the teacher as well as to motivate and instruct. Students lose interest when feedback is delayed, and teacher-corrected work, even when returned the next day, has little instructional value. In-class correcting gives immediate feedback on performance and errors. Aides and parent volunteers can check routine student work, but remember this caution: Students have the right to privacy regarding their work and progress.

Organizing Completed Work Some teachers use a folder system to keep track of student work. The folders are compartmentalized with labels such as *Unfinished Work, Ready for Checking,* and *Completed and Checked.* Folders are kept on students' desks. At the end of each day, the teacher reviews items in the *Ready for Checking* compartment and moves them into the *Completed and Checked* compartment.

In classes where folders are not used, monitors collect completed work, perhaps by tables, teams, or groups, and place it in a receptacle. The teacher or an aide checks the work and returns it the next day.

Vignette 7.2   Checking Student Papers

Ginny Lorenz, who teaches a 4/5 multi-age class, manages checking her students' work in this way: "I like to read carefully student work, but I am not willing to bury myself with thirty papers at a time. I have my thirty students divided into eight groups. Every two weeks, Mondays through Thursdays, I am able to collect, read, and give constructive individualized guidance and feedback to everyone's written work by closely look-ing at about four papers a day, and we all are able to enjoy Fridays and weekends."

UPON REFLECTION

What other methods have you seen teachers use to handle the volume of student papers and work for students in upper grades? for students in primary grades? How do you plan to handle the daily volume of student papers and work?

Acknowledging Good or Improved Work Student work that has been done well or evidences effort and improvement should be acknowledged, usually privately through comments or stickers. Barbara Coloroso suggests that teachers allow students to decide themselves if their work needs a sticker. Occasionally, good work should be posted for all to see. This provides a sense of success and is highly motivating to most students, though not to all. Be sure to ask the student for permission beforehand. Additionally, samples of completed work—both inferior and superior—should be kept privately in student folders to show caregivers at conferences or during open house. These work samples are intended to present a well-rounded and accurate profile of the habits and accomplishments of the student.

Student Accountability and Criterion of Mastery

As teachers review student work, they should consider both quality of work and student accountability. How much work is enough? How many math problems should students complete for homework? How many sentences should they diagram? Rather than require all students to complete the same amount of work, teachers should answer these questions in terms of a *criterion of mastery*.

Consider the difference in these two sets of instructions. Some teachers say, "Boys and girls, you are to solve the odd problems on this page. Problems you don't finish before recess will be homework." This statement supports a *criterion of speed*. Students will hurry with their work so they can enjoy recess and have no homework. Nothing the teacher said encourages students to be accurate or to learn the concept.

In contrast, other teachers say, "Boys and girls, you are to solve the odd problems on this page. You may stop when you correctly answer five problems in a row." Now students have a genuine interest in accuracy and perhaps even mastery. If they answer the first four problems correctly and miss the next problem, they must begin counting from number one again for their correct five in a row. With this simple instruction, the teacher has encouraged both mastery and student accountability. With each correct response, students become more invested in solving the next problem correctly.

Homework

Although educators and caregivers debate whether to give it, most teachers above early primary grades assign homework. The value of homework is not so much in learning new material as in (1) practicing and strengthening skills already learned, (2) developing an interest in more pleasurable learning activities, such as reading, and (3) allowing caregivers to participate in and show support for their child's education.

For the most part, homework should focus on activities such as practicing and applying math skills, reading library books or magazines, reading together with an adult, writing anecdotes and reports, drawing pictures related to schoolwork, or making up work missed because of absence.

Such work might encourage, but should not require, caregiver assistance in providing a workplace and insisting that the work be completed. This is particularly true when the caregivers speak a language other than English in the home. When students are weak in a particular skill, such as adding and subtracting or spelling, the caregiver can be asked to work with the child, perhaps with remedial drill games. Caregivers want to know about homework and how they can help. They should be told the best things they can do are as follows:

- Provide a quiet place for the child to work.

- See to it (good-naturedly) that the child does homework as scheduled.

- Read to or with the child.

- Play games with the child such as dominoes, Scrabble, Parcheesi, checkers, Yahtzee, and Rummikub that encourage spelling, math, and other types of thinking.

- Ask and answer questions about news events and a variety of other topics.

Closing Activities

Teachers who simply wait out the last 15 minutes of the day miss some rich opportunities for teaching and reflecting. Here are some ideas for ending the day: Spend five minutes taking care of closing assignments, notices, cleaning, and tidying so that the last ten minutes can be used for review and reflection. Have students give their views on what occurred during the day—accomplishments, high points, excitements, disappointments, things that went well, and things that could be done better next time. Review the day's events by creating a mind map with the students on overhead transparencies or chart paper. Give students a preview of what the next day will bring. Promise at least one interesting surprise and live up to it, so they will look forward to the next day with anticipation.

Providing Assistance

Student Assistants

Students can assist with many chores in the classroom. Often called *monitors,* these student assistants can take care of tasks such as watering plants, distributing worksheets, and any other routine chores in the room. Some teachers use "one-minute student managers" to handle the variety of jobs that arise from the particular needs for their class. For example, a kindergarten teacher may take advantage of a skilled youngster to serve as "shoelace manager." This student helps classmates tie their shoelaces and, in doing so, saves both time and the teacher's back. An upper-grade teacher may have a "materials manager," who is responsible for distribution of materials as they are needed. These managerial activities add mutual teaching and learning time to the day and allow students to become active partners in the classroom.

Student assistants can be assigned to most routine duties. For example, an upper-grade teacher might use these categories of responsibilities, to provide jobs for 32 students:

- Class president—manages class business and classroom meetings as needed.

- Flag monitor—leads the daily flag salute and other lessons and activities that have to do with the flag.

- Lights monitor—sees that the lights are turned on and off.

- Environmental assistant—sees that windows and doors are opened, closed, and shaded as necessary during the day.

- News, weather, and map reporters (two)—report on two or three news items per day, including weather forecasts for the city, state, and nation, and locate on the map where the news and weather events occur.

- Class news reporters (two)—make daily entries in the class log about highlights of the day. Kept as a class record, the log becomes a source for the teacher's monthly newsletter to caregivers. From time to time, the students reread the log to affirm their sense of history, accomplishment, and growth.

- Messenger—delivers messages to the office, library, and other teachers.

- Line leaders (two)—head lines and model good behavior for entering and leaving the room and for movement to other parts of the school.

- Physical education equipment managers (two)—distribute, collect, store, mark, and take care of equipment used on the playgrounds at recess and lunch.

- Table or group captains (five to six)—manage tables or identifiable groups of students, with such duties as taking attendance, distributing and collecting materials, seeing that the area is kept clean and orderly, and sometimes reporting as the group spokesperson.

- Plant and pet caretakers (two)—water and care for plants; clean and care for aquarium and feed fish; and feed and care for animals in the terrarium.

- Materials managers (two)—handle, store, distribute, and collect small materials such as workbooks, worksheets, pencils, paper, glue, and scissors.

- Audiovisual managers (two)—obtain, operate, and return VCRs and CD and DVD players and any other equipment that is used for instruction; manage models.

- Technical support providers (two)—assist other students and teacher with technical support.

- Librarians (two)—manage the class library and the system used for students to check out books, class videos, and other materials. Library assistants are trained to process checkout cards and to keep track of materials.

" I KNOW YOU WERE ELECTED CLASS PRESIDENT BUT THAT DOESN'T MEAN YOU'RE IN CHARGE..."

Permission by Dave Carpenter.

- Substitute teacher aides (two)—assist substitute teachers. The teacher keeps these monitors updated on daily routines, the locations of lesson materials, standards of behavior, and the discipline system used in the class.

- Greeter—welcomes classroom visitors and offers them seating.

Assignments to tasks are made in different ways. Some teachers arbitrarily assign the duties. Others allow students to choose, in alphabetical order or on a first-come basis. Still others have students make written requests or complete application forms and interview for the duties they wish to perform. In such cases, selection then can be made by the teacher or by class vote.

Directions and Feedback

As students work individually at assigned activities such as seatwork, they invariably encounter difficulties that require teacher help. Effective management requires that teachers provide this help quickly and efficiently so students can stay on task and complete work on time. Jones (2007) says that the teacher's job is to answer the question "What do I do next?" as efficiently as possible. This is accomplished best when the teacher (1) gives clear, understandable directions, (2) posts and reviews reminders and visual instructional plans, (3) uses signal systems for requesting assistance, (4) moves easily and quickly to students in need of help, and (5) provides assistance quickly and efficiently.

Directions and Reminders Earlier in this chapter, you saw how directions can be given briefly and clearly so students know exactly what they are supposed to do, how much time they have, what to do with completed work, and what to do while waiting for the next lesson or activity to begin. In Chapter 6 you saw a VIP for long division. By posting well-constructed VIPs on a wall, most students can work through their math problems or other work with little additional teacher help. Graphic models that show spelling rules, paragraph construction, math algorithms, and steps in conducting experiments also can be helpful. Teachers should have students review the graphic models before requesting further help. Other reminders that are not directly pertinent to a given lesson also may be posted, such as "*i* before *e* except after *c*," "Keep your area clean," and "Invert and multiply." These posted VIPs, graphic models, reminders, and written directions should answer most of the questions students are likely to ask during independent work.

Teacher Signals and Student Requests for Help Early in the year teachers should install a quiet signal they will use for attention—a raised hand, finger to the lips, flicking lights, ringing a bell or wind chime.

Students also should be taught nonverbal signals to alert the teacher about concerns. For example, students can extend one palm forward in a stop position or slowly lower their hand to communicate that the teacher is talking too fast. Students can skim their hands "over their heads" when the material is too complex or confusing. Thumbs up or clapping index fingers together can indicate silent approval or understanding; thumbs down can indicate the opposite.

We all remember scenes of students congregating at the teacher's desk or sitting dispiritedly at their desks with arms waving limply, waiting for teacher help. Confusion and arms in the air can be avoided through the use of signal systems that advise teachers when students need assistance. Some teachers use folded or colored construction paper that students place on the corner of their desk. A variation of this is for students to prioritize and signal their need for assistance by setting a red, yellow, or green cup on their desks.

Teacher Movement Teacher movement and proximity are key factors in managing assistance. The teacher must be able to reach each student as quickly as possible to minimize wasted time and forestall misbehavior. If the desks are arranged with an interior walking loop, or in modular clusters or shallow semicircles, the teacher will be fairly close to all students. Some teachers prefer to move in a predetermined pattern among the desks to be near students, comment on their work, and give help in regular rotation. Others prefer to observe from a central location and move quickly toward any student who shows signs of difficulty.

Efficient Help Assistance should be given very quickly—in no more than a few seconds time. Jones's research (2007) shows that teachers spend an average of about four minutes per student when giving individual help. In these mini-tutorials, teachers question the student and then wait for a reply, which may be erroneous, fumbling, or nonforthcoming. Jones claims that effective help can be given in 20 seconds or less, as follows: (1) at first contact, quickly find anything the student has done correctly and mention it favorably, such as "Good job up to here." (2) Give a straightforward prompt that gets the student working again, such as "Watch the decimal," "Borrow here," "Look at step three on the chart," or "That word means. . . ." (3) Leave immediately, being sure to pay brief attention to the work of nearby students who have not requested help. Although this third step may appear inconsiderate of the feelings of students needing help, Jones maintains that it has two positive effects: (a) rapid movement gives attention to a greater number of students during work time, and (b) it begins to lower the dependency syndrome and helpless hand raising in which students require the teacher's presence before they begin work. As Jones says, "Be positive, be brief, and be gone."

Student Requests for Help

We described some nonverbal signals students may use to request help as teachers give directions. Additionally, students may receive help from partners. Whether it comes from the teacher or a partner, it is important that students continue working or know what to do until help is available to them.

Vignette 7.3 When Students Constantly Ask for Help

Devora Garrison, a fifth-grade teacher, found this strategy to work with one of her students.

"I have one of those students this year who constantly is standing in front of me with a question. She never raises her hand, but feels the need to be under my feet the moment I give an instruction. I discussed ways she could get answers rather than relying on me to do her thinking for her. Finally, to get her to think, I gave her three sticks each day with 'Garrison/Anderson' written on them. Now when she comes up to Mrs. Anderson, my student teacher, or me, she has to give us a stick. When the sticks are gone, she's out of opportunities for the day. There has been an immediate drop in her leaving her seat."

UPON REFLECTION

What else might Mrs. Garrison do to help this student and others who frequently request teacher's help?

Partner Helpers In addition to using nonverbal signals when requesting help, teachers can teach students to be effective partner helpers. A hallmark in differentiated classrooms is that all students participate in respectful work, and when they can, they help each other. In classrooms that utilize cooperative learning teams, the strategy of team questions also works well—"Ask three teammates or other students, then me." Both these strategies, in particular, support student autonomy, prompt help from team members, and allow the teacher to circulate and monitor student work without feeling bogged down by "helpless hand raisers" and overly dependent students.

Continue Working While waiting for the teacher to arrive, students needing help should know they are to move ahead to the next problem or exercise. If this is not possible, they should take out a book and read silently until the teacher arrives to help.

Incidentals

Seating

As mentioned in Chapter 3, various seating arrangements have served teachers well—rows, U-shapes, circles, semicircles, and clusters of various kinds. To the extent larger class sizes allow, most elementary teachers today want space flexibility for different kinds of activities. They also want to use a good deal of cooperative team work and to be able to circulate easily among students. Modular cluster seating, with four to six students per cluster, usually serves these wants well.

It is best to begin the year with the teacher assigning students to seats and making tagboard name tags for each student. Students should not be allowed to select their own seats until they show that they are capable of self-control.

Entering and Exiting the Room

Most teachers still favor lines for entering and exiting the room and use various procedures to form them. Once the most common procedure was to have boys and girls form separate lines, but now boys and girls line up together in one or two lines. Let your students know how you want them to form lines and give them ample practice in doing so.

Usually, lines for entering the room are formed on a first-come basis. For exiting the room, teachers often excuse students according to (1) where the students sit, (2) alphabetical order by first or last name, (3) arbitrarily by work groups, or (4) as a reward for students or teams who have behaved or worked well. For occasional variety, teachers may have students move according to prompts: "Line up if you are wearing something I can see that is red," "If your birthday is in a month that begins with J," and so on.

Pencil Sharpening

Pencil sharpening can be very disruptive to class instruction. Some teachers keep a large container of pencils sharpened by a student assistant before the day begins. If lead breaks or wears down, the student simply exchanges the pencil. Thus, the pencil sharpener is not used during the day, and no time is lost because of noise, wandering, or waiting.

Other teachers feel that this system does not encourage self-responsibility. They allow students to keep two pencils in their desks and be responsible for sharpening them at appropriate times, such as before school. Whatever procedure you prefer, it is important to teach the routine to the students and then adhere to it.

Out-of-Room Passes

Passes are used when students must leave the room to go to the restroom, an outside drinking fountain, the library, or the office. Teachers should not allow students to leave the room—with or without permission—unless it clearly is necessary, because there always are students who will look for any excuse to leave the room as often as possible.

Some schools provide teachers with laminated passes on which are written the teacher's name and room number. When this is not the case, teachers provide their own. Some teachers simply purchase premade passes at a teacher supply store. Others make their own passes from large pieces of wood or laminated tagboard that students cannot inadvertently misplace. Six passes should be sufficient: one drink pass, one office/nurse pass, two library passes, and two for the restroom—one for boys and one for girls. The number of passes should be adjusted according to classroom need, but usually it is not a good idea to allow two or more students to go together to unsupervised areas such as drinking fountains or restrooms.

In past years, students in Julie DePew's fourth/fifth multi-age class used passes she created with clip art and then laminated (Figure 7.1). On the first day of school every student in Julie's class received a laminated pass with his or her name on it. Students were reminded at that time to use the bathroom before school, at recess, and at lunch. Every morning one student distributed the passes to the others. If students needed to leave the room, they returned their pass to a small basket near the door. However, if they needed to leave more than once, they had to sign in as a consequence. Students said, "We like that we can leave once a day if we need to." They also said, "We don't like to sign in, so this lets us be responsible."

Figure 7.1

An Example of a Pass for the Bathroom or Drinking Fountain

Source: Julie DePew. Reprinted by permission.

Noise Control

Some teachers tolerate noise well; others don't. Regardless of teacher tolerance, every class occasionally (sometimes daily) gets noisy to a degree that interferes with teaching and learning. If this happens in your room, you almost certainly will hear complaints from other teachers. If possible, you should check with your neighboring teachers when you anticipate that a lesson or activity will be a little noisy to be sure they have not planned a test or quiet activity at the same time.

To keep noise within acceptable limits, discuss with your students the negative effects that loud noise has on learning and instruction. Explain that different levels of noise are appropriate and allowable for different activities. For example, there should be no talking during silent reading. During discussions, one person at a time can talk in a normal voice. During cooperative work, quiet talking is allowed as needed. For other activities such as drama and singing, more noise is allowable. It's important to follow these discussions with

---

Vignette 7.4   Silent Signals

Kathryn Krainock teaches second grade in an open classroom. "Because there are no doors between classes, I developed silent waves, silent claps, and silent cheers so my students don't distract others. My students give silent waves (index finger gently waving) to a parent or administrator who comes into the room. They give silent claps (two fingers quietly clapping) and silent cheers (arms quietly moving up and down as though cheering) for fellow students when they give a speech or do other fantastic feats. These methods would work successfully in any classroom because they take minimal time and don't distract others."

UPON REFLECTION

Kathryn Krainock describes silent claps, cheers, and waves in her second-grade open classroom. How are students likely to respond to these in intermediate or upper grades or in self-contained classrooms?

---

practice so students can *hear* what is acceptable and what is too loud. Furthermore, it is important to have students practice refocusing their attention quickly back to the teacher when they are engaged in cooperative work.

You also should use a clear signal for indicating when the noise level is too high. Consider using a color signal system (visual) or a sound such as a bell or wind chime (auditory) whenever the noise level goes above acceptable limits. Another alternative is to play background music. When you can no longer hear the music, the noise level is too high.

Other Annoyances

Several other annoyances drive teachers crazy: procrastination, tattling, messiness, tardiness, and irresponsibility. Teachers also find themselves dealing with some behaviors that are more serious: cheating, lying or stealing, language (swearing), temper tantrums, and bullying. Teachers should model the appropriate behaviors continually and should quickly redirect students when signs of these behaviors occur. The following suggestions help bring these problem areas into manageable proportions.

Procrastination, Tattling, Messiness, Tardiness, and Irresponsibility

Procrastination   Procrastination, the exasperating habit of putting things off until the last minute, afflicts many students. Everyone has difficulty working at unexciting tasks, and most of us cannot maintain enthusiasm when tasks are overly long or complicated. But when students regularly fail to begin promptly and fool around instead of working, consider remedies such as the following:

- Keep instructional tasks as interesting and as short as possible while covering what is intended.

- Break long tasks into a series of short steps and place a deadline on the completion of each step. Say, See, Do Teaching, for example, involves students quickly and guides them actively through the learning process one step at a time.

- Insert timely brain breaks and energizers into your lesson. For example, have students stand and use their arms to write their spelling words in the air. Or have them stand and dance in their teams to music. "The Freeze" on the CD *We All Live Together* by Greg Scelsa and Steve Millang (1978) is such a movement energizer. Other songs the children enjoy will work for this as well.

- Emphasize a time limit and remind students as it passes. One idea is to call out the time occasionally. For example, the teacher might say, "Ten minutes. You should be working on problem number 4." A second idea is to use a Teach Timer, a management tool that displays time (either counting up or down) with an overhead projector onto the wall, whiteboard, or screen. Older students can monitor their progress and the time themselves when they can see the clock or timer from where they are in the classroom. Another idea is to use appropriate background music the children are familiar with and have them self-gauge their progress according to the music— "When this music ends, you should be about half finished." (Take a minute to review the discussion in Chapter 3 about using music to enhance the ambience in the classroom.)

- Use incentives. "As soon as you answer correctly five problems in a row [keeping in mind the criterion of mastery discussed earlier], you may. . . ." (some quiet preferred activity, such as free reading).

- If other remedies do not work, take the student aside and say, "You just are not getting your work finished. I know you can do it. I wonder what we can work out so you will complete your assignments."

Tattling Tattling can become a virulent disease that affects almost everyone in the class. It is habit-forming and causes students to focus on the negative, lose respect for each other, and forever look to an authority to adjudicate minor problems the students should settle or ignore. For teachers, tattling can become a major irritation. Fortunately, tattling can be controlled rather easily.

Barbara Coloroso (2002) stresses the importance of teaching children to think for themselves and to believe that no problem is so great it cannot be solved. To help students develop decision and problem-solving skills, she continually encourages them by saying, "You have a problem, you can solve it. What's your plan?" Of course, the children's age and maturity affect how they handle this conversation. When tattling occurs anyway, and if the matter is insignificant, as most are, proceed to the following steps:

- To help children discern the difference between tattling and telling, teach them this formula from Coloroso (2002): "If it will get another child *in* trouble, don't tell me— that's tattling. If it will get you or another child *out* of trouble, tell me. If it is *both*, I need to know" (p. 135).

- For older children, have the tattler write out the complaint, together with a constructive suggestion for resolving the problem.

- Ask the tattler to wait until lunch or after school to make the complaint, assuring the student that you will consider it carefully at that time.

- Have the disputants meet together to discuss the matter and come up with an acceptable solution with which they both can agree.

- Have class discussions or class meetings regarding the nature of tattling, its negative effects on cooperation and good feelings, and the desirability of solving one's own minor differences. Indicate that it is all right to inform the teacher when another student seriously violates one's rights by stealing, bullying, or inflicting physical harm. Then, as a class, have students role-play tattling behaviors and proper alternatives.

Nelsen, Lott, and Glenn (2000) suggest using classroom meetings as opportunities to practice effective problem-solving skills. Following discussion and role-play, students are taught to brainstorm ideas for logical consequences and nonpunitive solutions. Then they vote and act on a suggestion they think will be most helpful. After a reasonable trial period, students reevaluate their solution and make any adjustment that might be necessary.

Messiness   Messiness is a chronic problem for some students and is evidenced in their work and the care they give school materials. Messiness annoys teachers and reinforces unattractive habits in students. To deal with messiness, consider the following suggestions:

- Model neatness. Keep your own work area in order and tidy.

- Have class meetings or discussions about pride in oneself, schoolwork, and the classroom. Talk about how pride often relates to neatness.

- Let students know you are keeping their neatest papers to show caregivers.

- Establish an incentive system in which a series of neat papers earns a reward such as a certificate, sticker, or preferred activity.

- Encourage students to exchange ideas about organizing their desks for maximum neatness and efficiency.

Tardiness   Tardiness often occurs for legitimate reasons. However, when it is habitual, tardiness can be annoying and disconcerting, causing the student to miss out on important instruction and instilling a general lack of responsibility. When left unchecked, the habit often becomes worse. Chronically late students may blame their caregiver or an unending series of catastrophes, or they may have fallen into the tardiness habit because it is their nature to procrastinate, they have not yet accepted responsibility for their own educational process, or they find something very interesting to do on the way to school.

Although it is likely that one or two students will arrive late every day, the incidence of tardiness, especially for the chronically late, can be reduced through the following measures:

- Have class meetings or a discussion about student responsibilities in supporting and participating in the school program. Make sure students understand the need to arrive a few minutes before school begins.

- Make the opening activities attractive, enjoyable, and important so students will want to participate and will feel left out when they do not. Coloroso (1994) believes in sharing information that is "a little nice to know" first thing in the morning. For example, tell only the students who are present to answer just the even problems on the day's math quiz.

- Show you mean business by establishing consequences for tardiness and by giving rewards or preferred activity time for continued punctuality. Let students help decide the consequences and rewards and PAT.

- If other measures do not correct the problem, call the parents or guardians and ask for their input and help.

Irresponsibility   Irresponsibility refers to student disinclination to work up to capacity; mistreatment of materials, equipment, and facilities; and failure to live up to ordinary obligations. An important goal of education is to build within each student a sense of responsibility for one's own actions and for the common good. Responsibility is shown when obligations are fulfilled promptly and correctly with concern for others. To help instill this sense in students who are not otherwise inclined, consider the following:

- Periodically discuss with students what responsibility means and how it contributes to the good of everyone. Also discuss what students should do in the classroom to show they are being responsible.

- Assign specific responsibilities to all class members for helping manage the classroom, as with student assistants.

- Assign specific responsibilities to students when they work in cooperative teams. For example, as a team member, a student might act as leader, encourager, questioner, researcher, reporter, artist, summarizer, typist, materials collector, or time manager.

- Have students evaluate their own behavior on several points, such as being punctual, completing work, doing their best, taking care of assigned duties, and helping others when necessary. Have them fill out contracts for future improvement and reward them appropriately when they live up to their promises.

Cheating, Lying or Stealing, Swearing, and Temper Tantrums

Sometimes students cheat, lie or steal, swear, or have temper tantrums. Even in the best run classrooms teachers may not be able to prevent these events. However, some general practices are appropriate:

- Continually model and give opportunities for student to practice honesty, appropriate language, and anger management.

- Have class meetings or discussions about student responsibilities in modeling and supporting appropriate behaviors. Have students role-play behaviors and responses to these situations.

- To the extent possible, plan ahead to prevent the problems.

- Focus on solutions rather than punishment, blame, or shame.

- As you handle the situation, do all you can to keep everyone's dignity intact.

Cheating   Students cheat on tests or assignments for a variety of reasons. Some want to do well and get good grades. Some are afraid of punishment. Some don't want to disappoint their caregivers or their teacher, or they fear they won't have personal value if they don't do well. Others are motivated by rewards. To help students avoid the temptation to cheat:

- Give open-book tests rather than tests that require the memorization of facts, although you can have students quiz each other when they are ready on subjects that require memorization, such as the multiplication tables.

- Distribute sample or actual test questions in advance so students know what to study.

- Have students brainstorm ways to solve cheating problems.

- Rather than trying to trick a confession, speak directly to any student involved in cheating ("I noticed you cheated on the math test this morning"). Then invite the student to work with you on a solution so he or she can succeed without cheating.

Lying or Stealing   Young children may lie or steal because this is part of their natural development. They are learning the differences between what is real and unreal, right and wrong, and they are moving from an egocentric perspective to a broader view of the world. Some have not developed the interest or skills that would prevent them from lying or stealing. Sometimes children lie or steal because they feel hurt—they don't feel they get enough attention and want something from you or others; they don't have friends and try to fill a void by lying or stealing things; or they may feel materially or financially deprived. Some lie or steal because these are actions they observe in adults. Teachers can help students in several ways:

- Model honesty and share openly with the class how it makes you feel when someone lies to you or steals something from you.

- Give the student a chance to correct the untruth or return what was stolen by saying, "I'm not interested in blame or punishment. I just want the truth, or the item returned. I trust this will be done before school ends today."

- Avoid set-up questions ("Are you lying to me?" or "Did you steal this?"). Rather, ask what and how questions ("What happened?" "How do you feel about it?" "What did you learn from this?" "How can you use what you learned in the future?" or "What can you do to avoid the problem in the future?").

- Have the student who told the lie or stole something figure out a way to make restitution that is respectful of everyone. Younger children may need more help: "Would you like to put this where it belongs, or would you like me to?"

Language—Swearing   Actually, it is typical that four- and five-year-olds use this type of language when they are discovering and practicing a newfound skill, their ability to startle the adults around them. When adults deal with inappropriate language matter-of-factly and respond calmly, the language tends to disappear in a short time. Older students may continue to use inappropriate language because they still continue to feel rewarded by attention from startled adults, they want to gain status among their peers, or they hear the language elsewhere and really do not know appropriate alternatives. Consider these suggestions:

- Avoid expressing anger or dismay. Rather, simply state that such language is inappropriate, and let students know how this makes you feel: "I feel uncomfortable when you swear, and I will appreciate it if you choose another word to say what you mean."

- Ask questions to help students discern inappropriate language and consequences: "How does your grandmother feel about swearing?" "What do referees and umpires do when people swear?"

- Young children need guidelines for their behavior. Be firm but kind: "We do not use those words at school." Then walk the child away from the group, but invite him or her to return when he or she will use acceptable words.

- Either individually or in class meetings, have children brainstorm acceptable alternatives to swear words.

Temper Tantrums Tantrums may have a purpose. A child may want the teacher's attention or the opposite, to get the teacher to leave him or her alone. The child may want to hurt somebody or simply may want to have his or her own way. Sometimes tantrums are triggered when a child is on cognitive or emotional overload. And in some instances, the child may not know appropriate ways to communicate his or her needs. Read about neurological-based behavior and some appropriate management strategies and responses in Chapter 8. Briefly, to help avoid tantrums and soothe students:

- Support the child, not the behavior. Be there, offer quiet comfort, and speak reassuring words: "It's OK to be upset. It happens to everyone."

- Help the child identify ways to recognize the signs and find alternative ways to communicate: "We need to find a way to let me know how you are feeling without hurting yourself or others."

- Always pay attention to the safety of the child and others in the room, including yourself.

Bullying

Sadly, bullying is a regular occurrence at school, as we discussed in Chapter 4. Bullies are individuals who instill fear in others through physical, verbal, emotional, or sexual bullying, who intend to hurt, and who enjoy it. Elementary-aged bullies may use verbal or physical bullying, or they may ignore or exclude their victims with relational bullying. Bystanders and peers of victims often suffer effects from bullying, along with the victim. Bystanders may appear to follow or support bullies, or do nothing to stop the action, for several reasons: They may feel guilty or helpless because they didn't stand up to the bully. They fear associating with the victim because they are afraid of retribution from the bully. They may not report the incidents for fear of being seen as an "informer" or "snitch." Or they may feel unsafe, with loss of control and inability to take action. Teachers should approach bullying by doing the following:

- Continually infuse expectations for good character into the way you teach and model and provide practice for appropriate behavior and acceptance.

- Hold class meetings or discussions and conduct role-plays and other activities to reduce bullying. For example, create, teach, and practice an action plan to ensure that students know what to do when they observe a bully/victim episode.

- When bullying occurs, gather information directly from students. Do this anonymously and with sensitivity to the students' safety and needs. Establish or follow procedures to investigate reports of bullying and keep careful documentation. Additionally, listen to family members who report bullying.

- Ask the children what they need from adults to feel safe. Show genuine support and concern for students, and establish "friendship groups."

- Establish, practice, and follow clear school and classroom rules and consequences for bullying.

- Provide adequate supervision, particularly in common areas such as the playground and lunchroom.

- Inform caregivers and try to involve them in solutions of the problem.

This concludes our considerations of the management of students at work and directs us to an examination of how to manage the special needs of students in today's classrooms, the topic of Chapter 8. Before moving ahead, take time to explore these end-of-chapter activities.

Parting Thought

Never, never, never, give up.

—Winston Churchill

Summary Self-Check

Check off the following as you either understand or become able to apply them:

☐ Good management of students at work contributes greatly to time availability, class control, rapid learning, sense of responsibility, and sense of security.

☐ Routine management calls for attention to
  - Work routines
  - Opening activities: attendance; sharing; silent reading; journal writing; choosing; five-a-days
  - Signals for attention
  - Clear, succinct instruction for doing work
  - Movement in the room: traffic patterns, permission
  - Computers: computer stations and materials
  - Materials: storage and distribution, use and care, replacement, small and large materials
  - Completed work: what to do with students' completed assignments
  - Student accountability and criterion of mastery
  - Homework: its value and purpose
  - End-of-day closing: a rich instruction time

☐ Providing assistance
  - Student assistants: responsibility for everyone
  - Helpful directions and feedback: clear directions; visual instructional plans and posted reminders; rapid, effective assistance
  - Partner and team help

☐ Incidentals: seating (matched to the instructional program); entering and exiting the room; pencil sharpening; out-of-room passes; noise control

☐ Other annoyances: procrastination, tattling, messiness, tardiness, irresponsibility; cheating, lying or stealing, language (swearing), temper tantrums; bullying

Activities for Reflection and Discussion

1. Take a moment to review the statements in the Preview–Review Guide at the beginning of this chapter. Put a check mark in the *Review* column next to any statement with which you now agree. How have your thoughts changed since reading this chapter?

2. Interview at least two teachers about what they do to plan and manage their students at work. Ask them to describe what they do specifically to handle entering and exiting the room and passes, noise levels for various activities, and bullying, as well as some of the other annoyances that occur in their classes. Also, ask them what student assistants, if any, they have in their classroom and how they are selected, rotated, and trained.

3. Individually or in teams, describe what you would do to control at least two of the following: tattling, procrastination, messiness, irresponsibility, cheating, lying or stealing, swearing, temper tantrums, or bullying.

4. Think about the schedule of a normal school day for a specific grade level of your choice. (Refer back to Chapter 2 if necessary.) Decide on the level of noise that you would consider acceptable for the various activities. How would you discuss the topic of noise with the students? What signals, if any, would you use as reminders? How would you handle noise and signals if your students were in another grade (primary, intermediate, upper)?

5. For a grade level you select, decide what classroom monitor duties you want students to fill. How would you make the assignments? How would you instruct student assistants concerning their duties and responsibilities? What would you do if a monitor proved to be irresponsible? How would you handle monitors if your students were in another grade (primary, intermediate, upper)?

6. Make a list of the various work products that students regularly complete while in elementary school—tests, practice papers, compositions, artwork, and so on. What would you want your students to do with their completed work? Describe how you will communicate and carry out this process.

7. Custom design a 10- to 15-minute closing routine (not clean-up) that you consider most beneficial to your students and program. What variations might you make during the week? (Some districts provide one shorter day, or minimum day, each week to give teachers planning time without students. How would your routine for that day vary from the regular days? between Monday's routine and Friday's?) What variations might you make from month to month? Also, what variations would you make if your students were at another grade level (primary, intermediate, upper)?

Webliography

Directions and Feedback and Efficient Help

Fred Jones: http://www.fredjones.com

Bullying

Dan Olweus: http://www.olweus.org

Olweus Bullying Prevention Program; reprinted in Evertson & Emmer, 2001, p. 2009: http://www.stopbullyingnow.com

The school safety check book by the National School Safety Center, reprinted in Parkay & Stanford (2010), pp. 92–93: http://www.nsscl.org

References and Recommended Readings

Charles, C. (2011). *Building classroom discipline* (10th ed.). Boston: Allyn & Bacon.

Coloroso, B. (1994). *Kids are worth it! Giving your child the gift of inner discipline.* New York: Avon Books.

Coloroso, B. (2002). *The bully, the bullied, and the bystander.* Toronto, Ontario, Canada: Harper-Collins.

Jones, F. (2007). *Tools for teaching: Discipline Instruction Motivation* (2nd ed.). Santa Cruz, CA: Fred H. Jones & Associates.

Gardner, H. (1993). *Multiple intelligences: The theory in practice.* New York: Basic Books.

Kagan, S., & Kagan, M. (1998). *Multiple intelligences: The complete MI book.* San Clemente, CA: Kagan Cooperative Learning.

Meaningful work. (2010, September). [Special Issue]. *Educational Leadership, 68*(1).

Nelsen, J., Lott, L., & Glenn, H. (2000). *Positive discipline in the classroom.* Rocklin, CA: Prima Publishing.

Olweus, D. (1999). *Core program against bullying and antisocial behavior: A teacher handbook.* Bergen, Norway: Research Center for Health Promotion, University of Bergen.

Schwartz, F. (1981). Supporting or subverting learning: Peer group patterns in four tracked schools. *Anthropology and Education Quarterly, 12*(2), 99–120.

Wong, H., & Wong, R. (2009). *The first days of school* (4th ed.). Mountain View, CA: Harry K. Wong Publications.

Compact Disk

Scelsa, G., & Millang, S. (1978). *We all live together* (Vol. 2). [CD]. Los Angeles: Little House Music.

PEARSON myeducationlab

Go to the Topic: **Planning, Conducting, and Managing Instruction** in the MyEducationLab (www.myeducationlab.com) for your course, where you can:

- Find learning outcomes for **Planning, Conducting, and Managing Instruction** along with the national standards that connect to these outcomes.
- Apply and practice your understanding of the core teaching skills identified in the chapter with the Building Teaching Skills and Dispositions learning units.
- Examine challenging situations and cases presented in the IRIS Center Resources.
- Use interactive Simulations in Classroom Management to practice decision making and to receive expert feedback on classroom management choices.

Managing Special Groups

CHAPTER 8

There is only one child in the world and that child's name is ALL children.

—Carl Sandburg

Preview–Review Guide

Before you read the chapter, and based on what you know, think you know, or assume, take a minute to put a check mark in the **Preview** column if you agree with the statement. When you finish the chapter, take time to reread the statements and respond in the **Review** column. Reflective discussions can develop because many of the statements are not clearly "yes" or "no."

Preview   **Review**

1. _____ Fully Inclusive education is a fairly new concept, with little history or legal   _____
   support.

2. _____ Response to Intervention (RTI) is a multitiered means to determine   _____
   whether any student, regardless of type of disability, needs more intensive
   instruction.

3. _____ *Exceptionality* is the term used to identify children who are especially   _____
   bright, gifted, or talented.

4. _____ Attention deficit disorder (ADD) and attention deficit hyperactivity disorder   _____
   (AD/HD) are best treated with medication because the child is likely to
   outgrow the disorder.

5. _____ The term *neurological-based behavior (NBB)* refers to behavior that is   _____
   outside the student's control and related to the way the brain works.

6. _____ Children who are emotionally disturbed understand the signs and triggers   _____
   for their outbursts and can learn to control them.

7. _____ Language diversity describes the presence of more than one language   _____
   in the student's home and has little to do with ethnicity and race.

8. _____ Caregivers homeschool their children because of concerns with the   _____
   quality of instruction and safety in public schools.

9. _____ Children without permanent housing are more likely to attend school in   _____
   order to receive the adjunct services such as the free lunch program.

10. _____ Differentiated instruction is time-consuming and contributes little toward   _____
   managing diversity among students.

Chapter Objectives

After reading Chapter 8 (and Appendix B), students will demonstrate understanding of

■ legislation and civil rights acts that relate to inclusion

■ potential academic, physical, language, and social challenges of today's students

through their active participation in discussions and the end-of-chapter activities for reflection.

Diversity is prevalent in schools in the United States. Children in today's classrooms come with a wide range of academic and physical abilities, challenges, or other special needs. Some come with behavior disorders. Children also come to school from diverse cultures, family structures, and economic conditions. Some arrive speaking languages other than English. These are the realities of today's schools. The charge of educators is to provide the best quality education possible while meeting the needs of *all* children. A problem to solve or an essential or guiding question for this chapter might be: *Given the diversities and special needs of today's students, how can I best meet everyone's needs?*

We begin this chapter with discussions that relate to children with special education needs, be they academic, physical, or emotional needs. Later we will discuss children with other needs that arise from language and family diversities and economic circumstances.

As you continue reading, it is important to remember that the students we describe are real persons who have real challenges in life. Consequently, all references are made using person-first language, such as "students with visual impairments" rather than "blind students."

The Concept of Inclusion

Inclusion refers to the involvement of all students in the educational setting that best meets their needs, regardless of background, creed, or level of ability. The intended educational setting is the public school classroom. But inclusion has a broader meaning as well. It refers to a way of life, an attitude, a value, a belief system that holds that all children are entitled to the best education we can provide, *and* that an association of diverse students provides benefits for all. Schools and teachers who embrace the attitude of inclusion show it by their words, decisions, and actions. They strive to make all children feel welcomed and secure. They support the unique gifts and the needs of every child in their school and classroom communities. Their sincere goal is for every child to become successful.

Over the years, the federal government has enacted multiple legislations in its effort to uphold the guiding principles of our founding fathers for free and public education for all children. Perhaps of greatest legal impacts, though, are the Individuals with Disabilities Education Act (IDEA), the No Child Left Behind Act (NCLB), Assistive Technology Act (ATA or Tech Act), Section 504 of the Rehabilitation Act, and the Americans with Disabilities Act (ADA). More current education reform legislation is the American Recovery and Reinvestment Act of 2009 (ARRA) and President Obama's Race to the Top program. Refer

Case Study 8.1 Managing the Challenges of Diversity

FOCUS QUESTIONS

Where does the teacher begin? How can this teacher learn more about her students and their special needs? What is the process to access her students, and what support services are available for her and her students?

Mrs. Sanderson was hired to teach a multi-age fourth- and fifth-grade class. She was one of five teachers in this team. She began her year with 22 students in her class but soon added three more. She quickly found that her students had a wide range of ethnic, cultural, and language backgrounds, as well as differing academic and skill abilities.

In addition to her Caucasian students, ethnic and cultural diversity included students (or their families) from Germany, Japan, Korea, Mexico, Puerto Rico, and South Africa. The six students who were identified as English learners possessed a range of language ability. Two had minimal (preproduction) English-language ability; two were identified as having early production proficiency; and two were fairly fluent, with intermediate fluency. Three of these students lived in homes where family members predominately spoke a language other than English.

The children ranged in age from a young ten-year-old to a thirteen-year-old boy who had been retained in first grade. Four students were identified as gifted and talented (GATE). Most of the students read at grade level, although four read below and two read at the tenth-grade level.

Several students had identified disabilities. One of the girls was deaf, and although she could sign and read lips, a paraprofessional was with her in the mornings. One boy had autism and worked with the resource specialist three mornings a week. A third child was severely diabetic and had a service dog that was trained to alert her and others when an insulin reaction was imminent. A fourth student had severe asthma. Finally, two children were on behavior contracts.

Eight students lived in divorced or blended families, and another lived with her grandmother. The family of one student was homeless and had been staying in a nearby shelter for the past month.

to Appendix A to learn more about the basic tenets and requirements of the legislation associated with inclusion, the 2009 reform legislation, and the Response to Intervention (RTI) process.

Managing Exceptionality: Students with Special Needs

The U.S. Department of Education, the National Center for Education Statistics (NCES), and the Office of Special Education Programs (OSEP) publish regular reports regarding participation rates and time spent in general education classes for students with disabilities. Over the years, rates have consistently increased. In the 2006–2007 academic year, participation increased to 54 percent, although settings varied greatly across the states (Smith & Tyler, 2010, p. 43). Several reasons may explain the continuous gradual increase in services. These include the Education for All Handicapped Children Act Amendments in 1986 that mandated public school special education services for all handicapped children aged three to five; the increased number of children identified as having speech, language, or other impairments; the increased enrollment of children with autism and traumatic brain injuries; and the Child Find program that actively seeks infants, toddlers, and preschoolers with disabilities.

One way to categorize disabilities is according to the incidence in schools. IDEA '04, a federal law, identifies 14 categories of qualifying disabilities and sorts them into high- and low-incidence categories. Consequently, IDEA '04 lists specific learning disabilities, speech or language impairments, mental retardation, and emotional disturbance as high-incidence. It lists multiple disabilities, deafness, hearing impairment, orthopedic impairments, other health impairments, visual impairments, autism, deaf-blindness, traumatic brain injury (TBI), and developmental delay as low-incidence disabilities. Developmental delay, the newest category to be included under IDEA '04, refers to a general, non-disability-specific group of younger individuals.

Ysseldyke and Algozzine (1995) identified 27 different categories relating to exceptional students, those formerly labeled as learning-disabled. Kirk et al. (2006) consolidated the range of exceptional students that may be in a classroom into six broad groupings:

1. *Intellectual differences* include students who are slow to learn (such as mental retardation) and students who have superior intelligence (such as giftedness).

2. *Communicative differences* include students with communication, speech, or language disorders.

3. *Sensory differences* include students with auditory or visual limitations.

4. *Behavioral differences* include students who are emotionally disturbed or socially maladjusted.

5. *Physical differences* include students with orthopedic or mobility disabilities.

6. *Multiple and severe handicapping conditions* include children who have a combination of conditions (such as cerebral palsy and blindness).

Intellectual Differences

Students of Lower Ability

Some children have achievement rates in certain academic areas that are lower than their general ability levels would indicate. They are apt to be disorganized, forgetful, and frustrated, and they tend toward anger, hopelessness, or low self-concept. Teachers can support these students in several ways. In addition to differentiating content, process, or product to best meet student need and ability, teachers should provide predictable routines and structures, model and signal important information and assistance clues, and provide ample practice for smaller portions of information. Teachers should limit confusing activities and directions and have students repeat directions aloud. It also is important for teachers to emphasize students' achievements rather than their mistakes and for students to keep records of their own work and behavior.

Several assistive tools are available for teachers of children with lower activities. Teachers may use audio books, talking computers, captioned films and videos, and semantic mapping software to help students with their reading. Teachers may have students use word-processing programs with spelling and grammar checks to help them with their writing. Manipulatives and calculators can help students with math and problem solving. Personal organizers, electronic calendars, and a variety of organizing software programs are available to help students with their organization. Finally, the Internet and computer-based instructional programs can help students with their studying and learning.

Students of Higher Ability

Students of higher ability, sometimes referred to as gifted and talented (GATE), are those who significantly surpass the identified norms in achievement. The Gifted and Talented Students Act of 1978 defines gifted and talented students as "possessing demonstrated or potential abilities that give evidence of high performance capability in areas such as intellectual, creative, specific academics, or leadership abilities, or in the performing and visual arts, and who by reason thereof require services or activities not ordinarily provided by the school" (p. 8). The act distinguishes *gifted* as referring to above-average intellectual ability, and *talented* as referring to excellence in drama, art, music, athletics, or leadership. It further states that students can have these abilities separately or in combination.

Students who are identified as high achievers can be either self-starters or creative, divergent thinkers. In either case, these children generally require differentiated educational programs and services beyond those normally provided by the regular school.

Some students who are high achievers are self-starting, persistent, able to work independently, and resourceful. There is direction to their personal learning goals, and they need minimal guidance to proceed. For these students, management relates to the strong articulation of personal goals, of plans to accomplish them, and of tools to assess their progress.

Other students with higher ability, however, may appear more difficult to manage. They are likely to be divergent thinkers who approach situations and problems with perspectives different from those of other students. Teachers often view divergent thinkers either as very creative individuals or as noncompliant students with behavior problems.

Generally, students with higher abilities, both the self-starters and the creative, divergent thinkers, benefit most from open-ended activities. Such assignments allow students to adapt an assignment, a situation, or a problem to match their own uniqueness, ability, and interest. This can be highly motivating for both quality work and behavior. Guided conversations and jointly designed scoring rubrics that clearly set expectations and standards help teachers and students manage a nontraditional approach to curriculum and demonstrations of understanding.

Though these students have the potential to contribute to everyone's learning, they should not be made team teachers for lessons or be kept occupied with busy work. In other words, students who are high achievers should be given *other,* not *more,* and it is especially important that they feel valued and appreciated. With some caution and careful application, distance education technology (telecommunications) and online courses have been found to benefit students who are gifted. It also can offset a lack of programs and resources

"DO YOU WANT YOUR CHILD ENROLLED IN THE ROCKET SCIENTIST TRACK, BRAIN SURGEON TRACK, OR BILL GATES COMPUTER GEEK TRACK?"

© H. L. Schwadron. Printed with permission.

(Olszewski-Kubilus & Lee, 2008, in Smith & Tyler, 2010, p. 487). Additional ideas for students who are high achievers might include bonus activities, questions, and projects that are motivational, challenging, and meaningful. A helpful resource is http://www .nagc.org.

Communicative Differences

Students with Communication Disorders

Communication is a complex ability that enables individuals to receive, understand, and express information, feelings, and ideas. We communicate in varied ways—speech, voice, writing, nonverbally through facial expressions and body language, and manually with gestures and sign language. Additionally, a distinction exists between speech (expressive) and language (receptive) disorders. "*Speech* is the system of forming and producing the sounds that are the basis of language, and *language* is considered the system of communicating ideas" (Mastropieri & Scruggs, 2010, p. 52). In other words, speech problems relate to production of sounds and words, while language problems relate to difficulties with the linguistic code, rules, and conventions for connecting the sequences into meaning.

A communication problem exists when an individual's speech noticeably differs from the speech of others, interferes with the intended message, or causes distress or frustration for the listener or the speaker. Speech impairments include three major types of difficulties: articulation, fluency, and voice. *Articulation* relates to the production of speech sounds. Articulation problems can be identified with the acronym SODA—substitution, omission, distortion, addition. *Fluency* relates to the rate and flow of speech. Stuttering is a fluency problem. *Voice* relates to pitch, loudness, and quality of sounds. Problems with any of these aspects of speech result in abnormal speech that is unintelligible, unpleasant, or distracting to the listener, and can affect or interrupt the communication process. Physical conditions such as cleft palate or lip (sender) or middle ear infection (receiver) also can present a speech challenge.

Students with Speech Disorders

Many students with speech (expressive) or language (receptive) disorders receive individual help outside the classroom. The IEP team determines the frequency with which a qualifying student receives services. These services may be provided to individuals or small groups of students with the same speech or language difficulty.

Within the classroom, potential negative consequences of speech and language disorders may affect the child's self-concept and interpersonal relations with peers. It is important to prevent these consequences from occurring. This begins when teachers show acceptance for all children. Rather than make assumptions about what the student needs or wants, teachers should ask the student or caregiver what can be done to help. Teachers should model appropriate language, use open-ended questions and wait time to encourage all children to talk, and listen attentively to what all children have to say. Teachers might use a secret signal to alert students when they will be called on next to respond. Teachers also should adapt the environment, materials, and evaluation, and plan and deliver instruction so students can rejoin the class easily when they return from their time with the resource teacher.

Students with Language Disorders

Language disorders are the difficulty or inability to master language rules, and thus interfere with communication. Language disorders impede one or more of the three aspects of language. *Form* is the rule system that includes phonology, morphology, and syntax. *Content* is the intent and meaning of the message. *Semantics* is the system within language that governs content, intent, and meanings of spoken and written language.

Assistive technology provides a variety of alternative augmentative communication (AAC) devices for students with communication disorders. AAC devices can be made for individual students and are intended to supplement oral and written language production. They can be aided or unaided, electronic or nonelectronic, simple or complex. Communication boards are fairly low-tech. High-tech equipment such as speech synthesizers and speech talkers allow individuals with communication disorders to "talk." Machines that create speech and language use icon systems that are accessed by touch or switches. Now with technological advances, AAC devices are smaller (some can be worn on the wrist), more capable, and more affordable.

An important note must be made here. Given the reality of today's schools, cultural diversity and even regional dialects can affect communication in classrooms. But these are differences, *not* disorders. Today's world is mobile. Transfer students from other parts of the United States as well as students from different countries and cultural backgrounds may have speech or language differences that affect their ability to participate in class. We'll talk more about students who are learning English later in this chapter. For now, remember this: difference is not necessarily a communication disorder.

Sensory Differences

Students with Hearing Impairments

Hearing loss falls into two primary categories: deafness and hard of hearing (having partial hearing). The U.S. Department of Education (2006) and IDEA guidelines define *deafness* as a hearing impairment "that is so severe that the child is impaired in processing linguistic information through hearing, with or without amplification, that adversely affects a child's educational performance" (p. 1261). It defines *hard of hearing (hearing impairment)* as "an impairment in hearing, whether permanent or fluctuating, that adversely affects a child's educational performance but that is not included under the definition of deafness" (p. 1262).

Mild hearing loss may go unnoticed. However, once it is detected, children with hearing impairments usually function well in the classroom, provided certain accommodations are made. For example, some may require a paraprofessional to assist them during the day. Arrangements must be made to accommodate the paraprofessional. Others may use a hearing ear dog as a helper. It is crucial that the other children understand the dog is there to work, not play. It may help to have the owner introduce the dog to the class and share information about how the two work together.

To best help students with hearing impairment, teachers should ask the student or caregiver what can be done to help (rather than assume that their ideas are what the student needs or wants). Teachers should consider learning and using basic sign language and using adaptive devices such as microphones and receivers as appropriate and available. Several devices are listed below. Teachers should adapt the physical environment and noise, instruction, and evaluation. It also is a good idea to partner the student with others who are able to verbalize or model expectations and procedures and who will help in emergency situations. Finally, teachers should be alert in watching and listening to their students for signs of behavior, appearance, and complaints that might signal possible hearing impairment.

Assistive technologies for students who are deaf or hard of hearing allow them to experience instruction with amplification or through their other senses. Assistive learning devices (ALDs) include hearing aids, cochlear implants, and a variety of FM (frequency-modulated) transmission devices. With FM technology, the speaker uses a microphone that transmits directly to the student's receiver. This helps overcome the distance and noise problems of classrooms, including background noise that can interfere with appropriate hearing and the hearing of subtle language sounds. Speech-to-print systems, including the teletypewriter-printer device (TTY or TT), telecommunication devices (TDD), and captioning on broadcast and media presentations, are other available tools.

Students with Visual Impairments

Vision impairments can range from low vision to functionally blind to totally blind. The U.S. Department of Education (2006) defines *visual disabilities* as "an impairment in vision that, even with correction, adversely affects a child's education performance. The term includes both partial sight and blindness" (p. 1265). Individuals with *low vision* primarily use vision for learning. They can read print, although they may depend on optical aids to see better. Individuals who are *functionally blind* use their senses of sound and touch for understanding, and braille for efficient reading and writing. Individuals who are *totally blind* have no visual input, and must rely completely on their senses of sound and touch and braille for reading and writing.

Students with visual impairments usually function quite well with the use of supplementary aids and services. For example, they may use a cane or a guide dog, use a braille machine or computer, or have a paraprofessional who works with them throughout the day. As with the hearing ear service dog, the children must understand that the guide dog is there to work, not play. If a braille machine or refreshable braille displays are used, arrangements should be made in the classroom so the equipment is accessible to the child and not distracting to classmates. IntelliKeys is a newer alternative that enables children with visual (or physical or cognitive) disabilities to access curriculum. The system has a programmable alternative keyboard, a touch pad, braille overlay, and a variety of software applications so children can type, enter numbers, navigate on-screen displays, and execute menu commands with ease. Again, the other children must understand the purpose of the machine. Likewise, arrangements must be made to accommodate the paraprofessional who accompanies the child to class.

Considerations for helping students with visual impairments are similar to those for helping students with hearing issues. Again, teachers should ask the student or caregiver what can be done to help (rather than assume that their ideas are what the student needs or wants), and adapt the physical environment, instruction to include auditory and tactile experiences, and evaluation. In the case of visual impairment, it is a good idea to partner the student with others who can verbalize or model expectations and procedures and who will help in emergency situations. And teachers should be vigilant in watching and listening to their students for signs of behavior, appearance, and complaints that might signal possible visual impairment.

Assistive technologies for students who are visually impaired or blind allow them to experience instruction by means of enlarged print or through other senses. A handheld magnifying glass is very low-tech. Bar magnifiers and writing guide sets are relatively inexpensive visual aid tools. Closed-circuit television (CCTV) displays enlarged print on a monitor. Optical character readers (OCR) or scanners with special software help students who need a print document that is not available electronically. The Magni-Cam, a camera embedded in a mouselike tool that can be rolled over printed pages, also enlarges print. When it is connected to a computer, the computer screen displays the magnified image. Computer word-processing features allow changes to print style and fonts, and duplicating machines allow for adjustments in printing size. Modern braille machines are more compact, portable, and convenient than before. Older students may use JAWS, an online library catalog that reads aloud text on a monitor. With JAWS, students can listen to text, take notes on a braille note taker, and then scan their notes with an optical character reader to convert them to print. The Kurzweil 3000 is a personal computer and desktop reading software that turns print into speech. Audio books through Bookshare.org and publishers may be available on request.

Behavioral Differences

Behavior disorder is a general category in special education for students who exhibit serious and persistent inappropriate behavior that results in social conflict and personal unhappiness, and affects school performance. The term implies that the child is causing trouble for someone else. Sometimes behaviors are described as excesses and deficits. *Excess behaviors* are the more blatant behaviors, such as tantrums and frequent fighting that quickly attract teachers' attention. However, students with *deficit behaviors* (students who are shy or withdrawn, have few friends, or seldom participate in class) also need attention.

Current research into the brain and how it relates to learning has recognized that many students behave as they do because of the way their brains function. Behavior that is outside the control of the individual is referred to as *neurological-based behavior* (NBB). It appears that NBB results from chemical imbalances, congenital brain differences, brain injuries, or brain diseases that, in turn, impair normal brain functioning. Two major characteristics of NBB are inconsistency and unpredictability (Kranowitz, 1998). Some students have difficulties in processing information, and their resultant behavior is inappropriate. Students who are diagnosed with NBB or other "mental health issues" usually show high degrees of inattention, hyperactivity, impulsivity, excess emotionality, anxiety, inconsistent emotional responses, unpredictable intense mood swings, withdrawal, and episodes of rage (Kranowitz, 1998; Greene, 2001; Papolos & Papolos, 2002; Hall & Hall, 2003; Cook, 2004).

Students Who Have Attention Deficit Disorder and Hyperactivity Disorder

Volumes also have been written about attention deficit disorder (ADD) and attention deficit hyperactivity disorder (AD/HD)—what they are, how to recognize the conditions, and how to treat the problems—and it almost seems that the more we learn about the disorders, the more remains to be learned. IDEA '04 includes AD/HD as a subcategory under "other health impairments," rather than listing it separately. The term *AD/HD* applies to three subtypes: attention deficit disorder, hyperactivity disorder, and a combination. Caregivers and teachers say they readily can spot the symptoms. In primary grades, teachers will notice children with short attention spans or who are easily distracted. In the intermediate grades, these same children daydream or have difficulty staying focused on work.

Students with AD/HD generally have difficulties with attention, hyperactivity, impulse control, emotional stability, or some combination of these. Children who are hyperactive show excessive, almost constant movement. They jiggle and wiggle and squirm and fuss, blurt out comments and answers, and generally bother the teacher and other students with their noises and movements. Based on its criteria for classification of AD/HD, in 2002 the American Psychiatric Association (APA) published statistics showing that approximately 3 to 8 percent of all school-age children may have attention deficit hyperactivity disorder (Root & Resnick, 2003; Biederman, 2005). Figure 8.1 lists criteria identified by the *Diagnostic and Statistical Manual of Mental Disorders (DSM-IV)* for AD/HD.

Although attentional distractibility and behavioral hyperactivity often go together, their exact relationship fluctuates. During the 1970s, evidence suggested that distractibility was the key to the hyperactivity syndrome. Recent research suggests that many things

Figure 8.1

DSM-IV Diagnostic Criteria for AD/HD

Inattention
  a. Often fails to pay attention to details or makes careless mistakes in schoolwork, work, or other activities
  b. Often has difficulty sustaining attention in tasks or play activities
  c. Often does not seem to listen when spoken to directly
  d. Often does not follow through on instructions and fails to finish schoolwork, chores, or duties in the workplace (not due to oppositional behavior)
  e. Often has difficulty organizing tasks and activities
  f. Often avoids, dislikes, or is reluctant to engage in tasks that require sustained mental effort
  g. Often loses things necessary for tasks and activities
  h. Is often easily distracted by extraneous stimuli
  i. Is often forgetful in daily activities

Hyperactivity
  a. Often fidgets with hands or feet or squirms in seat
  b. Often leaves seat in classroom or in other situations in which remaining seated is expected
  c. Often runs about or climbs excessively in situations in which it is inappropriate
  d. Often has difficulty playing or engaging in leisure activities quietly
  e. Often on the go or acts as if driven by a motor
  f. Often talks excessively

Impulsivity
  a. Often blurts out answers before questions have been completed
  b. Often has difficulty waiting turn
  c. Often interrupts or intrudes on others

Source: Reprinted with permission from the *Diagnostic and Statistical Manual of Mental Disorders,* Text Revision, 4th ed. Copyright 2000 by the American Psychiatric Association.

contribute to AD/HD, including both genetics and nongenetics, psychosocial factors, and neurological-based factors (Kauffman & Landrum, 2009, in Mastropieri & Scruggs, 2010, p. 72). While exact causes still are unknown, here are three important things to remember: (1) ADD can be diagnosed without hyperactivity but one does not have hyperactivity without ADD, (2) for the most part these behaviors are not deliberate, and (3) it takes a long time for these children to learn ways to compensate for or control them.

Students Who Are Emotionally Disturbed

IDEA '04 uses the term *emotional disturbance* to describe students who make emotional or behavioral responses over a long period of time that differ from acceptable norms and that adversely affect their educational performance.

To better inform yourself about these students, you should read their school histories, if available, and consult with the school psychologist, administrators, and other teachers who are involved with the student, taking note of any recommendations. Children who are emotionally disturbed are easily frustrated, are prone to outbursts of temper, or may be withdrawn. They need your patience and help learning to manage their self-control.

For students who are emotionally disturbed, teachers should be proactive. They should differentiate content, process, or product to best meet student needs and abilities. They should learn to recognize behavior clues that signal outbursts in order to anticipate a student's loss of control. They should avoid dwelling on past outbursts and incidents, overlook minor inappropriate behavior, reinforce acceptable behavior, and reduce stressors. This even means temporarily adjusting expectations if the student is having a bad day. A goal is for the student to learn from the current incident to prevent future outbursts. To ensure everyone's safety when a tantrum or outburst occurs, the student needs a safe, supervised area to cool down, and the teacher needs an action plan with the principal, counselor, and others.

Computers have been found to be especially helpful assistive tools for children with emotional or behavioral disorders. Computers are emotionally neutral systems with which children can interact and engage actively in learning, have fun, and achieve success. Answers in computer-assisted instruction are simply right or wrong. In other words, computers provide safe environments in which children are not judged or criticized.

Students Who Display Conduct Disorders

"Conduct disorder consists of a persistent pattern of antisocial behavior that significantly interferes with others' rights or with schools' and communities' behavioral expectations" (American Psychiatric Association, 2000, quoted in Turnbull et al., 2010, p. 187). Conduct disorder may result from abuse or neglect, but generally presents itself as defiant behavior. More specifically, conduct disorders fall into four categories: "(1) aggressive conduct, resulting in physical harm to people or animals; (2) property destruction; (3) deceitfulness or theft; and (4) serious rule violations, such as truancy and running away" (*DSM-IV-TR* by the American Psychiatric Association, 2000, in Turnbull, Turnbull, & Wehmeyer, 2010, p. 187).

Physical Differences

Students with Physical and Health Impairments

Orthopedic impairments (OI) are skeletal and muscular problems that adversely affect a child's educational performance. These impairments might be congenital (such as a clubfoot or absence of a limb); caused by disease (such as bone tuberculosis); or the result of other causes (such as cerebral palsy, amputations, fractures, or burns) (*Federal Register,* 1977).

Other Health Impairments (OHI) involve limited strength, vitality, or alertness due to chronic or acute health problems (such as asthma, diabetes, epilepsy, heart condition, leukemia, tuberculosis, sickle cell anemia, and others) that adversely affect a child's education performance (*Federal Register,* 1977).

Many students with physical or other health disorders remain in regular classrooms. However, some of these students may need medication or they may miss school for long periods of time. Consequently, teachers must consider carefully both the academic as well as the social experience of the child. In addition to asking the student or caregiver what can be done to help, teachers should consult with the school nurse or physical or occupational therapist, teachers, and other resources to understand the condition. Supportive actions include adjusting instruction, assignments, and time considerations to allow students to participate and complete work. Also, to the extent possible, teachers should support the child who is hospitalized during the school year, and allow sufficient time for catch-up work when welcoming the child back to school from an illness.

Multiple and Severe Handicapping Conditions

This category includes children who have a combination of conditions that result in severe educational needs that require accommodations by multiple special education programs because the needs are beyond the scope of one of the impairments. Thus, these students will have significant impairments in two or more areas: intellectual functioning, adaptive skills, motor development, sensory functioning, and communication skills. IEP teams are tasked with developing individualized plans that focus on the conditions and on what the student can do, not just on the limitations and what the student cannot do.

Managing Students with Other Needs

Now we turn attention to managing students with a variety of other challenges. These are not students who are identified or qualified for special education programs. Rather, these are students who bring different challenges to the classroom because of their language, their family diversity, or the economics of their situation. Based on history, the numbers for all these categories are likely to be higher with the results from the 2010 census.

Students from Diverse Language Groups

Language diversity obviously includes the presence of a language other than English. In addition, however, it includes issues of slang, pronunciation, and usage within a single language, such as African American or Hispanic American English. The U.S. Census Bureau (2003) reported that one in six school-age children in the United States speak a language other than English at home. In 2001 the U.S. Department of Education reported that students in the United States spoke over 400 different languages, with Spanish being the most prevalent. Current census data indicate that 74 percent of school-age children from immigrant families speak English "exclusively" or "very well." According to fairly recent reports by the National Clearinghouse for English Language Acquisition (2008), the U.S. Department of Education estimates that more than 5 million school-age children in the United States are English language learners—this is more than 10 percent of all K–12 students. Exact numbers here are challenging because student profiles vary. Children may have been born in the United States, immigrated, or come as refugees. They may speak only their

© H. L. Schwadron. Printed with permission.

native language, be bilingual in both English and their native language, or may speak primarily English. For these students, the term *students who are learning English* is a more positive label that celebrates the student's resource advantage of having two languages instead of one. These numbers have great significance for teachers because they will likely have students who are learning English in their classes. Census 2010 results are likely to show an increase in these numbers.

Of further concern is the matter of wrongly identifying language differences as a disability. In 2006 the U.S. Department of Education reported that 3.8 million students—11 percent of the student population—received services to learn English during the 2003–2004 school year, and 12 percent of these students also received services in special education (in Turnbull, Turnbull, & Wehmeyer, 2010, p. 79).

Numerous programs have been used for instructing students who are learning English. On a continuum they range from a separate curriculum to total immersion. Teachers who follow current research of language acquisition understand language development differently than their predecessors. They understand that learners of a second language need many opportunities to practice both their basic interpersonal communication skills (BICS) and cognitive academic language proficiency (CALP), and the practice must be meaningful and involve low stress. These teachers front-load vocabulary to help language learners with content. These teachers also believe that listening, speaking, reading, and writing skills should be linked and developed at the same time. Differentiating instructional strategies and classroom environment can support language acquisition for students who are learning English.

Students from Diverse Family Structures

The areas of diversity that we just described are well recognized and documented. An additional area of diversity is on the rise and requires educators' attention. It has to do with variations in the structure of families from which students come, especially as concern single, separated, or divorced parents; blended families; multigenerational families; foster care; children who are abused or neglected; and children who are homeless or living in poverty. Certainly, not all children in these situations are at risk. Yet, their family and home experiences can, on occasion, affect their performance in school.

Children of Single-Parent Families, Separated or Divorced Parents, Blended Families, Multigenerational Families, and Foster Care   "Half of all children will witness the breakup of a parent's marriage. Of these, close to half will also see the breakup of a parent's second marriage" (http://www.divorcereform.org). As of 1997, one million children in the United States were involved in a new divorce every year (http://www.divorcereform .org). Between 1970 and 1996, the number of children under the age of eighteen living with one parent increased from 12 to 28 percent (Teachman, 2004). For some children this means two homes. They spend time with each parent, sometimes split by school year and vacations and summer. Others split times during the school year itself. With a rise in cohabitation, now one in three children is born to unmarried parents (http://www.divorcereform .org). Whatever the situation—divorce, cohabitation, or when a parent marries or remarries—children may find themselves members of blended families, with new brothers and sisters in addition to a new parent.

For reasons of economics or culture, some children live in households that have multiple generations. In these homes, grandparents, parents, and children interact daily and share responsibilities, sometimes even for one another's care and well-being.

Large numbers of students who reside in foster care are placed there for a number of reasons, including serious abuse or neglect. "About 30% of children in foster care have several emotional, behavioral, or developmental problems. Physical health problems are also common" (AACAP, 2005, p. 1). Many also have issues of blame or guilt, insecurity, feelings of helplessness or not being wanted, and mixed emotions about attachments.

Additionally, for a multitude of reasons, large numbers of children spend time outside school without adult supervision. Current statistics indicate that approximately one of every ten elementary school children spends 4.5 hours a week unsupervised by adults (although younger children may be supervised by an older sibling). This condition translates into serious realities. When compared to children who are supervised, these children are more likely to experience stress, are more afraid to be alone, are angrier, have more academic and social problems, skip school more frequently, and are more likely to commit antisocial acts founded in peer pressure (Long & Long, 1989; Dwyer et al., 1990).

So we find that, compared to in past years, more children in school have single, separated, or divorced parents, reside in foster care homes, or are unsupervised. Teachers of these students must be alert for the probability of adjustment and custody concerns. Both concerns can affect a child's behavior and academic achievement.

Teachers, as well as some communities and business organizations, are working with caregivers and children to reduce unsupervised time for children. Structured before- and after-school activities, boys and girls clubs, homework clubs, and mentors are in place for this purpose. As a constant adult for the child, teachers should also do the following: recognize and accept emotions; listen to and talk to the child, encouraging healthy expression of these emotions; be sensitive in activities and class discussions; when possible, consider the use of mentors; and to the extent possible, maintain communication with families and caregivers.

Children Who Are Homeschooled

The concept of homeschooling has evolved over the years. It has become an alternative to public schools that has grown in popularity in the last decades and now presents itself in varied forms, including public charter schools, private schools, district-sponsored schools, and online schools. Children who are homebound for health reasons also may be taught at home by district-paid itinerant teachers. In 2007 the number of homeschoolers had grown to 1.5 million (National Center for Education Statistics, 2008). Many children are home-schooled because of growing concerns by caregivers over the quality of instruction and safety in schools.

For the most part, homeschooling has strict guidelines. Most states require that (1) instruction is equivalent to what is taught in public schools, (2) the instructing adult is qualified (but not necessarily certified) to teach, (3) local school authorities receive system-atic reports, and (4) instruction occurs a minimum number of hours per day.

While not a requirement, children who are homeschooled may spend at least part of their day or week in public school classrooms. Teachers should welcome children who are homeschooled when they spend time in regular classrooms. As with all students, they should partner students with classmates who can help show them the ropes around the school and in the classroom, vary instructional strategies to align with student learning styles, and maintain communication with caregivers.

Children Who Are Homeless or Living in Poverty

In addition to the ravages of natural disasters (such as earthquakes, Hurricanes Katrina and Rita, tornados in the Midwest, floods in the southlands, and wildfires across the southwest-ern parts of the United States), the increasing poverty and subsequent homelessness among families have resulted from several causes: unstable employment, low wages, loss of benefits and lack of affordable health care, decline in public assistance, foreclosures and a diminish-ing supply of affordable housing, mental illness and addiction disorders, and the rise in domestic violence.

"*Homeless* refers to individuals who lack a nighttime home, cannot afford housing, or live in provided public or private shelters, cars, or elsewhere" (Heflin & Rudy, 1991, quoted in Mastropieri, 2010, p. 115). Fact Sheets published in July 2009 by the National Coalition for the Homeless estimate that the number of children and families with children are fast-growing segments of the homeless population, and the numbers are staggering. They esti-mate that the number of children who are homeless ranges from 800,000 to 12 million, and recent estimates state that one in 50 children in the United States is homeless (National Coalition for the Homeless, 2009).

It is important to remember that these numbers are approximations. A group referred to as the "unsheltered" or "hidden" homeless also exists. These persons are experiencing homelessness but are living with family or friends, or in motels, automobiles, camp-grounds, or other places that are not counted by researchers and in surveys.

Economically disadvantaged is synonymous with *living in poverty*. Both terms refer to households that must spend more than one-third of their disposable income for food ade-quate to meet the family's nutritional needs. Payne's research (2001) reveals that about one-fourth of all students in the United States presently fall into the category of living in poverty. In 2005, 35.7 percent of persons living in poverty were children (U.S. Bureau of the Census, 2007, cited by the National Coalition for the Homeless, July 2009 report, "Why are people homeless?"). This is significantly higher than the poverty rate for any other age group.

Children who are homeless face challenges to enrolling in school. The U.S. Department of Education (2004) reports that "residency requirements, guardianship requirements, delays in transfer of school records, lack of transportation, and lack of immunization records often prevent homeless children from enrolling in school." Those who are able to enroll find regular attendance challenging: "While 87 percent of children and youth are enrolled in school, only 77 percent attend school regularly" (National Coalition for the Homeless, 2006).

The consequences for children who are homeless can be substantial. Children without permanent housing may suffer physically, emotionally, and educationally. Children who live in cars, shelters, campgrounds, and other such places are more likely than other children who are impoverished to miss school because of higher mortality rates, more severe health problems, and fewer immunization opportunities.

Communities and programs have come together to support students who are homeless. For example, a magnet school and adult volunteers and mentors provide stability, support, and opportunity for students who are homeless throughout the Phoenix, Arizona, area. The McKinney-Vento Homeless Assistance Act (formerly known as the Stewart B. McKinney Homeless Assistance Act of 1987, amended in 1990 and 1994, and reauthorized January 2002) is a federal response to homelessness that protects the educational needs of children who are homeless. In addition to tracking the attendance and addresses of students who are homeless, the Homeless Education Resource Outreach (HERO) program, developed in 1993 in Nashville, Tennessee, provides programs and resources to help with the educational needs of children and families who are homeless or in transition. The After-School Corporation (TASC), established in 1998, grants money raised from contributions and foundations to community-based organizations to run after-school programs in schools. TASC's ultimate goal is to make quality after-school and summer programs available to every child in the United States. Federal and local programs such as these are working to curtail this cycle, but homelessness and poverty are growing realities, nonetheless, and teachers are faced with the challenges of students who appear at school one day and then miss the next because they do not have a permanent residence.

Teachers can be powerful forces in the lives of children who are homeless or live in poverty, helping them both emotionally and academically. On an emotional level, teachers can listen and talk to the children; be sensitive in activities and discussions that touch on personal situations; and, to the extent possible, maintain communication with caregivers and provide information regarding appropriate and available support services.

On an academic level, teachers may partner students with classmates who can help show them the ropes around the school and classroom; find volunteers or mentors who can tutor and support the child at the shelter; vary instructional strategies and offer nontraditional options for the child to display understandings; be informed of appropriate services from the school, such as the free lunch program; and provide shelter staff with copies of homework assignments, newsletters, and calendars.

This has been a discussion of a few of the many special challenges teachers face every day with their students. The list of potential special needs is far from exhausted. Important for teachers to remember is that all children are entitled to life, liberty, and the pursuit of happiness. Also important to remember is that all children have the right to free public education. Our job as teachers is to support these rights. We can begin by making all children feel welcome, wanted, secure, and successful.

Instructional Strategies for Individual Differences

We now consider some of the broader approaches to managing today's diversity, some of which were mentioned in the previous chapter on managing students at work. However, remember this: Before you do anything with your students, you must get to know them. It is essential that you observe and evaluate your students, and if appropriate to do so, talk with their caregivers and previous teachers, so you know their special gifts and needs. Then remember to reevaluate frequently the effort and progress of each student.

Assistive Technology

Assistive technology—tools and devices that enhance the functioning of individuals with special challenges—gives students with special needs access to instruction. The Assistive Technology Act of 2004 supports the use of state-of-the-art technology, particularly targeting assistance for children with speech and motor challenges. With appropriate assistance, regular education teachers are better able to include all students in instruction and learning. Some of the available assistive technology was discussed earlier in relation to specific challenges.

Universal Design for Learning (UDL) and Differentiated Instruction

UDL refers to the design of materials and activities to make the content accessible to *all* children. UDL often is rooted in technology, "creates alternatives open to all students; is part of the standard delivery of instruction; and provides multiple and flexible options for presentation, expression, and engagement" (Smith & Tyler, 2010, p. 36). Teachers who *differentiate instruction* use alternative ways to deliver content instruction. They also vary the process by which students can make sense of the content, or they provide various ways for students to demonstrate the understanding and learning they take away from the content.

Multi-Age Classes

When students of varying ages and abilities come together as a community, they are able to contribute to the learning environment. Successful multi-age classes practice differentiated instruction.

Looped Classes

Keeping teachers and students together for two or more years results in increased familiarity and understanding for the teacher, the students, and the caregivers. It increases the teacher's understanding of the students' needs and provides a better-matched academic program for them. It also increases student and caregiver confidence in the teacher.

Team Teaching

Teachers at the same grade level can agree to team teach. They share students, but because they teach specific subjects or ability levels, they may see different students at different times. Team teaching maximizes the teachers' instructional time and energies, but requires cooperation, planning, coordination, and flexibility.

Student Study Teams (SSTs)

The primary goal of the SST is to review the apparent needs of the student and develop a plan of action to further investigate and then best meet those needs. SSTs or similar meetings are part of the Response to Intervention process and occur prior to IEP meetings that, by law, require more formal documentation and action. In addition to the teacher, who initiates the SST, and the caregivers, the team may include former teachers, an administrator, a counselor or other service provider, and a student advocate.

Response to Intervention (RTI)

Intended to reduce the number of students mistakenly labeled as learning-disabled, the RTI process is a multitiered system of frequent assessments and multiple interventions used to determine whether any student, regardless of type of disability, needs more intensive instruction. Skill sequences are taught and assessed throughout the process. You can read more about the RTI process in Appendix A.

Individualized Education Programs (IEPs)

PL 94-142 describes the conditions of IEPs. Regular and special education teachers, caregivers, and other involved parties come together to develop educational plans for individual students who qualify for an IEP. IEPs must be referenced to the core curriculum. Also, they must include statements of the student's current performance, long- and short-range goals for the student, details of the nature and duration of instructional services for meeting the goals, as well as an overview of the intended evaluation methods.

Supplementary Pullout Instruction

Sometimes students are taught best when they leave their classroom for special instruction. Although this sounds contrary to the essence of inclusion, it is not. For some students, pullout instruction is used to reinforce skills being taught in the classroom. For students with higher abilities, pullout instruction can be another way to enrich their educational program.

Schedules are probably the biggest challenge related to pullout programs. They must be planned carefully so students do not miss or interrupt important instruction. Teachers must coordinate times with other teachers, service providers, and resource specialists, and stay on schedule in their own classrooms.

Transitions also require finessing so they are not disruptive. Teachers must think about students as they leave and return to the class. Because students need to be brought quickly into the instruction or activity that is in progress, teachers should establish and have all students practice routines for transitions: leaving and entering the classroom, locating appropriate materials, and the like. Teachers should post organizers and visual instructional plans for activities and assignments for students to refer to as they begin to work. They should arrange for partners or buddies to help returning or new students settle into the activity or assignment, or have shorter activities available for the rest of the class to work on while they help the returning or new students themselves.

Contracts

Contracts provide individualized agreements for a student's work, effort, and/or behavior. They include specific goals, objectives, or benchmarks; relevant materials; assessment expectations; and incentives. Furthermore, contracts are agreed to by the teacher and the student. Because contracts are individualized, they give the teacher and student the opportunity to modify the activity or assignment in ways that are best for the student. Contracts also may be extended to involve caregivers and align with home behavior and work expectations.

Learning Groups and Peer Learning

Partners or groups of up to six students often provide learning benefits. Spencer Kagan (Kagan & Kagan, 2009) describes four principles that are essential for true cooperative groups: positive interdependence, individual accountability, equal participation, and simultaneous interaction (PIES). Additionally, teachers should remember two other facts about groups: (1) Groups don't simply happen; group structure must be taught and rehearsed. To be successful, students must learn and practice the skills of cooperation such as listening, sharing, and being responsible. (2) Groups seem to work best when every student in the group has a specific job with specific responsibility to contribute to the group effort, and is accountable for that responsibility. For example, literacy circles in groups of five might have a discussion director, a character captain, a summarizer, an illustrator, and a materials manager. (You may wish to revisit the discussion of cooperative learning in Chapter 6.)

Peer and Cross-Age Tutors and Cross-Grade Partnerships

Most of us learn better when we have to teach someone else. Student tutors and partners provide another opportunity for individualized assistance and attention. The experience gives older students the opportunity to be a mentor and a role model to someone younger. The younger children enjoy individual attention from someone who is closer to them in age and experience.

Special Programs

Special programs involving community, businesses, and foundation partnerships exist around the country. Several of these were mentioned earlier in the chapter. These programs support academic achievement and social growth, and offer enrichment activities for all children.

This brings to an end our considerations for managing special groups of students. In our next chapter, we look deeper into how to manage overall student behavior. Before moving ahead, please take time to explore these end-of-chapter activities.

Parting Thought

Knowledge is of two kinds: We know a subject ourselves or we know where we can find information upon it.

—Samuel Johnson

Summary Self-Check

Check off the following as you either understand or become able to apply them.

☐ Inclusion is a way of life, an attitude that values all children.

☐ Legislation and civil rights laws affecting inclusion: Individuals with Disabilities Education Act (IDEA), No Child Left Behind (NCLB), Assistive Technology Act (ATA or Tech Act), Section 504 of the Rehabilitation Act, and the Americans with Disabilities Act (ADA).

☐ Response to Intervention (RTI) is intended to reduce the number of students mistakenly labeled as learning-disabled.

☐ Exceptionality includes a wide range of student abilities and challenges.

☐ Students with attention deficit disorder and attention deficit hyperactivity disorder (AD/HD) have difficulties with attention, hyperactivity, impulse control, emotional stability, or some combination of these.

☐ Language diversity is independent of ethnicity and race.
  - *Students who are learning English* is a more positive label that celebrates the student's resource advantage of speaking two languages instead of one.
  - Students who are learners of English need many opportunities to practice basic interpersonal communication skills (BICS), cognitive academic language proficiency (CALP), and listening, speaking, reading, and writing.

☐ Family diversity is a broad category of family and life situations that includes realities and challenges related to single, separated, or divorced parents; blended families; multigenerational families; foster care; children who are abused or neglected; children who are homeschooled; and children who are homeless or living in poverty.

☐ Tools and strategies for managing individual differences include assistive technology, universal design for learning (UDL) and differentiated instruction, multi-age classes, looped classes, team teaching, Student Study Teams (SSTs), the Response to Intervention (RTI) process, Individualized Education Programs (IEPs), supplementary pullout programs, contracts, learning groups, peer and cross-age tutors, and cross-grade partnerships.

Activities for Reflection and Discussion

1. Take a moment to review the statements in the Preview–Review Guide at the beginning of this chapter. Put a check mark in the *Review* column next to any statement with which you now agree. How have your thoughts changed since reading this chapter?

2. Interview at least two teachers about their experiences with students with special needs and the support they received from others (administrators, caregivers, support providers, doctors, and professional organizations) when the students were in their class.

3. In your opinion, which of the diversity issues discussed in this chapter pose the greater challenges to the teacher? to the students who are in those groups? to other students in the class? Describe how you will include those students (and their caregivers) in your class community.

4. You have two students who are struggling. Describe how the RTI process will be used to determine whether they require special education services.

5. Anticipate that you have a new fifth grader who is learning English. How will you instruct that student in language arts and reading? math? social studies or science? How will your instruction be different if the student is a primary student (K–2) rather than an intermediate or upper-grade student (3–6)?

6. How will you adapt your classroom, instruction, and activities to include a student who is in a wheelchair?

7. Describe how you will use peer and cross-age tutors and a buddy class for your first graders. What kinds of activities might you have the two classes work on together?

8. Write a sample contract to use with a student of higher ability who is interested in studying about immigration during the fifth-grade unit on the topic. Write a sample contract to use with a student of lower ability for the same unit.

Webliography

Assistive Tools

http://www.intellitools.com

Exceptionality (GATE and Special Education)

National Association for Gifted Children: http://www.nagc.org

National Center for Education Statistics: http://www.nces.ed.gov/pubs2009/2009030.pdf

National Center on Response to Intervention: http://www.rti4success.org

National Coalition for the Homeless. (2008, 2009). See link to Factsheets: http://www.nationalhomeless.org

The After-School Corporation: http://www.tascorp.org

U.S. Department of Education. (2006). *Fast facts: Students with disabilities:* http://www.nces.ed.gov/gasftfacts/display/asp?ID-64

What you need to know about IDEA 2004. Response to Intervention (RTI): New ways to identify specific learning disabilities: http://www.wrightslaw.com/info/rti.index.htm

Families and Foster Care

American Academy of Child & Adolescent Psychiatry: http://www.aacap.org/cs/root/facts_for_families/foster_care.

Americans for Divorce Reform. Divorce Statistics Collection: http://www.divorcereform.org.

National Center on Family Homelessness. *Homeless Children: America's New Outcasts.* **(1999):** http://www.familyhomelessness.org/pdf/fact_outcasts.pdf.

Miscellaneous Facts

National Center for Education Statistics: http://www.nces.ed.gov/pubs2009/2009030.pdf.

Partnerships (schools and families)

The After-School Corporation: http://www.tascorp.org.

Poverty and Homelessness

People and households. Poverty: http://www.ccnsus.gov/

National Coalition for the Homeless (2008, 2009). See links to Factsheets: http://www.nationalhomeless.org

- *NCH fact sheet #10: Education of homeless children and youth.* (2006).
- *NCH fact sheet #13: Homeless youth.* (2008).
- *Homeless families with children.* (2009).
- *Who is homeless?* (2009).
- *Why are people homeless?* (2009).
- *How many people experience homelessness?* (2009).

Legal Actions

Gifted and Talented Students Act of 1978, PL 95-561. (1978).

Individuals with Disabilities Act (IDEA) of 1990, PL 101-476. (1990). Reauthorization of IDEA. (2004).

McKinney-Vento Homeless Assistance Act. Formerly known as the Stewart B. McKinney Homeless Assistance Act of 1987. (Amended 1990 and 1994, Reauthorized January 2002).

Reports and Conferences

Federal Register. (1997, August 23). Washington, DC: U.S. Government Printing Office.

Institute of Education Sciences (IES). National Center for Education Statistics. (2008). Brief: *1.5 million homeschooled students in the United States in 2007.*

National Clearinghouse for English Language Acquisition. (2008). *The growing numbers of limited English proficient students: 1995/06-2005-06.* Washington, DC: Author.

U.S. Census Bureau (2003). *Language use and English-speaking ability: 2000.* Retrieved December 18, 2003, from: www.census.gov/prod/2003pubs/c2kbr-29.pdf.

U.S. Census Bureau Public Information Office. (2003, October 8). News release. Retrieved December 18, 2003, from: www.census.gov/Press-Release/www.releases/archives/census_2000/001406.html

U.S. Census Bureau. (2005).

U.S. Department of Education. (2004). Education for Homeless Children and Youth Program, 2004. Available at: http://www.ed.gov

U.S. Department of Health and Human Services. (2002).

References and Recommended Readings

American Psychiatric Association. (2000). *Diagnostic and statistical manual of mental disorders* (4th ed., revised). Washington, DC: Author.

Biederman, J. (2005). Attention-deficit/hyperactivity disorder: A selective overview. *Biological Psychiatry, 57*(11), 1215–1220.

Cary, S. (1997). *Second language learners.* Los Angeles: Galef Institute.

Cook, P. (2004). *Behavior, learning, and teaching.* Applied studies in FAS/FAE (Distance Education Curricula). Winnipeg, Manitoba, Canada: Red River College.

Crowe, C. (2008, November). Solving behavior problems together. *Educational Leadership, 66*(3), 44–47.

Dwyer, K., Richardson, J., Danley, K., Hansen, W., Sussman, S., Brannon, B., et al. (1990, September). Characteristics of eighth grade students who initiate self-care in elementary and junior high school. *Pediatrics, 86*(3), 448–454.

Good, T., & Brophy, J. (2008). *Looking into classrooms* (10th ed.). Boston: Allyn & Bacon.

Gorski, P. (2008, April). The myth of the "culture of poverty." *Educational Leadership, 66*(3), 32–36.

Greene, R. (2001). *The explosive child.* New York: HarperCollins.

Grimes, K., & Stevens, D. (2009, May). Glass, bug, mud. *Phi Delta Kappan, 90*(9), 677–680.

Hall, P., & Hall, N. (2003). *Educating oppositional and defiant children.* Alexandria, VA: ASCD.

Heflin, L., & Rudy, K. (1991). *Homeless and in need of special education.* Reston, VA: Council for Exceptional Children.

Improving instruction for students with learning needs. (2007, February). [Special Issue]. *Educational Leadership, 64*(5). Alexandria, VA: ASCD.

Kagan, S., & Kagan, M. (2009). *Cooperative learning.* San Clemente, CA: Kagan Publishing.

Kauffman, J., & Landrum, T. (2009). *Characteristics of emotional and behavioral disorders of children and youth* (9th ed.). Upper Saddle River, NJ: Merrill/Pearson.

Kirk, S., Gallagher, J., Anastasiow, N., & Coleman, M. (2006). *Educating exceptional children* (11th ed.). Boston: Houghton Mifflin.

Kranowitz, C. (1998). *The out-of-sync child.* New York: Skylight Press.

Long, L., & Long, T. (1989). Latchkey adolescents: How administrators can respond to their needs. *NASSP Bulletin, 73,* 102–108.

Mastropieri, M., & Scruggs, T. (2010). *The inclusive classroom: Strategies for effective differentiated instruction* (4th ed.). Upper Saddle River, NJ: Merrill.

Neuman, S. Use the science of what works to change the odds for children at risk. (2009, April). *Phi Delta Kappan, 90*(8), 582–587.

Papolos, D., & Papolos, J. (2002). *The bipolar child.* New York: Broadway Books.

Payne, R. (2008, April). Nine powerful practices. *Educational Leadership, 65*(7), 48–52.

Payne, R. (2009, January). Poverty does not restrict a student's ability to learn. *Phi Delta Kappan, 90*(5), 371–372.

Payne, R. (2001). *A framework for understanding poverty*. Highlands, TX: aha! Process, Inc.

Poverty and learning (2008, April). [Special Issue]. *Educational Leadership, 65*(7). Alexandria, VA: ASCD.

Root, R., & Resnick, R. (2003). An update on the diagnosis and treatment of attention-deficit/hyperactivity disorder in children. *Professional Psychology: Research and Practice, 34*(1), 34–41.

Sato, M., & Lensmire, T. (2009, January). Poverty and Payne: Supporting teachers to work with children of poverty. *Phi Delta Kappan, 90*(5), 365–370.

Smith, D., & Tyler, N. (2010). *Introduction to special education Making a difference* (7th ed.). Upper Saddle River, NJ: Merrill.

Smith, J., Fien, H., & Paine, S. (2008, April). When mobility disrupts learning. *Educational Leadership, 65*(7), 59-63.

Supporting English Language Learners. (2009, April). [Special Issue]. *Educational Leadership, 66*(7). Alexandria, VA: ASCD.

Teachman, J. (2004, January). The childhood living arrangements of children and characteristics of their marriages. *Journal of Family Issues, 25*, 86–111.

Turnbull, A., Turnbull, R., & Wehmeyer, M. (2010). *Exceptional lives: Special education in today's schools* (6th ed.). Upper Saddle River, NJ: Merrill.

Turnbull, R., Huerta, N., & Stowe, M. (2009). *What every teacher should know about the Individuals with Disabilities Education Act as amended in 2004.* (2nd ed.) Boston: Pearson.

Yell, M., & Drasgow, E. (2005). *No Child Left Behind A guide for professionals*. Upper Saddle River, NJ: Pearson Merrill.

Ysseldyke, J., & Algozzine, B. (1995). *Special education: A practical approach for teachers* (3rd ed.). Boston: Houghton Mifflin.

Zapt, S. (2008, November). Reaching the fragile student. *Educational Leadership, 66*(1), 67–70.

Trade Book

Sollman, C., Emmons, B., & Paolini, J. (1994). *Through the cracks.* Worcester, MA: Davis Publications.

PEARSON
myeducationlab)

Go to the Topic: **Managing Special Groups** in the MyEducationLab (www.myeducation lab.com) for your course, where you can:

- Find learning outcomes for **Managing Special Groups** along with the national standards that connect to these outcomes.
- Examine challenging situations and cases presented in the IRIS Center Resources.
- Use interactive Simulations in Classroom Management to practice decision making and to receive expert feedback on classroom management choices.

Managing Student Behavior

Everyone stood in awe of the lion tamer in the cage, with half a dozen lions all under the control of his "consequences." Everyone, that is, except the teacher . . .

—June Dostal

Preview–Review Guide

Before you read the chapter, and based on what you know, think you know, or assume, take a minute to put a check mark in the **Preview** column if you agree with the statement. When you finish the chapter, take time to reread the statements and respond in the **Review** column. Reflective discussions can develop because many of the statements are not clearly "yes" or "no."

Preview   **Review**

1. _____ For many years, discipline has been high on the list of teacher and public   _____
   concerns about education.

2. _____ Kounin says successful behavior management relates to withitness   _____
   and lesson management.

3. _____ Dreikurs and Albert believe that behavior comes from a need to belong,   _____
   and individuals may choose hidden goals in order to satisfy this need.

4. _____ The Canters insist that nothing should be allowed to interfere with   _____
   teachers' rights to teach and students' rights to learn.

5. _____ Glasser contends that cooperative learning teams help meet students'   _____
   needs for socializing.

6. _____ After studying teachers who seem naturally adept at discipline, Jones   _____
   was able to identify and focus on several clusters of teacher skills.

7. _____ Kagan, Kyle, and Scott explain that student positions—the conditions   _____
   for disruptive behavior—tell teachers *why* students do what they do.

8. _____ Coloroso responds to student mistakes, mischief, and mayhem by   _____
   applying three Rs (respect, responsibility, and reciprocity).

9. _____ Marshall says that positivity, choice, and reflection help students learn   _____
   to conduct themselves responsibly.

10. _____ A good discipline plan meets students' needs; teacher needs are   _____
    basically irrelevant to its success.

Chapter Objectives

After reading Chapter 9, students will demonstrate understanding of

- realities and challenges that affect student behavior

- evolution of programs to manage student behavior

- steps toward building a personal discipline plan

through their active participation in discussions and the end-of-chapter activities for reflection.

Gallup polls are published annually by Phi Delta Kappa, a professional organization for educators. According to the polls of teacher and public attitudes toward education, for nearly four decades, discipline (misbehavior in the classroom) has been listed among their top concerns in public education. (See Gallup polls concerning public attitude toward education, published annually since 1969, in *Phi Delta Kappan*.) Consequently, a problem to solve or an essential or guiding question for this chapter might be: *How can I best manage and help students manage misbehavior and other behavior issues?*

Formal attention to classroom discipline began in the early 1950s, and pioneer work at that time laid the foundation for much of today's classroom discipline. In the past, the approach to discipline was fairly strict and teacher-controlled. Teachers could demand, scold, speak sternly, threaten, and keep students after school—all to force students to conduct themselves appropriately. Teachers also had the backing of administrators, caregivers, and the community. Over time, programs evolved to be more student-centered. In fact, some would say that today's popular programs have gone to extremes in allowing students rather than teachers to make choices concerning students and school. Presently, a number of discipline programs are being used by educators to manage student behavior.

How Serious Is Disruptive Behavior?

Discipline is a serious and ever-growing problem. Many see undesirable trends and conditions in society as contributing factors. Some blame excessive attention to students' civil rights and due process over teachers' rights to teach in a productive and safe environment. Some, including education critic Alfie Kohn, criticize teaching and discipline that do things *to* students rather than *involve* student as partners in the process. Still others, including Canadian consultant Ronald Morrish, even blame current discipline programs, saying that they stress *management* and making the environment functional, rather than stressing discipline and teaching students to behave properly.

Disruptive behavior in the classroom is any behavior that interferes with productive teaching and learning. Charles (2011) defines disruptive behavior as any behavior that,

Case Study 9.1   A Typical Day for Some

FOCUS QUESTIONS

How typical do you believe the actions and behavior of Mr. Wilson's students to be?

What are the reasons that students are acting the way they are? What steps should Mr. Wilson take to install a discipline plan that will work for him and his students?

Mr. Wilson is a beginning third-grade teacher. He has 28 students in his class. It's November, and every day seems to be a little worse than the previous day.

His students are well intentioned, but most of the children have high energy, and most mornings they yell and push as they enter the room. This morning Zack and Ty are fighting as they enter.

Many of the students dawdle by the cubbies as they remove coats and put away their backpacks. Once they finally sit down at their desks, they conjure reasons to get up and move about the room: "My pencil is broken." "I have to go to the bathroom." "I need a drink of water." "I left my homework in my backpack." "Can I feed the gerbil?"

Often Mr. Wilson teaches lessons that are scripted in the teacher's edition of the textbooks. His routine is to present the new material and give students seatwork to practice the material.

On average, it takes about 10 minutes for students to line up for recess or lunch. Rather than cut lunch short, Mr. Wilson tells students to walk together in straight, quiet lines to the cafeteria.

Maddie often argues when Mr. Wilson assigns work or a task. Tim often says, "You can't make me do this." Sasha asks countless questions about every task. Becca pretends to work by doodling on her worksheet.

Finally, a bell rings and another day ends.

through intent or thoughtlessness, (1) interferes with teaching or learning, (2) threatens or intimidates others, or (3) oversteps society's standards of moral, ethical, or legal behavior. Fred Jones (2007) notes that teachers in a typical classroom lose about half their teaching time because of students' disruptive behavior. Such behavior is not always bad behavior. In fact, it usually is nothing more than talking, goofing off, or moving about the room without permission. However, disruptions, even those considered benign, lower achievement and often damage class morale. Consider the following:

- *Teachers' rights to teach.* Disruptive behavior interferes with the teacher's basic right to teach, which also affects student learning and produces much teacher frustration.

- *Students' rights to learn.* Students who make irresponsible choices disrupt learning for themselves and others, which in turn leads to lowered academic achievement.

- *Wasted time.* Teachers dealing with classroom disruptions lose enormous amounts of time that would and should be devoted to instruction—50 percent according to Jones's observations.

- *Stress, motivation, and energy.* Disruptive behavior increases stress and weakens motivation and energy by wearing on teachers and students, and perpetuating a poor attitude toward learning.

- *Classroom climate.* Disruptive behavior at times can produce a climate of fearfulness and stress for students and teachers alike.

- *Teacher–student relationships.* Disruptive behavior dissolves trust so cooperative relationships never develop adequately.

Many beginning teachers have naïve expectations of students—remember Alexa Smart in Chapter 1? They believe that if the teacher is caring, students will make responsible choices and will behave appropriately—they will be orderly, courteous, helpful, honest, respectful of property and others, willing to work, and relatively quiet. But what teachers often encounter are minor but ongoing misbehaviors and even unruliness that in some cases escalate to open hostility, defiance, and physical aggression. As Jones (2007) observed, although 95 percent of disruptive behavior involves little more than talking, moving around the room without permission, and simply wasting time, almost all teachers report that disruptive behavior interferes with their teaching, sometimes greatly.

The disquieting fact is that student behavior, reflective of society in general, continues to worsen. Curwin and Mendler (2002) have observed these trends:

- More students now are behaviorally and academically at risk of failing in schools.

- More students now are disruptive than in the past, and the rate is increasing.

- Children are becoming more disruptive at younger ages.

- Children are more violent.

- Many children lack any feeling of caring or remorse.

- Teachers describe students as more aggressive and hostile.

It is no wonder that teachers and the public have concerns.

Special Challenges Related to Economic Realities

A reality of today's society is that a growing number of students come from economically disadvantaged backgrounds. About one in four of all students in the United States are identified as students living in poverty. They are members of households that must spend more than one-third of their disposable income for food adequate to meet the family's nutritional needs (Payne, 2001). Some are students from generational—long term—poverty. Among the challenges related to poverty are survival, personal relationships, and entertainment. These children are more likely to be developmentally delayed, and they often feel undervalued and powerless. Poverty is a key factor that limits student success in school (Pellegrino, 2005), and these children are more likely to be early school drop-outs (Payne, 2001).

Students who come from poverty follow their own set of hidden rules to survive, rules that differ from the predominant values of schools and most teachers. Revisit the suggestions in Chapter 8 for working more effectively with students from disadvantaged backgrounds. In particular, keep these four suggestions in mind to help waylay or manage misbehavior:

■ Learn as much as you can about the students and their value systems—what they consider important, how they relate to each other and to adults, and how they relate to teachers and schools in general.

■ Learn as much as you can about the hidden rules that govern group and personal behavior.

■ Show acceptance of your students, their families, and their lifestyles.

■ Link the curriculum to students' out-of-school experiences.

Special Challenges Related to Neurological-Based Behavior

Chapter 8 included a discussion of atypical behavior that is neurological-based (NBB). Childhood mental health conditions now are very common. The major conditions of NBB diagnoses that adversely affect students and appear prominently in current literature were listed in Chapter 8. Other disorders include explosive behavior disorder, paranoia, obsessive compulsive disorder (OCD), substance dependence, phobias, eating disorders, and Tourette's syndrome.

On average, about one in five students has one or more mental health conditions that affect behavior in school (National Institute of Mental Health, 2008). Additionally, an estimated one in ten students is "notably erratic in selecting what they say and do" by displaying behaviors that are outside the usual boundaries of self-control (Charles, 2011). Neurological differences often are difficult to diagnose. Students may not receive the help they need until several years after they experience the onset of symptoms (Papolos & Papolos, 2002).

Overly simplified, students with these diagnoses behave as they do because of the way their brain works. Students have difficulties in processing information because of compromised cerebral functioning resulting from chemical imbalances, congenital brain differences, brain injuries, or brain diseases. In particular, difficulties in behavior, language, and/or academics may indicate NBB.

Inconsistency and unpredictability are two major characteristics of NBB (Kranowitz, 1998). Students may be inattentive, hyperactive, impulsive, anxious, or withdrawn. They may exhibit extreme or inconsistent emotional responses, unpredictable intense mood swings, or rage (Kranowitz, 1998; Greene, 2001; Papolos & Papolos, 2002; Hall & Hall, 2003; Cook, 2004).

Most NBB disorders are treated with medications, some of which may adversely affect students' ability to focus or concentrate (National Institute of Mental Health, 2008). Students diagnosed with any form of NBB present challenges to teachers and others. Review the suggestions in Chapter 8 for working more effectively with these students, but in particular keep these four suggestions in mind to help avert or manage misbehavior:

■ Learn as much as you can about the condition, including how individuals with the condition relate to each other, and how they relate to teachers and school in general.

- Establish a positive and nurturing rapport with the students and modify and structure the classroom environment and activities.

- Be accepting of students' limitations—you cannot change them through repeated criticism.

- When appropriate to do so, work closely with diagnostic and support staff and utilize any special services and resources to their fullest extent.

Another Growing Challenge—Bullying

We previously discussed bullying in Chapters 4 and 7. Bullying is a serious problem both in and out of school that affects not just victims and bystanders, but probably most members of the school community. Data from the National Center for Educational Statistics (2007) indicate the following (in Jones & Jones, 2010, pp. 5–6):

- Twenty-eight percent of 12- to 18-year-old students reported being bullied at school during the last six months. Of these,
  - 53 percent reported being bullied once or twice during this time period.
  - 25 percent said they had been bullied once or twice a week.
  - 11 percent reported being bullied once or twice a month.
  - 8 percent reported being bullied almost daily.
  - 19 percent reported that the bullying involved being made fun of.
  - 15 percent reported being the subject of rumors.
  - 9 percent said they were pushed, shoved, tripped, or spit on.
  - 24 percent reported they were injured.

- Seventy-nine percent reported being bullied inside the school building; 28 percent reported being bullied outside on school grounds.

- Older students report less bullying: 37 percent of sixth graders; 28 percent of ninth graders, and 20 percent of twelfth graders reported being bullied. In other words, bullying often begins in elementary school, peaks in middle school, and lessens in high school.

Horn et al. (2004, cited in Webb et al., 2010) published several realities. (1) Males tend to use physical bullying; females tend to use social bullying such as rejection, exclusion, slander, and rumors. (2) Victims/targets tend to be most susceptible to bullies because of "age, gender, physical weakness, timidity, insecurity, poor self esteem, mental capacity, or lack of protection from peers or teachers" (p. 256). (3) Bullying is most likely to occur where there is a lack of adult supervision and a structured environment, such as outside or in hallways, lunchrooms, and bathrooms.

The dynamics of bullying is a topic of interest for other researchers. Olweus is a prominent name in this area (one website is http://www.olweus.org). Also, Barbara Coloroso examines all the participants in the cycle of violence in her book *The Bully, the Bullied, and the Bystander* (2002). You also can visit her website at http://www.kidsareworthit.com.

Cyberbullying

Cyberbullying, the newest form of bullying, occurs online. Also called Internet harassment, cyberbullying involves the use of electronic media—technologies such as e-mails, instant messages (IMs), chat rooms, Web logs (blogs), websites, personal digital assistants (PDAs), and cell phones—to willfully harass or threaten individuals or groups with words or pictures.

A 2004 study by i-Safe America (in Larrivee, 2009, p. 94) found that 58 percent of fourth through eighth graders reported "having had mean or hurtful things said to them online" and 53 percent admitted to participating in this behavior with others. Nearly 33 percent had been threatened and 42 percent said they had been bullied online, but 58 percent of those who experienced harmful behavior did not inform parents of the incidents.

As we have said, the incidence of bullying is present in schools and communities, and is serious. Bullying is not a normal developmental stage for young people. Rather, it often is the harbinger of more serious behavior—violence, weapons, and assault offenses (Nansel et al., 2003, cited in Levin & Nolan, 2010, p. 60). Too often, however, teachers are unaware of bullying because they aren't present when and where it occurs, or they miss subtleties that may exist in the form of threatening stares, notes, or gestures.

Here's something else to think about. Take a moment to consider how much teachers and other adults may, in fact, actually exacerbate bullying. We tell students not to tattle. We tell students to get along with others and work out problems themselves. Over time, by doing so, we establish the foundation for a code of silence for students not to tell adults about problems, including when they witness or are the target of bullying (Larrivee, 2010, p. 93).

Early Signs, Prevention, and Intervention

Most school districts have adopted antibullying policies, and many public schools now have some program in place to prevent and/or reduce bullying and violence. These programs provide activities in and out of school, including meetings and role-playing to help students manage situations when bullying occurs. In addition to increased security, personnel, and equipment, most schools now provide

" NO DAVID, NO ONE SQUEALED ON YOU. I SAW YOUR PRANK ON YOUTUBE."

Permission by Dave Carpenter.

published discipline codes, life skills training, peer mediation, and conflict resolution programs.

These efforts are effective, but awareness and recognition of early warning signs, followed with appropriate referrals, are needed to waylay and end the cycle of violence. This means vigilance and follow-through by teachers, administrators, caregivers, and the community to spot the signs in troubled youth. Dwyer, Osher, and Warger (1998) identify early warning signs of potentially violent youth. The signs include social withdrawal; excessive feelings of isolation or rejection; history of discipline problems or impulsive, violent, or aggressive behavior; being a victim of violence, or feeling picked on and persecuted; and low self-esteem, low school interest, and poor academic performance. Gang membership and drug and alcohol use also signal potential behavioral problems (in Webb, Metha, & Jordan, 2010, p. 257).

Awareness is an essential first step in developing successful programs. However, experts concur that effective programs are organized and systematic and involve students, caregivers, the community, and the school. Thus, existing plans for prevention and intervention should be adjusted to meet the circumstances, population, and needs of individual schools, based on current needs assessments. Peterson and Skiba (2001, referenced in Bloom, 2009, pp. 208–209) attribute the following eight elements to successful programs:

- *Alternatives to conflict and violence.* Conflict resolution and social instruction can occur in class meetings, peer mediation, and formal teaching and guided practice of appropriate social behavior.

- *Classroom strategies to prevent and reduce disruptive behavior.* This includes prompt and efficient handling of minor misbehaviors before they become crises.

- *Partnerships.* Partnerships among the school, families and caregivers, and the community support successful programs.

- *Early identification and support.* Identification of early warning signs and screenings, and early positive behavior support can do much to avert more serious problems.

- *School and district records.* Records of disciplinary actions, referrals, suspensions, and expulsions help schools and officials evaluate disciplinary processes and identify risk factors.

- *Schoolwide disciplinary policies, rules, and procedures.* Teams develop, implement, and evaluate practices. Teams also can provide consistency, awareness, and communication to all students, staff, and the community.

- *Positive behavioral support teams.* Behavioral support teams can accomplish two things. In addition to assisting in planning, implementing, and evaluating positive behavior support, they can provide mandated IDEA assessments.

- *Crisis and security planning.* Proactively, schools should have appropriate plans for security, personnel, and equipment in place to handle crises should they occur.

The Movement Toward New Discipine

Villa, Thousand, and Nevin (2010) depict effective discipline as a pyramid (see Figure 9.1). Their revised five-level pyramid presents a system of teachers, community, and students

Figure 9.1

Self-Discipline Pyramid

Level V:
Wraparound
support (PBS)

Level IV:
Somewhere else to plan

Level III:
Long-term supports—life skills

Level II:
Recovery methods that maintain
student dignity

Level I:
Creating caring community

Source: Villa, R. A., Thousand, J. S., & Nevin, A. I. (2010). *Collaborating with Students in Instruction and Decision Making* (p. 172). Thousand Oaks, CA: Corwin. Reprinted by permission.

working together to develop self-discipline. The base and the strength of the pyramid rest on creating a classroom community that embraces caring and positive interdependence. This level goes a long way toward prevention. Level II in the pyramid consists of recovery methods. Here, student dignity and student reflection are key responses when class expectations are violated. Generally, these actions occur at the moment distractions or disruptions happen. Level III offers long-term supports such as teaching social skills and problem-solving methods. Extra assistance, such as individual contracts for students who need them, also occurs at this level. Implementation of Level IV occurs when a disruption cannot be resolved in the classroom. Children go "somewhere else," where they can calm down, think, and problem-solve under adult guidance in order to return to the classroom quickly. The apex of the pyramid consists of caring individuals who collaborate to establish plans to bring about long-term change in student behavior.

What Major Authorities Say about Discipline

A number of authorities, past and present, have made suggestions and devised techniques that greatly help teachers minimize disruptive behavior in the classroom. Here, we briefly review selected contributions.

Groundbreaking Authorities

Beginning in the 1950s, several authorities made notable contributions in the area of classroom discipline. Among these groundbreaking authorities were Fritz Redl and William Wattenberg, B. F. Skinner, Haim Ginott, Jacob Kounin, Rudolf Dreikurs, Linda Albert, Lee and Marlene Canter, and William Glasser.

Fritz Redl and William Wattenberg   Redl and Wattenberg (1951) studied and wrote about how group dynamics influenced behavior and were the first to formalize study in this area when they offered a systematic approach to classroom discipline based on human psychology and humane tactics.

B. F. Skinner   A behavioral psychologist, B. F. Skinner investigated how people's behavior and actions were influenced by what happened immediately after they performed an act. Skinner never concerned himself directly with classroom discipline. However, in the early 1960s, Skinner's followers created and popularized a program known as behavior modification that was widely used in teaching, child rearing, and human relations.

Haim Ginott   In 1971 Haim Ginott published *Teacher and Child*, in which he examined the role of communication—how teachers talk to and with their students—in discipline. Many still regard Ginott's book as one with great influence in the area of classroom discipline.

Jacob Kounin   Jacob Kounin (1970) was the first to present a detailed analysis of the effects of classroom and lesson management on student behavior, and his suggestions on lesson management are incorporated into most of the discipline systems used today. Kounin isolated two significant skills that showed teachers in charge. *Withitness* is knowing what is going on in every part of the classroom at every moment, in a way that is evident to students. *Overlapping* is the ability to deal with at least two issues simultaneously. For example, teachers working with a small reading group overlap when they correct disruptive behavior occurring elsewhere in the room without leaving the reading group or interrupting other classroom activity.

Kounin also identified skills for managing lessons, each of which, if not accomplished well, allows for inattentive dead time that encourages disruptive behavior. *Focus* is obtained by making sure students know what they are supposed to do and why. *Attention* is obtained through motivation and specific directions. *Accountability* (student responsibility) is obtained by calling on students to respond, interpret, comment, discuss, and demonstrate. *Pacing* depends on timing that ensures efficient coverage of activities and ending at the appropriate time. *Momentum* is evident in steady progression through the lesson, without slowdown or frantic rush. *Transitions* from one activity to another depend on established routines that ensure rapid changeover.

Rudolf Dreikurs   Psychiatrist Rudolf Dreikurs, a contemporary of Ginott and Kounin, was beneficial in developing student self-control and responsible behavior. Dreikurs viewed discipline as an ongoing process in which students learn to impose limits on themselves. He observed four underlying causes of misbehavior—the mistaken goals of seeking attention, seeking power, seeking revenge, or withdrawal and how to deal with them—as students acted out to satisfy their primary need to belong.

To eliminate most discipline problems, Dreikurs suggested that teachers establish democratic classrooms for students to gain their primary goal of belonging. When disruptive behavior does occur, teachers should identify the student's mistaken goal and confront the student with it: "You would like me to pay attention to you, wouldn't you?" or "Could it be that you want to show that I can't make you do this work?" Also, disruptive behavior always should be followed with reasonable consequences. These are activities students dislike but that are not hurtful, such as staying after school or completing an assignment at home that should have been finished in class.

Linda Albert   Building on Dreikurs's work, Linda Albert (2003) organized an approach called *Cooperative Discipline* that provides a process that teachers, students, administrators, and caregivers can implement easily. For Albert, behavior is based on choice; choices are based on the basic need for belonging; and for students to belong, they must feel capable, connected, and able to contribute to the group. Students unable to feel a sense of belonging misbehave in ways that correspond to Dreikurs's mistaken goals. Albert's program also includes a classroom code of conduct, cooperative conflict resolution, school and home action plans, and partnerships with student and caregivers. For more information about her program, visit Albert's website, http://www.cooperativediscipline.com.

Lee and Marlene Canter   Educators Lee and Marlene Canter (1976) set forth a revolutionary approach they called *Assertive Discipline,* which became an instant success. Overall, assertive discipline allowed teachers to apply positive support and corrective actions calmly and fairly. The Canters insisted on teachers' rights to teach and students' rights to learn and said that nothing, especially student misbehavior, should be allowed to interfere with either. They said that teachers have the right to a calm, quiet classroom; the right to expect students to behave in ways that do not defeat their best interests; the right to expect backing from their administrators and support from caregivers; and the right to productive classrooms where quality teaching and learning can occur. Their approach provided techniques for teaching students how to behave properly, for gaining student trust and cooperation, and for dealing with students whose behavior is difficult to manage.

William Glasser   Since 1969 psychiatrist William Glasser has continually developed, refined, and popularized approaches to teaching that provide motivation and help students make good behavioral choices while taking responsibility for their actions. Glasser presented his views in several highly acclaimed books, the most recent of which are *Choice Theory in the Classroom* (1998), *The Quality School: Managing Students without Coercion* (1998), *The Quality School Teacher* (1998), and *Every Student Can Succeed* (2001). The following are some of the main tenets of Glasser's theories:

- All behavior is our best attempt to control ourselves to meet five basic needs: survival, belonging, power, fun, and freedom.

- We can control no one's behavior except our own.

- We cannot successfully make a person do anything. All we can do is open possibilities and provide information.

- All behavior is understood best as *total behavior,* composed of four components: acting, thinking, feeling, and physiology (how we function).

- All total behavior is chosen, but we only have direct control over the acting and thinking components. In other words, we choose how to act and how to think. Feeling and physiology are controlled indirectly through how we chose to act and think.

- External control does not motivate students to act responsibly or learn. Primarily our actions are determined by what goes on inside us.

- Present-day schools and curriculum ignore the basic needs and emphasize memorization of isolated facts that are irrelevant to students' lives. Moreover, quality is judged by how many fragments of information students can retain long enough to be measured on tests.

- Cooperative learning groups help meet students' need for belonging.

- One way to improve behavior and learning is through clarifying what a quality existence would be like and plan the choices that would help that existence. In the classroom, this process occurs best when teachers establish warm, trusting relationships with students.

Contemporary Authorities

At present, several authorities are making very strong contributions to the science of classroom discipline. Among the most popular are the following.

Harry and Rosemary Wong   For years Harry and Rosemary Wong have written about the first days and weeks of school. Their very practical approach, published in *The First Days of School* (2009), is a compilation of valuable ideas from many sources.

The Wongs would have teachers develop a detailed plan of action to be implemented the very first day of school. The plan would be "scripted" (written out in detail) and would include strategies and procedures that enable students to work diligently, behave responsibly, and reach high levels of achievement. Here are some of their ideas regarding teaching, learning, and the first days and weeks of school.

- Poor classroom management, not poor discipline, is the main problem in teaching.

- How teachers manage the classroom is the most important element for student learning.

- The three most important things teachers must teach the first days and weeks of school are discipline, procedures, and routines.

- Beginning the first day of school, discipline plans should be written, posted, reviewed, and practiced with the students and should clearly state the kinds of behavior the teacher expects from students.

- Schools should be challenging, exciting, engrossing, and thought-provoking. Schools also must have structure to ensure success. Well-managed schools and classrooms are task-oriented and predictable.

- Effective teachers spend the first two weeks of school teaching students to follow classroom procedures. They decide what routines will be necessary for the intended activities; list the procedural steps students must follow in order to participate in and

---

Case Study 9.2   Planning for a Good Learning Environment

FOCUS QUESTIONS

Sarah Jondahl anticipates and plans for many things before she even meets her students. Brainstorm lists of specific routines and procedures for each of these broader categories. How will the lists be different for different grade levels (primary, intermediate, upper elementary)?

Classroom teacher Sarah Jondahl applies the Wongs' ideas as she anticipates each school year. She prepares the classroom before students arrive. She thinks about academic expectations, class schedules and time frames, and lesson plans and activities for the first days of school. She considers procedures and evidence to document and evaluate student practice and understanding. She plans steps for maintaining a good learning environment. She also plans ways to establish working relations with students and caregivers.

---

benefit from the activities; and then teach the procedures by explaining, rehearsing, and reinforcing.

The Wongs also offer a video series called *The Effective Teacher* and publish a column on http://www.teachers.net. Their website is http://www.effectiveteaching.com.

Fred Jones   Fred Jones (2007), formerly a clinical psychologist, developed and now directs popular training programs nationally in procedures for managing classrooms and discipline. Jones stresses that the goal of discipline is for students to assume responsibility for their actions. Jones's approach to discipline is effective, easy to implement, and able to produce results quickly.

Jones's research found that although most teachers fear crisis events such as fighting and blatant defiance to authority, these rarely occur, even in hard-to-manage classes. The reality is that about 80 percent of all disruptive behavior is little more than talking without permission, and another 15 percent is almost entirely students moving about the room when they should be in their seats, or generally goofing off by daydreaming, making inappropriate noises, and the like.

Jones also found that most teachers can regain teaching time that otherwise is lost. They arrange the room so they can work the crowd as they move among students during seatwork. They set clear limits through class agreements and effective body language. They use Say, See, Do Teaching and incentive systems. And they give efficient help.

Efficient *classroom arrangement* improves the likelihood of successful teaching, learning, and behavior. *Limit setting* involves clarifying the boundaries of acceptable behavior and then formulating *class agreements* of rules and incentives accordingly. For Jones, rules describe procedures—how students are to do their work, what they should do if materials are needed, what to do when unable to proceed on their own, and what to do when finished with an assignment. *Backup systems,* including the school discipline code, will be used when students misbehave seriously and refuse to comply with the rules or the teacher's requests.

Effective *body language* projects the message that the teacher means business. According to Jones, it is the teacher's most effective tool in enforcing boundaries on acceptable behavior. Jones claims that teachers can prevent 90 percent of normal discipline problems with nonverbal communication: calm breathing, physical proximity to students, body position, facial expression, tone of voice, and eye contact. Here are two examples:

An Li stops following the math lesson and is thinking about the new puppies at home. She hears Mr. Lassiter pause. She looks at Mr. Lassiter and finds him looking at her (eye contact). An Li straightens herself and waits attentively.

Sean stops working and talks to Isaac. Suddenly, he sees Mr. Lassiter's shadow (physical proximity). Immediately, he gets back to work, without anything said.

Say, See, Do Teaching keeps students actively involved during instruction by asking them to respond frequently to teacher input. *Incentive systems* work like carrots before a horse's nose. Jones suggests using preferred activity time (PAT) because it offers something students want, and students know they will get it only if they work and behave as they should. Mr. Lassiter tells his class that all who correctly finish their homework assignment every day for a week (reinforcing the criterion of mastery mentioned in Chapter 7) can participate in a game of Jeopardy at the end of the week. Game questions will reinforce what the students study during the week.

Providing efficient help is one of Jones's most useful suggestions. Suppose that Mr. Lassiter demonstrated a long-division algorithm and students practiced under his guidance before he assigned them problems to complete at their seat—and eight students soon raised their hands. Describing situations such as this one, Jones asked teachers how much time they thought they spent helping individual students during seatwork. Teachers thought one or two minutes, but Jones observed that the actual average was four minutes per student. This is a long time for other students to sit doing nothing—until they misbehave.

To keep students working instead of misbehaving, Jones offers two suggestions. First, teachers should use visual instructional plans and graphic reminders to which students can refer instead of calling for the teacher. Second, teachers should give students enough help in twenty seconds or less to get them back on track. Teachers give this help in three steps: (1) comment on what the student has done correctly (an optional step after the first interaction), (2) give a direct suggestion or clue to

"WE'D BETTER BE ON OUR BEST BEHAVIOR. SHE JUST PUT HER HAIR UP IN A SCRUNCHIE."

© Martha F. Campbell. Reprinted by permission.

get the student back on track, such as "The next thing to do is . . . ," and (3) leave immediately. This rapid procedure enables teachers to provide help to all who need it while deterring helpless hand raising and the dependency syndrome in which students rely on the teacher's presence before doing their work.

Jones offers a video course of study and a free online study guide entitled *The Video Toolbox* (2005), as well as a companion parenting program (available in both English and Spanish versions). The materials and updated workshop information are available through Jones's website, http://www.fredjones.com. The website also maintains an active bulletin board of ideas for PAT.

Spencer Kagan   For many years, Spencer Kagan's name has been associated with several facets of education and effective teaching and learning, including cooperative learning and multiple intelligences. His programs are presented internationally to teachers and administrators. In recent years, he has expanded his work to include discipline and has articulated his ideas in *Win-Win Discipline* (2007), a book he co-authored with Patricia Kyle and Sally Scott. Kagan says that the ultimate goal of discipline is for students to be able to manage themselves autonomously and meet their needs through responsible choices. He believes that responsible behavior links closely to curriculum, instruction, and the teacher, and that discipline is something acquired by students, not something done to them. Any behavior that interrupts the learning process reflects a lack of acquired discipline and is a good opportunity for teaching and learning skills of self-discipline and life skills.

Accordingly, win-win discipline emphasizes a "we" approach to working with students to produce long-term learned responsibility. This approach involves three fundamental principles that Kagan calls "the Three Pillars":

- Same Side: teacher understands where the student is coming from and teams with the student to find discipline solutions
- Collaborative Solutions: teacher and student share responsibility for co-creating discipline solutions
- Learned Responsibility: student acquires nondisruptive, long-term responsible behavior

Kagan shows teachers how to identify the type of misbehavior as well as the condition that is prompting students to misbehave at any given time. Nearly all disruptions can be categorized into four types of behavior: aggression, breaking rules, confrontation, and disengagement (ABCD disruptive behaviors). They tell teachers *what* students do. What Kagan refers to as *positions*—the conditions for the disruptive behavior—tell teachers *why* students do what they do. In other words, positions reflect a person's needs at the time he or she acts out. The seven positions are these:

- Attention-seeking—seeking to be recognized; to receive caring, concern, love
- Avoiding failure—seeking to avoid looking foolish or unsuccessful in front of others
- Angry—seeking to express one's anger
- Control-seeking—seeking to establish the sense of being in charge and able to make one's own choices

- Bored—seeking stimulation
- Energetic—seeking to release excessive energy
- Uninformed—not knowing which behavior is appropriate for the situation

Positions are neither right nor wrong; they simply are part of the human condition. We all regularly find ourselves in these positions. Identifying and understanding a student's position does not mean that the teacher allows or affirms the disruption. Nor does it mean that the teacher tries to change the position. Rather, the teacher deals with the disruption by validating the position and maintaining the student's dignity. The teacher's goal is to help the student toward responsible nondisruptive ways of behaving when in these positions.

Kagan emphasizes preventive strategies aligned with each position, and gives teachers hundreds of concrete structures—step-by-step sequences of interactions—to use for the moment of disruption, follow-up, and long-term solutions. He also places heavy emphasis on the importance of integrating life skills instruction as part of the discipline program. He advocates that teachers and students create jointly written class agreements of rules and responsible alternatives and that teachers develop parent and community alliances to make win-win solutions work for everyone. Additional information on win-win discipline, Kagan structures, and current workshops can be found at this website: http://www .kaganonline.com.

Barbara Coloroso Barbara Coloroso, who writes and consults widely on discipline, believes that all students are worth the effort teachers can expend on them—not just when they are bright, good-looking, or well behaved, but always. She asserts that in order for them

---

Vignette 9.1   Class Agreements

Fourth-grade teacher Ginny Lorenz believes that the best statement for allowing students a hand in the writing of classroom rules comes directly from the students. Every year Ginny asks her class to write a letter to the incoming fourth graders.

"Alex wrote this about class rules. 'I will always remember fourth grade because I finally felt good about me. When I came to fourth grade everybody didn't like me because I always got into trouble. Nobody would let me play at their house because they had heard about me at school. This year we talked about rules and picked the ones we wanted. I found out I could be good. I found out I could even be a good student.'

"Alex was correct; he found out that when he controlled his own behavior, he could be a good student. I did not control Alex's behavior. He and the other students took care of their own behavior because they felt that they had a say in what was important and they felt that they truly belonged."

UPON REFLECTION

What might Ginny say when she first meets her new class of fourth graders to involve them in creating a jointly written class agreement of rules and responsible alternatives?

to have good discipline, teachers must do three things: (1) treat students with respect and dignity, (2) give students a sense of positive power over their own lives, and (3) give students opportunities to make decisions, take responsibility for their actions, and learn from their successes and mistakes.

Proper discipline, according to Coloroso, does four things punishment cannot do. First, it shows students what they have done wrong, in contrast with punishment that merely tells. Second, it helps students develop an inner discipline by giving them ownership of their problems. Teachers must help students learn *how* to think, not just *what* to think by giving students responsibility and ownership, allowing them to make mistakes, and guiding them to accept the natural or reasonable consequences of their actions. The certainty, not the severity, of consequences will have an effect for students. Third, proper discipline provides students with ways to solve problems they encounter. And fourth, it leaves students' dignity intact.

Coloroso describes three categories of misbehavior and suggests what teachers can do to help students. *Mistakes* are simple errors that provide opportunities for learning better choices. When an excited Declan accidentally scribbles on the table rather than his paper, he can help scrub the table clean, and the teacher can cover the table with paper to avoid future mishaps.

Mischief, while not necessarily serious, is intentional misbehavior. It provides an opportunity to help students find ways to fix what was done wrong and to avoid doing it again, while retaining their dignity. When Cai tears apart a book because she likes the pictures and wants to keep them in her desk, she should work out a payment plan with the teacher and her parents to replace the damaged book.

Mayhem is willfully serious misbehavior and calls for application of the three Rs for guidance in helping students take responsibility and accept consequences. *Restitution* has the student repair or compensate for the damage. *Resolution* allows the student to identify and correct whatever caused the misbehavior so it won't happen again. *Reconciliation* helps students complete the process of healing the relationships with people who were hurt by the misbehavior. Consider fifth grader Marcy. When she was not selected for the soccer team, Marcy broke the arm of the team captain Amy by willfully pushing her against the wall. With the help of an insightful and supportive coach, Marcy offered to take notes for Amy, so she can keep up in class. In addition to apologizing to Amy and her parents, the coach, and the other team members, Marcy participated in an anger management program sponsored by the neighborhood youth club. There, she was able to clarify what she did, why she did it, and what she learned from the experience. She also was able to practice alternative anger management strategies so she could make better choices in the future.

Coloroso explains her ideas on discipline in her books and video series, *Kids Are Worth It! Giving Your Child the Gift of Inner Discipline* (1994) and *Parenting with Wit and Wisdom in Times of Chaos and Loss* (1999). Find out or more about her work at: http://www.kidsare worthit.com.

Marvin Marshall   Marvin Marshall, a former school administrator and now a worldwide consultant, believes the best way to ensure good classroom behavior is to help students learn to conduct themselves responsibly. He believes that almost all students are inclined to behave responsibly, although they may need help to do so. For Marshall, responsibility is another word for internal motivation to "do the right thing." He insists that students cannot be forced to learn or behave responsibly, but they can be influenced to do so through a non-coercive approach. According to Marshall, teachers help when they articulate clear behavior expectations, and establish a positive attitude in the classrooms by emphasizing positivity, choice, and reflection. Marshall says that these elements activate motivation.

Positivity is an emotion of optimism that focuses on the upside of things. Optimistic people tend to make others feel better. Unfortunately, students often perceive teachers and schools in a negative light because teachers unwittingly set themselves up as enforcers of rules rather than as encouragers, mentors, and role models. Teachers should infuse positivity into all aspects of teaching.

Choice empowers students by offering them options. When teachers speak to students about their behavior, Marshall suggests that teachers ask the students about the choices they had and how they could make better choices. A simple question would be, "What do you think we should do about the situation?" When the teacher is satisfied with the student's choice, the response would be, "I can live with that."

Reflection is a process of thinking about one's own behavior and judging its merits. It has a key role in changing one's behavior, but teachers must understand they cannot control students by asking for obedience, making demands, or imposing consequences. Teachers cannot force change in how students think, want to behave, or will behave once the teacher's presence is no longer felt. Students do these things for themselves.

What teachers *can* do is establish expectations in a noncoercive manner, and empower students to attain them, by asking questions that prompt students to think about how they are behaving. Teachers can prompt students to ask themselves questions such as, "If I wanted to be successful in this class right now, what would I be doing?" In most cases the answer will be apparent and students will begin to behave accordingly.

Some of Marshall's ideas are outlined in his book *Discipline without Stress, Punishments, or Rewards: How Teachers and Parents Promote Responsibility & Learning* (2007). His free monthly electronic newsletter, "Promoting Responsibility & Learning," is available via e-mail at http://www.MarvinMarshall.com. His other websites are http://www.AboutDiscipline.com and http://www.DisciplineWithoutStress.com.

Richard Curwin, Allen Mendler, and Brian Mendler Richard Curwin and Allen Mendler created an approach called *Discipline with Dignity* (1988, 2008), which has remained popular for over 20 years. Brian Mendler now works with them in writing and consulting widely on matters related to discipline and working with challenging youth. These educators assert that most students who chronically misbehave see themselves as losers with no hope that education will serve them, and these beliefs put students in serious danger of failing in school. Curwin, Mendler, and Mendler stress that helping students learn to behave acceptably in school is fundamental to teaching, and they ask teachers to do everything possible to instill hope and success in all students, including those who are behaviorally or academically at risk, in a way that preserves everyone's dignity. Teachers must explore ways to ensure success, motivate students, and make learning attractive, interesting, and worthwhile. To this end, Curwin, Mendler, and Mendler describe a systematic approach and offer concrete suggestions for dealing with challenging students and violence in the classroom and schools. You can find out more about their program and suggestions at their website, http://www.disciplineassociates.com.

Ronald Morrish   Ronald Morrish, a former school counselor and now a widely followed consultant, believes that today's teachers have been misguided in their approach to discipline. He believes teachers have been taught to focus on behavior management—making the environment functional—rather than on *real discipline*—by which he means teaching students to act appropriately, with respect, responsibility, and cooperation. He says students do not automatically know right from wrong; they do whatever works for them at the time without considering the rights or needs of others, and they do not consider consequences.

Morrish believes that teachers must reestablish their authority in the classroom, and that students must be trained to accept and comply automatically with rules, limits, and this authority. He believes that this is accomplished through direct instruction, insistence, do-overs, and practice until the behaviors become habit. *Insistence* is teachers' persistence until students do what they are told to do. *Do-overs* have students repeat the acceptable behavior. In addition to teaching students skills required for school and life success, the ultimate goal of real discipline is for students to be self-disciplined and able to conduct themselves properly even when the teacher is not present. Morrish's discipline tips can be found in his book *FlipTips* (2003) and on his website, http://www.realdiscipline.com.

How to Build your Discipline System

You have seen ideas for managing student behavior from several authorities. You can use these ideas to build a system of discipline that works for you and your students. Some teachers prefer to begin the year with their plan in mind and spend the first days and weeks of school teaching the elements of the plan to their students and having students practice. For this you would review existing discipline techniques, outline and fine-tune your ideas, and then present and practice your plan with your students. Other teachers believe a participative approach will serve them best. Participative discipline is a system in which teachers and students cooperate in making decisions about expectations, behavior, and consequences. To develop a participative discipline plan, you should review existing discipline techniques, outline your ideas for a plan that uses techniques you believe will work for you, and then fine-tune the plan with your students.

Review Techniques

Compile a list of discipline ideas and techniques that match your philosophy of working with students and that suit the needs of your students. For example, you might (or might not) include such ideas as basic rights to teach and learn, rules, withitness, student needs and positions, routines for opening and ending the day, good lesson management and transitions, efficient help, incentive systems, shared responsibility, and joint teacher–student ownership of the plan.

Outline and Launch Your Plan

Keeping in mind the age and maturity of your students, outline a basic plan. Then discuss your ideas for a class agreement or discipline plan with students. Ask them for their

Vignette 9.2   Positive Reinforcement through a Behavior Ladder

Betsy Goff has taught primary grades for 15 years. To inform parents of the behavior ladder she will use with her students, at the start of the year she sends home this general explanation of rewards and consequence expectations:

To keep our room a comfortable and happy learning place, we have a positive reinforcement program. You will find a "ladder" on the back file cabinet. Your child has a magnet that begins on level 3 each morning. Students may move up for good behavior or down for disruptive behavior throughout the day. Notices go home for the students who reach the top, level 5, and the bottom, level 1. If your child comes home with a level 3 or above, he or she had a great day!

UPON REFLECTION
What will be your plan to manage behavior, consequences, and rewards? How will your plan differ for students in primary grades? middle or upper grades? How will you document and inform caregivers of the daily behavior of your students?

reactions and suggestions. As you plan and discuss, keep in mind the seven elements discussed below. Some points are presented as sample dialogues to have with your students as you launch your plan with the class. Other points are general considerations before you finalize the plan.

Practicality As you anticipate, and certainly before you finalize the rules and consequences of your discipline plan, keep this point foremost in your mind: You have to live with the plan. It is supposed to serve your class; your class is not supposed to serve it. It must not be so complicated, difficult, or time-consuming that it enslaves you. Make sure the plan is easy to implement, serves its purpose, requires little extra time from you, and produces minimal irritation, resentment, and lost time.

Understanding Begin by talking with your students. "This is our class, and if we work together, we will create a place where each of us feels comfortable and where we all can enjoy the teaching and learning. I have a responsibility to create an environment where this can happen, but I need your help to really make it work. Each of you is an important member of this class with important responsibilities to help make this a pleasant place to be and where everybody's needs are met. I suggest we work together now to create a class agreement.

"We all have very important jobs in this class. Your job is to learn as much as you can. That means that you must try your hardest, do your best work, and help everyone in the class to do better. My job is to teach you as best I can, to help you, and to make learning as much fun as possible.

"We all have very important rights in this class, and we must not let anyone interfere with them. You have the right to learn without anyone bothering you. I have the right to teach without anyone bothering me. We must not allow any kind of irresponsible behavior to take away your right to learn or my right to teach.

MATH STORY PROBLEM

IF I HAVE 18 STUDENTS IN MY CLASSROOM AND I DECIDE TO SEND KEVIN AND JASON TO THE PRINCIPAL'S OFFICE BECAUSE THEY WILL NOT STOP MISBEHAVING, HOW MANY STUDENTS WILL I HAVE LEFT IN MY CLASSROOM?

Permission by Dave Carpenter.

"Throughout the year, we all must try to do the best we can do—the best teaching from me, the best learning from you, and the best work from all of us, so we can be proud and your caregivers can be proud of you. We can have a good time working together and getting along and doing excellent work. This is how we make the best of ourselves."

Balance "You need many things to happen in this room for you to do your best. You need good teaching from me, good things to learn, and pleasure in what we do together. I need many things in order to teach you best—a calm, quiet atmosphere, good manners from you, and cooperation and helpfulness toward each other. What I need must be balanced with what you need. We can't have a good class if we do everything only to suit me or only to suit you. We have to balance things so that all of us can have what we need to make this class exceptionally good. That means that all of us must be kind, considerate, and helpful to each other."

Formal Agreement "You and I need to be on the same side and work together to create a classroom where we all want to be and where everyone can learn. You will be able to have your say and make decisions about the class, so let's talk now about how we want our class to be. Suppose you were trying your best to learn something in this class. How would you want the other students to act while you were trying to learn? Let's name some behaviors that would make us happy to be in this class and able to get our work done. (Record student responses, guiding the process so the behaviors are stated positively and apply to everyone.) What are some examples of what these behaviors look, sound, and feel like?

"Do you think we need rules to help us remember how we should behave when I am trying to teach and you are trying to learn? (Discussion.) Let's see if we can think of a rule about how each of us will try to do our work and a rule about how each of us will behave toward others. (Discussion. Write the rules on the board.)

"Let's think about what they mean, about what they tell us to do and not do. How do you feel about this list? (Discussion.) You seem to like these rules, and I do, too. I believe they will help us. Are you willing to adopt them as our class agreement?

"Now suppose that most of us follow these rules, but one or two students don't. Suppose they talk loudly or run around the room. What should be done if that happens? (Discussion. Record student suggestions, guiding the process so they are stated positively, apply to everyone, and offer solutions, not punishments.) I think your suggestions will be good for our class.

"This year in our class we will learn and practice skills that are important for being citizens in a democratic society. Choosing responsible behavior will be one of the most important things we will learn. Tomorrow I'll have the class agreement, with the rules as well as what happens if they are broken, written on paper. We'll all sign our names to show that we agree with the rules and agree to follow them. Then I'll make copies for you to take home for your caregivers to see."

Vitality Ideally, your discipline plan is not separate from instruction. Rather, it is something that is incorporated into instruction, as essential and natural as directions and feedback. Assuming that students see your plan as fair (why you spend so much time discussing it and making sure students buy into it), it will serve wonderfully as you inject interest, novelty, fun, and importance into learning activities. It will earn continued support if you can stop disruptive behavior at once, invoke consequences, and follow through calmly and helpfully, showing the personal support that students prize. We said this before: For your students, it should not be the severity but the certainty of receiving the consequences that has impact. Further, administrators and caregivers will back the plan if it is humane, obviously serves students, and is communicated well.

Civility Despite the workload, frustration, and stress with which you always must contend, remember that it is your responsibility to ensure that the classroom is a place of decorum and civility, where students speak and act courteously, where no one's character is attacked, and where you, especially, serve as the finest model. If you and your students are to prosper, you must make and keep your classroom a good place in which to live and work. This requires ongoing modeling of the qualities of good character and behavior, as well as authentic opportunities for students to practice them.

Flexibility and Renewability You should begin with what you believe to be best for your students and yourself; then stick by your resolve so long as there is reason to do so. But at the same time, you must remain eminently flexible. If something is not working, try to change it so that it will. Discuss the problem with your students and together come up with an alternative that promises better results. Regular classroom meetings provide a good forum to discuss the class, discipline, and other topics of interest or concern. Some teachers take time at the end of every day for a short discussion of what went well and what did not, and when problems surface, they arrange times for longer discussions. They want to know students' views of how things are going and what needs to be done differently. These teachers are willing to make new beginnings when warranted, knowing that sometimes a simple change for change's sake is valuable.

This concludes our consideration of discipline—how to manage student behavior so quality teaching and learning can occur within an atmosphere of civility and helpfulness. Before we turn to the topic of how to manage the assessment of student progress, along with record keeping and reporting to caregivers and administrators, take time to explore these end-of-chapter activities.

Parting Thought

Simplicity is an acquired taste. Mankind, left free, instinctively complicates life.

—Katherine Fullerton Gerould

Summary Self-Check

Check off the following as you either understand or become able to apply them:

☐ Disruptive student behavior causes more wasted time, more teacher stress, and more teacher burnout than all other factors combined.

☐ Student behavior is growing worse, as evidenced by apathy, failure to work, disrespect, and open aggression.

☐ Bullying is not a normal developmental stage for young people and is a serious problem both in and out of school.

☐ The older disciplinary technique of authoritative teacher demands no longer works.

☐ Many valuable ideas in discipline have appeared in the past five decades:
- Pioneering research and work by Fritz Redl and William Wattenberg, B. F. Skinner, Haim Ginott, Jacob Kounin, Rudolf Dreikurs, Linda Albert, Lee and Marlene Canter, and William Glasser
- Harry and Rosemary Wong: the first days and weeks of school, procedures and routines
- Fred Jones: setting limits and body language; backup systems; Say, See, Do Teaching; incentive systems; efficient help
- Spencer Kagan: same side, collaborative solutions, learned responsibility; ABCD disruptive behaviors; student positions; life skills
- Barbara Coloroso: three categories of misbehavior (mistake, mischief, mayhem); three Rs of guidance (restitution, resolution, reconciliation); the bully, the bullied, the bystander
- Marvin Marshall: responsibility, positivity, choice, reflection
- Richard Curwin, Allen Mendler, and Brian Mendler: behaviorally and academically at risk, rediscovering hope, dignity
- Ronald Morrish: real discipline, teacher's authority, student compliance, do-overs

☐ Teachers typically construct or guide the formation of their own systems of discipline, consistent with their personality, philosophy, and needs, and the traits and needs of the students they teach.

☐ Steps in formulating a good personal system of discipline:
- Review preferred techniques.
- Outline and launch a plan that includes practicality, understanding, balance, formal agreement, vitality, civility, and flexibility and renewability.
- Fine-tune and publish the plan after discussion with students.

Activities for Reflection and Discussion

1. Take a moment to review the statements in the Preview–Review Guide at the beginning of this chapter. Put a check mark in the *Review* column next to any statement with which you now agree. How have your thoughts changed since reading this chapter?

2. Interview at least two teachers about their discipline plans. To what extent did the teachers and their student work together to create the class rules and consequences? What are their class rules? consequences? rewards? How are caregivers, administrators, and other teachers informed of the plan?

3. Brainstorm a list of disruptive behaviors that you might find in an elementary classroom. Categorize these behaviors according to ABCD.

4. Compile a list of specific discipline techniques that you feel best match your personality, philosophy, and needs. How is the list different for primary, intermediate, upper elementary students?

5. Virtually all elementary students will agree that they would like to learn. Why then do they so often misbehave and make no effort to do what teachers ask of them? Discuss in small groups or as a class.

6. When you were an elementary student, under which of the various systems of discipline described in this chapter would you have preferred to work? Explain.

7. Review the seven student positions that Kagan identifies. Create kinesthetic signs (and add sounds) to convey their meanings. Work in small teams and then teach the class.

Webliography

Authorities

Discipline Associates, LLC (Richard Curwin, Allen Mendler, and Brian Mendler): http://www.disciplineassociates.com

Dr. Marvin Marshall. *Discipline without stress punishment or rewards:* http://www.DisciplineWithoutStress.com

Dr. Marvin Marshall. *Discipline for Promoting Responsibility and Learning:* http://www.MarvinMarshall.com

Fredric H. Jones & Associates http://www.fredjones.com

Harry K. Wong Publications, Inc. (Harry and Rosemary Wong. http://www.EffectiveTeaching.com

Kids are Worth It! inc. (Barbara Coloroso): http://www.kidsareworthit.com

Kagan Publishing & Professional Development (Spencer Kagan): http://www.kaganonline.com

Maintained by Webmaster at Choice Theory.com (William Glasser): http://www.choicetheory.org/directory.html

Maintained by Webmaster at Choice Theory.com William Glasser: http://www.choicetheory.com/links.htm

Ronald Morrish (Real Discipline): http://www.realdiscipline.com
Tripod (Linda Albert, Cooperative Discipline): http://cdiscipline.tripod.com/

Bullying and Cyberbullying

Dan Olweus: http://www.olweus.org
i-Safe America. (2004). *Beware of the cyber bully:* http://www.isafe.org/imgs/pdf/education/Cyberbullying.pdf
Olweus Bullying Prevention Program; reprinted in Evertson & Emmer, 2001, p. 2009: http://www.stopbullyingnow.com
The school safety check book **by the National School Safety Center, reprinted in Parkay & Stanford (2010), pp. 92–93:** http://www.nssc1.org

Effects of Poverty

Pellegrino, K. (2005). *The effects of poverty on teaching and learning:* http://www.teachnology.com/tutorials/teaching/poverty/print.htm

References and Recommended Readings

Albert, L. (2003). *Cooperative discipline.* Circle Pines, MN: American Guidance Service.

Bloom, L. A. (2009). *Classroom management: Creating positive outcomes for all students.* Upper Saddle River, NJ: Merrill.

Canter, L., & Canter, M. (2001). *Assertive discipline: Positive behavior management for today's classroom* (3rd ed.). Los Angeles: Canter & Associates.

Charles, C. (2000). *The synergetic classroom: Joyful teaching and gentle discipline.* New York: Addison Wesley Longman.

Charles, C. (2009). *Today's best classroom management strategies: Paths to positive discipline.* Boson: Allyn & Bacon.

Charles, C. (2011). *Building classroom discipline* (10th ed.). Boston: Allyn & Bacon.

Coloroso, B. (1994). *Kids are worth it! Giving your child the gift of inner discipline.* New York: Avon Books.

Coloroso, B. (1999). *Parenting with wit and wisdom in times of chaos and loss.* Toronto, Ontario, Canada: Viking.

Coloroso, B. (2002). *The bully, the bullied, and the bystander.* Toronto, Ontario, Canada: HarperCollins.

Curwin, R., & Mendler, A. (1988). *Discipline with dignity.* Alexandria, VA: ASCD. Revised editions 1992, 1999, 2002. Upper Saddle River, NJ: Merrill.

Curwin, R., Mendler, A., & Mendler, B. (2008). *Discipline with dignity: New challenges, new solutions.* Alexandria, VA: ASCD.

Dreikurs, R., & Cassel, P. (1972). *Discipline without tears.* New York: Hawthorn.

Dreikurs, R., Grunwald, B., & Pepper, F. (1982). *Maintaining sanity in the classroom.* New York: Harper E Row.

Dwyer, K., Osher, D., & Warger, C. (1998). *Early warning, timely response: A guide to safe schools.* Washington, DC: U.S. Department of Education.

Dwyer, K., Richardson, J., Danley, K., Hansen, W., Sussman, S., Brannon, B., et al. (1990, September). Characteristics of eighth grade students who initiate self-care in elementary and junior high school. *Pediatrics, 86*(3), 448–454.

Glasser, W. (1969). *Schools without failure.* New York: Harper & Row.

Glasser, W. (1998). *The quality school: Managing students without coercion.* New York: Perennial Press.

Glasser, W. (1998a). *Choice theory in the classroom.* New York: HarperCollins.

Glasser, W. (1998b). *Control theory in the classroom* (rev. ed.). New York: Harper & Row.

Glasser, W. (1998c). *The quality school* (rev. ed.). New York: HarperCollins.

Glasser, W. (1998d). *The quality school teacher* (rev. ed.). New York: HarperCollins.

Glasser, W. (2000). *Every student can succeed.* Chatsworth, CA: Author.

Hall, P., & Hall, N. (2003). *Educating oppositional and defiant children.* Alexandria, VA: ASCD.

Horn, A. M., Opinas, P., Newman-Carlson, D., & Bartolomucci, C. L. (2004). Elementary school bully busters programs: Understanding why children bully and what to do about it. In D. L. Espelage and S. M. Swearer (Eds.), *Bullying in American schools: A social-ecological perspective on prevention and intervention.* Mahwah, NJ: Lawrence Erlbaum.

Jones, F. (2007). *Tools for Teaching: Discipline Instruction Motivation* (2nd ed.). Santa Cruz, CA: Fred H. Jones & Associates.

Jones, V., & Jones, L. (2010). *Comprehensive classroom management: Creating communities of support and solving problems* (9th ed.). Upper Saddle River, NJ: Pearson/Merrill, pp. 5–6.

Kagan, S., Kyle, P., & Scott, S. (2007). *Win-win discipline.* San Clemente, CA: Kagan Publishing,

Kohn, A. (2008, November). Why self-discipline is overrated: The (troubling) theory and practice of control from within. *Phi Delta Kappan, 90*(3), 168–176.

Kounin, J. (1970). *Discipline and group management in classrooms.* New York: Holt, Rinehart & Winston.

Kranowitz, C. (1998). *The out-of-sync child.* New York: Skylight Press.

Larrivee, B. (2009). *Authentic classroom management: Creating a learning community and building reflective practice* (3rd ed.). Upper Saddle River, NJ: Pearson Merrill.

Marshall, M. (2002). *Discipline without stress, punishment, or rewards: How teachers and parents promote responsibility and learning.* Los Alamitos, CA: Piper Press.

Marshall, M., & Weisner, K. (2004, March). Using a discipline system to promote learning. *Phi Delta Kappan, 85*(7), 498–507. Bloomington, IN: Phi Delta Kappa International.

McGrath, M. J. (2007). *School bullying: Tools for avoiding harm and liability.* Thousand Oaks, CA: Corwin Press.

Morrish, R. (2000). *With all due respect: Keys for building effective school discipline.* Fonthill, Canada: Woodstream Publishing.

Morrish, R. (2003). *FlipTips.* Fonthill, Canada: Woodstream Publishing.

Nansel, T., Overpeck, M., Haynie, D., Ruan, W., & Scheidt, P. (2003). Relationships between bullying and violence among US youth. *Archives of Pediatrics and Adolescent Medicine, 157*(4), 348–353.

Nelsen, J., Lott, L., & Glenn, H. (2000). *Positive discipline in the classroom.* Rocklin, CA: Prima Publishing.

Olweus, D. (1999). *Core program against bullying and antisocial behavior: A teacher handbook.* Bergen, Norway: Research Center for Health Promotion, University of Bergen.

Papolos, D., & Papolos, J. (2002). *The bipolar child.* New York: Broadway Books.

Payne, R. (2001). *A framework for understanding poverty.* Highlands, TX: aha! Process, Inc.

Peterson, R., & Skiba, R. (2001). Creating school climates that prevent school violence. *Social Studies, 92*(4), 167–176.

Redl, F., & Wattenberg, W. (1951). *Mental hygiene in teaching.* New York: Harcourt, Brace & World. Revised and reissued in 1959.

Shariff, S. (2008). *Cyber-bullying: Issues and solutions for the school, the classroom and the home.* London: Routledge

Siris, K., & Osterman, K. (2004, December). Interrupting the cycle of bullying and victimization in the elementary classroom. *Phi Delta Kappan, 86*(4), 288–291.

Skinner, B. F. (1954). The science of learning and the art of teaching. H*arvard Educational Review, 24,* 86–97.

Villa, R., Thousand, J., & Nevin, A. (2010). *Collaborating with students in instruction and decision making.* Thousand Oaks, CA: Corwin.

Webb, L. D., Metha, A., & Jordan, K. F. (2010). *Foundations of American education* (6th ed.). Upper Saddle River, NJ: Pearson/Merrill.

PEARSON
myeducationlab)

Go to the Topic: **Maintaining Appropriate Student Behavior** in the MyEducationLab (www.myeducationlab.com) for your course, where you can:

- Find learning outcomes for **Maintaining Appropriate Student Behavior** along with the national standards that connect to these outcomes.
- Apply and practice your understanding of the core teaching skills identified in the chapter with the Building Teaching Skills and Dispositions learning units.
- Examine challenging situations and cases presented in the IRIS Center Resources.

Managing Assessment, Record Keeping, and Reporting

CHAPTER 10

What we want to see is the child in pursuit of knowledge,
not knowledge in pursuit of the child.

—George Bernard Shaw

Preview–Review Guide

Before you read the chapter, and based on what you know, think you know, or assume, take a minute to put a check mark in the **Preview** column if you agree with the statement. When you finish the chapter, take time to reread the statements and respond in the **Review** column. Reflective discussions can develop because many of the statements are not clearly "yes" or "no."

Preview		Review
1. _____	Authentic assessment places less reliance on testing than traditionally has been the case.	_____
2. _____	Portfolios are synonymous with student work folders.	_____
3. _____	Assessment should be part of the instruction process and should help students learn.	_____
4. _____	Among assessments that guide improvements in student learning are those that teachers administer regularly in their classrooms.	_____
5. _____	Overall, test scores are the most useful records for teachers to keep, since those are what most caregivers understand.	_____
6. _____	Objectives are the activities students will do during instruction and ultimately direct the instruction and assessment.	_____
7. _____	Lists of standards and objectives, as well as continuums, can be found in curriculum guides and in teachers' editions of newer textbooks.	_____
8. _____	Students are motivated toward higher achievement when their teachers display comparison records of work and progress.	_____
9. _____	Generally, caregivers resent being asked to help with their child's schoolwork at home.	_____
10. _____	Performance should be observed during class time, but records entries should be made in the privacy of the teacher's home.	_____

Chapter Objectives

After reading Chapter 10, students will demonstrate understanding of

■ the nature and intents of multiple forms of
assessment

■ records needed for conferencing with
caregivers and other interested persons

through their active participation in discussions and the end-of-chapter activities
for reflection.

Assessment, record keeping, and reporting are necessary requirements of teaching, but few teachers enjoy dealing with them. Traditionally, these tasks have been seen as unpleasant burdens to be endured while experiencing the pleasures of teaching children. In recent years, legislation and the nationwide push for performance accountability for teachers and students, and higher student learning outcomes, have added to the pressures teachers feel about assessment. But while all this is true, new practices in teaching, assessment, and technology have helped to make these tasks more manageable and achievable for everyone concerned. A problem to solve or an essential or guiding question for this chapter might be: *How can I manage assessment, record keeping, and reporting with accuracy and efficiency?*

This chapter explores assessment methods that are under teacher control, and then discusses effective means of keeping records and reporting to caregivers, administrators, and others—both electronic and paper records. Most teachers now are able—and perhaps even expected—to keep electronic rather than paper records. The variety, practicality, and usability of newer program designs and accessibility to electronic software and programs allow them to do so. The following overview summarizes details relevant to the processes of assessment, recording, and reporting.

The Push for Better Assessment and Reporting

Nationwide movements continue to aim for positive and higher learning outcomes for our students. The tone for curriculum standards and the impetus for their development began with Goals 2000: Educate America Act (1994). Content-specific professional organizations, in their various publications, activities, and their Internet sites, have articulated national standards for each specific curriculum area. The No Child Left Behind Act (2001) and, more recently, Race to the Top (2009) continue to influence the movement. This national attention has led to the creation or revision of state learning goals, along with standards and benchmarks for each grade level. These standards relate to the broad areas of content, performance, and opportunities to learn. *Content standards* focus on what should be learned in various subject areas, as well as critical thinking and problem-solving skills. *Performance standards* attempt to answer the question "How good is good enough?" They specify the level of satisfactory performance when students apply and demonstrate what they know, often in authentic or real-world situations. *Opportunity-to-learn standards,* controversial because of the potential for more federal involvement, have to do with the condition and resources necessary to give students an equal chance to meet the performance standards (Morrison, 2002).

The Nature and Forms of Assessment

In education, *assessment* refers to the process of finding out, as objectively as possible, how well students are progressing. Because it should be ongoing, assessment often drives instruction as teachers use this information to plan their next steps in their instruction. Thorough assessment involves multitrait, multimethod, and multisource estimations of student status or progress. In contrast, *measurement* tends to be one-dimensional, often reduced to scores made on short-answer tests. *Grades* are the numbers or letters assigned at the end of a piece of work or a set period of time as a summary judgment statement of the level of student understanding or performance.

Different forms of assessments serve different purposes. *Diagnostic* or *placement* assessment considers "Where are the students now, and where do I begin with my instruction?" This form of assessment, including task analyses and pretests, helps teachers determine what knowledge and skills the students already have.

Other assessments are fundamental for helping students learn. *Formative assessments* are part of the instruction process. They help teachers determine if students are making satisfactory progress and whether the instruction needs to be modified. They relate directly to instructional goals and should align to national, state, and district standards. Because teachers are testing what they teach, these assessments provide immediate results about both student and instruction success. Examples of formative assessment include discussions and questioning, quizzes and tests, writing assignments, and other in-class work that teachers administer regularly.

Summative assessment, occurring at the end of the unit or lesson sequence, helps teachers to determine whether students met the objectives or mastered the content. Summative assessments probe learning the intended outcomes of instruction. They ask students to produce products and demonstrate skills and understandings in realistic situations and in a variety of ways—through discussion, role-playing, or performance; through conducting investigations or demonstrations; by completing projects or producing tangible products; and by analyzing ideas and procedures. Usually, summative assessment is the basis for assigning grades.

Because most formative and summative assessments are "teacher-created"—they assess what the teacher actually taught—they are considered to be *criterion-referenced*. Student learning is compared to clearly published standards and the content that was presented by the teacher to the class. Student learning is not compared to the work or performance of others. This contrasts with *norm-referenced* assessments that have teachers compare students with other students who are similar—at the same age or grade level—and then rank them in terms of their achievement.

Traditional testing helps teachers answer the question, "Do students know content?" (Parkay & Stanford, 2010, p. 385). In the past, test scores were entered and averaged in the teacher's paper or electronic grade book as evidence to support final grades. But in the movement toward accountability and more satisfactory means of assessment, evidence has been expanded to include the *quality* of student productivity, often in class or cooperative team assignments. Attempts are made to help students demonstrate nuances of understanding over time, indicate how they think and process information, and show their ability to apply learned skills realistically. Generally, this type of assessment is considered to be more genuine, less contrived, and less testlike than former attempts at measurement.

The current trend is to judge student learning with ever-increasing numbers of tests. The No Child Left Behind Act emphasizes standards, testing, and accountability. It also creates a greater push for standardized testing and paves the way for current controversy. The standardized testing movement emphasizes norm-based measurement (showing how students compare to one other) to establish national standards of performance. Since 1969 the United States has used the federally funded National Assessment of Educational Progress (NAEP) assessments as a national "report card" for educational achievement. Periodic tests, administered to representative samples of students, report achievement in several fields, including reading, writing, mathematics, science, history, and geography. Additionally, states now use other programs and tests such as the Standardized Testing and Reporting program (STAR), the Stanford Achievement Test (SAT 9), and the Indiana Statewide Testing for Educational Progress (ISTEP), intended to measure student achievement of grade-level content standards. Many educators dislike standardized tests because too often they measure only recall and knowledge and provide sparse insight into learning outcomes such as critical thinking and creativity. Furthermore, the tests usually are inadequately aligned with district and state curricula. Educators believe that as states continue to develop their own assessment tests, reliance on national standardized tests may decrease.

The Matter of Grades

As teaching and assessment practices change, a rethinking of grading also is occurring across the country. Marzano (2000) believes the primary purpose of grading is to provide timely corrective feedback that is as accurate and precise as possible so students can improve their work. Kohn (1999) and others argue that letter grades usually fall short of that goal. Letter grades are symbols, but generally they are not aligned to any common standard and they are essentially arbitrary in levels (A versus B versus C and so on). Further, letter grades do not provide much, if any, information about students' strengths and areas for growth or give any insight into how to help students improve. Consequently, often it is unclear what letter grades represent.

In some districts and schools, teachers are being asked to maintain ongoing records in Internet portals so caregivers can use their home computers to check on their child's homework, attendance, and scores, and track their child's progress daily. These programs are intended to strengthen the alliance between teacher and caregivers. To accomplish this, some publishers are providing to districts and teachers the needed software with adoption of their materials. In some schools, quarterly report cards will continue in addition to this program (Alphonso, 2003).

Educators are seeking better ways to report student accomplishments and areas of growth. Some current recommendations even go so far as to advocate the elimination of letter grades, particularly during the primary years. Teachers are encouraged to monitor student growth in terms of performance, work samples, and long-term projects that show students' capabilities in light of predetermined standards and intended learning outcomes. They then can report this with holistic narratives or continuum checklists of competencies. In the mid-1990s, Vermont was the first state to use portfolios in a statewide assessment program when it required all students in fourth and eighth grades to keep portfolios for writing and mathematics. Fourth and eight graders took a uniform test (timed writing samples and a series of mathematics problems) and presented their portfolios to demonstrate their progress and understandings over time. Well-crafted statewide curriculum standards were developed for judging the portfolios, and the state promoted writing rubrics and benchmarks based on state standards, statewide professional development meetings, yearly online calibration, and Web-based tools to compile the data. Portfolios no longer are collected for statement data because, as designed, they do not align well with NCLB. However, Vermont Department of Education personnel are working to redesign portfolios and assessments in hopes of their return in the next few years.

Standards-Based Grading

Standards-based grading is a relatively new grading practice that considers students' proficiency in relation to well-defined course objectives (Tomlinson & McTighe, 2006). While standards-based grading can be used in addition to traditional grades, some educators and districts believe for a variety of reasons that they can and should replace them.

As we stated earlier, letter grades A, B, C, D, and F connote vague meanings, although they traditionally connect to graduation credits and presumed learning. Traditional letter grades and points tend to overwhelm teachers, largely because of volume and meaningless paperwork. Standards-based grading reduces the volume because assessment aligns with objectives, not with artifacts of homework and test scores. Standards-based grades show what quality looks like and help teachers adjust instruction to better meet student learning and needs. Students have a clearer sense of when they meet proficiency goals or master a concept. Students who struggle are able to retest and use alternative assessments until they show proficiency, without the consequence of added time. Students who are identified as GATE are able to continue with more challenging work.

2008 Alejandro Yegros

YEGROS

I have tons of homework; you have lots of grading. Perhaps we can come to an understanding.

Alternative Assessments

While tests are and will continue to be major tools for assessing student learning, in recent years teachers also have begun to use alternative assessments. That is, when opportunity exists, teachers are using "forms of assessment that require the active construction of meaning rather than the passive regurgitation of isolated facts" (McMillan, 2001, cited in Parkay & Stanford, 2010, p. 383). Alternative assessments, made to align with national, state, and district standards, occur in several forms, including authentic assessment, portfolios, performance-based assessment, assessment for problem-based learning, peer assessment, and self-assessment.

Authentic Assessment

Authentic assessment, continuing to gain favor among educators, involves students in real-world challenges and experiences such as those they will face as members of society, the work force, and adult consumers. Unlike testing, authentic assessment is at the center of the teaching-learning process. Students are judged by what they do and produce during and after instruction. They do not have to try to translate what they learn into test responses. That fact makes authentic assessment appealing to teachers and students. Taking improvement into account makes the process even more appealing.

With feedback from their teachers and others, students analyze, refine, and improve their work over time. In this approach, a student essay might be written and rewritten until polished to high quality. You can see the contrast between this approach and what used to occur—the student wrote an essay, turned it in, received it back with red marks and a grade, and threw it away. Authentic assessment encourages students to investigate possibilities, make judgments, rethink efforts, and even redo work until the student considers it a quality product—remember Glasser's thoughts about quality in Chapter 5 and Jones's thoughts about a criterion of mastery in Chapter 7? It is the student, not the teacher, who decides when the work is good enough. The resultant improvement can be as objective an indicator of quality as are grades on tests.

Broad Grading Considerations for Authentic Assessments Portfolios, performance-based assessments, or assessment for problem-based learning are forms of authentic assessments. Teachers who plan for

Grade: C-
Timmy, your thesis was good, but you did not back it up with evidence from the text. Let's meet to talk about ways of improving this paper.

Grade: C-
Timmy, your thesis was good, but I don't like you. No matter how hard you work in this class, you'll never do well... because I don't like you.

WHAT TEACHERS WRITE

WHAT STUDENTS READ

Permission by Alejandro Yegros. http://alejandroyegros.com. Reprinted with permission.

and use authentic assessments as one means to judge student understanding and skill should consider the following general criteria (based on Paulson, Paulson, & Meyer, 1991, p. 60):

Depth: Evidence of personal growth through reflection, critical thinking, and insights

Breadth: Evidence of personal growth through multiple and varied experiences

Emphasis: All aspects of the work contribute to the theme of personal growth

Unity: Clear evidence of the process that supports the product of the study

Mechanics: Correct sentencing, spelling, capitalization, and punctuation

From the basis of these expectations, the teacher is able to make evaluations that ultimately may be converted to grades for records and report cards, described in the broadest terms as follows:

Exceptional achievement, earned by student work that is particularly well presented, well organized, insightful, and technically correct

Commendable achievement, earned by student work that is impressive and interesting but that is more loosely organized, less insightful, and not as informative as the exceptional work

Adequate achievement, earned by student work that, although acceptable, does not show good organization or display much critical thinking, insight, involvement, or growth

Minimal evidence of achievement, earned by student work that lacks depth and is weak in content, thought, and presentation

No evidence of achievement, earned by student work that is completely off-track, reveals no insights or other redeeming qualities, or is not the original work of the student

Student Portfolios

Students use portfolios to show their work, efforts, and talents, just as models, artists, architects, and others use portfolios to showcase their work. Portfolios play a central role in authentic assessment. Although the name can suggest a large and unwieldy container, a portfolio may simply be a file folder or a three-ring binder that contains organized work samples as well as written tests from most areas of the curriculum. The important thing is not how portfolios look, but how they are created, developed, and used.

A true portfolio requires *collection, selection,* and *reflection.* From a collection of all their work products, students select for inclusion in their portfolios pieces of work—not necessarily their A work—that they consider particularly noteworthy. Then they reflect and articulate orally or in writing why they selected each sample—why it is special and what they learned by completing it.

This process has significant benefits for students and teachers. Portfolios make students active participants in the assessment process. Portfolios show individual student's ranges of interests, abilities, and achievements over time. This provides teachers, students, and caregivers with much to discuss about student learning at school. The process of selection, articulation, and improvement over time provides a broad window into students' experiences and learning and can provide tangible profiles of their academic and personal growth.

Portfolios also provide concrete examples for teacher- and student-led parent conferencing. The teacher can say, "Here's what we'd like to accomplish. Here's where your child is. Here are some examples."

Portfolios in Different Subject Areas   Student portfolios are suitable for use in all subject areas and can easily be aligned with national, state, and district standards. Examples for the traditional areas of reading, writing, and arithmetic at the sixth-grade level might include:

For Reading

- Written responses to reading, such as character or problem analyses
- Book reports
- Literature-based projects or photographs with supporting details of projects
- Audiotapes, videotapes, or CDs of dramatic readings

For Writing

- Examples of free or creative writing
- Writing targeted for different audiences
- Writing for different purposes, such as persuasion, information, or entertainment
- Work in a variety of forms, such as poetry, journals, letters, and scripts

For Mathematics

- Math journals
- Projects and investigations
- Diagrams, graphs, charts

Grading Portfolios   Portfolios are whole efforts, not exhibits of individual items. It is important for teachers to view them as whole products. Although they are made up of individual samples of student work already reviewed and graded by the teacher, it is for the student to determine the items that are noteworthy and that provide evidence of progress and achievement. In addition to the general criteria listed above for authentic assessments, teachers would consider the following specific criteria related to the unity of the portfolio:

Unity: Clear evidence of the process of collection, selection, and reflection

---

Case Study 10.1   Portfolios in First Grade

FOCUS QUESTION

Nancy Rutherford describes how she uses portfolios with first graders. Brainstorm specific ways to use portfolios for assessment in intermediate and upper grades. What suggestions for evidence might students consider to include?

Mrs. Rutherford now uses portfolios with her first-grade students, but when she first heard about them, she thought they were too advanced a concept to be used in first grade. "I was put off by the logistics of storing the many oversized projects that are part of my curriculum. I also envisioned the portfolio as purely an assessment tool, so all in all their use didn't appeal to me.

"I've since changed my mind 180 degrees. I find portfolios to be a great asset in monitoring work in progress. My students realize that writing is not a one-time try. They learn to look at their work reflectively in terms of predetermined criteria, to assess strengths and weaknesses, and to rewrite accordingly. My favorite use of portfolios is to show individual progress. My students review their own work over time and generally are astonished at the differences they find. Even those who had top papers see how much they have improved."

Performance-Based Assessment

Simply, performance-based assessment uses observation and judgment (Stiggins, 2005; Parkay & Stanford, 2010, p. 384). Teachers focus on quality as they observe individuals or teams performing a task or using a skill, or as they examine student-made products. Focus here is on "students' ability to apply knowledge, skills, and work habits through the performance of tasks they find meaningful and engaging . . . [It] helps answer the question, 'How well can students use what they know?'" (Parkay & Stanford, 2010, p. 385). In addition to the broad considerations listed earlier in the chapter, teachers can use scoring rubrics when they assess performance work by students. Scoring rubrics, discussed later in this chapter, can be designed by teacher and students together to match the standards and the expectations for the performance task.

Problem-Based Learning Assessment

We described problem-based learning (PBL) as a teaching strategy in Chapter 6. There we highlighted teacher and student roles, along with limits, strengths, and usability of the strategy. Again, student work can be overlaid with the broad guidelines mentioned earlier in this chapter and scoring rubrics can be designed by teacher and students together.

Peer Assessment and Self-Assessment

Sometimes it is appropriate or efficient for peers to assess another's work. Sometimes self-assessment is appropriate.

"I won a lifetime achievement award today in kindergarten."

Bob Vojtko. Bob Vojtko Cartoons on Facebook. Reprinted with permission.

Peer assessment often occurs informally during class, as teachers read the correct homework or practice answers to objective questions. Peer feedback also can have value for reviewing student work such as essays. For this to be successful, time and practice must be given to teaching students the feedback and scoring expectations for the specific task or assignment. Students may be more accepting and understanding of the word choices and feedback of peers. Peer assessment also allows teachers to observe the process and provide any necessary input. However, most teachers prefer—and rightly so—to carefully review and grade work that is intended to demonstrate what and how much students learned.

Self-assessment has students assess both their work and their thinking as they did the work. Students can learn a great deal when they really take time to think about their work process. Self-assessment is a skill that must be taught and practiced in a way that is age- and ability-appropriate. No matter the approach used for self-assessment, it also is important to teach the scoring criteria to the students before they try to assess their own work. Younger students and those who are struggling can be taught to label their work as a traffic light: green has only minor problems but overall is good work; yellow needs some work but is OK; red has problems and the student would benefit from teacher help. While students with green and yellow assessments meet in small groups to help each other, the teacher holds minitutorials with students with red labels to work on their problems. For older or more advanced students, guiding questions can help direct student self-assessment: "What have I learned as a result of this activity? What problems did I encounter during my learning? How will I overcome these problems in the future?" (Parkay & Stanford, 2010, p. 384).

Rubrics and Their Use

A *rubric* is a scoring guide or assessment scale that is devised to match the standards, objectives, and learning goals of a specific assignment. Because rubrics reflect both broad evaluation standards and specific evaluation criteria, they provide clear descriptions of what students are expected to achieve.

Rubrics can be written for any subject and adapted to any grade level. They require teachers (and even students) to think more clearly about intended goals and quality work. Well-written rubrics help teachers to score students' work more accurately and fairly. Rubrics match student work to predetermined scoring standards rather than to other students' work (unlike standardized tests) or to expectations held for each individual student. Whether teachers actually develop rubrics with their students or simply share the scoring guides, students profit from clear knowledge of expectations, and that knowledge then guides their work. In fact, it can be very beneficial for teacher and students to discuss learning goals and from those discussions develop the rubrics together.

There are, however, things teachers don't like about rubrics. For one, rubrics don't neatly match other systems, such as letter grades. Also, rubrics can be difficult to explain to caregivers. In addition, it takes time to develop successful rubrics, especially those that describe multiple aspects of performance, each with its own criteria and attainment levels.

The right language is critical when developing rubrics because it must articulate clearly the qualities of student performance that distinguish the levels of work and effort. Over a period of time, teachers may write and refine a project or performance rubric several times in order to make it resemble closely what they actually expect to see in the student work. In order to ensure the integrity and quality of the rubric, in addition to high scores, students actually must be able to perform the task. If this does not occur, the criteria may be wrong and require revision or refinement. Depending on the grade level, a variety of broad

Vignette 10.1   Rubric to Guide Kindergarten Digital Storytellers

Linda Foote moved from her elementary classrooms to the Support Services department of her district office, where she works as a Technology Integration Specialist, and now is able to mentor teachers in curriculum planning based on student assessment outcomes.

"In this position I have the opportunity to work with teachers and coach them to align their teaching with the content standards and their students' needs. In the process we explore how to use technology to engage their students and increase student learning.

"In one kindergarten classroom, as students were beginning their work on a digital storytelling project, they analyzed digital stories to determine what elements made a story more powerful and interesting. From this work they developed a rubric that would help them create a digital story that would be strong in all critical elements: photos, camera shots, storyboard, fluency, costumes, and music.

"Unlike other rubrics that provide a continuum from poor to excellent, the students determined that no range except for excellent was acceptable to them on this project. So, their ranges became 'needs to improve,' (How can you make it better), 'is basically OK,' and 'is ready to go.' Their descriptors for each element defined excellence. They determined if any element of their digital story was less than 'ready to go,' according to their rubric, they would rework it until their project was excellent in all areas. Using this strategy, their digital story truly was amazing."

(Continued)

Let's Think About Great Digital Stories
(A Rubric to Guide Digital Storytellers)

Story: interesting, has a climax, solves the problem, "each page makes you wonder what is on the next page," has elements of humor and surprise	How can you make it better		
Music: sets the mood, matches the story and makes it better (speed, words, beat)	How can you make it better		
Make-up and Costumes: match characters' roles	How can you make it better		
Photos: help audience focus on important details, background doesn't distract, Ken Burn's effects help the story and don't distract or make you dizzy	How can you make it better		
Use of close-ups capture the viewer's attention and show the storyline or emotion	How can you make it better		
Transitions: Support the story and don't distract the viewer	How can you make it better		
Speakers: speak clearly, with lots of expression, not too fast, not too slow	How can you make it better		

Source: Linda C. Foote. Reprinted with permission.

UPON REFLECTION

Rubrics are key to successful projects. Ask several teachers for rubrics they have developed or used for assignments and projects. If they developed the rubric, to what extent did they involve students in creating the rubric? What challenges did they encounter in the process?

descriptors can be used to label very specific expectations for the elements of the task that are being assessed:

- Exemplary achievement, commendable achievement, adequate achievement, limited or minimal achievement, no response
- Exemplary, proficient, progressing, or not meeting the standard

As we have suggested, successful rubrics are designed to match specific assignments and tasks. Figure 10.1 shows a sample rubric for a very specific multimedia project that was developed with teachers who were learning to create a PowerPoint presentation to use with their students.

Figure 10.1

Sample Rubric for a Multimedia Project: Nonlinear PowerPoint Presentations

The following rubric was created with teachers who were learning to create nonlinear PowerPoint presentations to increase student learning.

CATEGORY	4	3	2	1
Content	Covers topic accurately, in-depth, with details and examples. Subject knowledge is excellent.	Includes essential knowledge about the topic. Subject knowledge appears to be good.	Includes essential information about the topic but there are 1 or 2 factual errors.	Content is minimal AND/OR there are several factual errors.
Standards and Essential Questions	Standards are clearly addressed. Responses to essential, engaging questions demonstrate student understanding of the topic.	Standards are partially addressed. Somewhat engaging essential questions and good responses are present, although they show less insight and student understanding of the topic.	Standards are aligned with video and project. Limited essential questions and responses show minimal insight and understanding of the topic.	Standards are not addressed clearly. Few or no essential questions are present. Little or no evidence of student understanding of the topic.
Nonlinear Elements	Main concept is clear. Nonlinear elements clearly demonstrate student's understanding of the concept.	Main concept is clear. Some of the nonlinear elements support student's understanding of the concept.	Main concept is stated. The nonlinear elements may not all support or build understanding of the concept.	Main concept is unclear. The non-linear elements do not all support student's understanding of the main concept.
Attractiveness	Presentation is enhanced through excellent use of font, color, graphics, and effects.	Presentation is enhanced through good use of font, color, graphics, and effects.	Font, color, graphics, and effects are used, but occasionally they detract from the presentation content.	Font, color, graphics, and effects are used, but often they detract from the presentation content.

Source: Linda C. Foote, Technology Integration Specialist, Poway Unified School District, CA. Reprinted with permission.

- *Four-point rubric:* 4 points, exceeds standard (E); 3 points, meets standard (M); 2 points, below standard, improvement required (B); 1 point, below standard, requires major improvements (B)

Four-level rubrics such as these avoid a safe, "average" response. Occasionally, a six-point rubric is needed to indicate finer gradations of quality:

- *Six-point rubric:* 5–6 points, exceeds standard (E); 4 points, meets standard (M); 3 points, below standard, improvement required (B); 2/1 points, below standard, requires major improvements (B)

And sometimes a simple three-level rubric such as the following is appropriate, especially for younger children:

- Star (✶), smiley face (☺), or straight face (☹)

Records and Record Keeping

Ongoing assessment and good records of student progress must be kept to promote effective instruction, good learning, and efficient reporting to caregivers and administrators. Other reasons for keeping accurate records are to furnish data to other schools, to keep attendance (on which financial aid is based), to show student achievement, and to evaluate and modify the district and school curriculum periodically. Additionally, the No Child Left Behind Act requires that records be used in evaluating schools and districts for accountability. Specifically, NCLB focuses on two concerns: (1) increasing the academic performance of all students enrolled in public schools and (2) improving the performance of low-performing schools.

What Teachers Want Records to Show

From the teacher's perspective, good records can indicate quickly, at any time during the year, where individual students stand academically, socially, and behaviorally. Teachers need this information for teaching, evaluating students, planning for the future, and conferring with and reporting to caregivers and other interested individuals. Records should show the following for individual students: instructional level; progress; unreached standards, goals, and objectives; strengths and weaknesses; and social and behavioral adjustment.

Instructional Level A student's instructional level in any part of the curriculum is the level at which new learning is challenging yet possible. These levels are especially important in classrooms where differentiated instruction or Response to Intervention (RTI) procedures are being used. Instructional level is determined through observation, ongoing monitoring of student performance, and occasionally, formal testing. The scores, work samples, and anecdotal comments that serve as indicators are recorded in formats that will be discussed later.

Progress Teachers, students, and caregivers appreciate evidence that the student is making genuine progress. But lack of progress must be noted as well, for this is where replanning, corrective instruction, and second chances begin. Second chances help determine whether the corrective instruction was effective, and they give students another opportunity to be successful in their learning. Progress can be shown in several ways. One of the most common ways is to compare pre- and posttest scores, useful in spelling and math. Another way is to compare samples of work, as in writing and art, done a few weeks apart. Yet another way is to show increased performance through standards and objectives that have been reached and through books that have been read. Also, student progress in the RTI process is carefully monitored. Whatever the method, results should be individual and private to avoid showing a student in a bad light when compared to others.

Unreached Standards, Goals, and Objectives Caregivers are interested in their child's progress, as well as in what remains to be accomplished. Well-managed records provide this information, either in a list of standards or objectives that can be checked off when attained or in notations of material to be covered in textbooks.

Strengths and Weaknesses Student strengths and weaknesses become apparent by examining test scores, other records, and the contents of portfolios or work folders. Teachers note error patterns as they analyze student work, develop ideas for appropriate corrective instruction, and provide opportunities for students to have a second chance to be successful in their learning. Occasionally, specialists may be asked to administer diagnostic tests to individual students. Such tests reveal specific weaknesses and error patterns as well as general overall scores. When needed, the RTI process provides tiers of intervention. Student progress in the general education class is carefully monitored. Intensity and more individualized instruction and support are increased as student needs require. (Read more about the RTI process in Appendix A.)

Social Adjustment and Behavior The abilities to relate acceptably and work cooperatively and productively with others are among the most important outcomes of schooling. Evidence of social adjustment and responsible behavior is obtained on an informal basis by the teacher, who observes and notes how a student gets along with classmates, shows manners and courtesy, cooperates, takes turns, accepts responsibility, and abides by class rules. Teachers compile this evidence by entering brief comments on progress forms for each student. Documentation by teachers of irresponsible behavior, along with the history of intervention and remediation efforts, also is helpful to teachers, administrators, and caregivers who share concern for a child. All this information is of special interest to caregivers, most of whom want their child to behave, cooperate, and learn as much as possible.

As students work more and more in cooperative learning groups and teams, they should be taught to judge the quality of their own work and the efforts of their team. The teacher can help by providing a review sheet such as that shown in Figure 10.2. Note that the contributions of every member are recorded as positive comments. If a member makes no contribution, the space is left blank.

Future Instructional Plans In every parent–teacher conference, attention should be given to future instructional plans for the student. For the most part these plans will be carried out at school, but sometimes they require assistance at home from the parents or

Figure 10.2

Contributions Review

Project Activity _____   Date _____

Leader _____   Contributions _____

Recorder _____   Contributions _____

Member _____   Contributions _____

Member _____   Contributions _____

Member _____   Contributions _____

Member _____   Contributions _____

Problems: Describe any problems the group had and tell what you did to help correct the
problem. _____

guardians. Student records substantiate the need for assistance, indicate the areas in which
it should be provided, and describe how caregivers can help provide assistance.

Forms and Formats for Good Record Keeping

Computer programs exist for electronic record keeping, and many districts now provide—
and expect—teachers to use them. GlobalScholar and the Northwest Evaluation Association (NWEA) are two companies that offer assessment packages to districts for purchase.
GlobalScholar, at http://www.pinnaclesuite.com, offers Pinnacle Suite to help educators
meet the needs and support individual needs of learners. Their modules include numerous
tools: grade book, curriculum and assessment, analytics, student information system, professional development, and accelerated learning. NWEA also offers programs to districts
through its website, http://www.nwea.org. NWEA provides an online reporting suite that
shows growth on assessments given in the fall, winter, and spring. It determines where each
student, class, or grade level is performing in relation to district performance, international
performance, and personal performance. For each student, data are available that show pre-
dicted growth and instructional statements that describe what he or she is ready to learn.
Thus, participating districts and teachers are able to access valuable data that can be used to
plan most efficiently and effectively for their students.

Standards and Continuums It is crucial for teachers to know the state standards, the
district expectations and benchmarks, and what is expected on the district report cards.
Standards or benchmarks may be listed as written statements or checklists in newer curriculum guides and textbook teachers' editions. Objectives are written statements that precisely describe the intended outcomes of instruction—what students should know or be
able to do because of the instruction and supporting experiences. Standards or objectives

Figure 10.3

Portion of a Kindergarten Math Skills Continuum

Student Names	Identify and complete pattern	Match set members	Identify set with most	Match set of 6 to numeral	Identify set 1 less than 5	Identify set 1 more than 2	Identify greatest numeral	Identify counting order (1–4)	Identify counting order (11–13)

form what is called a *continuum* when they are organized into a particular order or sequence. Continuums are helpful to teachers in tracking student progress. Normally, they simply are checked off when attained, although codes may be used to better qualify level of mastery. For example, a slash (/) indicates that a concept or skill was introduced. When mastery occurs, the slash is crossed to make an X. Other systems may indicate the date of mastery, the number of attempts before mastery, and the degree to which the standard or objective was attained—for example, mastery or proficient (M or P), satisfactory (S), and improvement needed (I). Figure 10.3 shows an excerpt from a portion of a kindergarten math skills continuum.

Individual Records Folders Personal records folders contain all essential information about students and are indispensable when conferencing with caregivers and administrators, as well as with students themselves. They may include graphs that indicate progress in math, spelling, and other areas, and updated samples of student work. Folders should be kept current and in a secure location when not in use.

Progress Forms and Graphs Forms such as Figure 10.4 give a general summary of student progress in all subjects. Anecdotal narratives identify the evidence for progress (or lack thereof) for each subject of the elementary curriculum. Graphs are an easy visual depiction of progress in increments over time.

Work Samples Samples of student work show accomplishments, progress, and challenges over time. They are useful in judging and documenting student performance, but

Figure 10.4

Student Progress Sheet

Name _____

	Pretest	Midtest	Posttest

Reading
 San Diego Quick—level
 Oral Reading Test—level
 Silent Reading Test—level
 Word attack needs _____

Mathematics
 Math grade-level test—
 Basic facts (see graphs)
 Word problem application _____

Language
 Spelling placement
 Word lists and scores (see graphs and samples)
 Capitalization, punctuation, grammar _____
_____

Composition and Penmanship (see samples) _____
_____

Social Studies _____
_____

Science & Health _____
_____

Art (see samples) _____
_____

Music _____
_____

Physical Education (see graphs) _____
_____

Character Education Community _____

Technology _____

Other _____

Social Behavior _____
_____

some areas, such as physical education/movement and character education/community, do not yield useful work samples. Always try, however, to include something in math, language, social studies, and art, as appropriate for the grade level.

Records for Various Curriculum Areas

Different areas of the curriculum involve different content standards, benchmarks, and goals. Consequently, they call for different records.

Mathematics Several records are useful for mathematics. Continuums provide an overview of the program and indications of progress as student skills and progress are checked off. Records sheets can track student competencies and errors on different types of math problems. Graphs show a record of timed exercises in addition, subtraction, multiplication, division, and word problems.

Language Arts The elementary language arts program encompasses multiple areas of study in reading and writing, each with its own needs for effective record keeping.

Reading Useful reading records show assessment scores in comprehension and fluency, standards or objectives continuums, and lists of books and other materials read by the student. Instead of simply listing titles and dates, many students find it motivating to add segments to a bookworm of books read or add leaves or ornaments to a picture of a tree. A form of grade-appropriate skills in language arts (similar to the math skills shown in Figure 10.3) can be used to document specific standards, benchmarks, or objectives reached and not reached by the student.

Running records of students' reading help teachers to assess reading fluency. By calculating the percentage of words the student reads aloud correctly, the teacher can determine how well the text matches the student's level at the time. The teacher also analyzes miscues or errors for possible patterns in order to plan minilessons, tutorials, and other word study activities. Running records, such as that shown in Figure 10.5, are made easier when the teacher makes notations directly on a duplicate copy of the text as the student reads.

Spelling Records show scores on weekly spelling tests and work on special word lists or bonus words. Teachers also need to assess spelling in written work—are words mastered on the spelling test carrying over to a student's written work?

Grammar and Vocabulary Anecdotal appraisals and comments are best for this part of the language arts curriculum. *Grammar* refers to general language usage, both oral and written, including sentence structure, subject-verb agreement, correct verb tenses, and so forth. The teacher notes errors that seem to recur and makes comments, if needed, on the student's progress sheet (Figures 10.4).

Writing Comments about penmanship and composition are entered here. Composition is further divided into expository and creative writing. *Expository writing* emphasizes clear and sequential expression of ideas and involves skills in organization, paragraph construction, the

Figure 10.5

Individual Reading Inventory (IRI)

Student _____ Grade _____ Teacher/Rm _____

Date _____ Recorder _____ Comments _____

Competencies (circle predominant behaviors)
1-to-1 matching   Directionality   Fluent Reading

At an unknown word				**Calculations**
Makes no attempt	Seeks help	Reruns	Reads on	Error Ratio $\underline{RW} = 1$
Attempts using . . .	Visual	Meaning	Structure	E

Accuracy % 91%

After an error				S/C Rate $\underline{E + SC} = 1$
Ignores	Seeks help	Reruns	Attempts S/C	SC
Self-corrects using . . .	Visual	Meaning	Structure	Level: Easy Instr Hard

						Cues	Used
Level: 4	**RW: 53**			**Totals:**			
Page	**Cues Used** **Title:** Where Is My Hat?		**Words:**	**E**	**SC**	**E**	**SC**
2	"Where is my hat?" said Ben						
3	Ben looked under his bed. "It is not here," he said.						
4	Mom looked in the closet. "It is not here," she said.						
5	Ben looked in his toybox. "It is not here," he said.						
	He looked and looked.						
6	Mom looked behind the chair.						
7	"Here it is!" she said.						

use of topic and subordinate sentences, and so forth. *Creative writing* stresses the artistic side of writing—expression, novelty of presentation, and varied forms of prose and verse. In both cases, before and after samples show student progress, although if the work is handwritten, the student's penmanship can influence the contrast.

Social Studies Content and skills vary according to grade level. Samples of project work often reflect team or group effort and are best kept as records with photographs or video or CD recordings. Narrative appraisals on a progress form describe the type of work done, the student's level of involvement, quality of participation, and any extra efforts that might have been undertaken. A compilation video or CD of all the students as they work on various projects throughout the year makes a nice addition to the class library and an enjoyable feature at the spring open house.

Science and Health These subjects are similar to social studies in that they usually involve large units of study and group projects. Consequently, similar record keeping is appropriate.

Art If it has not been cut for budget reasons, the art program usually consists of appreciation and production. Because art appreciation is difficult to measure, simple records that note experiences are appropriate. Production art, however, provides samples that show artistic growth.

Music This is another subject that might be cut for budget reasons. Neither appreciation nor music production gives scores or products that show attainment of objectives or growth. Thus, simple notations about experiences are appropriate.

Physical Education In elementary schools, physical education rarely is presented through formal instruction. Students are taught to play various games and more or less fend for themselves while an adult supervises their play. Before budget cuts, some teachers and schools offered programs in running, cardiovascular fitness, and individual sports that promoted coordination and muscle tone. For these programs, time, distances, numbers or repetitions, and so forth could be recorded and graded.

Simplify Records Management

Good complete records can be kept rather easily. Record keeping need not be a distasteful and overwhelming burden. Consider the following suggestions:

1. As budgets, resources, and accessibility allow, save time and work by using computers and software programs to assess and record. Or adapt spreadsheets for this purpose. They can help organize and manage grades, log standards and objectives that are attained by the student, and send or print record forms and progress notes for caregivers. Learning to make use of the enormous capabilities of electronic record keeping programs can be pleasant and efficient for teacher and students alike. Attitude is the key.

2. Relate all records directly to the standards, benchmarks, or objectives used in the district, curriculum guides, and/or teachers' editions of textbooks.

3. Use record-keeping forms or electronic programs that require minimum marking or data entry.

4. Supplement the forms or data entries with samples of student work that show progress toward standards, benchmarks, and objectives.

5. Do the record keeping while at school. When working with paper records, have aides or volunteers help. To the extent possible, involve students, as such participation motivates, shares responsibility, and conveys ownership to students of their own education. It also makes for more timely feedback. Remember, however, that students have the right to privacy regarding their work and progress, and because records are legal documents, you alone are legally responsible for their management, recording, and accuracy.

6. Make the individual records folders and portfolios sources of pride for students. They show student accomplishments, capabilities, and progress. Help students see them as extensions of themselves.

Vignette 10.2   Record Keeping with Technology

Lynne Harvey teaches fourth grade in a district that has collaborated with the Northwest Evaluation Association (NWEA) in Seattle to develop and provide districtwide formative assessment and communication options to educators, students, and caregivers.

"Our grade-level teams use a formative assessment program called Measurement of Academic Progress (MAPS) to set short- and long-term curriculum goals. MAPS focuses on reading, math, and language, and is aligned with the STAR tests. We set and are able to monitor benchmark guidelines for every student every trimester.

"A paper-pencil version of MAPS once existed; however, our students now take a computer-adapted version three times a year in a computer lab setting. An advantage of computerized testing is that students and teachers are able to view results immediately. Then in a few days NWEA provides us with more elaborate data of the students' progress. Once the data are available, teachers, parents, and students are able to access personal learning ladders that identify areas for growth and provide programs to raise scores in areas of lower achievement.

"With MAPS we also are able to articulate curriculum decisions across grade levels. In this way we avoid redundancies and omissions in the elementary curricula. Additionally, we are better able to place students for the next year."

UPON REFLECTION

Technology can benefit or hinder a teacher's ability to assess, record, and track student work and progress. In what ways can electronic record keeping be helpful? In what ways can it hinder? Take a few minutes to check out the MAPS program at the following website: http://www.nwea.

Records Needed for Conferencing

Most teachers personally conference with caregivers at least once a year. Some conference more frequently, and there are times as well when student study teams, IEP meetings, and conferences about particular students must be held with administrators and specialists. The quality of input that regular education teachers bring to these conferences is sharply increased by good records. Suggestions for communicating and conferencing with caregivers are presented in Chapter 4 and Chapter 11. The following materials will help you feel well prepared for any conference.

The Individual Student Folder The individual student work folder provides your most useful set of materials for conferencing with or about a student. Progress forms that succinctly describe the curriculum, either paper or electronic, can be attached inside the front cover or placed on top of the other content. Progress forms also should show scores and comments about how the student is doing in each area. Graphs that show evidence of progress can be attached to the back cover. Work samples and lists that provide concrete evidence of student effort, accomplishments, and progress are inside the folder.

Notes about Future Plans Student strengths and weaknesses, revealed in the records folder, may suggest future instructional plans for the student. Take a moment before the conference to make notes concerning such plans to discuss with the caregiver or administrator.

Notes about Suggestions for Help at Home Caregivers should be informed if necessary about how they can help at home with future plans. Their assistance might consist of setting definite uninterrupted study times, working for short periods of time with drill or spelling, listening to their child read aloud, or discussing with the child the plot of a story or book that is being read. Remind caregivers that their involvement normally serves to increase their child's achievement. This information should be made available to parents and guardians in their primary language.

Student-Involved Conferencing Some teachers have found student-involved conferences to be very valuable and powerful. These may be goal-setting conferences in the early fall or progress and sharing conferences later in the year. Both teacher and student participate in sharing information with the caregivers, although the teacher's role and degree of participation vary with the purpose of the conference.

For fall goal-setting conferences, students begin a 15-minute conference time by sharing their personal goals, describing their learnings, and presenting some of their work. Student, teacher, and caregivers recognize strengths demonstrated by the student's work, and then each identifies an area or two that the student needs to work on. The student states one or two personal goals for future work, and the teacher and caregivers promise specific help toward meeting the goals. The teacher then answers questions, summarizes, and concludes the conference.

Conferences that occur later in the school year usually serve a much different purpose. This is when students use their own portfolio with preselected work samples and artifacts to share accomplishments and progress. In preparing for this type of conference, students self-assess and are able to provide remarkable insights into the quality of their work and what they need to do to improve.

Before scheduling student-led conferences, teachers must prepare students carefully. These conferences are most successful when students have actual rehearsal opportunities. For older students, peers, parent volunteers, and the teacher can listen to the rehearsal. Cross-age tutors and cross-grade partners can be taught to provide helpful feedback to younger students.

It is essential that students and caregivers understand both the learning goals and their roles for either type of conference. Furthermore, they all must be willing to give thought to the student's strengths and areas for growth and how they can participate toward improvement. In any event, student-led conferences bring the focus back to the children.

Ancillary Materials The records folder and notes usually are sufficient. However, during the conference, you should have standards, benchmarks, and objectives continuums; a curriculum guide and textbooks; and workbooks and sample worksheets nearby. These materials should not be referred to unless there are questions about standards, benchmarks, objectives, materials, or activities.

This concludes the review of assessment considerations that fall to the teacher's control—alternative and authentic assessments, management of high-quality electronic and paper records, and preparation for reporting to parents and guardians. Before moving ahead to Chapter 11, which deals with managing communication with students, caregivers, and others, take time to review these end-of-chapter activities.

Parting Thought

I have learned that success is to be measured not so much by the position that one has reached in life as by the obstacles he has overcome while trying to succeed.

—Booker T. Washington

Summary Self-Check

Check off the following as you either understand or become able to apply them:

- □ Assessment, record keeping, and reporting are requirements of teaching that few teachers enjoy, although now with alternative and authentic assessments and technology tools, the tasks are becoming less burdensome and, for some teachers, even enjoyable.
- □ Assessments that relate directly to what teachers cover in the class help teachers test more accurately what they teach.
- □ Types of assessment: standardized and normed testing, teacher-created, diagnostic or placement, formative, summative, alternative or authentic.
- □ Corrective instruction is part of the instructional process and helps students learn.
- □ Standardized tests, which help teachers determine whether students know the content, are an effort to respond to public concern regarding accountability, but may alter curriculum by making teachers teach to the test.
- □ Alternative and authentic assessments minimize the use of tests while emphasizing products that result from student work. Those products provide greater insight into student abilities and accomplishments than do tests, and help teachers determine how well students can use what they know.
- □ Alternative and authentic products can be judged objectivity with the use of carefully designed rubrics.
- □ Records of student performance should reflect the following for any student at any time: academic instructional levels, specific strengths and weaknesses, progress that has occurred, social adjustment and behavior, future instructional plans.
- □ Record management simplified: use technology and software programs, relate records to specific standards and objectives; use record forms and electronic programs that require minimum marking or data entry; make entries while at school; make individual records folders a source of pride for students.
- □ Records are legal documents and teachers alone are legally responsible for their management, recording, and accuracy.
- □ Records during conferencing: use the individual student folder to describe strengths, needs, and progress; make notes about future plans for the student; make notes about how caregivers can help at home.
- □ Student-led conferences for personal goal setting (early in the year) and accomplishments (later in the year) reveal much about student progress and learning.

Activities for Reflection and Discussion

1. Take a moment to review the statements in the Preview–Review Guide at the beginning of this chapter. Put a check mark in the *Review* column next to any statement with which you now agree. How have your thoughts changed since reading this chapter?

2. Interview at least two teachers about their assessment and record-keeping practices. In what ways do they involve students in assessment? What information and records do they find necessary and helpful to keep? How do they use and manage electronic tools to help with their record keeping?

3. Describe how you will balance standardized testing and authentic assessment alternatives in a grade of your choosing.

4. Organize a record-keeping system for a grade of your choice. Set it up so all of the required work can be done at school.

5. Explain how you would use a student records folder to describe to a caregiver in 10 minutes or less a child's achievement and needs in your class.

6. You are to conference with caregivers who have a history of criticizing and berating teachers for unfairly assigning grades to their child. What have you included in the child's folder to counter or forestall the expected criticisms? Explain.

7. Briefly describe a social studies project for a grade of your choice. Create a rubric to score the project objectively.

Webliography

Assessment Tools from the Northwest Evaluation Association: http://www.nwea.org
Discovery Software, LTD. *Rubrics:* http://www.rubrics.com
MidLink Magazine. *Rubrics:* http://www.ncsu.edu/midlink/ho.html
National Center for Education Statistics: http://www.nces.ed.gov
Pinnacle Suite Assessment Package by GlobalScholar: http://www.pinnaclesuite.com
Rubrics: http://ed.web.sdsu.edu/webquest/rubrics/weblessons.htm,
    www.ncsu.edu/midlink/ho.html and http://www.rubrics.com
The Source for Learning, Inc. Webquest 101 – *Putting Discovery into the Curriculum:*
    http://www.teachersfirst.com/summer/webquest/quest-b.shtml.

References and Recommended Readings

Alphonso, C. (2003). *The Globe and Mail: A poor student's worst nightmare*. Retrieved August 8, 2003 from http://www.globetechnology.com/servlet/ArticleNews/TPStory/LAC/20030808/USTUDNO

Brookhart, S., Moss, C., & Long, B. (2008, November). Formative assessment that empowers. *Educational Leadership, 66*(3), 52–57.

Cooper, B., & Gargan, A. (2009, September). Rubrics in education: Old term, new meanings. *Phi Delta Kappan, 91*(1), 54–55.

Easton, L. (2007, January). Walking our talk about standards. *Phi Delta Kappan, 88*(5), 391–394.

Fisher, D., & Frey, N. (2007). *Checking for understanding: Formative assessment techniques for your classroom.* Alexandria, VA: ASCD.

Glasser, W. (1998). *The quality school teacher* (rev. ed.). New York: HarperCollins.

Informative assessment. (December 2007–January 2008). [*Special Issue*]. *Educational Leadership, 65*(4). Alexandria, VA: ASCD.

Kohn, A. (1999). *Punished by rewards.* Boston: Houghton Mifflin.

Marzano, R. (2000). *Transforming classroom grading.* Alexandria, VA: ASCD.

McMillan, J. (2001). *Classroom assessment: Principles and practice for effective instruction* (2nd ed.). Boston: Allyn & Bacon.

Morrison, G. (2002). *Teaching in America* (3rd ed.). Boston: Allyn & Bacon.

Multiple Measures (2009, November). [Special Issue]. *Educational Leadership, 67*(3). Alexandria, VA: ASCD.

Parkay, F., & Stanford, B. (2010). *Becoming a teacher* (8th ed.). Upper Saddle River, NJ: Merrill.

Paulson, F., Paulson, P., & Meyer, C. (1991). What makes a portfolio a portfolio? *Educational Leadership, 48*(5), 60–63.

Popham, W. An unintentional deception. (2008, October). *Educational Leadership, 66*(2), 80–81.

Scriffiny, P. (2008, October). Seven reasons for standards-based grading. *Educational Leadership, 66*(2), 70–74.

Stiggins, R. J. (2004, September). Assessment for learning: New assessment beliefs for a new school mission. *Phi Delta Kappan, 86*, 22–27.

Stiggins, R. (2005). *Student-involved assessment for learning* (4th ed.). Upper Saddle River, NJ: Pearson/Merrill Prentice Hall.

Stiggins, R. (2007, May). Assessment through the students' eyes. *Educational Leadership, 64*(8), 22–26.

Tomlinson, C., & McTighe, J. (2006). *Integrating differentiated instruction and understanding by design: Connecting content and kids.* Alexandria, VA: ASCD.

Wiggins, G. (1994, November). Toward better report cards. *Educational Leadership, 52*(2), 28–37.

Trade Books

Dr. Seuss, Prelutsky, J., & Smith, L. (1998). *Hooray for Diffendoofer Day!* New York: Alfred A. Knopf.

Finchler, J. (2000). *Testing Miss Malarkay.* New York: Walker & Company.

PEARSON **myeducationlab**

Go to the Topic: **Planning, Conducting, and Managing Instruction** in the MyEducationLab (www.myeducationlab.com) for your course, where you can:

- Find learning outcomes for **Planning, Conducting, and Managing Instruction** along with the national standards that connect to these outcomes.
- Apply and practice your understanding of the core teaching skills identified in the chapter with the Building Teaching Skills and Dispositions learning units.
- Examine challenging situations and cases presented in the IRIS Center Resources.
- Use interactive Simulations in Classroom Management to practice decision making and to receive expert feedback on classroom management choices.

Managing Communication with Students, Caregivers, and Others

11

The most important thing in communication is to hear what isn't being said.

—Peter F. Drucker

Preview–Review Guide

Before you read the chapter, and based on what you know, think you know, or assume, take a minute to put a check mark in the ***Preview*** column if you agree with the statement. When you finish the chapter, take time to reread the statements and respond in the ***Review*** column. Reflective discussions can develop because many of the statements are not clearly "yes" or "no."

Preview   **Review**

1. _____ It is the student's responsibility to communicate with the teacher when concerned about something in the classroom.   _____

2. _____ The main purpose of the four-way test is to ensure that what you are saying is factual.   _____

3. _____ Parallel communication in elementary classrooms means that both teacher and student use the "adult" style, as described by Berne.

4. _____ Supportive feedback and encouragement, as well as appropriate corrective feedback, are valuable to others.   _____

5. _____ Teachers tend to give less attention to students who behave properly and do their work consistently.   _____

6. _____ The main purposes of parent–teacher conferences are to become acquainted and to give caregivers the opportunity to talk.   _____

7. _____ The purpose of win-win conflict resolution is to find a good solution without either disputant feeling put down.   _____

8. _____ Glasser and Nelsen suggest that class meetings be scheduled whenever the teacher senses a problem that involves the class.   _____

9. _____ Communication skills—both verbal and nonverbal—contribute more to the quality of teaching than any other skill.   _____

10. _____ When telephoning caregivers, teachers should try to draw out their feelings, even though the process might take some time.   _____

Chapter Objectives:

After reading Chapter 11, students will demonstrate understanding of

- various forms of communication that teachers use with students and others

- Bloom's revised taxonomy of the cognitive domain and its connections to questioning and student work

through their active participation in discussions and the end-of-chapter activities for reflection.

What are your memories when you think back to your best school experiences, to those classes or rooms where you learned most and you found yourself most engaged in education? Chances are you recall teachers and others who were there, more than what you actually were taught. That's because so much of school learning occurs from exchanges with others. This phenomenon, also present in work and leisure, helps us understand that interaction with others is what makes life most rewarding and memorable. A problem to solve or an essential or guiding question for this chapter might be: *How can I manage the many forms of communication I will use daily with my students and others?*

The Value of Communication

When it comes to teaching, communication—the interchange of information, thoughts, and feelings—is the vehicle that moves education forward. It is the means by which teachers motivate, inform, guide, encourage, meet needs, build relationships, and otherwise stir the educational pot. Most individuals think of communication as verbal—what we say and hear, what we write and read, and now even what we send and receive electronically. In Chapter 4 we pointed out that a fairly small percentage of what individuals communicate to others is done with actual word choices. A much larger percentage of communication is done through the sounds of words and through facial expressions and body language. In other words, much of what we communicate is nonverbal; we convey powerful messages through proximity and facial and body cues (Jones, 2007).

Teachers must communicate routinely with students, caregivers, colleagues, support providers, and administrators. Those who do it well earn cooperation, respect, and even esteem. It is not farfetched to say that communication contributes more to the quality of teaching than does any other skill. It is no accident that teachers who enjoy the greatest success in teaching also happen to be good managers of communication.

Despite its obvious importance, communication rarely is emphasized in teacher education. Most teachers have to learn how to manage it while on the job. This chapter is intended to help by offering an overview of communication requirements and suggestions for their successful accomplishment.

Uses of Communication

Throughout the school day, good communication is repeatedly necessary. Consider the following:

- Giving directions—making them brief and clear
- Conducting instruction—teaching clearly, gently, and patiently

- Holding class discussions and meetings—being receptive, nonthreatening, positive, and helpful
- Meeting with student support providers—being open and collaborative
- Corresponding electronically or meeting in person with staff, administrators, beginning teacher support providers, and other teachers—shedding all defensiveness and applying the four-way test, which follows
- Corresponding electronically or meeting individually with administrators and colleagues—being pleasant, helpful, and supportive
- Contacting electronically or conferencing with caregivers in person or by telephone—treating them as equals who prize their child above all else

The Four-Way Test

The four-way test asks four direct questions that all people should consider silently as they work on their communication skills. Teachers should keep these questions in mind when they communicate electronically or speak in person with students, caregivers, and others:

1. Is what I am saying or writing true?

2. Is it helpful?

3. Would my silence hurt?

4. Will my saying or writing this build good relationships?

To better understand the magnitude of communication that occurs within the domain of school—to what, how, and to whom school communication applies—review the grid shown in Figure 11.1. Notice the groups of persons—students, caregivers, colleagues, and administrators—with whom teachers regularly communicate and the five primary purposes served by communication—to inform, instruct, build relationships, maintain class control, and build esprit de corps. These points will be explained in the sections that follow.

Figure 11.1

A Classroom Communication Grid

	Persons			
Purposes	**Students**	**Caregivers**	**Colleagues**	**Administrators**
1. Inform	x	x	x	x
2. Instruct	x			
3. Relate	x	x	x	x
4. Control	x			
5. Spirit	x	x		

Although communication is a dynamic two-way engagement, understand that teachers must guide the process. The remainder of this chapter is divided into three parts representing the three groups to whom teacher communication is aimed: (1) students, (2) caregivers, and (3) colleagues and administrators.

Communicating with Students

In 1964 Eric Berne identified three "states" individuals exhibit when talking with others: the child state, the parent state, and the adult state. The *child state* is shown when we talk with someone to whom we feel inferior. We defer to authority and perhaps behave emotionally. The *parent state* is exhibited when we talk with someone to whom we feel superior. We tend to act as our parents probably did to us—we lecture, correct, admonish, and moralize. In the *adult state,* used when talking with others on a basis of equality, we express our thoughts logically and firmly, without hostility. We should always try to use the adult state of parallel communication when we talk with anyone. The examples of exchanges between teacher and student presented in this chapter reflect adult–adult parallel communication.

Informing Students and Conducting Instruction

Informing   Informing students is mentioned here because teachers do this regularly. All it means is giving routine information orally, and then checking that students understand.

Case Study 11.1   Three States of Talking

FOCUS QUESTIONS
According to Berne, which adult is using the child state when talking to Luke? the parent state? the adult state? How could the two adults change their comments so they talk to Luke in the adult state?

Luke is having a frustrating day. It seems that everyone is talking to him in a different way.

On the way to school, Daniel, the bus driver, wanted Luke to sit down and stay seated: "Luke, I'm tired of telling you every single day to sit down. Don't you ever listen to anyone? Sit down. Now."

Then Luke had a scene with Ms. Janice on the playground before school even began: "Luke, if you don't listen to me this minute, I will not let you play with your friends at recess for the rest of the week. You will have to sit by yourself by the wall."

He liked his teacher Miss Hummel, though. She always talked to him in a grown-up way, even when he did something wrong. Today when the class went to the library for new books, he told her that he had left his library book at home. Students cannot check out books until they return the ones they have. Miss Hummel simply said, "Luke, it sounds like you have a little problem. What do you think you can do to solve it?" Then she listened as Luke made some suggestions.

Conducting Instruction When they instruct, teachers use communication to gain student attention, provide motivation, give directions, explain concepts and procedures, pose questions, provide feedback, reteach by providing corrective instruction and second chances, and redirect inappropriate behavior.

Gaining Attention Frequently, attention is gained by making statements such as:

- "All eyes on me."
- "Everyone, fold your hands and look at me."
- "Freeze!" (to gain the attention of a boisterous class).

    Often, nonverbal signals such as these are used:

- Bell tone, rain stick, wind chime, or piano chord
- Flicking lights
- Rhythmic hand clapping

    Students should be taught—and practice—to respond immediately to these words or signals, and no new task or lesson should be started without the attention of every student.

Providing Motivation Under ideal circumstances, motivation is inherent in most well-structured lessons. Teachers provide motivation with statements such as:

- "Boys and girls, have you ever imagined what it would be like to . . . ?"
- "This is a contest lesson to see if you can set a new record for yourself, your team, or the class."
- "Friends, there is a surprise hidden somewhere in this lesson. Watch and listen for it."

Giving Directions Good directions prevent a multitude of problems. Therefore,

- Make directions very clear.
- Keep them short.
- Model what you mean and, if appropriate and available, show examples.
- Check to make sure students understand by asking them to repeat the instructions back to you.
- If more than two steps are involved, consider writing reminders on the board, using visual instructional plans, or using Say, See, Do Teaching, all described in Chapter 6.

    Here are two examples of directions:

- "When I say 'begin,' open your workbooks to page 23 [write page number on the board]. On scratch paper do problems 2, 4, and 6 [write problem numbers on the board]. This is for practice only. I'll come around to see how you are doing. All right, let's get to work."

- "Study your map with your team. You may discuss, but use soft voices only [write 'soft voice' or place marker on the soft voice symbol]. Using the map, find the answers to the five questions I have given you. When you finish, you may read your library book."

Explaining Concepts and Procedures Like giving directions, explaining can help with student understanding; therefore, clarity is essential. For concrete concepts and procedures, common in elementary education, it is best to demonstrate the procedure as you explain orally. For example,

- "We will cut out our rabbits by starting here at the tail and cutting up and around [demonstrate]. Cut along the line, like this. Jorge, please show us where to begin cutting. Amelia, where do we try to cut? Now let's all do that."

- "When we multiply two negative numbers, the product is a positive number. Watch what I do [demonstrate on board or overhead $-2 \times -2 = +4$]. Minus times minus equals plus. Now try this one: minus 4 times minus 2. [Wait about five seconds.] Kwan, what did you get? Why? Remember class, minus times minus equals plus."

Posing Questions Questions keep students focused and active. For example, the teacher might ask a question such as the following to encourage student participation: "Who can tell me what *e pluribus unum* means? Thumbs up if you know." (Wait and look around before calling on anyone.)

Questions can force students to use different levels of thought. The hierarchy of six levels of the cognitive domain, originally developed by Benjamin Bloom in 1956, was revised in 2001 (Anderson et al., 2001). The revision accomplished several things: It provided the opportunity to (1) use "cleaner," clearer verb labels for all level names, (2) rename three levels, and (3) switch the order of the top two levels. Consequently, the revised taxonomy retains six levels, now labeled and ordered: remember, understand, apply, analyze, evaluate, and create (Sousa, 2006). As you instruct your students, consider posing questions at multiple levels of the hierarchy:

- For students to show ability to *remember* information, ask factual and literal questions: "In what year did the Spaniards finally drive the Moors from Spain? What else of importance to us happened that year?"

- To show *understanding*: "Suppose you have the colors red, yellow, and blue, but you need some green. How could you make green from the colors you have?"

- To show ability to *apply* learnings: "Let's say you have just written a story. How could you make certain you spelled all your words correctly?"

- To show ability to *analyze* learnings: "What do you think the colonists were trying to accomplish when they dumped tea into the harbor?"

- To show ability to *evaluate*: "Do you think Peter Rabbit was doing a good thing when he got into Mr. McGregor's cabbage patch? Why did he do that?"

- To show ability to *create* from learnings: "How would you go about constructing a map of an imaginary island so we could locate it and identify its various features?"

Some teachers prefer to sort their questions into three categories: literal (find the answer); thinking or reasoning (figure it out); and evaluating, reacting, or feeling (give your opinion). They then teach their students a simple formula to help them identify the types of responses they are expected to make to questions they are asked: "Read the lines," "Read between the lines," and "Read beyond the lines."

Providing Supportive and Corrective Feedback

Making helpful comments, sometimes publicly and sometimes privately, while directing a lesson or circulating during student work can provide both supportive and corrective feedback. Comments may focus on errors and corrections, observations, or encouragement. In general, comments should be private if they single out a student and public if they give reminders of procedures or are appropriate to the entire class. Here are a few examples.

Private (Individual Focus)

- "This is some of the best work I've seen you do."
- "You've made a mistake here. How can you correct it?"
- "No, look here: a plus times a minus gives a minus."
- "I don't feel as though you're trying today. I wonder if something else is on your mind. How can I help?"

Public (Group Focus)

- "This is some of the best work we've done."
- "It seems that many of you are making the same mistake. Look up here. Let me go through this again before we continue."
- "The secret to doing this correctly lies in looking at the time the driver uses. Think of the problem from that angle."
- "I see improvement today. I see good improvement. We are getting there."

Remember that with very few exceptions, feedback should be positive and helpful rather than faultfinding. When you must reteach, also remember that corrective instruction and second chances support students' success in their learning.

Redirecting Inappropriate Behavior

Usually, when students become inattentive, noisy, disgruntled, or reluctant, or when they dawdle, daydream, and play with objects instead of working, they need only gentle reminders. Negative consequences need not be invoked unless the behavior becomes flagrant or is continually repeated. Normally, students can be put back on course through redirection such as the following:

- "Joaquin." (Just say the student's name quietly.)
- "You need to be finished in five minutes."
- "I know you're tired, but let's see if we can finish this. I'll help you."
- "Please remember our rule about working."

Building Positive Relationships

Another important role of communication is that of building positive relationships. Previous chapters, especially Chapter 4, have explained that students have a primary need to belong, and they should be reassured that they have place, purpose, and acceptance in the class. Students also have a need to be noticed and acknowledged. The quality of their behavior and work merits comments, always with courtesy and consideration.

Emphasizing Belonging and Importance

What most of us want, really, is to feel appreciated. As a practicing rule, you should make comments that show you value the presence of every student. (Even if you don't, be a convincing actor for the student's sake and yours.) You may even find that such expressions help troublesome students become less troublesome. Be very free with comments such as:

- "We are very glad you are in this class, Trish."
- "I like your drawing, Miguel. May I put it on the display board?"
- "Class, I just want to tell you how pleased I am with our agreement to make everyone in this room feel comfortable and important."
- "We can't do our best work in these groups unless everyone contributes. We need that from everybody."

Speaking Personally with Each Student

Teachers good in communication try to speak personally to each student at least once a day. You might feel this personal contact occurs naturally, without conscious effort on your part, but in practice teachers tend to give more of their attention to the few brightest students in their class and to those who disrupt or fail to work. In doing so, they overlook other students—usually, the majority—who follow directions, complete their work, behave themselves, and show no particular flashes of brilliance.

What do teachers say in these personal communications? They ask questions and make observations, as appropriate. Interactions need not take long, really only a few seconds, and they can be accomplished without using instructional time. Here are some examples:

- "I heard you have new puppies at your home, Teisha. What kind are they?"
- "Today is a hot day, isn't it, Manny? Were you too hot on the playground?"
- "Class, Jimmy has a new baby brother. What's his name, Jimmy? What's it like to be a big brother?"
- "I really appreciate how nicely you worked today, Caitlin. Thank you."

Commenting on Quality of Behavior and Work

Almost all students like to receive positive comments about their good behavior and work. Younger students like those comments made publicly; older students may prefer that they be made privately so others won't tease them about being teacher's pet or worse. Conversely, no student likes to receive negative comments, especially in front of the class.

It is important that students know when their efforts are appreciated as well as when they are not. Except for routine comments or sticky notes on their desks that tell students

---

Case Study 11.2   Phone Calls the Night before School

FOCUS QUESTION

Often children are anxious before the start of the new school year. They worry about many things: Will my teacher be nice? Will I know anyone in my class? Is fourth grade going to be really hard? When class rosters are delivered a few days before the first day of school, Karen O'Connor chooses to call all of her students the night before school begins. Write a short script of what she might say to each of them. How do other teachers make students feel welcome?

Karen O'Connor is a fourth-grade teacher who takes time to introduce herself and make each student feel welcome before she meets her class for the first time.

"I know that I can't alleviate all of their concerns, but I believe I am able to relax them considerably on the eve of the new school year by calling my students and personally welcoming each of them to fourth grade and to my class. Each call takes me about four minutes. I tell them how much I am looking forward to meeting them and I highlight a few of the major activities and areas of study. I end the phone call by allowing the children to ask questions and by suggesting that they have a good night's sleep so they can be ready for a terrific year.

"Although phone calls to thirty or more students take the better part of the evening, I believe the rewards are great. In fact, parents tell me how excited their child was to receive a phone call from the new teacher and they thank me throughout the year. On the first day of class, the children are less anxious because they have already 'met' me. For me, these phone calls are a great way to set the tone for the year."

"good," "fine," "thank you," "right," "you're on target," and so on, personal appraisals should be kept between teacher, individual student, and the student's caregivers. If a student does well, find a quiet moment and say:

- "You really helped our class today with your comments, Pedro. Thank you for that."
- "Sarah, your paragraph showed that you have learned a great deal in the past week. Keep up the good work."

If the student does poorly, feedback should be honest, even if sugarcoated:

- "I don't think you did your best today, Anna. Is there a problem I can help you with?"
- "I was really bothered by your behavior in class today, Cassie. I wasn't able to teach well because of it. I think we should come up with a plan so we won't have this problem again."
- "Kevin, you missed eleven spelling words. I'd like to ask your mother to help you at home. I will send her an e-mail with the list of words and ask if she will work with you tonight." (Or, "I've written a note for her that lists these words and asks if she will work with you tonight.")

Sometimes the teacher may choose to e-mail a message directly to the caregiver. It's important to do this for successes, too. Too often, caregivers hear only what their child did wrong. If students are aware when you send an e-mail or a note to a caregiver, it is a good idea to tell them about the content or let them read the message so they won't feel uneasy.

Stressing Courtesy and Consideration Classes tend to reflect the personality of their teachers. Good character among students is more likely when it is infused into the way teachers teach. For example, classes behave much more humanely when courtesy and civility are emphasized as prime goals, incorporated into class rules, and intentionally taught, modeled and practical.

Younger students readily accept instruction in good manners, meeting people, speaking courteously, saying please and thank you, and offering help.

"IT's A NOTE FROM MY TEACHER, AN EXAMPLE OF WHAT CAN HAPPEN WHEN THE ALPHABET FALLS INTO THE WRONG HANDS."

© Martha F. Campbell. Reprinted by permission.

Older students may snicker and groan, but privately they like learning and practicing these things, too. Class meetings and situational role-plays offer opportunities for guided practice.

- "Don, would you please help Preetha? Thank you."

- "Boys and girls, I'd like to introduce Mrs. Santos, Claire's mother. Welcome to our room, Mrs. Santos."

- (After instruction on how to introduce people) "Craig, please introduce our guest."

- "Class, what should you say when someone helps you or does something nice for you? That's right, 'thank you'. Today I will listen to hear if any of you say thank you to another student. You listen, too. At the end of the day, we'll discuss what we heard."

- "Room 12, I believe we have been acting very discourteously during our kickball games. I think this goes for winners and losers alike. No one likes to lose, but usually somebody does. How should we act at such times? How should winners act? Let's practice your suggestions before we go outside today to play."

Maintaining a Sense of Community

Sense of community is emphasized as a means of encouraging students to take initiative, show responsibility, and provide support for each other and the teacher. Class meetings help provide a sense of community in the classroom.

Class Meetings William Glasser (1969, 1998) feels that most major problems teachers and students face in the classroom can be resolved with class meetings. Many other authorities in classroom management also place heavy emphasis on classroom meetings. These whole-class meetings are conducted with students and teachers seated in a tight circle so they can see and talk easily with each other. The teacher participates with students but does not criticize or try to direct.

A common purpose of class meetings is to find constructive solutions to problems identified by students—too much noise during work time, assignments too difficult or no fun, students picking on each other, not enough time to complete work, or too much homework.

Three rules are required for meetings to function as intended. First, only positive and constructive solutions can be considered—no complaining, faultfinding, or backbiting is allowed. (This is the only time when the teacher should step in strongly.) Second, every person has the right to express an opinion without being slighted or put down by others. Third, the teacher plays a subdued rule, participating to clarify and encourage but not to dominate, lead, or criticize.

Jane Nelsen, Lynn Lott, and H. Stephen Glenn (2000) describe eight building blocks that lead to effective class meetings. Each building block targets a specific skill: forming a circle, practicing compliments and appreciations, creating an agenda, developing communication skills, learning about separate realities, solving problems through role-playing and brainstorming, recognizing the four reasons people do what they do, and applying logical consequences and other nonpunitive solutions.

Win-Win Conflict Resolution Even in the best-managed classes, conflict occurs between students and between the teacher and students. Often in resolution of those conflicts, one person emerges as winner with an urge to gloat, and the other as loser with a penchant to pout and hold hard feelings. To improve that situation, Spencer Kagan, Patricia Kyle, and Sally Scott (2007) developed a win-win approach, where all involved get at least part of what they want. For win-win resolutions to occur, teacher and students need to be on the same side, working together toward the same end, and sharing responsibility in the learning process.

Communicating with Caregivers

Caregivers are parents, guardians, foster parents, or any others who are in charge of children at home. Elementary teachers who are most successful—and who enjoy the highest reputations within the community—are those who communicate well with caregivers. For most caregivers, their child is their most precious possession, the best reflection of themselves, and their best extension into the future. Although appearances nowadays sometimes seem to be contrary, most caregivers expect teachers to hold little Johnny or Jennifer central in their thoughts, and it's no matter that there may be 19 to 35 other children in the class whose caregivers expect the same. The wise teacher keeps this reality in mind.

What Caregivers Expect from Teachers

Caregivers don't expect you to turn their child into an Albert Einstein, a Langston Hughes, a Jade Snow Wong, or an Amy Tan. But they rightfully expect you to:

- *Care* about their child and give attention to him or her as a person, which you show through acknowledgment of the child's interests, joys, fears, capabilities, and special needs.

- *Excite* their child about learning.

- *Instruct* their child in the basics—literacy and life skills; something of the human condition; responsible ways of behaving; and the good, right, and beautiful.

- *Encourage and support* their child's efforts by nurturing, prodding, and encouraging.

- *Control* their child to prevent self-defeating behavior, and especially to prevent mistreatment by others.

- *Inform* them about their child's educational program and progress.

- *Be dedicated* to doing the best you can for their child.

What Caregivers Need to Know, Will Ask, and Will Say

Caregivers need to know a number of things about their child in school but often never ask about what they really need to know. They tend to shy away from school after their child completes kindergarten and first grade. Many feel they shouldn't meddle. Many feel insecure about approaching the teacher. They don't want to feel embarrassed, or their culture doesn't support such actions. Many would like to help but don't know how. If English is not their first language, some do not feel able to help. If you take time to inform caregivers about what they need to know, you will earn their esteem and support.

Anticipate the questions caregivers are likely to ask, and be prepared to answer them as though their child were always in the center of your thoughts:

- "How's my child doing in school?"

- "What is a typical day like?"

- "What knowledge and skills is my child expected to master this year?"

- "How do you evaluate and grade my child?"

- "Is my child progressing as well as expected?"

- "Does my child seem happy?"

- "How does my child get along with others?"

- "How does my child react to trying new things? to making mistakes?"

- "What is my child best at? What is my child weakest in?"

- "My child has some challenges. How do you help him or her be successful?"

- "Does my child cause problems?"

- "What after-school programs and opportunities are there for my child?"

- "Is there anything I can do to help?"

Most caregivers listen to the teacher's answers but then may respond with additional comments. Teachers who communicate most successfully with caregivers listen carefully and make comments such as the following to the replies caregivers are likely to make:

- "He was never that way before." (Even though he was, your reply should be, "I hope I can count on your help, because I know you don't want him behaving this way.")

- "She was well liked in her other school." (This may or may not be true, but your reply should be, "She will be well liked here, too, if together we encourage her to be more friendly to others. I'm sure with your help we can.")

- "He is just like his father, who has never learned to pick up after himself." (Your reply should be, "Let's see if we can work on this. How can you help?")

- "Her mother is the same way, just loves to talk." (Your reply should be, "I really like her. It's just that her talking sometimes disturbs the class and keeps her from getting her work done. I'm sure you want her to learn, just as I do.")

A Note on Communicating with Caregivers Most caregivers see teachers as professional, knowledgeable, and communicative. They don't want to think of teachers as wishy-washy, silly, or disorganized, nor do they want to see them behave as long-lost best pals. Of course, they don't want teachers to be gruff and intimidating either.

Focus on how you communicate with caregivers. You want to be approachable and nice, but brief, plain, and businesslike. Be considerate, remain approachable, and show caregivers that you value their collaboration. This is no time to show off your impressive vocabulary or your command of complex sentence structure. Nor is it a time to impress caregivers with the number of acronyms you know (GATE, ELP, IEP, RTI, SDAIE, ADHD, and so on ad infinitum). Don't be wordy, but at the same time, don't talk down to caregivers. Use short, direct sentences with words everyone understands.

Means and Opportunities for Communicating with Caregivers

Even with the sign-in policies and procedures now in place in most school offices, you never know when a caregiver may appear at your classroom door and want to talk. When that happens, be sure the unexpected visit does not interrupt your instruction time, and then mostly listen. But for occasions you set and for which you have time to prepare, consider the following opportunities for communicating well with caregivers.

Back-to-School Night As mentioned in Chapter 2, your school will invite caregivers to visit, and you will be expected to talk about the following:

1. The educational program you plan to provide in your class—a summary of your curriculum, the subject area standards, and special activities. (This doesn't mean that your entire program is to be communicated all at once. You should continue to describe your program through the year using newsletters, websites and homepages, and other means that we explain here.)

2. The expectations you hold for the children, including class work, behavior, homework, attendance and tardiness, makeup work, and so forth.

3. How you intend to enforce your expectations—your discipline system.

4. What caregivers can do to help further the program of their child.

5. Information about special activities and events.

After your presentation, caregivers may have questions and wish to speak with you individually about their child (refer back to questions caregivers ask). It's good practice to schedule this meeting at another mutually convenient time.

Questionnaire Some teachers send a questionnaire (written in English and translated into the primary language used in the homes of their students) in order to receive specific information from caregivers regarding their child and family. Questions might include: Does your child use the same last name as you? What do I need to know to best work with your family? (Are parents separated or divorced? Are there stepparents? Is this a blended family? Are separated parents able to meet together, or is it best to have separate communications with each?) What special needs does your child have (health, allergies, medications)? What limits do I need to know? Do you have access to a computer and the Internet? Will we be able to communicate through e-mails? How will you be able to participate in the classroom (sharing a special interest, helping with field trips or special activities, donating wish list items)? Also, asking caregivers to describe their child to you can be particularly insightful.

CDs and DVDs Some teachers find opportunities to tape students as they work on projects and activities in class and then make the tapes available in the class library for children to check out and share at home. Children are taped only after the teacher receives signed permissions from caregivers. For these teachers, then, CDs and DVDs, or videos of the class,

---

Vignette 11.1   Class Videos

Kindergarten teacher Linda Monedero uses videotapes to communicate with parents and guardians. "To prepare parents for this communication, I send a letter home to each family listing the purposes of the videotape program and encouraging their participation (which is not mandatory). Caregivers are asked to return signed permissions for their child to be taped. I tell them that the completed videos are usually less than 15 minutes long, which allows families to view tapes when they come home in spite of busy schedules. I encourage each family to keep videos for one or two evenings and return them to school as soon as possible so that other families can view them. The rotation for each video varies because children put their names on slips of paper and the helper of the day draws the name of the student. Video checkout cards or lists are kept in a special location as a record of who has which videotape.

"I believe three basic rules are necessary to make a video program successful. First, the person filming the video is reminded that the tape will go home with each child; therefore, each child should be taped about the same amount of time. Second, children are told that only acceptable student behavior will be taped. This fosters positive behaviors without having to emphasize the negative, which leads to better overall behavior. Third, a short list of desired activities to be recorded is given to the filming volunteers so that the tapes always show children actively involved in learning."

UPON REFLECTION

Describe how you might use videos or CDs in order to communicate with parents. What would you want to be taped? Who would do the actual taping? How, then, would the tapes be made available to others?

classrooms, and homes where technology still consists of videotapes, provide a nice alternative option for communicating with caregivers. Many caring adults work outside the home and can no longer volunteer in classrooms during the day. However, they still have the desire to know what their child is doing in school. CDs, DVDs, or videos of the class and activities give parents and grandparents the gifts of time and presence.

Weekly Reports Teachers can create a simple form such as the one developed by Karen O'Connor (Figure 11.2). On Thursday afternoons, she rates each student's behavior/self-control, and his or her completion of class work and homework for the week. She then adds a

Figure 11.2

Sample Weekly Report   **Name: Johnathan**

E = Excellent
S = Satisfactory
N = Needs to Improve
U = Unsatisfactory

Week Ending:	Behavior/ self-control	Class work Completion	Homework Completion	Comments:	Parent Initials
4/2	S	S	E	Great job on Academic Sharing!	
4/11	E	S−	F	Missing pronoun review sheet. Field trip on Tuesday-bring sack lunch.	
4/18	N	S+	E	Two sign-ins for not following directions-all class work complete.	
4/23	S+	E	E	Much better, more focused week!	
4/30	F	E	E	6x tables not mastered yet. Please practice 10 min each night. Great week!	
5/7	S+	E	E	Passed 6x tables, got 95% on science test. Please sign and return.	
5/14	E	E	E	☺Excellent week-parent newsletter enclosed.	

Source: Karen O'Connor, California Teacher of the Year 2000. Reprinted with permission.

personal comment note and sends the reports home with students on Friday. Parents initial the report to indicate that they received and read the report, and return it with their child on Monday. This is an easy way to provide ongoing, timely feedback about every student in your class, while keeping a record of home/school communication. It also helps with record keeping should the need arise for a meeting with the parent or a student study team.

Newsletters Because of inherent teaching and learning opportunities, many teachers still send home newsletters every month—or more frequently if possible. In particular, older students can assist with the production of the newsletter within the language arts and computer programs. Results come in the form of parental interest, involvement, and support—well worth the effort.

It is better if newsletters are short and to the point, and caregivers can anticipate them on the same day or week of the month. They should include items such as calendar dates of

---

Vignette 11.2   Teaching and Communicating with Technology

Lynne Harvey teaches fourth grade. At her school, teachers are able to use several electronic devices and programs to enhance their instruction.

"In my classroom, my students and I use technology daily to ensure that everyone participates in the lessons. Interactive whiteboards have changed the way I present lessons and have increased student participation. Every student has available a handheld response device and is able to respond to my questions, thus giving everyone in the class a voice. Student responses are tallied and displayed in graph form, and I can adjust my instruction instantly.

"My district uses a form of Blackboard, which we call Learning Point. This is a secure districtwide Web-based portal that requires both a user name and password. The navigation structure of Learning Point allows me to manage several things. I post announcements and important reminders to parents on my homepage. I also post nightly homework in the 'Communications' section.

"Parents can access an 'Updates' folder. Here I am able to keep parents informed about both specific and general information. For example, I

update parents about our pilot program for using computers in the classroom (all my students have individual netbooks at their desks for instruction and responses). My newsletter, which is more general, goes to parents in this section as well.

"Learning Point has several other features that are helpful to teachers and students. I am able to maintain a calendar—parents can link to the calendar of events for my classroom. Additionally, I can build tests here, which the program then scores and posts to each student's personal grading page that is accessible by students and parents for instant feedback."

UPON REFLECTION

How do teachers go about setting up communication in your local school district or school? If you are able to use electronic programs such as Blackboard, what features would you like to have available for yourself and caregivers and students? If you are not familiar with features on Blackboard, take a few minutes to investigate by going to these websites: http://www.blackboard.com and http://www.en.wikipedia.org/wiki/Blackboard_Learning_System.

field trips and other special activities and class accomplishments. Newsletters also may include a question, learning activity, or website of the week. They never should disintegrate into breezy notes that single out a few students.

Websites and Homepages More and more schools, teachers, and caregivers are taking advantage of computer technology. Many teachers create webpages for their class and are thereby able to stay in contact with caregivers who have computer and Internet access. Webpages do not have to be fancy or elaborate, but should include helpful items for caregivers, such as announcements, homework assignments, and other news and information that may be of interest.

Setting up a webpage is not as difficult as it sounds. First, you need someone to host the page. Free space is available on the Internet if the school district doesn't have its own server and site dedicated for this purpose. Scholastic, United Streaming, and YouTube are examples of free hosts. Many service providers now include a free website in their service package. You should be able to find several from which to choose by searching the key words *free space* or *free Web hosting*.

Although the size of the site may be limited, there generally is plenty of room to have several pages of your own. You also will need a way to edit your page. Where your site is housed will determine this. Free sites often include the necessary software and instructions online, or you can use a website-editing package such as Microsoft FrontPage. To include student work and photos, you will need access to a scanner or digital camera.

Most districts will have a form for caregiver permissions, but if they don't, you can make your own. It's helpful to get separate permissions giving caregivers and students several options: to include work with first name identification only, to include a photo with no name identification, or to include a photo and name identification.

"MY MOM GETS A NOTE FROM THE TEACHER EVERY DAY. I'LL BE GLAD WHEN HER SUBSCRIPTION RUNS OUT."

© Martha F. Campbell. Reprinted by permission.

Messages—Notes and E-Mails Personal notes and e-mails are helpful for sending brief messages to caregivers, for reminders about snacks and money, and for calling attention to responsible student behavior and accomplishments. Of course, if appropriate, these messages should be translated into the primary language of the caregivers.

Telephone Calls Sadly, many caregivers only receive messages from teachers when their child is in trouble. It is good to surprise them occasionally with brief, friendly messages. When you finish a phone contact, simply say good-bye and hang up, thereby avoiding a lengthy chat from what certainly will be an appreciative caregiver.

Below are two examples of contacts that can be made either as an e-mail or a phone call. In the first the teacher shares an appreciation with the caregivers; the other shares a concern. Messages about concerns should be delivered in a way that requests help.

Mrs. Yee, this is Miss Cabrera, Ming's teacher. I just wanted you to know that Ming did excellent work in math this week. We all can be very proud of him. Please tell Ming I said so. Thank you for your support, and I'll call you again before long.

Mrs. Engels, this is Mr. James, Leo's teacher. I am calling to let you know there's a problem at school that I need your help with. Leo has received four playground citations in the past two weeks and I am concerned about him. I know you don't want him misbehaving on the playground and endangering himself and others. I am talking with him about following school rules and I'd like to ask you to do the same at home. We don't want to punish Leo. All we want is for him to follow the rules, for his safety and benefit as well as for others. May I count on your support in helping Leo?

Performances and Displays Like many teachers, you may wish to put on student performances and displays of student work to be attended by caregivers, relatives, and friends. These events include musical productions, plays, choral readings, readers' theatre, science fairs, art exhibits, and athletic events. Caregivers may turn out in numbers for these occasions, especially for the younger children. These events allow teachers to explain further the special activities that contribute to the children's well-rounded education and let them show off what they and the students have done. They also contribute strongly to teachers' good reputations.

Newer and remodeled schools may have the technology capabilities to broadcast events over the Internet with video streaming. Video streaming via the Internet requires a media program such as RealPlayer, a free downloadable program that includes a video-streaming tool. Family and friends anywhere are able to view the production online through the school website.

Parent–Teacher Conferences

As mentioned earlier, most schools regularly schedule fall conferences that bring the teacher and caregivers together to confer about each child's progress. In Chapter 10 we looked at two types of student-involved conferences. Conferences, both teacher- and student-led, can be very productive if they are properly organized. In traditional parent–teacher conferences, that duty falls to the teacher, who must set caregivers at ease, communicate without causing affront, draw out the caregivers' ideas, and when necessary, suggest a plan for improving the progress of the child. The following suggestions help make the conference agreeable and useful:

Before the Conference

- Prepare a folder for each child with the child's name attractively written on it.
- In the folder include a summary of work covered to date; a profile of the child's performance in that work; samples, good and bad, of the child's work; and tests and other products that back up your evaluation.
- Include notes to yourself about anecdotes that provide insight into the child's behavior and progress.

When Caregivers Arrive

- Greet them in a friendly and relaxed manner.
- Sit side by side with the caregivers at a table rather than behind a desk. This conveys a message of cooperation.

During the Conference

- Begin by chatting about the child as a worthwhile person. Mention good traits. This reassures the caregivers.
- Guide them through the student's folder, commenting on the work samples it contains.
- Encourage them to talk. Listen carefully. Be accepting. Do not argue or criticize. Caregivers cannot be objective about their own child, and you do not want to cause resentment.
- Keep in mind that caregivers can be your strongest allies. Let them know you believe this. Show that you, like the caregivers, want the best possible for the child.
- If appropriate, work together to create a home action plan for them and their child.

Ending the Conference

- End the conference by summarizing what you all accomplished in this meeting, and describing your plans for the student's future progress. Earnestly request their help in supporting your efforts. Thank them for talking with you about the child.

Forming Home Alliances and Home Action Plans

Teachers may find it helpful to involve caregivers as partners to work with the student's progress and behavior. Certainly, caregivers can reinforce what teachers do in the classroom. In fact, many current discipline practitioners and authorities stress the importance of home alliances and partnerships and build home communication and cooperation into their programs for managing student behavior. To win their cooperation, it's important to talk to caregivers about behavior in clear, objective, nonjudgmental terms; to ask for what is possible to do; and to anticipate success.

Keeping Track of Communication with Caregivers

In your electronic management database, or on index cards or individual sheets of paper, maintain a record or create a chart such as the one in Figure 11.3, for keeping track of contacts with caregivers and to serve as a reminder for contacting them.

For teachers who prefer to keep paper records, a simple variation of the communication log would be to use a telephone message book such as those found in office supply stores. Every entry is duplicated automatically on carbonless paper. The duplicate record remains in the message book as a running chronology of all contacts and comment notes; the original copy is placed in individual student folders.

Figure 11.3

Date and Type of Communication for Paper Records

Surname	Date	Ns	T	Nt	C	U	UCA
———	——	—	—	—	—	—	—
———	——	—	—	—	—	—	—
———	——	—	—	—	—	—	—

Ns = newsletter, T = telephone; Nt = note; C = conference; U = unscheduled talk;
UCA = unsuccessful contact attempt.

Communicating with Colleagues and Administrators

Much was said in Chapter 4 about how you ought to speak with and conduct yourself around colleagues and administrators so as to ensure support and good working relationships. If you remain concerned about this topic, you might wish to refer back to that chapter. Otherwise, we will bring this chapter to a close with the following brief reminders.

Administrators should be kept informed about programs and problems in your classroom. You may communicate this information orally or via e-mail unless otherwise directed. They may or may not be able to offer help, but in any case, administrators like to know what's going on in the school. They detest being caught off guard by calls from upset parents or guardians and not knowing what the caregiver is talking about.

Administrators want to know about your plan for managing student behavior, and you should furnish a written copy. Administrators also want to know in advance about class parties, programs, and field trips and may want to see copies of your newsletters or Web announcements before they are sent to caregivers. Occasionally, administrators will rule against your discipline system or an event you want to organize. By tactfully asking them to suggest alternatives that would accomplish the purpose you had in mind, administrators will feel obliged to help you.

Colleagues such as fellow teachers, paraprofessionals (including service providers for students with special needs), beginning teacher support providers, substitute teachers, student teachers, clerical staff, librarians, nurses, psychologists, custodians, lunchroom and playground staff, and others should also be informed of any activities or needs that might impose on them. They do not appreciate your taking their professional duties for granted, especially when they must change plans for your benefit. On the other hand, when you take pains to communicate such matters fully and they are able to help you, most will do so willingly, and your efforts in communicating will have paid off in friendliness, helpfulness, and mutual respect.

This ends our consideration of the effective management of communication. Before moving ahead to Chapter 12, which deals with how to manage the work of other adults—paraprofessionals, substitute teachers, and student teachers—and contacts with advocates, take a moment to explore these end-of-chapter activities.

Case Study 11.3   Grade-Level Team Meetings

FOCUS QUESTION

Grade-level teams can disagree on many things: how something is taught, which supplemental materials are most bene-ficial to the unit, quality evidence for assessment, and behavior systems. Identify one area of potential disagreement and describe what teachers can say to negotiate a solution so everyone feels they win.

Ginny Lorenz is a member of a fourth-grade team of teachers.

"Before we began our year at a new school, my team met to discuss grade-level expectations, the grading system, school and classroom rules, and other such matters. The discussion went well until we began to identify the classroom behavior system and classroom rules. I felt strongly that students need to be involved in making the class rules if they are to 'buy in.' Another team member, however, felt just as strongly that the teacher must be the rule maker. I was afraid we had come to an impasse, but I managed to convince one of my other team members to try my way of writing rules and consequences. While my one colleague still insisted she had to write the rules, she did agree to identical consequences. This way was not a perfect solution, but at least we had some consistency.

"At the end of the year we reflected on our successes, our challenges, and our solutions. Everyone on our team agreed that the compromise regarding the behavior system and rules worked quite well. Substitutes told us that it was very easy to substitute in any of our classrooms because of the grade-level behavior system. Both students and parents seemed to feel that there was a genuine concern for the needs of all students. And in hindsight, we all felt far less frustrated about the need to constantly correct negative behaviors."

Parting Thought

What most of us want, really, is simply to feel appreciated.

Anonymous

Summary Self-Check

Check off the following as you either understand or become able to apply them:

☐ Good communication is what makes good education possible.

☐ Good communication is especially needed in giving directions, conducting instruction, holding class discussions, holding individual conferences with students, conferencing with caregivers, and having staff meetings and individual conferences with administrators and colleagues.

- ☐ When communicating, remember the four-way test:
  - Is this true?
  - Is this helpful?
  - Will my silence hurt?
  - Will this build good relationships?
- ☐ Always use parallel (adult–adult) communication with students and everyone else.
- ☐ Communication considerations when conducting instruction: gaining attention, providing motivation, giving directions, explaining concepts and procedures, posing questions, providing supportive and corrective feedback, reteaching using corrective instruction and offering second chances, redirecting inappropriate behavior.
- ☐ The revised Bloom's taxonomy of the cognitive domain is helpful as teachers prepare questions and activities to check student understanding.
- ☐ Communication for building positive relationships: emphasize belonging and importance, speak personally with each student, focus on the quality of work and behavior, stress courtesy and consideration.
- ☐ Communication for maintaining responsible behavior: win-win conflict resolution, class meetings.
- ☐ Communication with caregivers:
  - What caregivers need to know from teachers: the educational program, expectations for students, means of enforcing rules, how their child is doing, how they can help, routine information
  - Style of communication with caregiver: friendly but businesslike, clear with no jargon
  - Opportunities for communicating with caregivers: fall back-to-school night (the educational program, expectations, means of enforcing rules, how they can help), newsletters, websites and homepages, notes and e-mail messages, telephone calls, performances and displays, parent–teacher conferences
  - The importance of forming home alliances and home action plans
- ☐ Communicating with administrators and colleagues: keep everyone informed, never take another's services for granted, beginning teacher support providers.

Activities for Reflection and Discussion

1. Take a moment to review the statements in the Preview–Review Guide at the beginning of this chapter. Put a check mark in the *Review* column next to any statement with which you now agree. How have your thoughts changed since reading this chapter?

2. Interview at least two teachers about their communication with others. How do they communicate with caregivers? How do they communicate appreciations to caregivers? How do they communicate concerns? What do they include when they prepare for parent–teacher conferences? What do they include in a newsletter or on a webpage?

3. What advantages do you see in applying the four-way test to what you say? What dangers do you see? Illustrate with scenarios that involve talking with caregivers, students, and administrators.

4. For a grade of your choice, identify typical contents of a class newsletter you would want to produce. Outline the format. How would you mention and/or include student work? How would you mention as many student names as possible?

5. Write out the telephone or e-mail message you might want to deliver to caregivers concerning (a) Aisha, whose work quality has been declining; (b) Brigit, who has frequent squabbles with other girls in the class; (c) Carla, who always behaves well and offers to help; and (d) Domino, who seems to try hard but continues to do poorly in spelling.

6. You are due to have a routine evaluation conference with your principal. The principal has observed you only three times, and on two occasions your students were abnormally unruly. You expect to be criticized for poor class control. (a) How will you intend to conduct yourself in the conference? (b) What will you say in response if you are criticized for class control? (c) What, if anything, will you say concerning your feeling that you have not been observed sufficiently? (d) What would you intend to say at the conclusion of the conference?

7. Assuming you are able to create one, describe what you would like to include on a webpage. What special considerations and permissions will you obtain in order to proceed with this tool? How will you do this?

Webliography

A to Z Teacher Stuff: http://www.atozteacherstuff.com/Tips/Parent_Teacher_Conferences.
Blackboard, Inc.: http://www.blackboard.com
Education World, Inc. *Parent involvement in schools*: http://www.educationworld.com/
a_special/parent_involvement.shtml
TeacherVision, part of Family Education Network: http://www.teachervision.fen.com/
parent teacher conferences/teaching-methods/3683.html
Wikipedia, a registered trademark of Wikimedia Foundation, Inc.: http://www.en.wikipedia
.org/wiki/Blackboard_Learning_System

References and Recommended Readings

Anderson, L. (Ed.), Krathwohl, D. (Ed.), Airasian, P., Cruikshank, K., Mayer, R.., Pintrich, P.,
Raths, J., & Wittrock, M. (2001). *A taxonomy for learning, teaching, and assessing: A revision
of Bloom's Taxonomy of Educational Objectives* (Complete edition). New York: Longman.
Berne, E. (1964). *Games people play.* New York: Grove Press.
Coloroso, B. (1999). *Parenting with wit and wisdom in times of chaos and loss.* Toronto, Ontario,
Canada: Viking.
Glasser, W. (1969). *Schools without failure.* New York: Harper & Row.
Glasser, W. (1998). *The quality school teacher* (rev. ed.). New York: HarperCollins.
Jones, F. (2007a). *Tools for teaching: Parent edition.* Santa Cruz, CA: Fredric H. Jones &
Associates.

Jones, F. (2007b). *Tools for teaching: Discipline Instruction Motivation.* Santa Cruz, CA: Fred H. Jones & Associates.

Jones, F. (2007c). *Tools for teaching: Discipline Instruction Motivation* (video series). Santa Cruz, CA: Fred H. Jones & Associates.

Kagan, S., Kyle, P., & Scott, S. (2007). *Win-win discipline.* San Clemente, CA: Kagan Publishing.

Nelsen, J., Lott, L., & Glenn, H. (2000). *Positive discipline in the classroom* (3rd ed.). Rocklin, CA: Prima Publishing.

Sousa, D. (2006). *How the brain learns* (3rd ed.). Thousand Oaks, CA: Corwin Press.

PEARSON
myeducationlab

Go to the Topic: **Working with Families** in the MyEducationLab (www.myeducationlab.com) for your course, where you can:

- Find learning outcomes for **Working with Families** along with the national standards that connect to these outcomes.

- Apply and practice your understanding of the core teaching skills identified in the chapter with the Building Teaching Skills and Dispositions learning units.

- Examine challenging situations and cases presented in the IRIS Center Resources.

Managing the Work of Paraprofessionals, Substitute Teachers, Student Teachers, and Contacts with Advocates

CHAPTER **12**

It's easy to get good players. Getting 'em to play together, that's the hard part.

—Casey Stengel

Preview–Review Guide

Before you read the chapter, and based on what you know, think you know, or assume, take a minute to put a check mark in the *Preview* column if you agree with the statement. When you finish the chapter, take time to reread the statements and respond in the *Review* column. Reflective discussions can develop because many of the statements are not clearly "yes" or "no."

Preview   **Review**

1. _____ A classroom paraprofessional is someone who takes the place
of the teacher.   _____

2. _____ Substitute teaching is considered one of the most difficult teaching jobs.   _____

3. _____ Teachers are expected to provide detailed lesson plans for their
substitute teacher.   _____

4. _____ Legally, paraprofessionals may administer, correct, and record
student tests and scores.   _____

5. _____ Substitute teachers should be encouraged to teach some of their
own lessons that they particularly like.   _____

6. _____ Student teachers technically are paraprofessionals.   _____

7. _____ Paraprofessionals, substitutes, and student teachers, like contracted
teachers, can be dismissed from their jobs for reasons of incompetence.   _____

8. _____ The same standards of professionalism are expected equally of
paraprofessionals, substitutes, student teachers, and regular teachers.   _____

9. _____ Paraprofessionals and substitutes are advised to discipline students in the
way they deem best, so long as they do not infringe on students' rights.   _____

10. _____ Parents of children with special needs may call advocates when
they disagree with how the regular and special education teachers
are meeting the needs of their child.   _____

Chapter Objectives

After reading Chapter 12, students will demonstrate understanding of

- the roles and responsibilities other adults may have in a teacher's classroom

- expectations for professionalism for all adults in the classroom

through their active participation in discussions and the end-of-chapter activities for reflection.

Enterprising teachers have always looked for help in operating their classrooms. In the old one-room schools, the older, more advanced students helped the younger, less advanced. In today's classrooms, students help each other in cooperative learning teams, differentiated and multi-age classes, cross-grade partnerships, and cross-age tutoring. Increasingly, other adults also help teachers run their program. Now it is rare to find an elementary teacher who does not count on the assistance of another adult in the room, at least occasionally. These helpers range from mothers who assist with a class party to full-time employed aides. On occasion when the regular teacher must be away, substitute teachers are present to teach the class and make the day productive for the students. Student teachers also may work in a classroom as teachers-in-training. And advocates may participate in IEP meetings with teachers and parents to develop successful learning experiences for children with special needs. With this in mind, a problem to solve or an essential or guiding question for this chapter might be: *How can I maintain my need for effective communication with other adults who are involved with my program?*

Adult helpers who undertake regular, assigned duties commonly are referred to as *paraprofessionals. Para* means "alongside of"; *professional* refers to the teacher. Teachers have come to rely on paraprofessionals for a variety of tasks. They do clerical work; tutor students; monitor the work of small groups; and supervise in the library, on the playground, and elsewhere in the school. At times, paraprofessionals also deliver basic instruction under the teacher's supervision. Paraprofessionals fall mostly into the following groups: (1) paid instructional aides, (2) paid support providers for students with special needs, (3) caregiver volunteers, and (4) community resource volunteers (such as business liaison volunteers and senior citizens). Student teachers also provide help in many classrooms, but are not referred to as paraprofessionals. The same is true for substitute teachers; district technology, curriculum, and instruction mentors; and adults brought in for special purposes, such as to read to children or help supervise them on outings. All these adult helpers work under the direction of, or in conjunction with, the teacher, whose responsibility, then, is to manage the schedules, duties, and activities of these helpers.

Paid Instructional Aides and Support Providers

Instructional aides and support providers have regular work schedules, are salaried, and are held to the same standards of reliability and professional demeanor as contracted teachers. They are recruited, selected, paid, and sometimes trained by the school district before being assigned to or scheduled by individual teachers. The supply of paid aides waxes and wanes in accord with economic conditions and special programs and grants. When schools have money, they hire more aides. Mandated programs such as special and bilingual education usually provide money to hire skilled support providers. Because of the individual attention required by young students, paid aides are more common at the primary level than in intermediate or upper grades.

Caregiver and Family Volunteers

The prime source of volunteer help is from caregivers and other relatives of students in the class. In fact, some schools even require caregivers to spend time helping in their child's classroom. Grandparents and older adults are especially excellent because they have more available time and usually relate well to the young. Such is the case for the Senior Motivators in Learning and Educational Services (SMILES) program in the Salt Lake City School District, which began in 1977. However, relatives tend to be hesitant about volunteering their services, so some gentle recruitment may be needed. This can be accomplished informally through mention of need via notes or e-mails, or postings on the class website or homepage, asking for specific kinds of volunteer help. These gentle requests should specify dates and times that help is needed and should include a response or option form.

Caregivers and family volunteers are an extremely valuable, though sometimes a frustrating, source of classroom help. These volunteers may be highly educated and skilled—or barely literate. They may be conscientious or negligent, reliable or undependable. They genuinely may want to help, or they may have little else to do with their time. They may be good models of language, self-respect, exemplary character, and attitude toward others, or they

---

Vignette 12.1   One Classroom Paraprofessional—An Interpreting Aide

As the interpreting aide for children who are deaf or hearing-impaired, Mary Brewer is one type of paraprofessional with whom teachers may interact.

"I work as an interpreting aide in classrooms. My role is not to teach, but rather to act as the voice for students who are deaf or hearing-impaired. I provide ongoing sign interpretation of all voiced communication to those students. Classroom teachers, therefore, must learn how to use my

services as interpreter effectively. Toward that end, it is important that we, the teacher and I, clearly understand our respective roles in working in the classroom."

UPON REFLECTION
What paraprofessionals/student support providers are available in your local school or district? What considerations must the teacher make to support students and best use the services of these adults?

may fall short in these regards. Not all turn out to be what you might hope, but when you get a good volunteer, it's like finding buried treasure.

Community Resource Volunteers

Community resource volunteers can make marvelous contributions to your program, but rarely can you consistently count on their help. They may be representatives from businesses or agencies. They may represent programs such as Newspapers in Education. Or they may be volunteers with local programs such as the Rolling Readers or another literacy program. Frequently, they are retired persons who held occupations that receive attention in the class. Sometimes they are musicians or artists who like to help with the music and arts programs. These individuals tend to be interesting and good communicators, but because they lead busy lives, you cannot count on them regularly.

Case Study 12.1   Parent Volunteers

FOCUS QUESTIONS

Many parents now deliver their children to school every morning, and Karen O'Connor uses this to her advantage. How will you invite and manage parent volunteers for students in primary grades? in intermediate or upper grades?

Every year Karen O'Connor invites parents to spend a few minutes in her classroom and participate in her Morning Readers program.

"Parents may drop in to my classroom any time during the first hour of school to read. Consequently, some days I may have several volunteers; on other days, one volunteer may read with several children. Morning Readers has advantages for both the children and the teacher. For the children, the program gives developing readers a daily opportunity to work on fluency and comprehension while they read one-on-one with someone. For me, quality instructional time with my class continues without interruption, and reading time for my developing readers is easier to implement and monitor. Early in the school year, I train parents on reading strategies and give them sample comprehension questions to use.

"I keep appropriate books, each with a student's name written on a note card and visible to volunteers, in a basket near the door. Parent volunteers take the book that is in front and go with the student to a prechosen reading spot. They read with the student for about 20 minutes, stopping at appropriate times to reread, clarify, and ask questions. Volunteers note the ending page on the card and return the book and card to the back of the basket. The next volunteer knows who reads next, and where to begin with the reader. When students finish a book, the volunteer asks them to notify me to choose a new book for them to read. I find that the program runs itself, and I am able to continue with the class."

What Is Expected of Paraprofessionals

A common view persists that paraprofessionals mostly do clerical work and help children with their shoelaces and coats, but the actual range of their contributions is almost as broad as that of the teachers. True, they spend substantial time duplicating materials, checking papers, and keeping records, but many also perform quasi-instructional duties such as directing instructional games and activity centers, monitoring and assisting individual students during seat work, coaching student rehearsals for presentations and student-led conferencing, and working with small groups to provide additional practice in basic skills. They may help teachers prepare instructional materials such as flash cards, art supplies, visual aides, and worksheets; organize displays and bulletin boards; administer tests; and even supervise playground activities. In other words, they perform innumerable other duties assigned by the teacher. Or, they simply may be another caring adult with whom students can relate.

Although the primary intent is to provide services that supplement and assist the teacher's efforts by handling many of the miscellaneous time-consuming tasks, skilled professionals clearly supervise most—and in some cases all—of the instruction in art, music, and physical education. It is common to see paraprofessionals who, at least in particular segments of the curriculum, are as skilled in instruction as the elementary teacher.

It is true that paraprofessionals add to the complexity of teachers' lives, which prompts questions about whether they are worth the extra time, energy, and attention they require. Most teachers say they definitely are worth having because paraprofessionals help make their educational programs fuller, richer, and more student-oriented. Teachers are quick to point out, however, that good planning is necessary if the paraprofessional is to be used to best advantage.

Not all teachers enjoy using paraprofessionals and volunteers. It is perfectly acceptable if you prefer to rely on your own abilities to provide a sound educational program. There is no reason to use an aide unless your program is improved by doing so. Sometimes paraprofessionals and volunteers get in the way of instruction, and many teachers do not like dealing with the assorted trials and tribulations that seem to accompany the other adults.

On the other hand, if you enjoy working with other adults, and particularly if you like to provide activities such as plays, field trips, exhibits, and so forth—activities for which aides are especially useful—let your interests be known. Good aides are available. It simply is a matter of connecting with them.

How Volunteers and Paraprofessionals Are Obtained

As mentioned, family members and members of the community often volunteer in classrooms. Other individuals, aides and support providers for students with special needs, are the only regular paraprofessionals to receive pay, and they are recruited, selected, and given orientation training by the personnel department of school districts. Other aides—caregivers, community resource persons, and student tutors—volunteer their services and receive only the pleasures from their work and contribution. Other arrangements are made for substitutes and student teachers.

Some teachers are known for their ability to attract and maintain an unending supply of qualified paraprofessionals and volunteers eager to work in their rooms. How do they do this?

Word of Mouth   Word gets around about teachers who like to work with volunteers and are skilled in doing so. Caregivers talk among themselves about teachers and programs. A number of these caregivers, and others to whom they talk, like to work in elementary classrooms. They hear about and gravitate toward teachers who treat people kindly and in whose rooms children seem to have fun while learning.

Universities and High Schools   Local universities and high schools have many students willing and eager to help in elementary classrooms. Often these students are seriously considering a career in teaching. Before admission to teacher credential programs, university students may be required to provide documentation of experience in elementary classrooms. High school students may be in future teachers clubs that maintain connections with elementary schools. Volunteers obtained through these sources tend to be highly motivated to do well and to learn as much as possible about teaching.

PTA and PTO Bureaus   Schools with active parent–teacher associations (PTAs) and organizations (PTOs) may have bureaus run by parents that are able to furnish qualified parent volunteers to aid in classrooms. Usually, teachers provide some basic training for these parent volunteers.

Community Agencies   Especially in larger cities, community agencies may provide liaison persons from among their employed personnel who make school and classroom presentations upon request. Zoos, museums, newspapers, hospitals, and fire and police departments often have educational departments that provide this service.

Other Helpers in the Room

As we noted, many other people who are not considered to be paraprofessionals also provide important help to the teacher. They include cross-grade partners, cross-age tutors, substitute teachers, and student teachers. Teachers also may find themselves working with advocates.

Cross-Grade Partners and Cross-Age Tutors

Just as you might have seen in a one-room schoolhouse 100 years ago, older students in the school can offer valuable assistance to teachers of younger grades. Also, a hallmark of differentiated and multi-age classrooms is the belief and practice that students help students. As with using cross-grade partnerships, teachers can differentiate instruction in their classrooms in such a way that classmates help one another.

Supporters believe that the use of cross-grade partners and cross-age tutors results in increased achievement and positive attitudes in both the children who are helping and the children being helped. The responsibility and status of helping can be very motivating to older students. For younger children it can be very motivating to have older students sit beside them, read to them, play with them, and help them with their work. Many teachers say that cross-grade partners and cross-age tutors are among their most reliable, conscientious, patient, and valued helpers.

Cross-grade partners are students from higher grades who befriend and provide encouragement to students in lower grades. In many schools, teachers organize liaisons between older and younger students. These cross-grade experiences are done primarily for moral support, assistance, and helping young students feel there are older students in the school who will help and listen to them, not just provide additional instructional help.

Cross-age tutors provide younger students help in learning. Some schools have formally established cross-age tutor programs. Where that is not the case, primary teachers desiring tutors should check first with the principal, and then approach teachers of older grades for suggestions. In this way, students best suited for tutoring can be obtained.

By fifth or sixth grade, some students think they might want to become teachers. They enjoy younger children, and the young enjoy them in return. Primary teachers prize such students, who are recognized and selected because of their skills, personality, and reliability. However, some teachers are reluctant to make frequent use of these students for fear of causing them to miss out on important parts of the educational program offered by their own teachers. To this end, some primary and upper grade teachers form *cross-grade partnerships*. As a regular part of their program, the teachers have both classes come together from time to time to work on projects and share reading, stories, and other experiences.

Substitute Teachers

Substitute teachers fill in when the regular classroom teacher is ill or excused for other duties. With current economy and employment concerns, many retired teachers and administrators return to the classroom as substitutes. A few districts may still hire interested persons who have earned, minimally, a bachelor's degree, but in most districts, qualified substitute teachers must successfully interview in order for their names to even appear on an approved master list. Substitutes may also be required to participate in an orientation or training before they can work in the district.

Teachers can request a substitute any time of the day or night. While substitutes may be called directly by a clerk in the district office, most districts now use a twenty-four hour telephone hotline system or a district online job-finder. Approved substitutes have the opportunity to check the hotline and job-finder throughout the day and accept positions at any time. Substitutes may still receive a morning call from this electronic "subfinder" for last-minute requests.

Substitute teachers have two main obligations—to keep order in the classroom and to further the class's instructional program. The second obligation, which most people consider the more important, cannot occur without the first. Substitutes fulfill these two primary obligations by being prepared, arriving early and obtaining information from the office staff, and generally making the day productive for the students. Substitutes make the

"I AM MRS, POWELL, YOUR SUBSTITUTE, AND I HAVE 911 ON MY SPEED DIAL."

© Martha F. Campbell. Reprinted by permission.

day productive when they take charge in the classroom, clarify expectations about how students are to behave, and emphasize to the students the importance of learning.

Teachers hope that when they must be absent, their substitute will control the class and make a normal day's progress in the curriculum. Substitutes hope that they will find good lesson plans and discipline standards. They also hope they will have the opportunity to use their own special skills—even teach a favorite lesson or two not in the teacher's plans. An ideal relationship between teacher and substitute incorporates their mutual hopes. The teacher's responsibilities, then, are to:

- Plan well.
- Leave an up-to-date paper or electronic substitute folder or easy access to lesson plans and a copy of the discipline plan, current seating chart, and class roster with notations of relevant student information (behavior, students with special needs and any support providers, medication, special schedules and routines, and so on), class schedule and current duty schedule, classroom monitor and volunteer lists, and school map.

- Teach their students how to treat and work with substitutes, and hold students accountable for their behavior.

The substitute teacher's responsibilities are to:

- Follow the teacher's plans carefully unless otherwise allowed.
- Follow the teacher's system of discipline, or if a plan is not available, quickly establish one before doing further work.
- Have special lessons ready at all times.
- Creatively use good time-filler and transition activities.

Student Teachers

Before teachers are certified, they complete coursework in a teacher credentialing program. They also student teach, probably in one or two classroom settings, where they are able to transfer the theory into practice. Student teachers work with tenured master or cooperating teachers. For many certification programs, student teachers are required to successfully complete field experiences in both primary (K–2) and intermediate or upper (3–6)

Case Study 12.2   A Teacher and a Substitute

FOCUS QUESTIONS

Teachers and substitutes sometimes have different expectations of how the day should go when the teacher is absent. How closely do Janet Beyea's expectations align with Ms. Young's expectations? Will she be able to look back and say that her days in Ms. Young's classroom were productive and successful?

When second-grade teacher Candace Young needs a substitute teacher, she usually wants the substitute to follow her schedule as much as possible. "However, I recognize the opportunities substitutes can bring to my class. As often as I can, I make it clear that variations are not only acceptable but often desirable. Substitute teachers often bring delightful learning activities with them. Some play the guitar and teach new songs; some bring favorite stories; some speak of faraway places; and some teach wonderful games, which the children then teach me when I return. Far more than covering material from point A to point B, I expect a substitute in my class to keep students engaged, successful, safe, and I hope, happy."

As a regular substitute in primary grades, Janet Beyea is accustomed to anticipating a different experience every day she goes to school. "I know firsthand that the unexpected is the norm in substituting, and that flexibility and creativity are required.

"Substitutes always anticipate walking into a classroom and finding no lesson plans. Once I showed up to teach music and ended up teaching a sixth-grade class for a week with no plans, no roll book, and no set routines. Because the class had had four teachers in the first six weeks of school, even the students didn't know what they were studying in class.

"When I find no lesson plans, I remind myself that I am not expected to be a miracle worker, and then turn to several resources. I look around the classroom and often find the classroom schedule, the discipline rules, and a job chart posted somewhere. I try to find the teacher's editions of the textbooks because I know they will be filled with suggestions. I use the students and other teachers for guidance. Also, I always have my briefcase where I keep a book of games and art projects for all grades and some easy-to-use lessons. I consider that I was successful if, at the end of the day, the room is tidy, I've had no major discipline problems, and the students had some fun."

classroom settings. Because they are training to be elementary teachers, student teachers are present every day and responsible for portions of the educational program as guided by the cooperating classroom teacher and a university supervisor.

Arrangements for student teachers usually are made by the credentialing university or by the district. Occasionally, student teachers may request their field placements, although when doing so, they must be certain that the experience will fulfill all the state and university requirements for the student teacher to receive a teaching license.

Usually, the duties of student teachers are quite clear-cut. While student teachers often carry out some of the same duties as paraprofessionals, there are two main differences: (1) Student teachers are training to be teachers, not teacher helpers. (2) The primary goal for student teachers, as they progress through their field experiences, usually is to be assigned fewer clerical and supervisory tasks and to assume ever-increasing amounts of the instructional program. As teacher trainees, they should eventually assume all classroom responsibilities, from curriculum planning and instruction to management. Under the guidance of the classroom teacher and university supervisor, student teachers typically do the following:

- Plan lessons and units.

- Teach lessons to the whole class and to small groups and individual students.

- Take responsibility for managing student behavior.

- Communicate with caregivers.

- Confer with teachers and university supervisors for suggestions, guidance, and detailed analyses of their efforts and progress.

- Perform on a reduced scale most of the professional activities performed by teachers. These may include extra duties such as lunch or bus supervision.

- Observe and participate for the same hours (contracted hours) as the teachers.

It is important to understand the role the master or cooperating teacher plays in partnership with student teachers. Teachers who are perceived to be highly skilled in instruction

---

Case Study 12.3   A Master Teacher and Her Student Teacher

FOCUS QUESTION

Ask several teachers about their student teaching experience. You will read that cooperating teachers are expected to help with orientation, induction, guidance, cooperation, and reflection. To what extent did the teachers perceive this help during their field experience?

Ginny Lorenz has taught for more than 20 years and has been a master teacher working with student teachers many times. "Over the years I have seen the education pendulum swing from one side to another and back again, but I've seen that one thing remains constant—the need for a master teacher with whom a student teacher can train and from whom a student teacher can learn.

"I sincerely believe that master teachers must be willing to mentor student teachers through all aspects of the educational system. From experience, I know that this mentoring process takes a great deal of time and effort, and I ask myself whether it is worth it. When I am approached to mentor a student teacher, I struggle with a variety of questions and emotions: *Do I have enough time to work with a student teacher? Will we (student teacher and I) get along? Will the student teacher have potential? Do I really want to share my students, my class, my time? If the student teacher is not doing well, do I have the expertise to help him or her succeed?*

"Despite my questions, I ultimately always have agreed to the mentoring process because I feel that if we truly believe in the educational system, we owe it to the new generation of teachers to provide them with a safe place to hone their skills. I believe that veterans—master teachers—must share their love and enthusiasm for teaching and learning. It is through teaching that we learn. And it is through learning that we continue to grow. Mentoring a student teacher allows veteran teachers to do both."

and management may at times be asked to have student teachers in their classroom. In this capacity they may be called master, cooperating, or lead teacher, and as such, they mentor, coach, and counsel individuals enrolled in a teacher credentialing program. The cooperating teacher is perhaps the most important resource for the student teacher during the field experience. The cooperating teacher works closely with the student teacher and university supervisor to provide the best guidance and field learning experience possible. Effective cooperating teachers are expected to do many things. They help student teachers understand the role the classroom plays in their development as professionals and help ease them into the school setting. They help students and caregivers understand the valuable role the student teacher plays in the classroom. Cooperating teachers also help with the following:

- Orientation—helping the student teacher locate key persons; resources; materials; equipment; and state and district curriculum standards, guidelines, and programs

- Induction—helping the student teacher understand the full-time teaching realities and responsibilities, how children learn, district expectations, and available supports

- Guidance—helping the student teacher with planning, evaluation, lesson delivery, and management; providing demonstration teaching

- Cooperation—through sharing ideas, conferencing and coaching, and accepting and respecting the student teacher both as a learner and a coworker

- Reflection—sharing critical assessments of the student teacher's experience and progress, modeling self-assessment through reflection, and encouraging the student teacher to use self-reflection productively

Advocates

Ideally, teachers and caregivers form collaborative partnerships to benefit students. Each has expertise, knowledge, and skills that can be blended to meet student needs effectively. Sometimes, however, caregivers of children with special needs—many of the exceptionalities included in Chapter 8—reach out to other individuals—advocates—for additional help and support. Advocates can provide a positive service, although sometimes their approach is described as "fighting," "being armed," and "using ammunition" by teachers and even the caregivers themselves.

Teachers of students with IEPs should meet with the resource teacher (RT) and/or case manager (CM), and together review the IEP and prepare a confidential single-page resource sheet that includes both details of the disability or challenge and bulleted modifications that are the

"MY MOTHER COULDN'T MAKE IT. THIS IS MY LAWYER."

Bob Schochet. Reprinted by permission.

Case Study 12.4   Working with Student Advocates

FOCUS QUESTIONS

What do you understand the role of student advocates to be? How might teachers see their presence in an IEP meeting as adversarial? supportive? Mrs. Teudt's experiences with advocates have been largely positive and productive. Ask several teachers about their experiences with advocates.

As a special education teacher, Debbie Teudt works with students in grades K–5, who come to her with a range of special needs. She also works with their caregivers and occasionally with advocates and attorneys.

"It rarely is easy whenever a parent brings an advocate or an attorney into an IEP meeting. Often, they are anxious to find answers that will help their child and are willing to go to any length to find them. It is important to remember not to take this personally—easier said than done. And it takes time and experience to learn how to do just that. We all work so hard to do not only what the law says we must do, but to do anything and everything within our power as special educators to provide the best possible learning environment for our students. Having an advocate or attorney present has the potential to create an adversarial situation. Learning how to not let this get to you is vital to long-term success as a special educator.

"I've taught for many years, and situations with advocates and attorneys have taught me how to look at various situations with a different set of eyes. The first time an advocate attended an IEP with me was absolutely nerve-wracking! *Why are they here? Does this mean the parents are unhappy with the school? What did the parents hope to gain by asking this person to the meeting? How much knowledge of the child do they have? Do they really 'get' the world of special education?* Unfortunately, even well-intended advocates don't always have a background in or experience with students with special needs or the field of special education. I've been fortunate to have worked with advocates and attorneys that truly were advocates for the child and who were willing to work collaboratively with our team to create a successful learning experience for the child. Mutual respect, whether we agree or disagree, makes a positive impact on the work that we do. Effective communication is vital to creating a positive working environment to all who are involved in the child's education.

"It is so important to understand that parents go through a process, almost like grieving, when their child first qualifies for special education services. What they once dreamed of for their child is changed. They worry about long-term implications for their child and family. How the parents are able to process and make sense of the situation varies widely—and the range of their responses may vary as well. Stressful and uncomfortable situations can and do arise in our careers. It's important to remember to step back, breathe, and not take things personally. It takes time and patience to get to a place where you can do this, but don't worry; we all will get there. The parents only want what is best for their child, but may have difficulty expressing that to you, the teacher. Ask for support from colleagues and administrators. Perhaps the best advice I've heard came from Dr. Ernest Mendes, who said at a conference, 'We cannot change what has happened, but we can change how we respond to it.'"

responsibility of the classroom teacher. Teachers "armed" with this quick reference sheet are better able to manage an IEP meeting and can refer to accommodations in place with more confidence. Parents and advocates see the tool and recognize the teacher's earnest efforts to meet the needs of the child.

Several goals are met when advocacy is positive and effective. All parties work collaboratively to provide successful learning experiences for children with special needs and to prevent problems. They look at the student and existing situations with open minds. They identify problems and document them without any judgments. They value all perspectives. They consider options and look for solutions that are win-win, so everyone's needs are satisfied to the extent possible. "Communication, respect, and equality all contribute to win-win solutions" (Turnbull, Turnbull, & Wehmeyer, 2010, p. 119). The bottom line for advocacy experiences should be to do what is in the best interest of the child.

Requirements for Paraprofessionals and Volunteers

The requirements for paraprofessionals and volunteers are not stringent, but all persons under consideration should understand two things from the beginning. First, their services are needed to support the educational program. Their presence at school is not for socializing, drinking coffee in the lounge, or laughing about inappropriate things children sometimes do. This point is tactfully made to prospective helpers, of course. Second, once they are given responsibilities, professional standards apply to them just as to other school personnel. A discussion of professionalism follows. This point also is tactfully made so that no offense is given. With these two understandings in place, teachers look for three additional traits in paraprofessionals and volunteers: (1) a sincere desire to work with students and to help provide a quality educational experience, (2) a personality suited to working with children and other adults in the school, and (3) an assurance of reliability—that the person can and will appear regularly as scheduled.

Optimum Number of Paraprofessionals and Volunteers

One paraprofessional or volunteer per classroom is desirable; two per room, if they are good, may be better. With more than two, the situation is likely to be counterproductive, cumbersome, and confused. With the exception of support providers for children with special needs, ideally a class profits substantially from the presence of a teacher, one paid paraprofessional present every morning or every day, and one caregiver or university student volunteer scheduled as needed. Cross-grade partners and cross-age tutors may be used as needed to work directly with students who require extra help. This amount of assistance permits good instruction and monitoring, individual attention to children, and adequate help so the teacher isn't run ragged.

Ground Rules for Paraprofessionals and Volunteers

There are many expectations of paraprofessionals and volunteers with regards to behavior, authority, and dealing with children. They will not know automatically what is expected of them, especially in professional appearance and demeanor. They will almost certainly know little about legal requirements and danger points. You should be prepared to inform and instruct paraprofessionals and volunteers under your direction, so they are able to function well.

Often expectations of paraprofessionals are stated in handbooks prepared by school districts, and if these are available where you teach, you should see that your adult paraprofessionals receive copies. You should ask that they read the guidelines and discuss the contents with you afterward. If you use parent volunteers, cross-grade partners, or cross-age tutors, take time to explain carefully what you expect. Make sure you discuss with all paraprofessionals and volunteers your expectations concerning authority, reliability, instruction, discipline, communication, professionalism, and legal requirements.

Authority

Adult paraprofessionals and volunteers should be made aware of the lines of authority within the school, which normally flow in the order depicted in Figure 12.1. As the chart illustrates, the principal is in charge of everyone at the school. Below the principal and on an equal level are teachers, librarians, clerical staff, custodians, and district resource personnel such as specialists and psychologists. Classroom paraprofessionals and volunteers function under the authority of the principal and classroom teacher but are directly responsible to the teacher in whose room they work.

Paraprofessionals have authority over students only in areas delegated by the teacher. Usually, that authority is limited to the classroom and the playground. It should clearly be understood that although the adult may be given considerable latitude, the teacher has the final say in all matters related to the class duties of the paraprofessional or volunteer, including instruction, clerical work, the learning environment, and dealings with children and their caregivers.

Reliability

Reliability is essential in paraprofessionals and volunteers. Those who are not reliable in attendance or performance of duties are of no value. They need to understand that they

Figure 12.1

Lines of Authority within the School

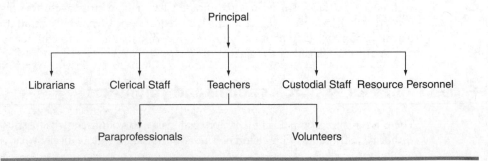

must be prepared, that they must function consistently, and that they must let nothing except emergency situations interfere with the performance of their obligations.

Naturally, people become ill and cannot or should not report for work in the classroom, and unexpected emergencies happen to everyone. When these situations occur, paraprofessionals are obligated to inform the teacher as early as possible so the teacher can make other arrangements.

Teachers should not spring surprise duties on paraprofessionals or volunteers that cannot be handled well or gracefully. And teachers always should anticipate the possibility that the aide may be absent. With a backup plan always in mind, such as change of activity or use of a volunteer, cross-grade partner, or cross-age tutor, the teacher need not panic when an aide will not be present.

Instruction

The instructional program is to be planned and delivered under the direction of the classroom teacher. Many paraprofessionals and volunteers are very good at teaching and do so regularly, but always with the presumption that the teacher has provided suitable guidance. The classroom teacher is not to turn over complete responsibility for significant portions of the instructional program to any paraprofessional or volunteer. The teacher is legally and professionally expected to be in charge of instruction and is responsible for instructional outcome.

Discipline

Technically, paraprofessionals and volunteers are not to discipline students. Discipline is the province of the teacher, principal, and other credentialed persons. In practice, however, teachers cannot expect a paraprofessional or volunteer to work with students but do nothing to manage or help students manage their own behavior. When it is necessary to correct disruptive or irresponsible behavior, the paraprofessional or volunteer should always do so within the parameters of the discipline system in effect in the classroom and with the teacher's permission. By no means should paraprofessionals or volunteers physically punish students, berate them, detain them after school, or force them to do unpleasant tasks as punishment for disruptive behavior. Consequences for disruptive or inappropriate behavior are always for the teacher to decide.

Teachers know that students often consider substitutes fair game. Therefore, they should talk seriously with students about class behavior during the teacher's absence. Teachers should make it clear that the substitute will report on the behavior of the class and individual students. Students should be informed that the substitute may use the teacher's discipline plan or an altogether different one, but that, in either case, students are to behave and be as helpful as possible to the substitute.

Most student teachers arrive at their field placements with ideas about curriculum, instruction, and discipline from their university program coursework and textbooks, as well as from their own school experiences. Ideally, the practicum nature of the field experience makes this a time for student teachers to find out what works and doesn't work for them, with a safety net of sorts provided by the cooperating teacher and university supervisor.

Vignette 12.2   The Substitute CD

Linda Monedero uses a CD (formerly a video-tape) activity to prepare her young students and the substitute for a successful day.

"The CD, created by my students, shows the daily schedule and the class rules and is included as part of the materials left for my substitute when I am away. The substitute and my class view this five-minute CD together at the beginning of the school day. My students are accountable because they were involved in making the CD and they hear and see it with the substitute.

"My students work in cooperative groups to make the short CD. Each group draws and labels two signs, one for a subject area (such as 'Reading 9:00–10:30') and another for a class rule. The CD then shows each cooperative group reading its signs. The signs for subject areas are presented in time line order."

UPON REFLECTION

Linda teaches kindergarten. How well do you believe this activity would work for intermediate or upper level students? Remember substitute Janet Beyea in Case Study 12.2? How likely is it that she would have a productive and successful day with Linda's students?

Consequently, student teachers might hope to develop and present their own discipline system. This would be done only with the guidance and support of the cooperating teacher.

Communication

Paraprofessionals and volunteers should be taught how to communicate with your students—to speak in a calm, reassuring tone of voice, using words that students understand, and to serve as models of correct grammar and polite language. If your paraprofessional, volunteer, or tutor has a problem in this regard, very tactfully explain that you have a certain way of speaking to children, and you would like his or her help with this. Then demonstrate what you say and how you speak. When you notice improvement, acknowledge the effort with genuine thanks.

Communication between teacher and paraprofessional, volunteer, substitute, student teacher (and the university supervisor), or advocate must be open. This openness permits an easier resolution of problems than when secrecy or hurt is involved, provided neither person is put on the defensive. It is good to remember Berne's three states of communication that were mentioned briefly in the previous chapter—the child state, the parent state, and the adult state. Using adult–adult parallel communication, teachers must take the lead in communicating openly and tactfully. Just as they are mindful about how they talk with students, teachers should take great care when communicating with paraprofessionals, volunteers, student teachers, and advocates to avoid sounding brusque, disparaging, or judgmental.

Professionalism

Paraprofessionals and volunteers, certainly those who are paid for their services, are expected and may need to be taught how to behave in a professional manner—that is, with a positive and sincere attitude toward one's status, work, and the children in the class. Professionalism includes dependability and the acceptance of responsibility. In addition, professionalism reflects the styles of dress, speech, and demeanor considered proper for school personnel.

We shared cautions regarding the teachers' lounge in Chapter 4, but it's worth repeating the cautions here. Be sure that you take a moment to discuss with paraprofessionals and volunteers the dangers inherent in gossip and negativity. The fact that over 90 percent of the informal talk that occurs in teachers' lounges is negative in nature is a daunting concern. Negative talk that criticizes programs, students, administrators, caregivers, colleagues may be entertaining, but invariably it is counterproductive. It encourages further negativism, diverts energy from productive work, and can lead to personal conflicts. Paraprofessionals and volunteers should be helped to understand clearly that they should either keep quiet or speak positively about children and programs to prevent irreparable damage.

Occasionally, frank talk is called for between teacher and paraprofessional, volunteer, or student teacher. Sometimes shortcomings must be discussed, but even then, the teacher must try to point to positive solutions and to better ways of doing things without denigrating the character of others. If you hear paraprofessionals or volunteers at your school speaking derogatorily of the school, programs, students, or personnel, take immediate steps to correct the problem. Handle the problem yourself if your own paraprofessional or volunteer is guilty and consider including the university supervisor if your student teacher is guilty. If others are involved, take up the matter with the principal as a school problem. Don't point blame at fellow teachers.

The way one dresses also demonstrates professionalism. Adult paraprofessionals and volunteers and, occasionally, student teachers need to be encouraged to dress neatly, more or less in keeping with how teachers in the school and grade level dress. They will want respect, like everyone else, and they should understand that respect is influenced by appearance. Of course, this consideration applies to a lesser degree for cross-grade partners and cross-age tutors.

Responsibility and dependability have already been mentioned as aspects of professionalism. Responsibility is shown in the assumption of duties and their follow-through without having to be asked. It also is shown through the use of common sense, such as paying attention to children when on playground duty. Dependability refers to living up to expectations—doing what one is supposed to do when one is supposed to do it. Of course, it is the teacher's responsibility to clearly inform paraprofessionals, volunteers, and student teachers of expectations, routines, and duties.

Legal Requirements

Paraprofessionals, like teachers, will not be allowed to keep their jobs if they are shown to be incompetent or insubordinate or to have engaged in criminal or certain immoral activities.

Incompetence refers to an inability or failure to perform satisfactorily those duties normally expected. To be substantiated, this failure must occur repeatedly over a period of time and be documented by the teacher. *Insubordination* means refusal to follow direct, reasonable orders given by a person in authority, or the breaking of a valid school rule in a willful and defiant manner. Generally, *criminal acts* are those activities categorized as felonies under the law—for example, robbery or sale of illegal drugs, but not jaywalking or speeding.

Immoral or otherwise unacceptable acts come into play only when they directly impact one's job performance or reputation, such as intoxication or drinking while on the job, obscene language at school, inappropriate sexual activity around the school premises or on the Internet.

Paraprofessionals, like teachers, need to be careful about what they say. While the Supreme Court in 1969 guaranteed teachers and students freedom of expression in the schools, that guarantee does not apply as fully for school personnel as for ordinary citizens. For example, teachers are allowed to speak out on controversial matters, including conditions and policies of the schools. They may not, however, make false or reckless accusations that disrupt the educational process, or make abusive and scornful attacks on school officials. Nor are they allowed to use profanity or tell off-color stories within students' range of hearing. It also is forbidden to use the classroom as a forum for expressing personal convictions in sensitive matters such as religion, politics, abortion, gender preferences, or sex education.

Liability for student injury or loss is another legal matter of which paraprofessionals and volunteers should be aware. School personnel have a legal responsibility to protect students from harm and injury. For example, if a student is hurt on the playground and suit is brought to show that the injury occurred at least partly because of negligence, the court will try to determine three things: (1) who was supervising the student at the time of the injury, (2) whether the supervisor exercised reasonable foresight in anticipating danger to the student, and (3) whether the supervisor acted in a reasonable and prudent manner. Teachers, paraprofessionals, and volunteers will not be found negligent unless it can be shown that they violated the requirements of reasonable foresight (e.g., not allowing students to play where there is broken glass or an excavation) and prudent manner (e.g., keeping watch over the students instead of slipping into the lounge for a cup of coffee).

Paraprofessionals and volunteers working in supervisory capacities therefore must be clearly informed that they must be present and attentive, that they must not allow students out of their line of sight while supervising, and that they must make sure students do not play in unsafe areas or use equipment that is obviously unsafe. Paraprofessionals and volunteers should always be informed of legal danger areas and given suitable instruction on conduct.

When Paraprofessionals Must Be Absent

Most student teachers genuinely want successful field experiences and see them as rich and practical learning opportunities. Many paraprofessionals and volunteers are completely dependable and miss work only out of dire necessity, and they inform the teacher as soon as possible of their pending absence. However, others take all the available paid absences, plus a few extras. Volunteers tend to be even less reliable. And to the teacher's distress, absences appear to occur at times when the aide seems indispensable, causing the teacher to scramble for alternative plans.

This need not be the case. Since you know that your paraprofessionals, volunteers, or student teacher may, at any time, be unavailable, be open to arranging for substitute aides or extra cross-grade or cross-age tutors. And when that is not possible, have ready some backup instructional plans.

Training Paraprofessionals and Volunteers

As mentioned earlier, some school districts provide training for the paid paraprofessionals they employ. Such training typically deals with the foregoing matters. However, most paraprofessionals, and almost all volunteers, cross-grade partners, and cross-age tutors, are trained on the job, in the classroom by the teacher. As teachers in training, student teachers also receive on-the-job training as the cooperating teacher models, mentors, and coaches the routines, management, and instruction of the classroom. As for advocates, it is a reality that even well-intentioned advocates may not have a background in or experience with students with special needs or the field of special education, and will need some guidance in these areas.

On-the-job training is acceptable—even preferable in most cases—because the duties of paraprofessionals and volunteers vary from classroom to classroom. Usually, training done by teachers includes an orientation to the classroom; instruction in specific duties; details of where volunteers are to be stationed, work, or circulate; and a demonstration of how duties are to be performed. Professional, ethical, and legal regulations are spelled out clearly. As the paraprofessional or volunteer works in the manner indicated, the teacher provides necessary feedback, both corrections and appreciations.

Paraprofessionals and aides who are regulars in the classroom quickly learn procedures and become able to discharge their duties without direct supervision. Still, it is the teacher's responsibility to plan all work and materials included in the instructional program and to supervise these adults at work. Student teachers also learn procedures and over time become more able to perform with less direct supervision, although it is the shared responsibility of the cooperating teacher and university supervisor to guide and oversee their progress.

Assigning Space and Work Duties

All regular paraprofessionals, student teachers, and aides, whether paid, volunteer, cross-grade, or cross-age, should have a place in the classroom designated as their own. Adults should not be asked to sit in small chairs at low tables used by young children. Consequently, if one is available, they should sit at an adult desk or table where the teacher provides their notes, materials, or other items.

Paid paraprofessionals are assigned to the classroom for a specific number of hours. Volunteer work time is scheduled by agreement with the teacher, typically for certain days and times, according to teacher need. Volunteers should not be left to simply hang around and observe, not knowing what to do with themselves. When a volunteer offers unexpected help, the teacher should accept the offer if it is convenient, but only if there is something productive for the volunteer to do, such as organizing materials, helping individual children, or sorting and filing papers. Otherwise, the teacher should thank the volunteer, explain that no help is needed at the moment, and ask permission to call for help in the future.

Oral instructions are sufficient when the duties of the paraprofessional or volunteer are mostly supervisory or clerical. However, many teachers write specific work assignments on

Vignette 12.3 Parent Volunteers

During her 15 years of teaching primary grades, Betsy Goff has been able to involve parent volunteers with overall success. She has developed a simple plan that works. It keeps parent volunteers happy and active in her classroom and at the same time provides clear expectations that allow her to work without disruption.

"When I was a new teacher, I quickly realized that parent volunteers can be quite helpful or very disruptive to a classroom routine. Without proper direction they can destroy classroom supplies, break expensive equipment, disrupt the best planned lesson, and create quite a commotion with small groups of students. However, with a little guidance and proper planning, they can lighten my workload, provide essential support to struggling students, and assist with special labor-intensive activities.

"At Back to School Night I send home a survey asking parents if they are interested in volunteering and if they prefer to do paperwork or work with students. I find that volunteers will be successful if I place them in their area of confidence. I explain that I will have volunteers at a specific time, and for only 1½ hours each day.

I also try to schedule only one parent each day, which sometimes means that parents work every other week instead of weekly. This eliminates parents becoming distracted. And it simplifies my schedule and eliminates confusion.

"Once I set up a schedule for the year I meet with the group of volunteers one day before or after school to explain my organizational system. I explain that I have a file box on a table in my room that is divided into the following sections: classroom preparation, copies, correcting, individual students, and small groups. At the front of each folder I place a card with step-by-step expectations of how to complete the task. Behind each card I place projects or lists of students, and the specific details needed to complete that activity. When parent helpers come into my room, they go immediately to the box and begin working. Rarely do I need to stop my instruction to give any directions."

UPON REFLECTION

How will you locate volunteers for your classroom? How will you schedule and train your volunteers? What specific tasks might you ask of a volunteer?

cards for their paraprofessionals and volunteers to avoid or minimize misunderstandings. These notations need not be made in detail but should indicate duties, sequence, materials, and time allocations. An assignment card might look something like the one in Figure 12.2. Teachers should provide more details on the cards when they first begin to work with the paraprofessional. Later, when duties are understood, brief notes suffice, such as:

Reading: Tom to center, read story to you; record errors.

Math: Photocopy tomorrow's papers; score today's and enter.

Spelling: Give practice test.

Language: Help monitor.

Figure 12.2

Assignment Card for Paraprofessional

Name: _____   Date:_____

Reading: Take Tom to center and have him read the story aloud to you; keep a record of the errors he makes.

Math: Duplicate tomorrow's papers. Collect today's papers and score them. Enter scores in record book.

Spelling: Give today's practice test to the class. Collect and mark the papers.

Language: Help me monitor students as they write their stories. Help with spelling or other questions they have.

When duties involve record keeping, remember these earlier cautions: Students have the right to privacy regarding their work and progress; records are legal documents; and you, as the contracted teacher, are legally responsible for their management, recording, and accuracy.

Maintaining Morale among Paraprofessionals and Volunteers

Good morale, easily overlooked, is as necessary to paraprofessionals, volunteers, and student teachers as it is to teachers. It affects the quality of their work and the amount of satisfaction derived from it. To keep the morale level high for paraprofessionals and volunteers, give attention to the following:

1. Acceptance—a sense of belonging to the classroom and educational program, which grows out of appreciative attention and communication from the teacher, and is furthered by assigning specific tasks and work space.

2. Meaningful work and clear directions—paraprofessionals and volunteers should not always do menial or tedious tasks; give sufficient guidance so that the work can be done properly.

3. Sense of accomplishment—helps paraprofessionals and volunteers to see that their work has been done well and progress was made.

4. Evidence of appreciation—for contributions made to the instruction program; need only be a sincere thank-you, but an occasional card or small gift always is welcomed.

Remember that student teachers are learners and need morale boosts, too. It is as important for them to hear about what they do well as it is to know what they need to change, correct, or improve. Specific positive feedback can be given during planning or conferences, in an interactive journal, or in short notes to the student teacher.

This concludes our consideration of managing the work of paraprofessionals, volunteers, substitutes, student teachers, and other helpers in the classroom. Before moving ahead to Chapter 13, which deals with how to manage two kinds of stress—the stressful emotions of unexpected events and trauma and job-related stress that so badly afflicts teachers—take time to explore these end-of-chapter activities.

Parting Thought

Determine that the thing can and should be done, and then . . . find the way.

—Abraham Lincoln

Summary Self-Check

Check off the following as you either understand or become able to apply them:

☐ Paraprofessionals and volunteers are individuals who work in the classroom with the teacher to help provide the educational program. Usually, they fall into the categories of paid paraprofessional, caregiver or university student volunteer, cross-grade partner or cross-age tutor, or community resource person. Substitute teachers and student teachers are other adults who might work in a classroom.

- What paraprofessionals can do: tutor, test, supervise, correct papers, duplicate, record, file, prepare instructional materials, assist as directed by the teacher.
- How paraprofessionals are obtained: recruited by schools or by teachers from caregivers, friends, and relatives of students; from high schools and universities; from older elementary and secondary students; from PTAs and PTOs; from senior citizens' groups; and from community agencies and companies.
- Other helpers: cross-grade partners, cross-age tutors, substitute teachers, and student teachers.

☐ Substitute teachers are hired to teach when contracted teachers must be away from the classroom.

- Teachers leave a paper or electronic substitute folder with lesson plans and a copy of the discipline plan, current seating chart and class roster with notations of relevant student information, class schedule and current duty schedule, classroom monitor and volunteer lists, and school map.
- The teacher's obligations: inform students about teacher absences, substitute teachers, how to work helpfully with substitutes, duties of substitute teacher monitors.
- The substitute teacher's obligations: further the program and make the day productive for the students; maintain discipline.
- Mutuality: the ideal relationship between teacher and substitute.

☐ Student teachers are teachers in training, not paraprofessionals.

- What student teachers can do, as abilities and responsibilities increase with time and experience: plan and teach lessons; take responsibility for discipline; communicate with parents and guardians; confer with teachers and university supervisors; observe, participate, and perform most of the teacher's activities.

☐ Advocates may be present at IEP meetings to help create successful learning experiences for children with special needs.

☐ Ground rules for paraprofessionals and volunteers:
- Authority belongs to the teacher but can be delegated to the paraprofessional.
- Reliability is an essential trait.
- Instruction can be provided by paraprofessionals under the teacher's supervision.
- Discipline is the province of the teacher.
- Communication is needed for good relationships.
- Professional standards are explained and exemplified by the teacher.
- Legal requirements require that attention be given to incompetence, insubordination, criminality, immorality, liability for student injury or loss; freedom of expression and subsequent restrictions.
- When paraprofessionals must be absent: utilize substitute, cross-grade partner or cross-age helper, backup plan.
- Training paraprofessionals: by schools for paid aides; on-the-job training by teachers.
- Work space and assignments: designated personal area; work assignments clearly set forth; record-keeping duties closely checked and verified.
- Morale of paraprofessionals and student teachers maintained through acceptance, meaningful work and clear directions, sense of accomplishment, evidence of appreciation.

☐ Important cautions when the duties involve record keeping: Students have the right to privacy regarding their work and progress. Records are legal documents and the contracted teacher is legally responsible for their management, recording, and accuracy.

Activities for Reflection and Discussion

1. Take a moment to review the statements in the Preview–Review Guide at the beginning of this chapter. Put a check mark in the *Review* column next to any statement with which you now agree. How have your thoughts changed since reading this chapter?

2. Interview at least two teachers about their use of paraprofessionals and volunteers in their classroom. How do they locate and schedule volunteers? When and how do they "train" volunteers? What tasks and responsibilities do they request of their volunteers? How do they show their appreciation?

3. You are told you can choose a paid paraprofessional and a substitute teacher from among four available candidates. List in order the criteria you would use in making your selections. How would you determine the extent to which each candidate meets your criteria?

4. You are provided with a paid paraprofessional for two and a half hours a day. For a grade level of your choice, put in order of importance what you would have your aide do during that limited amount of time. Give your reasons.

5. You are ready to instruct your paraprofessional on the ground rules of discipline and professionalism. What would you say and what training would you give, if any?

6. Compile what you will provide in a substitute folder to ensure that the substitute and students have a productive day.

7. Suppose you teach second grade. Two talented but somewhat troubled sixth-grade boys (they talk back to their teacher and sometimes fight with other boys on the play-ground) think it would be "cool" to work in your room as cross-grade tutors. Their teacher believes the experience would be good for them. You hesitantly agree to give them the opportunity. What ground rules would you establish for them? If they proved to be good and worthwhile for your program, how would you let them know that you appreciate their work?

Webliography

Disability Rights Organization: http://www.dralegal.org
National Substitute Teacher Alliance: http://www.nstasubs.org
Senior Motivators in Learning and Educational Services (SMILES) found in Eric Resources Information Center: http://www.eric.ed.gov/ERICWebPortal/record Detail?accno=ED346983
SMILES Program: http://www.slc.k12.ut.us/depts/communiv/schoolvols.html

References and Recommended Readings

Allen, R. (2002, November). Teachers and paraeducators: Defining roles in an age of accounta-bility. *Education Update, 44*(7). Alexandria, VA: ASCD.

Kagan, S. (2000). *Silly sports and goofy games.* San Clemente, CA: Kagan Publishing.

Turnbull, A., Turnbull, R., & Wehmeyer, M. L. (2010). *Exceptional lives: Special education in today's schools* (6th ed.). Upper Saddle River, NJ: Merrill.

Trade Books

Allard, H. (1977). *Miss Nelson is missing!* Boston: Houghton Mifflin.

Thaler, M. (1989). *The teacher from the Black Lagoon.* New York: Scholastic.

PEARSON
myeducationlab

Go to the Topic: **Communication Skills** in the MyEducationLab (www.myeducationlab .com) for your course, where you can:

- Find learning outcomes for **Communication Skills** along with the national standards that connect to these outcomes.
- Examine challenging situations and cases presented in the IRIS Center Resources.

CHAPTER 13

Managing Emotional Trauma and Job-Related Stress Productively

There have been no dragons in my life, only small spiders and stepping in gum.
I could have coped with dragons

—Author unknown

Preview–Review Guide

Before you read the chapter, and based on what you know, think you know, or assume, take a minute to put a check mark in the **Preview** column if you agree with the statement. When you finish the chapter, take time to reread the statements and respond in the **Review** column. Reflective discussions can develop because many of the statements are not clearly "yes" or "no."

Preview   **Review**

1. _____ Current brain research suggests that all three parts of the brain work   _____
   equally in times of stress.

2. _____ The main purpose of crisis intervention and critical incident stress   _____
   management is to handle situations that are beyond the resources
   of the individual or site.

3. _____ Distress is bad for you; however, eustress is good for you.   _____

4. _____ Teaching is considered to be high on the list of stressful occupations.   _____

5. _____ Discipline problems and lack of time are two of teachers'   _____
   greatest stressors.

6. _____ When prioritizing, it is advisable to finish the easy tasks first so you   _____
   can concentrate on the more difficult ones.

7. _____ Selective avoidance is one way to reduce the stress of teaching.   _____

8. _____ Good cooperation and quality achievement almost certainly render   _____
   a high level of class synergy.

9. _____ A good place to cut back if your workload is too heavy is on   _____
   communication with caregivers, provided there are no serious problems
   with students.

10. _____ If the work you assign students is important enough for them to do, then   _____
    it is equally important that you correct it carefully.

Chapter Objectives

After reading Chapter 13, students will demonstrate understanding of

- the nature and handling of emotional stress that comes from unexpected events and trauma

- the nature and handling of job-related stress issues

through their active participation in discussions and the end-of-chapter activities for reflection.

In this chapter, we explore two aspects of stress. We begin with a topic that relates ever more strongly to our lives today—the effects of emotional stress that result from unexpected events such as tragedy and trauma, with attention to managing that stress. Later we explore suggestions concerning management of stress that normally accompanies teaching. Thus, a problem to solve or an essential or guiding question for this chapter might be: *How can I manage the emotional stress that may arise from tragedy and trauma, as well as the stressors that come from the responsibilities of my job?*

Managing Emotions of Trauma and Unexpected Events

"The best laid plans of mice and men . . ." How many times have we planned and prepared and showed up ready to instruct, only to find that something or someone has put an enormous obstacle in our path? It may be something as simple as having to change the schedule for the day, despite its effects on your program. Certainly, the move of a best friend or the death of a pet can affect a child's attention and interrupt the flow of your plans. But other obstacles can take on an imposing nature as well: an accident with fatalities involving a school bus and its passengers; the sudden death of a beloved teacher; the kidnapping and death of a local child; the shooting at a local high school; terrorist attacks on New York City and Washington, DC; deployments of family members and friends to fight a war that is half-way around the world; natural devastations such as fires, earthquakes, hurricanes, tornadoes, and floods; and the other disasters that overflow today's news. All such events produce strong emotional reactions in our students and us. While we can't change the events, we can manage the associated emotions in a way that allows our students and us to cope with them more easily.

State laws give districts the legal responsibilities for emergency preparedness, school safety, and risk management. The Field Act of 1933 requires that schools be available as postdisaster shelters. To this end, districts have plans in place for such major events. Generally, public school employees are sanctioned as disaster service workers, and as such, teachers are responsible for giving care and support to students in a crisis. In other words, teachers may have to deal with the effects of trauma and emotional stress.

Important Definitions

In order to understand the nature and results of events that require special care or intervention, we should be familiar with the following terms.

Stress *Stress* is anything that causes continuing physical, mental, or emotional strain or tension. Later in this chapter, we will explore how stress can be positive (eustress) or negative (distress). Here, we focus on distress.

Trauma *Trauma* is a physical or emotional injury or shock from experiencing a disastrous event outside the range of usual experience. Devine and Cohen (2007) sort trauma into three categories. *Single-incident trauma* comes from experiencing a disaster—natural or man-made. Single-incident trauma can lead to posttraumatic stress disorder (PTSD). Victims—or witnesses—of abuse, neglect, violence, or extensive bullying can experience *chronic trauma.* Incidents of *high-stress trauma* involve stressful home and family situations, such as divorce or the serious illness of a family member. In this chapter, we focus on the emotional manifestations an individual or group displays to a disastrous or traumatic event. Anyone can experience high emotions when traumatic events occur. Teachers are faced with two important questions: How can we manage these emotions, especially in our children? And how do we take care of ourselves as well?

Critical Incident and Crisis Intervention Childs (2002) defines a *critical incident* as "any emotionally significant event that overwhelms the coping abilities of exposed individuals or groups" (p. 3). *Crisis intervention* is the "assistance rendered after a critical incident" (p. 3). As a short-term response to a critical incident, a crisis intervention has several goals:

- Interventions attempt to decrease or relieve adverse reactions of individuals or groups affected by trauma.
- They are intended to impact or address the individual's or group's ability to cope, and they assist in identifying and assessing available support structures.
- They normalize reactions to the event or crisis.
- They assess the individual's or group's capabilities and need for further support or referral.

Crisis intervention is not therapy for the individual or group. Teachers are not trained for that task. Rather, the goal of crisis intervention is to assess and then assist with the immediacy of the event in order to return the individual or group to a normal level of functioning.

Critical Incident Stress Management (CISM) *Critical Incident Stress Management* is a systematic crisis intervention model that has become a standard of care for traumatized persons. The model and its structure were conceived by Dr. Jeffrey Mitchell, a military doctor who studied emotional trauma of individuals involved in crisis. For additional information and links to related articles, resources, workshops, and training opportunities regarding CISM, go to http://www.icisf.org.

Stress and the Triune Brain

Knowledge about human brain physiology helps us understand how to provide crisis intervention. In the 1980s, Paul MacLean, the former director of the Laboratory of the Brain and Behavior at the United States National Institute of Mental Health, introduced the triune brain theory. MacLean describes the human brain as being three brains in one, having evolved in that manner in response to various needs. Although each of the three brains, or layers, specializes in a separate function, all three layers interact.

Simplified, the three areas of the brain work in this way. The primary function of the brain stem and cerebellum, also called the reptilian complex, controls physical survival and body maintenance (digestion, reproduction, circulation, breathing, and movement). The middle brain controls emotion and survival acts such as eating, drinking, and sleeping. The outer brain (neocortex) is responsible for language, higher-order thinking, and the ability to see ahead and plan for the future. The neocortex seeks a balance of emotions (meaning none becomes extremely high), and until this balance exists, the cortex has a reduced capacity to process information and use logical reasoning.

Here is how all this relates to stress. In times of threat or undue stress, the brain tends to bypass reason. Instead of allowing us to assess situations and plan ahead, it hammers us first with a fight, flight, or hide response—we fight back or we try to escape or hide from the situation. In others words, we react first, after which logic, reasoning, and decision making seem to follow. This explains why we may behave the way we do in a crisis—why we may forget the name of our best friend or feel driven to clean the house and polish the silver.

"CATEGORY FIVE CLASSROOM."

Signs and Symptoms of Emotional Stress

Fear and anxiety are debilitating emotions for everyone. Reactions to disaster differ from person to person, with individual behaviors shifting from calm and quiet to arousal to alarm, fear, and terror, to acting out. In general, under situations of threat or excitement, humans attempt to cope or adapt by making changes to their mental state, their thinking, and/or their body's physiology. Their bodies undergo chemical changes—rapid pulse, increased blood pressure, muscle tension, and perspiration. Along with the mental, cognitive, and physical adaptations, adults reacting to disastrous events often engage in a natural grieving process that begins with denial, then anger, and finally a degree of resignation. If their distress is great, they may demonstrate symptoms of what now is called posttraumatic stress disorder (PTSD), in which they reexperience the event, either in dreams or in a related context; avoid talking about it; numb their emotions; or assume a high-alert state of being.

Children's reactions to trauma also may be varied. For example, they may detach from the pain of the moment in emotional shock and be seen as having an apparent lack of feelings. They may regress into immature behaviors, needing to be held or rocked, or to remain close and clinging to a caregiver or someone important to them. They may act out behaviorally, venting feelings of anger, terror, frustration, or helplessness. They may repeatedly ask questions or require a lot of extra reassurances.

Perry (2006) studied brain development of children in crisis. He found that children who are traumatized and in a state of alarm are likely to be easily distracted and anxious. They also are more likely to pay greater attention to nonverbal cues such as tone of voice, body posture, and facial expressions.

The Nature of Crisis Intervention

Critical incidents generally involve traumatic loss (death, serious injury, hostage situations), social unrest or racial conflicts, and man-made or natural disasters. Critical incidents are judged by the reaction to the incident, not by the magnitude of the event.

Today many districts and schools have teams of district and community members trained to assist in the aftermath of a critical incident. A *crisis response team* (*CRT*) is called when the event overwhelms the school's ability to handle a situation, and operates with the consent and concurrence of the site administrator. The CRT command leader meets with administration and keeps them informed as the team carries out the approved plan. Typically, the team provides direct crisis intervention services to students in the classrooms, in whole- or small-group settings, and to individual students as needed. The team also is prepared to assist teachers and school personnel in handling student reactions and provide personal support to them. Additionally, the CRT can provide consultation services to administration and give information and community resources to parents and guardians.

The CRT responds to what individuals need right in the moment. Their interventions deal with the here and now, are designed to prevent further emotional and behavioral disturbances, and are short-term. Team members are facilitators who use active listening and direct strategies and responses. CRT members are not counselors, nor are they bound to invest in long-term care and treatment. They will make referrals to counselors and other community resources, as needed, so individuals receive the best long-term support.

When Crisis Teams Are Not Available

Crisis response teams are not always available when needed. In those cases, it is up to the teachers and school personnel to help others cope. Most school districts provide some advice concerning how personnel should function at those times, recognizing that they do not have adequate training or understanding. Here are some things educators do. When applying any of these tactics, one must keep in mind students' emotional maturity and needs.

Through a question and response guide, Berman et al. (2003) coach teachers and caregivers about ways to discuss exceptional events with children. These discussions are varied in accordance with the age and maturity of the children, as well as their personal connection to the event. Most children appreciate talking with adults they trust and see as supportive, caring, and sensitive. Among the guidelines for discussions are the following:

- Ask the children what they already know, what they think they know but are not sure about, and what questions they have. Ask open questions: "What do you know about . . . ?" "What is upsetting you the most?" "Are you saying that . . . ?"

- Listen and respond to their questions and concerns with facts, in simple language, and without extraneous details for which the children may not be ready. Simply and factually correct misinformation. Allow children to respond to each of your comments.

- As you listen to and observe the children, respond to what you hear and see in a calm, supportive, and sensitive way. Children are reassured when they know you are listening and you care about them.

- Avoid talking to children about adult concerns that would likely raise new questions and fears, limit their own expressions, or simply be over their heads.

- Use active listening to clarify without judgment, help you understand the children, and help the children sort out their ideas. Because children may be unable to say what they feel, or what they say may mean something different to you than they intended, paraphrase what you hear and invite them to elaborate or clarify: "I heard you say that . . ." "Can you tell me more about that?" or "What do you mean by that?"

- In addition to talk, provide children with opportunities to explore and express themselves through writing, play, drawings, and props such as clay or puppets.

- Look and listen for nonverbal messages such as facial expressions, gestures, posture, and fidgeting; also notice voice rate and tone and watch for significant increases in anxiety, distractibility, despair, or fear.

Case Study 13.1   Responding to Crisis

FOCUS QUESTION
What action plan does your local school or district have in place to handle serious or crisis events?

Sherry Coburn, a sixth-grade teacher, is also the team coordinator who prepares the yearly telephone tree that is used to contact all staff when a serious event warrants their knowledge. She describes crisis response at her school.

"Gilmore's crisis response team originally was designed to aid students in crisis—suffering from such losses as a sibling, parent, or relative. As time has gone on, its purpose has increased. We have been called on to service children who had been friends with someone shot and killed as a result of gang involvement and gang retaliation. We once had to deal with many students when a popular student was hit by a train and killed. We also had an incident in which a teacher was killed due to domestic violence.

"Our crisis team has had to branch out within the past few years to anticipate problems and work out situations prior to their happening in order to make our school a safe place for both students and staff. We devised and held the first intrusion drill in our state and continue to hold them on a monthly basis. We believe that this drill must be second nature to our students, just as a fire drill is.

"Last year when a large fight broke out in the hall, we devised a plan to deal with this new type of incident. We called it a 'Code Hall Sweep.' When teachers hear this over the PA system, they close their classroom doors and do not allow anyone in. Administrators and hall assistants then can handle the situation by rounding up anyone involved."

- Help children explore their feelings. Listen closely for underlying concerns such as personal and family safety.

- Validate that their feelings are OK: "You seem sad when we talk about this. I feel sad, too."

- When closure to a discussion of feelings is difficult, simply thank the children for sharing and affirm that you care.

- Identify and monitor children with personal connections to the event and inform the counselor.

- Finally, look for and accept support from other adults who can help you (a caregiver, mentor, and others).

Of the numerous strategies that have been proven effective, several are fairly easy to remember and implement by teachers, including the SEA-3 method and the SAFER method, described below. As you read about these strategies, keep in mind that they can be applied to anyone in need, adults as well as children. Also remember that as the classroom teacher, you know your students. Because you are familiar with your students' behavior and maturity prior to situations of stress or trauma, you will be able to gauge any of the changes listed in the paragraphs that follow.

SEA-3 Method

This is a method that considers five areas to assess the functioning of individuals—children or adults—in situations of stress or trauma. SEA-3 stands for speech, emotion, appearance, alertness, and activity.

- *Speech*. Listen to the child's speech. To what degree is it slurred or rapid?

- *Emotion*. Evaluate the child's emotion, considering both mood and affect. For example, to what degree is the child depressed or euphoric? Is the child's display of emotions flat or inappropriate? What emotions, if any, are being expressed? Does the child laugh or make jokes about a sad or bad situation? Does the child show overwhelming emotion, such as excessive crying or hysteria?

- *Appearance*. Consider the child's appearance—neat or disheveled?

- *Alertness*. Pay attention to the child's alertness. Do the child's thoughts seem natural? What is the child's level of abstraction—concrete or conceptual? Is the child hallucinating? How accurate is the child's orientation to time, place, and others? What are the child's judgment and capacity for insight? The teacher can assess the child's alertness and judgment by using nondirective responses to what the child says, such as "Let's talk a little more about what happened."

- *Activity*. What is the child's activity—lethargic or hyperactive?

SAFER Method

This is a very useful intervention method that teachers often use without knowing they do. SAFER stands for stabilize, acknowledge, facilitate, encourage, restore or refer. The SAFER method is designed to stabilize the situation by (1) removing the person in crisis from the source of stress, (2) reinforcing cognitive processing and what is natural in time and place, (3) reinforcing the individual's own coping skills, and (4) referring the person for additional care, if necessary. This process may take only a minute or less to perform. In simplified terms, here is what you do:

1. *Stabilize the situation.* Reduce the situational stressors by removing the child from the situation. Turn the child away from the scene or take him or her into another room.

2. *Acknowledge the crisis.* Ask the child to describe what happened or describe personal reactions. The teacher's role is to assist the child in talking about what happened and selecting the right words to express their reactions and emotions. This needs to be done carefully, without making assumptions or putting words in the child's mouth. Using active listening, the teacher would ask the child to describe what happened and then retell what he or she heard the child say ("I heard you say . . .").

3. *Facilitate understanding.* Using language appropriate to the developmental and emotional maturity of the child, explain what is going on. This helps the child understand the situation. Validate the child's reactions as being natural, but avoid the word "normal." For example, you might say something like: "That was probably really scary for you to hear the siren when they came into the parking lot."

4. *Encourage adaptive coping.* While continually assessing the child's ability to function, teach the child reasonable and appropriate basic stress and crisis management strategies. Identify appropriate coping skills ("What do you do when you are scared?"); consider personal, school, family, and community resources ("Is there someone at home who can come for you?"); and develop a reasonable action plan ("Would you like to put some water on your face or lie down in the nurse's office for a few minutes before you go back to class?" "I know Sarah is your friend. I just talked to Sarah's mother, and after school you can go to their house until your parents arrive home.")

5. *Restore or refer.* Your goal is to help the child return to regular functioning. If you feel your efforts are not producing that result, you should consider referring the child for additional care.

Attention-Refocusing Strategies

Attention-refocusing strategies also assist teachers as they work with children in stressful situations. This can be done by asking questions that require the person in distress to use the five senses or that draw attention to the outdoor natural environment. The teacher or helper may begin this strategy by telling the person in distress, "I'm going to ask some silly questions to help you become less upset." Before returning the child to the class or situation, it's important for the helper to ask, "Do you feel you are ready to go back to class?"

Upshifting

Upshifting strategies are intended to shift the child from an emotional focus to a cognitive focus. These strategies involve quick actions and sounds, such as having students echo rhythmic clapping led by the teacher, or blend counting with a word. For example, as students count in sequence, they replace every multiple of five with the word *buzz*.

Other Subtle Techniques

Several other subtle techniques can be used to advantage. Examples include:

- Physical contact by gently touching the individual's hands or shoulders
- Physically turning the individual from the event or distraction
- Speaking in a calm, quiet, unemotional voice
- Prompting deep rhythmic breathing
- Practicing tension-release muscle exercises and stretches, moving from head, face, and neck downward to the toes
- Focusing in the present, what has to be done right now
- Returning to a predictable pattern of routine
- Giving some choice or element of control in activity or interactions with others
- Relating only relevant facts, not details
- Paraphrasing the individual's last sentences and using nondirective responses
- Asking specific questions to check what the individual understands and how the individual is doing
- Asking the individual what has helped in past upsetting situations
- Asking the individual what he or she needs to help settle down now
- Reiterating the paradigm: Who was involved? What happened? What comes next?

Throughout the entire contact, the teacher or helper behaves calmly, naturally, and authentically.

Taking Care of Self

Through all these efforts, it is crucial that teachers and helpers take care of themselves and each other, whether they are individual teachers working with their own students or members of a trained crisis response team. This is necessary because helpers and team members are susceptible to direct or vicarious traumatization when responding to a crisis event or when providing support services for victims.

Self-Care Make sure that all adult helpers utilize tools to help them manage their own stress more effectively. Those tools include proper diet, exercise, and rest; journaling and/or counseling for themselves; reduction of other distractions; and moderate use of alcohol and medication.

Debriefing Debriefing is a structured process through which adults involved in crisis intervention are helped to process their experience in such a way as to avoid symptoms of

PTSD or vicarious traumatization. Debriefings, conducted by trained personnel, are essential for everyone's well-being and should occur regularly.

Managing Job-Related Stress

Now we turn attention to stress normally associated with teaching. Teaching can be a good and rewarding job, one that contributes to individual and collective good and brings participants into contact with many fine people. But it is no secret that teachers' lives are filled with stress. Instructing makes one nervous and tired, and if students do not behave or perform well, teachers are certain to experience headaches, anxiety, apathy, and an occasional desire to escape from it all.

Artwork reprinted courtesy of Jody Bergsma Galleries: http://www.bergsma.com.

It seems that instructing used to be easier than it is now; certainly, the potential stressors were very different. Sixty years ago, nearly all teachers taught to age 65. Many retired at that time, but others continued on to age 70 and beyond. Now you rarely see a teacher remain in service until 65. Many now accept reduced pensions and retire much earlier, just to escape the pressure. Teachers say the job wears them out, especially now that they no longer can count on the success, respect, and dignity that once came with teaching.

What has caused this unfortunate change? Most teachers say students have become less focused on learning and increasingly difficult to motivate and manage. Today's students are influenced by the media and countless interests outside of school, often lack a cohesive family structure, are less responsive to adult authority, and are more willing to test limits, which they do with regularity. Increasingly, caregivers either seem to do little to support the school program and their child, or are overbearing and demanding in their expectations.

But teachers are not only worn down by unruly students or difficult caregivers. For some it's part or a combination of the educational crises mentioned in Chapter 4: declining academic performance and achievement; achievement gaps among different races and socioeconomic groups; discrimination and racial tensions; and general lack of character, virtues, and social skills (Kagan & Kagan, 2009). In the 1990s, surveyed teachers considered the school setting and workload pressures more stressful than direct contact with students (Pullis, 1992). Teachers everywhere still complain of too much to do and too little time to do it. They see the curriculum change yearly, for varied reasons—sometimes academic, sometimes political. They constantly are required to retool in order to teach in accord with programs, standards, and tests that come into vogue. The No Child Left Behind Act, Race to the Top, and national and state tests and standards mentioned in Chapters 2 and 10 all are examples of prevailing political influences. Teachers also are responsible for fulfilling nonteaching duties that were unheard of 60 years ago. Add to that shrinking funds for supplies; inclusion of students with special needs, including children with physical and emotional challenges, into regular education classes, English language learners, and exceptionally difficult-to-handle students; endless in-service and professional development workshops; and the increased criticism they endure because of lackluster student performance and achievement—and you can see why teachers feel they are expected to do more and more with less and less, and get less respect for it. Such perceptions, correct or not, bring with them heavy loads of stress.

Stress and Its Effects

We have noted that stress is a state of bodily and mental tension. At times the pressures associated with stress become intense. This is not to say that stress is always bad. Life without any stress at all would be incredibly dull. Stress prepares us for action. As suggested earlier, under situations of threat or excitement, our bodies undergo chemical changes that manifest as rapid pulse, increased blood pressure, muscle tension, and perspiration. In modest amounts, these changes give us vim and vigor. Stress only becomes harmful when it reaches such proportions that it produces deleterious effects.

What Bothers Teachers Most

You might think that teachers would be energized by conditions opposite to those that bring stress—that is, they would be very happy if given adequate time, well-behaved students, high student achievement, close affiliation with colleagues, and cooperation from satisfied caregivers. It has been found, however, that while removal of major stressors results in job satisfaction, it does not in itself motivate teachers to invest greater amounts of effort into their work.

Sadly, few schools make significant efforts to provide positive motivation for teachers. Teachers rarely have the opportunity to do work in areas of special personal interest. They have almost no opportunity to advance unless they move from teaching into administration or counseling. Given those facts, teachers must find job rewards within teaching itself. Teachers sometimes have classes, and frequently several students, who are fun to work with. Occasionally, caregivers express gratitude, sometimes students thank their teachers and show appreciation, and once in a while administrators or fellow teachers make favorable comments. Some teachers are recognized as master or lead teachers and asked to work with and mentor student and beginning teachers. But self-satisfaction, in these hectic days of teaching, is too weak to motivate a continual push for excellence in most people. Slowly, most teachers begin to question the value of their efforts, especially as frustration builds.

Over the years, conditions of teacher burnout have been documented. Three main reasons seem to be attributed to teacher burnout: (1) emotional exhaustion, (2) depersonalization, and (3) lack of personal accomplishment (Friesen, Prokop, & Sarros, 1988). In 1983 Gmelch focused on a specific type of professional burnout and coined the term *rustout*. He used rustout to describe teachers who no longer see themselves as passionate learners. The condition can be temporary or permanent, but either way teacher enthusiasm is low or missing.

Stress Management for Teachers

Consider viewing stress management in three stages: prevention, at the moment, and long-term coping. *Prevention strategies* focus on situational and physiological factors. We will discuss many situational strategies below: prioritizing, accepting less than perfect, using selective avoidance, time management, and so on. Physiological factors relate primarily to adequate rest, diet, exercise, and relaxation. Attention to situational and physiological factors can help minimize stressors. *At-the-moment strategies* are what teachers can do for some quick and immediate relief. These would include isometric exercises, stretches, brain breaks, even a short daydream. *Long-term coping strategies* are essential for healthy minds and bodies. Sustained attention to the strategies that assist with prevention help with long-term coping. Self-awareness and internal talk also can help with coping.

2008 Alejandro Yegros

Alejandro Yegros. http://alejandroyegros.com. Reprinted with permission.

Much can be done to make teachers' professional lives better, despite the increasing number of stressors with which teachers must contend. There remains hope that someday school districts may accept the likelihood that education proceeds better when teachers are contented and hard-working than when they are stressed and struggling for survival. To accomplish a transformation in teachers' lives, schools need only free up time for teachers, require less busy work, trust teachers' judgment concerning how to instruct and manage student behavior, support home and community alliances that lighten teachers' burdens, and energize teachers through recognition of effort and success.

But let's be practical. If teachers want to improve their existence, they must take charge of the matter themselves. Among steps they can take to prevent, even relieve, much of their stress are prioritizing, accepting a new perspective regarding perfection, selective avoidance, time management, discipline, communication with caregivers, and maintenance of physical well-being. Discipline and communication, though discussed previously, are mentioned here once more.

Prioritizing To prioritize is simply to put things in order of importance and then to focus on items that require immediate attention while leaving those of lesser importance until later on. It means considering the best use of time at this moment. Most persons operate the other way—they attend to inconsequential matters first, thinking that when they get them out of the way, they can concentrate better on more important matters. Unfortunately, with time restrictions being what they are, the important matters never receive the attention they should. Stress comes from not getting to the matters that really need attention, or that others expect one to do expeditiously. It doesn't come from skipping the junk mail.

Accepting Less Than Perfection Many teachers want perfection. They want students to be perfect and they want themselves to be perfect. They set high goals and push everyone to reach them. Certainly, nothing is wrong with holding high expectations. The stress arises when individuals fall short, and they will, for a variety of reasons. Therefore, it is best that we acknowledge that perfection simply isn't possible. Football coach Vince Lombardi summed it up this way: "Practice doesn't make perfect. Only perfect practice makes perfect."

Using Selective Avoidance At a conference that dealt with the major problems that teachers have to face, one speaker suggested several ways teachers could deal with stress, the best of which simply is to avoid it. The audience laughed, but the speaker was serious. He explained that teachers can learn to say "no" as a way to prevent overburdening themselves in an insupportable load of tasks. They can avoid associating with chronic complainers who find fault with everyone and everything, and thus adversely affect the attitudes of those around them—remember our discussions in Chapters 4 and 11 about teachers' lounges. They can set aside the trivial matters that consume so much time. They can learn not to take work home with them every night—discussed more in this chapter and Chapter 10—and begin to enjoy the luxuries of a personal and family life, and thinking and talking about nonschool topics. Finally, they can give students greater responsibility in helping to manage the classroom and the instructional program with assistant roles such as those we listed in Chapter 7. Here are some suggestions.

Say "No" Most teachers, particularly new teachers, are unwilling to say "no" to their principal, and most are reluctant to say "no" to colleagues and caregivers. They want to impress others with their willingness to shoulder the load; they want the principal, colleagues, and caregivers to think and speak highly of them. And often they are afraid that a displeased administrator will give them bad evaluations or assign them to unpleasant duties. That eventuality is unlikely if the teacher says, "I'd like to help, but my schedule is packed. I'll do it if you can help me get a little more time." (Often, administrators can reduce a teacher's duties to make the time available.) Similarly, teachers frequently are afraid that colleagues and caregivers will dislike them if they decline personal requests. Again, say, "I'd like to be able to help you, but I'm so pressed for time. Do you have any suggestions?" Sometimes

"TODAY, I WAS VISITED BY NINE STUDENTS AND TWO TEACHERS."

Permission by Dave Carpenter.

colleagues and caregivers will surprise you with their willingness to relieve you of certain tasks in order to obtain your assistance with their problems.

Remember this—teachers by nature want to be helpful. After all, they have chosen a profession that is based on helping others. But sometimes one has to say "no" to balance rewards against the ravages of overload. It's also important to remember that there are many tasks that teachers simply must assume. You can't say "no" to meetings, maintaining good records, completing required reports, planning lessons, obtaining necessary materials for teaching, and so forth. But if you list the incredible number of tasks that teachers routinely contend with, you would find that many of them could be put aside without any negative consequences.

Seek Occasional Solitude Teachers probably can accomplish far more if they find a space that is quiet and away from the activity of others. The space should be furnished adequately with the materials and supplies they need for the task at hand.

Avoid Time Robbers and Use Time Savers Too much to do and not enough time to do it—that is a chronic complaint of teachers. But let us now bring up a matter that teachers tend to overlook. Most of them could save large amounts of time simply by not wasting time they have available.

Time robbers eat up a large portion of teachers' time and give little in return. One such robber is teachers' tendency to deal with matters that could be delegated or even left aside indefinitely. Often dealing with the trivial, talking instead of working, and working in a disorganized way compound the reality of time robbers.

In contrast to time robbers, time savers are steps and shortcuts that enable teachers to get necessary work done, while leaving some time for personal needs, including quiet time to relax and socialize in a positive way with colleagues. The most valuable time savers are working efficiently, delegating work, reducing paper checking, and controlling the number and length of faculty meetings.

Efficiency begins with prioritizing tasks as described earlier, giving attention only to tasks that are absolutely necessary—such as planning, preparing instructional materials and activities, reviewing selected papers, keeping adequate and accurate records, and preparing for conferences with students and caregivers. Difficult tasks should be completed first and the fun work left for later.

Once you establish priorities, work hard during the time you have set aside. Avoid the temptation to chat, gossip, daydream, or gaze out the window. Though these activities are

Case Study 13.2   Time Robbers

FOCUS QUESTION

Here Mr. Monroe gives in to several time robbers. List them. How could he better organize his tasks and time to avoid them?

Mr. Monroe, a sixth-grade teacher, works in his room for two hours each day after school. Two hours of concentrated work should be more than enough time to take care of all the matters that significantly impact his program. But Mr. Monroe spends the time reading memos, e-mails, notices, advertisements, and other pieces of mail received at school. He goes to the faculty lounge for coffee and on the way stops to talk with the custodian about a ball game. In the lounge he finds the principal and they chat, tell jokes, and talk about politics. Then he returns to his room, waters the plants, feeds the hamsters, and cleans their enclosure. He dislikes messes, so he picks up scraps, arranges books, cleans the sink, and tidies his desk. While looking for reference materials for the next day's lesson on ancient Greece, he comes across interesting material on money, coins, mints, and various monetary systems, which he reads though they have nothing to do with Greece. Before he knows it, five o'clock arrives and only a few of his necessary tasks have been done. He still has papers to grade, so he takes them home.

quite restful and valuable, they should come after the work is finished. Review papers and update records quickly and efficiently and then plan for the next day. Normally, you can do this in an hour of concentrated work. However, remember that a quick brain break or physical stretching is good for when you are engaged in a task that requires focus for a longer time.

Assign routine tasks such as watering plants, cleaning the room, feeding animals, dusting, straightening, and so forth to students. It's good for them. If students are too young, have aides or volunteers help.

Be Realistic about Paper Checking Checking work students turn in consumes monumental amounts of time for most teachers. This task can be greatly reduced with no detriment to students. Most teachers believe that if they assign written work, they are honor-bound to mark every single paper carefully. But there are strong counterarguments to this view. First, many written tasks are given to students for practice only. By circulating during independent practice time, you can observe students at work and know how they are doing, identify problems they are encountering, and immediately provide the help they need. Two side benefits accrue from circulating around the room. You are close to students and proximity helps maintain discipline. Also, by working the crowd, you can provide efficient help (in the 20 seconds or less that Fred Jones advocates). When students have completed their work and you have made notations as necessary on your clipboard, collect the papers and discard them later.

A reality is that students profit little, if any, from the marks and notations you make so conscientiously and meticulously. Even by the next day, students will have lost the context of what they were doing and your marks and notes will mean little to them. Their errors should be corrected as they are being made. Moreover, students do not like to receive marked-up papers. Their first and often final inclination is to crumple it and throw it away, unless of course it has a star or happy face on it. If you insist on going to such lengths in scoring student papers, you need to review the papers with the students, in detail, when you return them. Students don't like this, but that's the only way you can help them learn much from all your hard work.

This is not to say that you should never carefully correct student papers. Toward the end of units, when students are asked to show what and how much they have learned, you can expect them to do their very best work, which you should check carefully.

A note of caution, however: If you send corrected papers home with your students, make sure you mark them accurately! Caregivers invariably find the mistakes you make.

Streamline Record Keeping As discussed in Chapter 10, tasks related to record keeping can consume great amounts of time. You can reduce this workload by doing four things: (1) keep only those records that truly are necessary, (2) use available electronic technology for records management, (3) train students to assist in keeping their own records, and (4) have an aide or volunteer help with recording and filing. Remember these two cautions, however—students have the right to privacy regarding their work and progress, and you are legally responsible for the accuracy of these records.

Take a Proactive Role in Faculty Meetings If faculty meetings at your school tend to be too long and tedious, you can take steps to shorten them. You can request agendas for the meetings, and when discussions stray from the agenda, you can suggest that, in the interest of time, the agenda be followed. Faculty members can ask to be excused from the meetings when the topics do not apply to them—for example, there is no need for primary teachers to attend meetings that deal with sixth-grade outdoor camp. Also, teachers can agree as a staff to limit the length of discussions.

Vignette 13.1   Managing Student Work

Ginny Lorenz teaches a 4/5 multi-age class of 32 students.

"During my first year of teaching upper grades, I read student papers four nights a week. During my second year of teaching this grade, however, I did something new. I added a Writer's Workshop where caregivers helped with the editing of student work. When students had a piece in 'final' draft form, they put a check next to their name on the board. Once I had eight or ten names with check marks, I took those papers home and read them for grades. This worked well for both me and my students."

UPON REFLECTION

Ginny Lorenz described another procedure for managing student work in Chapter 7 (Vignette 7.2). Compare both her methods with what you have experienced or have seen other teachers do.

Remove the Stress from Teaching Disruptive student behavior not only severely cuts into teachers' time but also is a major source of frustration and stress. You can use a number of different tactics (many described in Chapter 9) to reduce dramatically the stress usually associated with discipline. You and your students will very much appreciate the results.

Streamline Communication with Caregivers In Chapter 11 you were urged to communicate well with caregivers as a means of securing family and home support for your efforts. Although they can be time-intensive, avoid the temptation to bypass communications with caregivers as you look for ways to free up some time. Rather, remember that communication with caregivers is worth the effort involved and should be given high priority. You can streamline the communication process by using a class website that describes expectations you hold, your discipline system, and how caregivers can help. You also can update information and even add photographs (with permission, as we discussed in Chapter 11) regarding class activities and assignments. If caregivers have Internet access at home or work, add e-mail capability so they can initiate or exchange communication with you, to which you should respond promptly and briefly. If you need to call a caregiver on the phone, say, with the utmost courtesy and respect, something like, "Hello, Mrs. Nichols. This is _____, Tara's teacher. How are you this evening? I'd like to talk with you for a moment about Tara. I only have five minutes right now. Is this a convenient time for you?" Prior to calling, rehearse what you want to say and anticipate questions and comments from the listener.

Keep Yourself Physically Fit Make sure you have adequate rest, good nutrition, some recreation, and some physical exercise, all of which help in combating stress. Drink plenty of water to keep your brain hydrated. Get enough sleep because sleep is critical for the brain to process, think, and remember. Also, do some isometric exercises and stretches throughout the day. When possible, work in natural light; fluorescent lights may cause eye strain and anxiety. Additionally, involve students. It will help them, too.

Take Occasional Brain Breaks Throughout your daily class routines, take time to nourish your brain (and your students' brains as well). Your brain needs food (glucose) and oxygen, and exercise and brain breaks help with this. Human brains are not designed to hold constant focus on something for lengthy periods of time. Brain breaks involve short periods of rest, listening to calming music, thinking about something entirely different, telling a joke or story, and standing and stretching.

Activities That Produce Positive Stress

The first part of this chapter concentrated on the damaging effects of emotional stress caused by trauma and unexpected events. The next dealt with on-the-job stress, and gave you a number of suggestions for removing unwanted stress in your work. We now turn our attention to what you can do to increase the positive useful stress known as *eustress*.

Moderate amounts of stress energize us, give us a sense of direction, make us pleased with our jobs and ourselves, and provide a sense of accomplishment and importance, and in so doing positively affect our morale. The following sections review sources of eustress that teachers find most readily available in teaching—professional learning communities and group efforts; student achievement; webpages, newsletters, and literary journals; public performances and exhibits; shared responsibility; and class synergy.

Professional Learning Communities and Group Efforts

The sense of belonging is a basic human need, and teachers hope to feel part of a caring and supportive community. Many teachers enjoy working with other teachers. In the past, however, unless they belonged to a collaborative grade-level team, they seldom had the incentive to do so. Now professional learning communities (PLC) are finding their way into public schools. Through PLCs, teachers work together to learn and help each other. They look at student work and together find ways to improve instruction and student learning. The eustress they experience is inherent in the process, but another good payoff is student gain. Remember, teachers can be resources to one another; they simply need to learn to ask and learn to share.

Teachers also might enjoy appreciations and thoughtful small gifts from a secret pal or secret admirer. By drawing secret names early in the school year and having random appreciation schedules, teachers contribute to mutual support and encouragement of their colleagues. Appreciations and gifts need not be expensive. They can be an actual token such as a gift certificate from the giver to a local coffee shop. Or the giver can deliver a note from an appreciative caregiver or an invitation from a student to share lunch.

Student Achievement

Achievement is mainly what schooling is all about. Teachers of high achievers usually feel successful, while those of lower abilities feel somewhat defeated. It is important to realize that student achievement actually can be increased through the way recognition is given. For example, when outstanding student work products such as art, compositions, and scale models are put on public display, students become motivated to accomplish work of still higher quality. When students keep personal charts that graphically depict how much they have read or how skilled they have become in math, they strive to reach even greater heights, especially when the results are communicated to caregivers.

To emphasize student achievement, you need to discuss with students what achievement—and quality—mean, show them what makes both possible, illustrate how progress is documented, and explain how results are shown to caregivers and others. Then as students strive to achieve and later to surpass previous levels of achievement, you will find that everyone's motivation to excel increases.

Webpages, Newsletters, and Literary Journals

Teacher- and student-produced webpages and newsletters, described in Chapter 11 as vehicles for communicating with parents and guardians, also provide marvelous opportunities for enlivening teaching and learning. The same is the case for class literary journals. Older students can contribute to the writing and production of newsletters and journals as writers, designers, and artists, with their names listed somewhere in the work. Teachers can assist in primary grades, but from the third grade onward students can do most of the work in print, and they are highly motivated to do their best writing, spelling, grammar, and artwork. Caregivers eagerly read such materials. They take pride in their child's work and credit the teacher for the documented accomplishments.

Public Performances and Exhibits

Many schools encourage teachers and their classes to present performances such as plays, readers' theatre, holiday skits, and musicals, as well as exhibits of art, science projects, and social studies projects. Generally, these events produce high levels of excitement and motivation, and students willingly work hard to prepare for them.

Most often performances and exhibits are seen in conjunction with back-to-school and open house nights. But displays of student work for students, teachers, and visitors to see, such as artwork and models, can be posted at any time in various locations in the school. Some performance events may even be broadcast through a local cable station or via the Internet. Some people may think of exhibits and performances as frills outside the core program, but once you see the level of motivation and pride they engender, you will want to make them prime components of your class's educational program.

Sharing Responsibility with Students

From the beginning of the school year, you should impress on your students the roles and responsibilities they are to assume in regard to their own education. Students can be shown

---

Vignette 13.2   Class Newsletters

Kindergarten teacher Kay Ballentine creates a short weekly class newsletter titled *Kindergarten Korner.* "It tells about activities during the week and upcoming events I want parents to be aware of. I try to mention as many children by name as possible each week, and I make sure every child is mentioned frequently. Parents read the newsletter avidly and go out of their way to write or tell me about it. They seem to think it proves that I care about their child, which of course I do."

Ronda Royal is a third-grade teacher who uses her newsletter to keep everyone informed. "I always give a copy of my newsletter to the principal and to any volunteers who do not have children in my room. My weekly newsletter is solely my production, although I often include snippets of student work to show parents what the children are creating in my room. I always write my news in complete sentences and full paragraphs. Many parents say they appreciate this type of complete communication because it shows that I am putting effort into informing them of events in my room, of ways to assist their child, and of upcoming guests and activities."

UPON REFLECTION

Both Kay and Ronda use newsletters to communicate with caregivers. Describe how you would use newsletters. What would you include? How would you involve students in their production?

how to take an active stance in learning to be participants rather than recipients. As they move into this shared responsibility, a spirit of self-direction and self-responsibility develops that teachers find very satisfying.

Achieving Class Synergy

When you are able to bring about an attitude of shared responsibility and then add to it the desire for significant accomplishment and evidence, that elusive condition of class synergy may occur—when members of the class energize each other through cooperative group efforts (Charles, 2000). This effect binds students together, spurs them on, and makes school a time of pleasure and fulfillment. Synergy, or esprit de corps, is one of the best things that can happen in a classroom. Classbuilding and teambuilding activities do much to foster synergy. Class work becomes joyful instead of tedious, and students involve themselves rather than comply lethargically. School days end with a satisfied glow instead of wretched fatigue. As students experience synergy, they provide much positive energy to teachers. As a bonus, word quickly gets to caretakers, who react positively to their child's educational program, and become in the process more supportive of the teacher.

Before moving ahead to Chapter 14, the epilogue ("It's Your Turn"), take time to explore these end-of-chapter activities.

Parting Thoughts

Yet do I hold that mortal foolish who strives against the stress of necessity.

Euripedes

Rule #1: Don't sweat the small stuff. Rule #2: It's all small stuff.

Dr. Michael Mantell

Summary Self-Check

Check off the following as you either understand or become able to apply them:
- ☐ Stress—some is needed, but too much is harmful.
  - ● Distress—inability to cope; overwhelming, hurtful.
  - ● Eustress—a challenge; interesting, helpful.
- ☐ Stress and trauma affect teachers and students.
- ☐ Critical incident—any emotionally significant event that overwhelms coping abilities.
- ☐ Crisis intervention—short-term response to a critical incident with the goal of helping.
- ☐ Crisis intervention is not therapy.
- ☐ Critical Incident Stress Management (CISM)—a systematic crisis intervention model.
- ☐ The three areas of the triune brain interact as we react to a critical incident.

- □ Signs and symptoms of emotional stress: children may shut down their feelings, regress to immature behaviors, act out behaviorally, ask questions, require lots of extra reassurances.
- □ What teachers and schools can do:
  - SEA-3 method: speech, emotion, appearance, alertness, activity.
  - SAFER method: stabilize the situation, acknowledge crisis, facilitate understanding, encourage adaptive coping, restore or refer.
  - Attention-refocusing strategies.
  - Upshifting.
  - Subtle techniques.
  - Take care of yourself.
  - Debriefing.
- □ Stress management has three stages: prevention, at the moment, and long-term coping.
- □ Stress can result in burnout or rustout:
  - Burnout—emotional exhaustion, depersonalization, and lack of personal accomplishment.
  - Rustout—temporary or permanent lack of enthusiasm or desire to continue learning.
- □ What stresses teachers most: disruptive student behavior, lack of time, too much to do, lack of student success, poor relationships with caregivers.
- □ What energizes teachers most: student achievement, recognition, interesting work, possibilities for professional growth and advancement.
- □ Stress management for teachers: prioritize (take care of important matters first), accept that perfect isn't possible, avoid selectively (learn to say "no"; learn to hide), manage time efficiently (avoid time robbers), develop a nonconfrontational discipline system, communicate well with caregivers, give close attention to your physical well-being.
- □ Steps toward positive stress: engage in professional learning communities and group efforts; work toward student achievement; produce webpages, newsletters, and journals; have your class put on public performances; work for shared responsibility with students; seek class synergy.

Activities for Reflection and Discussion

1. Take a moment to review the statements in the Preview–Review Guide at the beginning of this chapter. Put a check mark in the *Review* column next to any statement with which you now agree. How have your thoughts changed since reading this chapter?

2. Interview at least two teachers about their experiences with stress, both stresses that come from unexpected or traumatic events, as well as on-the-job stresses. Also ask what activities bring them eustress as opposed to distress. How do they deal with the things they find stressful, through prevention, in-the-moment, and long-term coping strategies?

3. Investigate the crisis response plan at a local school and share your findings with your class.

4. List six important tasks that call for your attention today. Prioritize those tasks by their importance. List nonessential tasks that try to draw you away from your important tasks. How will you deal with them?

5. Do you know a teacher who appears to have reached burnout (or rustout)? Assess that person as to how he or she looks, talks, relates to students and others, prepares for teaching, maintains discipline, and participates in school activities. Share your observations with your class.

6. The text suggests that your teaching life would be more enjoyable if your class produces a webpage, newsletters, and journals, and puts on public performances and displays. Evaluate that contention objectively. To what extent would those suggestions *add* stress rather than reduce it? List and discuss your pros and cons.

7. Suppose you are put in charge of teacher morale and appreciation in your school. Within reason, what would you do and emphasize in order to make teachers' professional lives more joyful and rewarding? Explain your program to the class.

Webliography

International Critical Incident Stress Foundation, Inc.: http://www.icisf.org
PBS Parents. *Talking with kids about war and violence*: http://www.pbs.org/parents
PTSD: http://www.helpguide.org/mental/post_traumatic_stress_disorder_symptoms_
treatment.htm

References and Recommended Readings

Berman, S., Diener, S., Dieringer, l., & Lantieri, L. (2003). *Talking with children about war and violence in the world.* http://life.familyeducation.com/war.parenting/36559.html.

Charles, C. (2000). *The synergetic classroom: Joyful teaching and gentle discipline.* Boston: Addison Wesley Longman.

Childs, G. (2002). *Workshop and crisis response team guidebook: Critical Incident Stress Management Program.* Poway, CA: Poway Unified School District.

Devine, J., & Cohen, J. (2007). *Making your school safe: Strategies to protect children and promote learning.* New York: Teachers College Press.

Friesen, D., Prokop, C., & and Sarros, J. (1988). Why teachers burn out. *Educational Research Quarterly 12*(3), 9–19.

Lavaree, B. (2009). *Authentic classroom management: Creating a learning community and building reflective practice* (3rd ed.). Upper Saddle River, NJ: Pearson.

Perry, B. (2006). *Maltreated children: Experience, brain development and the next generation.* New York: Norton.

Pullis, M. (1992). An analysis of the occupational stress of teachers of the behaviorally disordered: Sources, effects, and strategies for coping. *Behavioral Disorders 17*(3), 191–201.

PEARSON
myeducationlab

Go to the Topics: **Creating Positive Student-Student Relationships If Creating Positive Student-Teacher Relationships** in the MyEducationLab (www.myeducationlab.com) for your course, where you can:

- Find learning outcomes for **Creating Positive Student-Student Relationships If Creating Positive Student-Teacher Relationships** along with the national standards that connect to these outcomes.

- Apply and practice your understanding of the core teaching skills identified in the chapter with the Building Teaching Skills and Dispositions learning units.

- Use interactive Simulations in Classroom Management to practice decision making and to receive expert feedback on classroom management choices.

CHAPTER 14

Epilogue: It's Your Turn

You've got to do your own growing, no matter how tall your grandfather was.
—Irish proverb

Every child is an artist. The problem is how to remain an artist once he grows up.
—Pablo Picasso

Pulling Everything Together

Now it's your turn to pull together everything you have read, observed, discussed, and analyzed. In the preceding chapters you investigated good management skills, and it is hoped that they will help you step confidently into your first classroom. The activities that follow are additional broad extensions to the text. The problem to solve or the essential or guiding question for this chapter might be: *Given what I now know about managing elementary classrooms, how can I put it all together into a program that will work well for me and my students?*

But first, look at the problem-based learning (PBL) Capstone Activity below. Although you can complete the activity individually, it is designed for you to work in grade-level teams. It poses an authentic problem to you or your team: *How will you manage the details and minutiae that affect your ability to teach well?* Here you have the opportunity to reflect on the nature and operation of your own classroom.

PBL Capstone Activity: Grade-Level Management Plan

The Problem Your school site supports the tenets of a professional learning community. Working in small teams, select a grade level and outline the management details of the minute components of classroom management you will employ in your overall operation of the classroom. Ideally, all elementary grades will be covered, and all management plans will be available electronically to all members of the class. In an introductory overview section for this task, the team must explain briefly the general needs and characteristics—academic, physical, emotional, and social—of students at the selected grade level. For this PBL, remember to apply PIES (refer back to Chapter 6 if you need to review). To demonstrate individual accountability, each team member must identify at least five specific management components he or she writes about and explain briefly how the responses reflect personality and personal beliefs about teaching and learning.

Outcomes

- This PBL is intended to strengthen understandings of the realities of teaching, particularly as related to classroom management in elementary schools and at a designated grade level.

- The PBL is designed to provide an authentic collaborative grade-level team experience.

- The PBL also is intended to assist teachers as they subsequently plan for their first year of teaching.

Process Steps and Requirements

- To guide thinking regarding management considerations, students will work in grade-level teams of no more than five members to complete the management grid.

- While this is a team problem, individual responsibility and accountability also will be assessed for a minimum of five management considerations.

Key Skills/Knowledge That Will Be Evaluated

- Evidence of understandings of the realities of teaching, as particularly related to grade-level management considerations in an elementary classroom setting.

Cooperative Summary Worksheet

- Team members are to complete the Cooperative Summary Worksheet (Figure 14.1). One worksheet may be submitted with consensus as a team, or by individual team members in the form of personal worksheets.

Resources

- Charles, C. M., & Senter, G. W. (2012). *Elementary classroom management* (6th ed.) and other books about classroom management, including prior editions of *Elementary Classroom Management*.

Figure 14.1

Cooperative Summary Worksheet

(A Cooperative Summary Worksheet is to be completed and submitted by individuals or the team for every group activity/project.)

Activity/Project: _____   Date _____

WHAT EACH MEMBER DID TO PREPARE AND PRESENT (ORAL, WRITTEN):

Team member	Contributions to the project

OUTCOMES EVALUATION:

Task achievement:
Group functioning:
Suggestions for teamwork next time:

An Example of Assessment Point Distribution for a Grade-Level Management Plan

For a PBL that is weighted as 20 percent of the final grade (20 points of 100 total points):

- *Grade-level team accountability.* Completed management plan grid and completed Cooperative Summary Worksheet   10 points
- *Individual accountability.* Details for a minimum of five considerations within the management Plan   10 points

The course instructor should make available an online template for the entire management plan grid. When the PBL is completed, grade-level teams can publish their ideas for others to download and use as a beginning resource.

For easy reference, the components of the management plan grid are given below. Management concerns are sorted into categories that relate to chapters in the text. Teams and individuals are to elaborate on the details—how and what the teacher will do to manage the concern, and the explanation why, plus support or resources for action choices. Thus, the actual grid (set up in landscape orientation) might look like this:

My Management Plan   Grade level _____
Getting Started

Procedures	Details: How/What	Explanation: Why/Plus Support
Beginning the class		
Supplies 　Teacher 　Student		
Leaving seat in class		
Taking attendance 　Tardies 　Absences		
Other administrative (lunch count, etc.)		
Other considerations		

Managing Student Behavior

Consideration	Details: How/What	Explanation: Why/Plus Support
How/who makes the plan?		
Class agreements/rules	1. 2. 3. 4. 5.	
Action plan: In-the-moment interventions		
"Consequences"		
"Rewards"		
Other considerations		

Managing Students at Work

Consideration	Details: How/What	Explanation: Why/Plus Support
Opening activities		
Giving instructions for doing work		
Movement in the room		
Obtaining, using, and replacing materials Borrowing materials		
Providing assistance during work time		
Collecting/returning completed work		
Correcting completed work		
Homework		
End-of-day closing		
Monitors		
Differentiation		
Group work		
Other considerations		

Adaptations and Modifications for Individual Differences

For this section, each team member is to write about (at least) one exceptionality or special need. Describe the conditions of the exceptionality, accommodations to be made, and support for these choices.

Exceptionality	Conditions of the exceptionality	Accommodation: How/What/ Plus Support
1.		
2.		
3.		
4.		
5.		

Use of Technology

Purpose	Details: How/What	Explanation: Why/Plus Support
For instruction—teacher		
For learning—student		
For record keeping		

Incidentals

Procedures	Details: How/What	Explanation: Why/Plus Support
Seating		
Entering and exiting the room		
Pencil sharpening		
Out-of-room passes		
Signals for attention		
Noise control		
Procrastination		
Tattling		
Bullying		
Other considerations		

Communications

With whom	Details: How/What	Explanation: Why/Plus Support
With grade-level team members		
With teaching partners		
With support providers for students		
With volunteers		
With caregivers		
With administrators		
With others		

Assessment, Record Keeping, and Reporting

Content areas	What kinds of assessments are needed?	Explanation: Why/Plus Support

Language arts
  Reading
  Writing
  Spelling		

Math		
Social studies		
Science		
Art		
Music		
Physical education/movement		
Technology		
Character education/community		
Other considerations		

Activities for Reflection and Discussion

1. *Appendix A: The Legislation of Inclusion: A Primer.* Take time to review the synthesis of legislation that has affected inclusion and school reform. Discuss in small groups or as a whole class.

2. Contact various professional organizations and inquire about their mission, cost of membership, and benefits. (Usually, this can be done via the Internet or at the local level by contacting organization representatives or members for information.)

3. Obtain copies of five or six widely read professional journals and teacher magazines in education. Review and compare the contents. Present your reviews, along with subscription information, for class information and discussion.

4. Visit five or six teacher-related websites. Review and compare their contents. Present your reviews for class information and discussion.

5. Obtain five or six good resource books for teachers. Review and compare their contents. Present your reviews for class information and discussion.

6. Either locate state Departments of Education on the Internet or obtain a reference that outlines teacher certification requirements in various states. Compare the requirements for four or five states and present the results to the class.

7. Obtain a resource that provides information on overseas employment. (Your university or college placement office probably can furnish this information.) Share the information with the class. If possible, speak with a teacher or professor who has taught abroad and obtain his or her impressions of the advantages and challenges of the experience.

Webliography

Blackboard, Inc.: http://www.blackboard.com.

PEARSON
myeducationlab

Go to the Topic: **Models of Classroom Management** in the MyEducationLab (www.myeducationlab.com) for your course, where you can:

■ Find learning outcomes for **Models of Classroom Management** along with the national standards that connect to these outcomes.

Appendix A

The Legislation of Inclusion and School Reform: A Primer

I was still learning when I taught my last class.
—Claude M. Fuess, Phillips Academy educator

As a result of persistent legislation, students with varied special needs, languages, skin colors, facial features, heritages, values, and ceremonies now are able to come together for their formal education.

The United States has long held that all children have the right to education. Over the years, the federal government has enacted multiple legislations in its effort to uphold the guiding principles of our founding fathers for free and public education for all children. However, debates continue as to the best educational approach to meet the diverse needs of all students. In recent years, children with special needs have been recognized, supported, and included in regular classrooms (to the extent their abilities allow) for a maximum portion of their day. Thus, children with special, intellectual, and physical challenges are able to join a teaching and learning community where everyone's individual needs are met.

Perhaps of greatest legal impacts, though, are the Individuals with Disabilities Education Act (IDEA), the No Child Left Behind Act (NCLB), Assistive Technology Act (ATA or Tech Act), and the most current reform legislation: The American Recovery and Reinstatement Act of 2009 (ARRA) and President Obama's Race to the Top (RTTT) program. Also, civil rights laws have had impact: Section 504 of the Rehabilitation Act, and the Americans with Disabilities Act (ADA).

IDEA: Individuals with Disabilities Education Act

In 1975 Congress enacted P.L. 94-142, the Education for All Handicapped Children Act. The law guaranteed that all students are entitled to a free appropriate public education (FAPE). To this end, it provided for inclusion of all students in "the least restrictive environment" (LRE), "to the maximum extent appropriate," and "with the use of supplementary aids and services." It also required each student to have an individualized educational program (IEP). Since then Congress has made several amendments to the law, all true to the intent and goals of the original version. The most recent amendment, the Individuals with Disabilities Education Act, known simply as "IDEA," was enacted in 2004. Presently, 20 U.S. codes begin with Section 1400 of the 2004 reauthorized law.

IDEA '04 has four parts:

Part A declares the barriers, solutions, and national policy for educating students with disabilities. Part B authorizes funds to educate students ages 3–21. Under Part B, students receive a free appropriate public education (FAPE). Part C authorizes funds to educate infants and toddlers ages birth/0 to 3. Part D authorizes national research, training, demonstration, and technical assistance. (Turnbull, Huerta, & Stowe, 2009, p. 1)

IDEA '04 has six guiding principles:

1. *Zero reject.* Every child with a disability under IDEA is entitled to a free appropriate public education (FAPE).

2. *Nondiscriminatory evaluation.* Students who may have a disability and who may be entitled to IDEA's benefits can be evaluated without bias after they enter school and when the school or others believe they might be eligible for benefits.

3. *Appropriate education.* Students will receive individualized programs to help advance them toward the national proficiency goals.

4. *Least restrictive environment.* Education will take place in typical settings and with students who are not disabled.

5. *Procedural due process.* Parents can hold schools accountable for their child's education. Also, schools can hold parents accountable for their child.

6. *Parent participation.* Parents, students, and educators can be partners in the child's education.

As defined by federal law, IDEA '04, children are considered to have disabilities if they have any or a combination of the following 14 conditions. Note, however, that some states have established and continue to follow their own guidelines for the identification and qualification of handicapping conditions:

1. Autism, affecting verbal and nonverbal communication and social interaction

2. Deafness

3. Deafness-blindness

4. Serious emotional disturbance (SED), including schizophrenia

5. Hearing impairment (DHH)

6. Mental retardation (MR), significantly below-average general intellectual functioning, together with inadequate adaptive behavior

7. Multiple disabilities, simultaneous impairments such as mental retardation and blindness

8. Orthopedic impairment (OI)

9. Other health impairment (OHI), chronic or acute health problems, such as a heart condition, asthma, or diabetes, that limit strength, vitality, or alertness

10. Specific learning disability (SLD), visual and auditory processing difficulties including dyslexia and central auditory processing disorder (CAPD)

11. Speech or language impairment (SLI)

12. Traumatic brain injury (TBI), caused by external physical force rather than congenital or degenerative injuries

13. Visual impairment (VI), including blindness

14. Developmental delay

Developmental delay is the newest category to be included under IDEA '04. Its intent is "to avoid incorrectly labeling young children—[under eight years old]—as either having a disability when they do not or identifying them with the 'wrong' disability" (Müller & Markowitz, 2004; U.S. Department of Education, 2006, quoted in Smith & Tyler, 2010, p. 19). The category "developmental delays" refers to a general, non-disability-specific group of younger individuals.

An "established medical disability" also can be a qualifier for special education services. This is defined as a disabling medical condition or congenital syndrome that the individual education program (IEP) team determines has a high predictability of requiring special education and services [California Education Code Section 46441.11(d)].

You can visit the following websites for additional information about IDEA '04 and the qualifying conditions: http://www.pai-ca.org/pubs/505101.htm, http://www.cec.sped .org, and http://www.ed.gov/offices/OSERS/IDEA.

The current amended IDEA '04 aligns with the No Child Left Behind Act (NCLB), and with general education and disability civil rights laws.

NCLB: No Child Left Behind Act

NCLB was enacted in 2001 and signed into law in 2002 for the purpose of improving the education of *all* children in all public schools in the country. It was not written specifically for students with disabilities, but it has several important implications for students and special education. NCLB has six major principles:

1. *Accountability.* Schools should educate all students in elementary and middle schools to at least a level of academic proficiency in core subjects (including English and math) as demonstrated on standardized state or local assessments. NCLB stresses adequate yearly incremental progress (AYP) toward the goal of 100 percent proficiency in reading, math, and science for all students by the end of the 2013–2014 school year.

2. *Highly qualified teachers.* All teachers must meet federal and state standards of proficiency to teach.

3. *Scientifically based intervention* (also referred to as evidence-based intervention). Using research-based curricula, instructional methods, and scientifically based assessments, these highly qualified teachers will provide all students with appropriate education.

4. *Local flexibility.* State and local educational agencies will have some discretion about their use of federal monies to reach NCLB outcomes.

5. *Safe schools.* To better ensure safe schools, IDEA '04 provides procedures and standards for disciplining students with disabilities.

6. *Parent participation and choice.* All parents should have the opportunity to participate in their child's education. This includes their right to remove their child from unsafe or failing schools.

ATA or Tech Act: Assistive Technology Act

This act first appeared as the Technology-Related Assistance to Individuals with Disabilities Act of 1988. In 2004 it was amended and renamed the Assistive Technology Act. The essence of the act is of great importance to the futures of individuals with disabilities—in the community and workplace, as well as in school. Assistive technology (AT) helps individuals by increasing technology and removing barriers that previously limited their lives. Assistive technology can be very expensive. The Tech Act offers loan programs, training activities, and ongoing research and improvements in assistive devices. (See http://www. section508. gov/docs/AT1998. html.)

ARRA: American Recovery and Reinvestment Act of 2009

This is the newest education reform legislation. In February 2009 President Barack Obama signed into law the legislation designed to stimulate the economy, support job creation, and invest in critical sectors, including education. The ARRA lays the foundation for education reform by supporting investments in innovative strategies that are most likely to lead to improved results for students, long-term gains in school and school system capacity, and increased productivity and effectiveness (Race to the Top Executive Summary, 11/09).

Race to the Top (RTTT) is a competitive grant program funded with ARRA monies. The program provides incentives to states that invest in education innovation and reform. It also will help states that improve student outcomes and show significant gains in achievement, closures in achievement gaps, improved high school graduation rates, and stronger preparation for success in college and careers. Additionally, RTTT includes plans for four core areas of education reform:

- Adopting standards and assessments that prepare students to succeed in college and the workplace and to compete in the global economy;

- Building data systems that measure student growth and success, and inform teachers and principals about how they can improve instruction;

- Recruiting, developing, rewarding, and retaining effective teachers and principals, especially where they are needed most; and

- Turning around our lowest-achieving schools. (Race to the Top Executive Summary, 11/09)

Civil Rights Laws: Section 504 of the Rehabilation Act and the Americans with Disabilities Act

In addition to NCLB and IDEA, which are "grant-in-aid" laws that authorize federal funds to state and local educational agencies, two other laws help to ensure the education rights of all children. These are civil rights laws. Section 504 of the Rehabilitation Act Amendments was enacted in 1973 and required accommodations for persons with disabilities. This is why sidewalks have curb cuts, and public buildings have ramps, wide doorways, clear aisles, and nonprint signs. For education, this means that schools must provide accommodations to students with disabilities or conditions that have some special needs, but who do not require special education services.

The Americans with Disabilities Act (ADA) was enacted in 1990 and revised in 2000 and again in 2008. These two laws prohibit discrimination in education against students with disabilities, and promote the right to reasonable accommodations. The laws are not grant-in-aid laws; they do not authorize any federal funds to be used for educating students with disabilities. ADA "broadens the definition of disability and provides that impairments or conditions that could limit a major life activity but are not in remission still be considered disabilities" (Smith & Tyler, 2010, p. 14). Consequently, Section 504 and ADA classifications identify and protect more students for accommodations than the 14 classifications listed for IDEA '04 eligibility.

What Is the Discrepancy or Failure Model?

Some states use a traditional discrepancy or failure model to identify students who need special education services. Basically, the model says that in order to qualify for services, students must show a severe discrepancy between IQ (measured by an IQ test) and academic achievement (measured by standardized achievement tests) *and* must have a processing disorder.

The discrepancy model has its criticisms. Some argue that it is biased against students who score lower on IQ tests because of their ethnic or racial backgrounds. Others believe that detection for younger children (nine and younger) is not possible because of possible developmental delays in achievement. Additionally, discrepancy formulas vary from state to state; consequently, data accuracy is questionable.

What Is the Response to Intervention (RTI) Model?

"Response to Intervention (RTI) is a means to determine whether any student, regardless of type of disability, needs more intensive instruction" (Turnbull, Turnbull, & Wehmeyer, 2010, p. 58). RTI evolved as a reaction to an increasing dissatisfaction about using intelligence tests—or intelligence—to identify students with learning disabilities. RTI can be applied to any academic area, but because approximately 80 percent of students referred for special education services are referred for reading problems, RTI gives most attention to reading. The intent of RTI is to reduce the number of students who are mistakenly labeled as learning-disabled. Prior to IDEA '04, the identification of struggling students and students with learning disabilities was based on information about their classroom performance. Students were referred by the teacher, tested, and identified. Following IDEA '04, states and districts were able to use a prereferral step in the IEP process to gather information needed to identify students with learning disabilities (Smith & Tyler, 2010; Turnbull, Turnbull, & Wehmeyer, 2010). Consequently, RTI is a multitiered method that uses frequent assessment and multiple interventions that "filter" children through learning opportunities. Because the intensity of instruction and interventions increases over time, educators can better identify students who are "resistant to treatment," or who do not make sufficient progress or meet benchmark goals (Smith & Tyler, 2010).

Although some schools have added levels to the process, the RTI model usually involves three tiers of intervention. After a universal screening and assessment, all students receive quality instruction on basic academic skills and social skills in the *Tier 1* level. Students move to *Tier 2* when their documented behavior and skills performance indicate the need for additional support and instruction. Students receive this support through general education and data-based practices, and their progress is carefully monitored. Students who continue to show insufficient progress in their classroom performance receive *Tier 3* assistance—more intense and individualized interventions. Figure A.1 depicts three tiers of prevention and intervening services as they might occur for students who show insufficient progress.

Figure A.1

Multitiered Prevention and Early Intervening Services

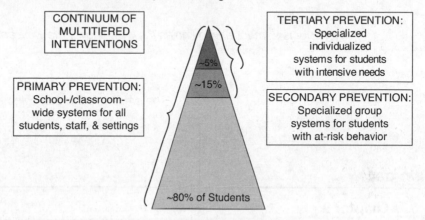

CONTINUUM OF MULTITIERED INTERVENTIONS

PRIMARY PREVENTION: School-/classroom-wide systems for all students, staff, & settings

~5%

~15%

~80% of Students

TERTIARY PREVENTION: Specialized individualized systems for students with intensive needs

SECONDARY PREVENTION: Specialized group systems for students with at-risk behavior

Source: Adapted from *What Is School-Wide PBS?* Center on Positive Behavioral Interventions and Supports, 2007, University of Oregon, www.pbs.org/schoolwide.htm. Used by permission.

Throughout the RTI process, skill sequences are taught and assessed until mastery is achieved. Thus, *mastery measurement* uses frequent, sometimes even daily, measures of individual student performance and progress. Students move to the next skill sequence when they achieve mastery. Additional interventions are used when the learning is not sufficient. *Curriculum-based measurement* (*CBM*) measures and assesses individual progress in all skills directly from the curriculum. In both cases, assessment influences instruction because skill acquisition and mastery align with the curriculum, are measured frequently, and provide immediate information about the student's performance and success in the curriculum.

Webliography

Council for Exceptional Children: www.cec.sped.org

IDEA '97. archived information: http://www.ed.gov/offices/OSERS/IDEA

Protection and Advocacy, Inc. publications: http://www.pai-ca.org/pubs/505101.htm & Democracy, Inc publications.

Section 504: http://www.wrightslaw.com/info/sec504.index.htm Hosted by Peter W. D. Wright and Pamela Darr Wright

Race to the Top Executive Summary: http://iss.schoolwires.com/1531107121081787/lib/1531107121081787/RTTT-Executive Summary.pdf

White House Fact Sheet. The Race to the Top: http://www.whitehouse.gov/the-press-office/fact-sheet-race-top

Appendix B

Comprehensive List of Websites, References, and Recommended Readings

A teacher is someone who knows the way, shows the way, and goes the way.
—Author unknown

The present is the only thing that has no end.
—Erwin Schrodinger

Webliography

Chapter 2

Character Counts! http://charactercounts.org
Curriculum Designers: http://www.curriculum21.com
U.S. Department of Education (2003). *U.S. Re-enters UN's education arm—UNESCO.* Speech of U.S. Secretary of Education to UNESCO General Conference: http://www.edwatch.org/updates06/022006-unesco.htm
Partnership for 21st Century Skills: http://www.21stcenturyskills.org
YouTube, LLC (viewed 3/27/2010): http://www.youtube.com

Chapter 3

Broadcast Music, Inc.: http://www.bmi.com

Chapter 4

Jack Pearpoint, Lynda Kahn, & Cathy Hollands, Inclusion Press International & The Marsha Forest Centre: http://www.inclusion.com
Kagan Publishing & Professional Development: http://www.kaganonline.com
Positive Discipline: http://www.positivediscipline.com

Chapter 5

Harvard School of Education. *Project Zero* **(Howard Gardner):** http://www.pz.harvard.edu/index.htm

Maintained by Webmaster at Choice Theory.com (William Glasser): http://www.choice
theory.com/links.htm

Kathy Curtiss and Company (William Glasser): http://www.kathycurtissco.com

Fredric H. Jones & Associates (Fred Jones): http://www.fredjones.com

Kagan Publishing & Professional Development (Spencer Kagan): http://www.kagan
online.com

Chapter 6

Cooperative Learning

Kagan Publishing & Professional Development: http://www.kaganonline.com.

Teachnology, Inc.: http://www.teach-nology.com

Problem-Based Learning: Activities

Sun Associates, 2003. A project-based learning activity about Problem-Based Learning:
www.sun-associates.com/lynn/pbl/pbl.html

Johnson, L. & Lamb, A. (site managers), 2007. Project, Problem, and Inquiry-based learning: http://eduscapes.com/tap/topic43.htm

The 21st Century Learner. Problem-based learning activities: http://the21stcentury
learner. webnode.com

Class Brain.com: http://www.classbrain.com/cb_games/cb_gms_bag/lemonade.html.

Lemonade Stand: http://www.legalzoom.com/legal articles/Top-Ten-Small-Business-Owners
.html.LegalZoom.com

National Park Service and U.S. Department of the Interior. Archeological Dig: http://
www.nps.gov/history/archeology/PUBLIC/kids/index.htm

Problem-Based Learning: What Is It?

[no host listed] What is Project-Based Learning (PBL)? http://imet.csus.edu/imet2/
stanfillj/workshops/pbl/description.htm

USC California Science Project. Problem-Based Learning (PBL): http://www.usc.edu/
hsc/dental/ccmb/usc-csp/Quikfacts.htm

WestEd Regional Technology Education Consortium. Exemplary Projects: Other Great
Projects: http://www.wested.org/pblnet/other_gp.html

Study Guides

Site is "researched, authored, maintained and supported by Joe Landsberger as an international, learner-centric, educational public service.": http://www.studygs.net/pbl.
htm

Visual Instructional Plans

Fredric H. Jones & Associates: http://www.fredjones.com

Other

The Cochrane Collaboration. *IT Literate or Retired (nd):* http://cochrane.org

Chapter 7

Directions and Feedback and Efficient Help
Fredric H. Jones & Associates: http://www.fredjones.com

Bullying
The school safety check book by the National School Safety Center, reprinted in Parkay & Stanford (2010), pp. 92–93: http://www.nssc1.org
Dan Olweus: http://www.olweus.org
Olweus Bullying Prevention Program; reprinted in Evertson & Emmer, 2009, p. 200: http://www.stopbullyingnow.com

Chapter 8

Assistive Tools
Cambium Learning Group: http://www.intellitools.com

Exceptionality (GATE and Special Education)
National Association for Gifted Children: http://www.nagc.org
U.S. Department of Education. (2006). *Fast Facts: Students with disabilities:* http://nces.ed.gov/fastfacts/display.asp?id=64
Department of Education. (2009). *Fast Facts: Students with disabilities:* http://nces.ed.gov/fastfacts/display/asp?id=64
National Center on Response to Intervention: http://www.rti4success.org
What you need to know about IDEA 2004. Response to Intervention (RTI): New ways to identify specific learning disabilities: http://www.wrightslaw.com/info/rti.index.htm

Families and Foster Care
American Academy of Child & Adolescent Psychiatry: http://www.aacap.org/cs/root/facts_for_families/foster_care
Americans for Divorce Reform. *Divorce Statistics Collection:* http://www.divorcereform.org
National Center on Family Homelessness. *Homeless Children: America's New Outcasts.* **(1999):** http://www.familyhomelessness.org/pdf/fact_outcasts.pdf

Miscellaneous Facts
National Center for Education Statistics: http://www.nces.ed.gov/pubs2009/2009030.pdf

Partnerships (Schools and Families)
The After-School Corporation: http://www.tascorp.org

Poverty and Homelessness
U.S. Department of Commerce. *People and households.: Poverty:* http://www.census.gov

National Coalition for the Homeless (2008, 2009). See links to Factsheets: http://www
.nationalhomeless.org

- *NCH Fact Sheet #10 Education of Homeless Children and Youth (2006)*
- *NCH Fact Sheet #13 Homeless Youth* (2008)
- *Homeless Families with Children* (2009)
- *Who Is Homeless?* (2009)
- *Why Are People Homeless?* (2009)
- *How Many People Experience Homelessness?* (2009)

Chapter 9

Authorities

Tripod (Linda Albert, Cooperative Discipline): http://cdiscipline.tripod.com

Kids are worth it! inc. (Barbara Coloroso): http://www.kidsareworthit.com

Discipline Associates, LLC (Richard Curwin, Allen Mendler, and Brian Mendler): http://
www.disciplineassociates.com

Maintained by Webmaster at Choice Theory.com (William Glasser): http://www.choice
theory.org/directory.html

Maintained by Webmaster at Choice Theory.com (William Glasser): http://www.choice
theory.com/links.htm

Fredric H. Jones & Associates: http://www.fredjones.com

Kagan Publishing & Professional Development (Spencer Kagan): http://www.kagan
online.com

Dr. Marvin Marshall. *Discipline for Promoting Responsibility and Learning:* http://www
.MarvinMarshall.com

Dr. Marvin Marshall *AboutDiscipline.com:* http://www.AboutDiscipline.com

Dr. Marvin Marshall. *Discipline without stress punishment or rewards:* http://www
.DisciplineWithoutStress.com

Ronald Morrish (Real Discipline): http://www.realdiscipline.com

Harry K. Wong Publications, Inc. (Harry and Rosemary Wong): http://www.Effective
Teaching.com

Bullying and Cyberbullying

The school safety check book by the National School Safety Center, reprinted in Parkay &
Stanford (2010), pp. 92–93; http://www.nssc1.org

i-SAFE America. (2004). *Beware of the cyber bully:* http://www.isafe.org/imgs/pdf/education/
Cyberbullying.pdf

Dan Olweus: http://www.olweus.org

Olweus Bullying Prevention Program; reprinted in Evertson & Emmer, 2009, p. 200:
http://www.stopbullyingnow.com

Effects of Poverty

Pellegrino, K. (2005). *The effects of poverty on teaching and learning:* http://www.teach-
nology.com/tutorials/teaching/poverty/print.htm

Chapter 10

National Center for Education Statistics: http://www.nces.ed.gov
Assessment tools from the Northwest Evaluation Association: http://www.nwea.org
Pinnacle Suite Assessment Package by GlobalScholar: http://www.pinnaclesuite.com
The Source for Learning, Inc. *Webquest 101—Putting Discovery into the Curriculum:*
    http:// www.teachersfirst.com/summer/webquest/quest-b.shtml
MidLink Magazine. *Rubrics:* http://www.ncsu.edu/midlink/ho.html
Discovery Software, LTD. *Rubrics:* http://www.rubrics.com

Chapter 11

Blackboard, Inc.: http://www.blackboard.com
Wikipedia, a registered trademark of Wikimedia Foundation, Inc.: http://www.en
    .wikipedia.org/wiki/Blackboard_Learning_System
Education World, Inc. *Parent involvement in schools:* http://www.educationworld.com/
    a_special/parent_involvement.shtml
TeacherVision, part of Family Education Network: http://www.teachervision.fen.com/
    parent-teacher-conferences/teaching-methods/3683.html
A to Z Teacher Stuff: http://www.atozteacherstuff.com/Tips/Parent_Teacher_Conferences

Chapter 12

Disability Rights Organization: http://www.dralegal.org
Senior Motivators in Learning and Educational Services (SMILES) found in Eric
    Resources Information Center: http://www.eric.ed.gov/ERICWebPortal/recordDetail?
    accno=ED346983
National Substitute Teacher Alliance: http://www.nstasubs.org

Chapter 13

International Critical Incident Stress Foundation, Inc.: http://www.icisf.org
PTSD.: http://www.helpguide.org/mental/post_traumatic_stress_disorder_symptoms_
    treatment.htm. Helpguide.org
PBS Parents. Talking with kids about war and violence: http://www.pbs.org/parents

Chapter 14

Blackboard, Inc.: http://www.blackboard.com

Appendix A

U.S. Department of Education *(November 2009):* http://iss.schoolwires.com/153110712
    1081787/ lib/1531107121081787/RTTT-ExecutiveSummary.pdf
Community Alliance for Special Education (CASE): http://www.caseadvocacy.org
Council for Exceptional Children (CEC): http://www.cec.sped.org
U.S. Department of Education. *IDEA '97. Archived information (August 26, 2002):* http://
    www.ed.gov/offices/OSERS/IDEA

U.S. Department of Education; Office of Special Education and Rehabilitative Services (OSERS). *Archived information (August 26, 2002):* http://www2.ed.gov/about/offices/list/osers/index.html

U.S. Department of Education, Office of Special Education Programs (OSEP). *Archived information (August 26, 2002):* http://www2.ed.gov/about/offices/list/osers/osep/index.html

Protection & Advocacy Inc. Publications: http://www.pai-ca.org/pubs/505101.htm

The White House: http://www.whitehouse.gov/the-press-office/fact-sheet-race-top

Peter W. D. Wright and Pamela Darr Wright: http://www.wrightslaw.com/info/lre.osers.memo.idea.htm

References and Recommended Readings

Albert, L. (2003). *Cooperative discipline.* Circle Pines, MN: American Guidance Service.

Allen, R. (2002, November). Teachers and paraeducators: Defining roles in an age of accountability. *Education Update, 44*(7).

Alphonso, C. (2003). *The globe and mail: A poor student's worst nightmare.* Retrieved August 8, 2003 from http://www.globetechnology.com/servlet/ArticleNews/TPStory/LAC/20030808/USTUDNO.

American Psychiatric Association. (2000). *Diagnostic and statistical manual of mental disorders* (4th ed., revised). Washington, DC: Author.

Anderson, L. (Ed.), Krathwohl, D. (Ed.), Airasian, P., Cruikshank, K., Mayer, R., Pintrich, P., Raths, J., & Wittrock, M. (2001)). *A taxonomy for learning, teaching, and assessing: A revision of Bloom's Taxonomy of Educational Objectives* (Complete edition). NY: Longman.

Armstrong, D., Henson, K., and Savage, T. (2009). *Teaching today An introduction to education* (8th ed.). Upper Saddle River, NJ: Merrill.

Badke, W. (2009, March). Stepping beyond Wikipedia. *Educational Leadership, 66*(6), 54–58.

Berman, S., Diener, S., Dieringer, L., & Lantieri, L. (2003). *Talking with children about war and violence in the world.* http://www.life.familyeducation.com/war.parenting/36559.html

Berne, E. (1964). *Games people play.* New York: Grove Press.

Bernstein, D. (1992). *Better than a lemonade stand: Small business ideas for kids.* Hillsboro, OR: Beyond Words Publishing, Inc.

Berry, M., principal investigator. (2002). Healthy school environment and enhanced educational performance, prepared for Carpet and Rug Institute. Report is available at www.jjcommercial.com/pdf/10-CharlesYoungElementary.pdf.

Biederman, J. (2005). Attention-deficit/hyperactivity disorder: A selective overview. *Biological Psychiatry, 57*(11), 1215–1220.

Bloom, L. A. (2009). *Classroom management. Creating positive outcomes for all students.* Upper Saddle River, NJ: Merrill.

Brookhart, S., Moss, C., & Long, B. Formative assessment that empowers. *Educational Leadership* (2008, November), 66(3), 52–57.

Brophy, J. (2004). *Motivating students to learn.* Mahwah, NJ: Lawrence Erlbaum.

Building classroom relationships (2003, September). Special Issue: *Educational Leadership, 61*(1).

Bureau of Education. (1918). *Cardinal principles of secondary education.* Bulletin #35. Washington, DC: Department of the Interior, Bureau of Education.

Campbell, D. (2000). *The Mozart Effect for children: Awakening your child's mind, health, and creativity with music.* New York: HarperCollins.

Campbell, D. (2002). *The Mozart effect: Tapping the power of music to heal the body, strengthen the mind, and unlock the creative spirit.* New York: HarperCollins.

Canter, L., & Canter, M. (2001). *Assertive discipline: Positive behavior management for today's classroom* (3rd ed.). Los Angeles: Canter & Associates.

Cary, S. (1997). *Second language learners.* Los Angeles: Galef Institute.

Chan, T., & Petrie, G. (1998). The Brain Learns Better in Well-Designed School Environments. www.nea.org/teacherexperience/braik030312.html.

Charles, C. (2000). *The synergetic classroom: Joyful teaching and gentle discipline.* Boston: Addison Wesley Longman.

Charles, C. (2009). *Today's best classroom management strategies: Paths to positive discipline.* Boston: Allyn & Bacon.

Charles, C. (2011). *Building classroom discipline* (10th ed.). Boston: Allyn & Bacon.

Childs, G. (2002). *Workshop and crisis response team guidebook: Critical Incident Stress Management Program.* Poway, CA: Poway Unified School District.

Coloroso, B. (1994). *Kids are worth it! Giving your child the gift of inner discipline.* New York: Avon Books.

Coloroso, B. (1999). *Parenting with wit and wisdom in times of chaos and loss.* Toronto, Ontario, Canada: Viking.

Coloroso, B. (2002). *The bully, the bullied, and the bystander.* Toronto, Ontario, Canada: HarperCollins.

Cook, P. (2004). *Behavior, learning, and teaching.* Applied studies in FAS/FAE (Distance Education Curricula). Winnipeg, Manitoba, Canada: Red River College.

Cooper, B. & Gargan, A. (2009, September). Rubrics in education: Old term, new meanings. *Phi Delta Kappan, 91*(1), 54–55.

Crowe, C. (2008, November) Solving behavior problems together. *Educational Leadership, 66*(3), 44–47.

Cruickshank, D., Jenkins, D., & Metcalf, K. (2006). *The act of teaching* (4th ed.). Boston: McGraw-Hill.

Curwin, R., & Mendler, A. (1988). *Discipline with dignity.* Alexandria, VA: ASCD. Revised editions 1992, 1999, 2002; Upper Saddle River, NJ: Merrill.

Curwin, R., Mendler, A., & Mendler, B. (2008). *Discipline with dignity: New challenges, new solutions.* Alexandria, VA: ASCD.

Devine, J. & Cohen, J. (2007). *Making your school safe: Strategies to protect children and promote learning.* New York: Teachers College Press.

Dlott, A. (2007, April). A (Pod)cast of thousands. *Educational Leadership, 64*(7), 80–82.

Doll, R. (1995). *Curriculum improvement: Decision making and process* (9th ed.). Boston: Allyn & Bacon.

Dreikurs, R., & Cassel, P. (1972). *Discipline without tears.* NY: Hawthorn.

Dreikurs, R., Grunwald, B., & Pepper, F. (1982). *Maintaining sanity in the classroom.* NY: Harper Row.

Dwyer, K., Osher, D., & Warger, C. (1998). *Early warning, timely response: A guide to safe schools.* Washington, DC: U.S. Department of Education.

Dwyer, K., Richardson, J., Danley, K., Hansen, W., Sussman, S., Brannon, B., et al. (1990, September). Characteristics of eighth grade students who initiate self-care in elementary and junior high school. *Pediatrics, 86*(3), 448–454.

Easton, L. (2007, January). Walking our talk about standards. *Phi Delta Kappan, 88*(5), 391–394.

Eisner, E. (1985). *The educational imagination: On the design and evaluation of school programs* (2nd ed.). New York: Macmillan.

Evertson, C., & Emmer, E. (2009). *Classroom management for elementary teachers* (8th ed.).

Fisher, D., & Frey, N. (2007). *Checking for understanding: Formative assessment techniques for your classroom.* Alexandria, VA: ASCD.

Fraser, B., & O'Brien, P. (1985). Student and teacher perception of the environment of elementary school classrooms. *Elementary School Journal, 85*(5), 567–560.

Freiberg, J. H. (Ed.). (1999). School *climate: Measuring, improving and sustaining healthy learning environments.* New York: RoutledgeFalmer.

Friesen, D., Prokop, C., & Sarros, J. (1988). Why teachers burn out. *Educational Research Quarterly, 12*(3), 9–19.

Gardner, H. (1991). *The unschooled mind: How children think and how schools should teach.* New York: Basic Books.

Gardner, H. (1993a). *Multiple intelligences: The theory in practice.* New York: Basic Books.

Gardner, H. (1993b). *Frames of mind* (10th ed.). New York: Basic Books.

Gardner, H. (1993c*). Multiple intelligences: The theory in practice.* New York: Basic Books.

Gee, J., & Levine, M. (March 2009). Welcome to our virtual worlds. *Educational Leadership, 66*(6), 48–52.

Ginott, H. (1972). *Teacher and child.* New York: Macmillan.

Glasser, W. (1969). *Schools without failure.* New York: Harper & Row.

Glasser, W. (1998a). *Choice theory in the classroom.* New York: HarperCollins.

Glasser, W. (1998b). *Control theory in the classroom* (rev. ed.). New York: Harper & Row.

Glasser, W. (1998c). *The quality school* (rev. ed.). New York: HarperCollins.

Glasser, W. (1998d). *The quality school teacher* (rev.ed.). New York: HarperCollins.

Glasser, W. (2000). *Every student can succeed.* Chatsworth, CA: Author.

Glickman, C., Gordon, S., & Ross-Gordon, J. (2007). *SuperVision and instructional leadership.* Boston: Pearson.

Good, T., & Brophy, J. (2008). *Looking into classrooms* (10th ed.). Boston: Allyn & Bacon.

Goodlad, J. (1984, 2004). *A place called school: Prospectives for the future.* New York: McGraw-Hill.

Gorski, P. (2008, April). The myth of the "culture of poverty." *Educational Leadership, 65*(7), 32–36.

Greene, R. (2001). *The explosive child.* New York: HarperCollins.

Grimes, K., & Stevens, D. (2009, May). Glass, Bug, Mud. *Phi Delta Kappan, 90*(9), 677–680.

Hall, P., & Hall, N. (2003). *Educating oppositional and defiant children.* Alexandria, VA: ASCD.

Hathaway, W., Hargreaves, J., Thompson, G., & Novitsky, D. (1992). A study into the effects of light on children of elementary school age—A case of light robbery. Unpublished manuscript, Planning and Information Services, Alberta Department of Education, Edmonton, Alberta, Canada.

Heflin, L., & Rudy, K. (1991. *Homeless and in need of special education.* Reston, VA: Council for Exceptional Children.

Horn, A., Opinas, P., Newman Carlson, D., & Bartolomucci, C. (2004). Elementary school bully busters programs: Understanding why children bully and what to do about it. In D. Espelage and S. Swearer (Eds.), *Bullying in American schools: A social-ecological perspective on prevention and intervention.* Mahwah, NJ: Lawrence Erlbaum.

Hunter, M. (1982). *Mastery learning.* El Segundo, CA: TIP Publications.

Improving instruction for students with learning needs (2007, February). Special Issue: *Educational Leadership, 64*(5).

Informative assessment. (2007, December–2008, January). Special Issue: *Educational Leadership* 65(4).

Jacobs, H. (1989). *Interdisciplinary curriculum: Design and implementation.* Alexandria, VA: ASCD.

Jacobs, H. (1997). *Mapping the big picture: Integrating curriculum and assessment K-12).* Alexandria, VA: ASCD.

Jacobs, H., ed. (2004). *Getting results with curriculum mapping.* Alexandria, VA: ASCD.

Jones, F. (2007). *Tools for teaching: Discipline Instruction Motivation.* Santa Cruz, CA: Fredric H. Jones & Associates.

Jones, F. (2007). *Tools for teaching: Parent edition.* Santa Cruz, CA: Fredric H. Jones & Associates.

Jones, F. (2007). *The video toolbox.* Santa Cruz, CA: Fredric H. Jones & Associates.

Jones, V. & Jones, L. (2010). *Comprehensive classroom management: Creating communities of support and solving problems* (9th ed.). Upper Saddle River, NJ: Pearson/Merrill , pp. 5–6.

Joyce, B., & Weil, M., with Calhoun, E. (2008). *Models of teaching* (8th ed.). Boston: Allyn & Bacon.

Kagan, L. (2007). *The successful dynamic trainer: Engaging all learners course workbook.* San Clemente, CA: Kagan Publishing.

Kagan, L., Kagan, M., & Kagan, S. (1997). *Cooperative learning structures for teambuilding.* San Clemente, CA: Kagan Cooperative Learning.

Kagan, M., Robertson, L., & Kagan, S. (1995). *Cooperative learning structures for classbuilding.* San Clemente, CA: Kagan Cooperative Learning.

Kagan, S. (2000). *Silly sports and goofy games.* San Clemente, CA: Kagan Publishing.

Kagan, S. (1994). *Cooperative learning.* San Clemente, CA: Kagan Cooperative Learning.

Kagan, S., & Kagan, M. (1998). *Multiple intelligences: The complete MI book.* San Clemente, CA: Kagan Cooperative Learning.

Kagan, S., & Kagan, M. (2009). *Cooperative learning.* San Clemente, CA: Kagan Publishing.

Kagan, S., Kyle, P., & Scott, S. (2007). *Win-win discipline.* San Clemente, CA: Kagan Publishing.

Kauffman, J., & Landrum, T. (2009). *Characteristics of emotional and behavioral disorders of children and youth* (9th ed.). Upper Saddle River, NJ: Merrill/Pearson

Kirk, S., Gallagher, J., Anastasiow, N., & Coleman, M. (2006). *Educating exceptional children* (11th ed.). Boston: Houghton Mifflin.

Kohn, A. (1999). *Punished by rewards.* Boston: Houghton Mifflin.

Kohn, A. (2008, November). Why self-discipline is overrated: The (troubling) theory and practice of control from within. *Phi Delta Kappan, 90*(3), 168–176.

Kounin, J. (1970). *Discipline and group management in classrooms.* NY: Holt, Rinehart & Winston.

Kozol, J. (2007, September). Letters to a young teacher. *Phi Delta Kappan, 89*(1), 8–20.

Kranowitz, C. (1998). *The out-of-sync child.* New York: Skylight Press.

Lavaree, B. (2009). *Authentic classroom management: Creating a learning community and building reflective practice* (3rd ed.). Upper Saddle River, NJ: Pearson.

Lever-Duffy, J., & McDonald, J. (2008). *Teaching and learning with technology* (3rd ed.). Boston: Allyn & Bacon.

Long, L. & Long, T. (1989). Latchkey adolescents: How administrators can respond to their needs. *NASSP Bulletin, 73,* 102–108.

Marshall, M. (2002). *Discipline without stress, punishment, or rewards: How teachers and parents promote responsibility and learning.* Los Alamitos, CA: Piper Press.

Marshall, M., & Weisner, K. (2004, March). Using a discipline system to promote learning. *Phi Delta Kappan 85*(7), 498-507. Bloomington, IN: Phi Delta Kappa International.

Martinez, D., & Harper, D. (2008, November). Working with tech-savvy kids. *Educational Leadership, 66*(3), 64–69.

Marzano, R. (2000). *Transforming classroom grading.* Alexandria, VA: ASCD.

Maslow, A. (1943). A theory of human motivation. *Psychological Review, 50,* 370–396.

Mastropieri, M., & Scruggs, T. (2010). *The inclusive classroom: Strategies for effective differentiated instruction* (4th ed.). Upper Saddle River, NJ: Merrill.

McGrath, M. (2007). School bullying: Tools for avoiding harm and liability. Thousand Oaks, CA: Corwin Press.

McMillan, J. (2001). *Classroom assessment: Principles and practice for effective instruction* (2nd ed.). Boston: Allyn & Bacon.

McTighe, J., & Wiggins, G. (2004). *Understanding by design: Professional development workbook.* Alexandria, VA: ASCD.

Morrish, R. (2000). *With all due respect: Keys for building effective school discipline.* Fonthill, Canada: Woodstream publishing.

Morrish, R. (2003). *FlipTips.* Fonthill, Canada: Woodstream Publishing.

Morrison, G. (2002). *Teaching in America* (3rd ed.). Boston: Allyn & Bacon.

Müller, E. & Markowitz, J. (2004). Disability categories: State terminology, definitions and eligibility criteria. Washington, DC: Project Forum, National Association of State Directors of Special Education.

Multiple measures (2009, November). Special Issue: *Educational Leadership, 67*(3).

Mustacchi, J.(2009, March). R U Safe? *Educational Leadership, 66*(6), 78–82.

Nansel, T. R., Overpeck, M., Ramani, S. P., Ruan, W. J., Simons-Morton, B., & Scheidt, P. (2001). Bully behaviors among US youth: Prevalence and association with psychosocial adjustment. *Journal of the American Medical Association 285*(16), 2094–2100.

Nansel, T., Overpeck, M., Haynie, D., Ruan, W., & Scheidt, P. (2003). Relationships between bullying and violence among US youth. *Archives of Pediatrics and Adolescent Medicine 157*(4), 348–353.

Nelsen, J., Lott, L., & Glenn, H. (2000). *Positive discipline in the classroom* (3rd ed.). Rocklin, CA: Prima Publishing.

Neuman, S. (2009, April). Use the science of what works to change the odds for children at risk. *Phi Delta Kappan, 90*(8), 582–587.

Olweus, D. (1999). *Core program against bullying and antisocial behavior: A teacher handbook.* Bergen, Norway: Research Center for Health Promotion, University of Bergen.

Papolos, D., & Papolos, J. (2002). *The bipolar child.* New York: Broadway Books.

Parkay, F. & Stanford, B. (2010). *Becoming a teacher* (8th ed.). Upper Saddle River, NJ: Merrill.

Partnership for 21st Century Skills. (2009). *P21 framework definitions.* Tucson, AZ: Author. http://www.21stcenturyskills.org.

Paulson, F., Paulson, P., & Meyer, C. (1991). What makes a portfolio a portfolio? *Educational Leadership, 48*(5), 60–63.

Payne, R. (2001). *A framework for understanding poverty.* Highlands, TX: aha! Process, Inc.

Payne, R. (2008, April). Nine powerful practices. *Educational Leadership, 65*(7), 48–52.

Payne, R. (2009, January). Poverty does not restrict a student's ability to learn. *Phi Delta Kappan, 90*(5), 371–372.

Pearpoint, J., & Forest, M. (1992). Foreword. In S. Stainback & W. Stainback (Eds.), *Curriculum considerations in inclusive classrooms: Facilitating learning for all students* (pp. xv–xviii). Baltimore: Paul H. Brookes.

Perry, B. (2006). *Maltreated children: Experience, brain development and the next generation.* New York: Norton.

Peterson, R., & Skiba, R. (2001). Creating school climates that prevent school violence. *Social Studies, 92*(4), 167–176.

Popham, W. (2008, October). An unintentional deception. *Educational Leadership, 66*(2), 80–81.

Poverty and learning (2008, April). Special Issue: *Educational Leadership, 65*(7).

Pullis, M. (1992). An analysis of the occupational stress of teachers of the behaviorally disordered: Sources, effects, and strategies for coping. *Behavioral Disorders, 17*(3), 191–201.

Rauscher, R., Shaw, G., Levine, L., Ky. K., & Wright, E. (1993). Music and spatial task performance. *Nature, 365,* 611.

Redl, F., & Wattenberg, W. (1951). *Mental hygiene in teaching.* NY: Harcourt, Brace & World. Revised and reissued in 1959.

Roblyer, M., & Doering, A. (2010). *Integrating educational technology into teaching* (5th ed.). Boston: Allyn & Bacon.

Rogers, C. (1969). *Freedom to learn.* Columbus, OH: Merrill.

Root, R., & Resnick, R. (2003). An update on the diagnosis and treatment of attention-deficit/hyperactivity disorder in children. *Professional Psychology: Research and Practice, 34*(1), 34–41.

Rosales-Dordelly, C., & Short, E. (1985). *Curriculum professors' specialized knowledge.* Lanham, MD: University Press of America.

Sapon-Shevin, M. Learning in an inclusive community. *Educational Leadership, 66*(1), 49–53.

Sato, M., & Lensmire, T. (2009, January). Poverty and Payne: Supporting teachers to work with children of poverty. *Phi Delta Kappan, 90*(5), 365–370.

Schwartz, F. (1981). Supporting or subverting learning: Peer group patterns in four tracked schools. *Anthropology and Education Quarterly, 12*(2), 99–120.

Scriffiny, P. (2008, October). Seven reasons for standards-based grading. *Educational Leadership, 66*(2), 70–74.

Shariff, S. (2008). *Cyber-bullying: Issues and solutions for the school, the classroom and the home.* London: Routledge.

Simkins, M., Cole, K., Tavalin, F., & Means, B. (2002). *Increasing student learning through multimedia projects.* Alexandria, VA: ASCD.

Siris, K., & Osterman, K. (2004, December). Interrupting the cycle of bullying and victimization in the elementary classroom. *Phi Delta Kappan, 86*(4), 288–291.

Skinner, B. (1954). The science of learning and the art of teaching. *Harvard Educational Review, 24,* 86–97.

Smith, D., & Tyler, N. (2010). *Introduction to special education: Making a difference* (7th ed.). Upper Saddle River, NJ: Merrill.

Smith, J., Fien, H., & Paine, S. (2008, April). When mobility disrupts learning. *Educational Leadership, 65*(7), 59–63.

Sousa, D. (2006). *How the brain learns* (3rd ed.). Thousand Oaks, CA: Corwin Press.

Sternberg, R. (2008, October). Excellence for all. *Educational Leadership, 66*(2), 14–19.

Stiggins, R.J. (2004, September). Assessment for learning: New assessment beliefs for a new school mission. *Phi Delta Kappan, 86,* 22–27.

Stiggins, R. (2005). *Student-involved assessment for learning* (4th ed.). Upper Saddle River, NJ: Pearson/Merrill Prentice Hall.

Stiggins, R. Assessment through the students' eyes. (2007, May). *Educational Leadership, 64*(8), 22–26.

Supporting English Language Learners (2009, April). Special Issue: *Educational Leadership, 66*(7).

Teachman, J. (2004, January). The childhood living arrangements of children and characteristics of their marriages. *Journal of Family Issues, 25,* 86–111.

The positive classroom. (2008, September). Special Issue: *Educational Leadership, 66*(1).

Tomlinson, C. (2000, September). Reconcilable differences: Standards-based teaching and differentiation. *Education Leadership, 58*(1), 6–11.

Tomlinson, C. (2002, September). Invitation to learn. *Educational Leadership, 60*(1), 6–10.

Tomlinson, C. (2008, November). The goals of differentiation. *Educational Leadership, 66*(3), 26–30.

Tomlinson, C., & McTighe, J. (2006). *Integrating differentiated instruction and understanding by design: Connecting content and kids.* Alexandria, VA: ASCD.

Turnbull, A., Turnbull, R. &Wehmeyer, M. (2010). *Exceptional lives: Special education in today's schools* (6th ed.). Upper Saddle River, NJ: Merrill.

Turnbull, R., Huerta, N., & Stowe, M. (2009). *What every teacher should know about the Individuals with Disabilities Education Act as amended in 2004.* (2nd ed.). Boston: Pearson.

Tyler, R. (1949). *Basic principles of curriculum and instruction.* Chicago: University of Chicago Press.

Villa, R., Thousand, J., & Nevin, A. (2010). *Collaborating with students in instruction and decision making.* Thousand Oaks, CA: Corwin.

Wagner, T. (2008, October). Rigor redefined. *Educational Leadership, 66*(2), 20–24.

Webb, L., Metha, A., & Jordan, K. (2010). Foundations of American education (6th ed.). Upper Saddle River, NJ: Pearson/Merrill.

Wiggins, G. (November 1994). Toward better report cards. *Educational Leadership, 52*(2), 28–37.

Wiggins, G., & McTighe, J. (2005). *Understanding by design* (expanded 2nd ed.). Alexandria, VA: ASCD.

Wong, H., & Wong, R. (2009). *The first days of school* (4th ed.). Mountain View, CA: Harry K. Wong Publications, Inc.

Yell, M., & Drasgow, F. (2005). *No Child Left Behind: A guide for professionals.* Upper Saddle River, NJ: Pearson Merrill.

Ysseldyke, J., & Algozzine, B. (1995). *Special education: A practical approach for teachers* (3rd ed.). Boston: Houghton Mifflin.

Zapt, S. (2008, September). Reaching the fragile student. *Educational Leadership, 66*(1), 67–70.

Legal Actions

Gifted and Talented Students Act of 1978, PL 95-561. (1978).

Individuals with Disabilities Act (IDEA) of 1990, PL 101-476. (1990).

McKinney-Vento Homeless Assistance Act. Formerly known as the Steward B. McKinney Homeless Assistance Act of 1987. (Amended 1990 and 1994)

Reauthorization of IDEA. (2004).

Reports and Conferences

Federal Register. (August 23, 1997). Washington, DC: U.S. Government Printing Office.

Institute of Education Sciences (IES). National Center for Education Statistics. (2008). Brief: *1.5 million homeschooled students in the United States in 2007.*

National Clearinghouse for English Language Acquisition (2008). *The growing numbers of limited English proficient students: 1995/06-2005-06.* Washington, DC: Author.

National Coalition for the Homeless:

- *NCH fact sheet #13: Homeless Youth* (2008).

- *Homeless Families with Children* (2009).

- *Who Is Homeless?* (2009).

- *Why Are People Homeless?* (2009).

- *How Many People Experience Homelessness?* (2009).

U.S. Bureau of Census (2005).

U.S. Census Bureau (2003). *Language use and English-speaking ability: 2000.* Retrieved December 18, 2003, from www.census.gov/prod/2003pubs/c2kbr-29.pdf

U.S. Census Bureau Public Information Office. (2003, October 8). News release. Retrieved December 18, 2003, from www.census.gov/Press-Release/www.releases/archives/census_2000/001406.html

U.S. Department of Education. (2004). Education for Homeless Children and Youth Program, 2004. Available at http://www.ed.gov

U.S. Department of Education. (2006, August 14). 34 *CFR* Parts 300 and 301. Assistance to States for the Education of Children with Disabilities and Preschool Grants for Children with Disabilities: Final rule. *Federal Register,* Washington, DC.

U.S. Department of Health and Human Services (2002).

Trade Books

Allard, H. (1977). *Miss Nelson is missing!* Boston: Houghton Mifflin.

Collins, M., & Tamarkin, C. (1990). *Marva Collins' way.* New York: G.P. Putman's Sons.

Dr. Seuss, Prelutsky, J., & Smith, L. (1998). *Hooray for Diffendoofer Day!* New York: Alfred A. Knopf.

Finchler, J. (2000). *Testing Miss Malarkay.* New York: Walker & Company.

Sollman, C., Emmons, B., & Paolini, J. (1994). *Through the cracks.* Worcester, MA: Davis Publications.

Stuart, J. (1949). *The thread that runs so true.* New York: Simon & Schuster.

Thaler, M. (1989). *The teacher from the Black Lagoon.* New York: Scholastic.

Index